*"Come and see
what God has done ..."*

PSALM 66:5

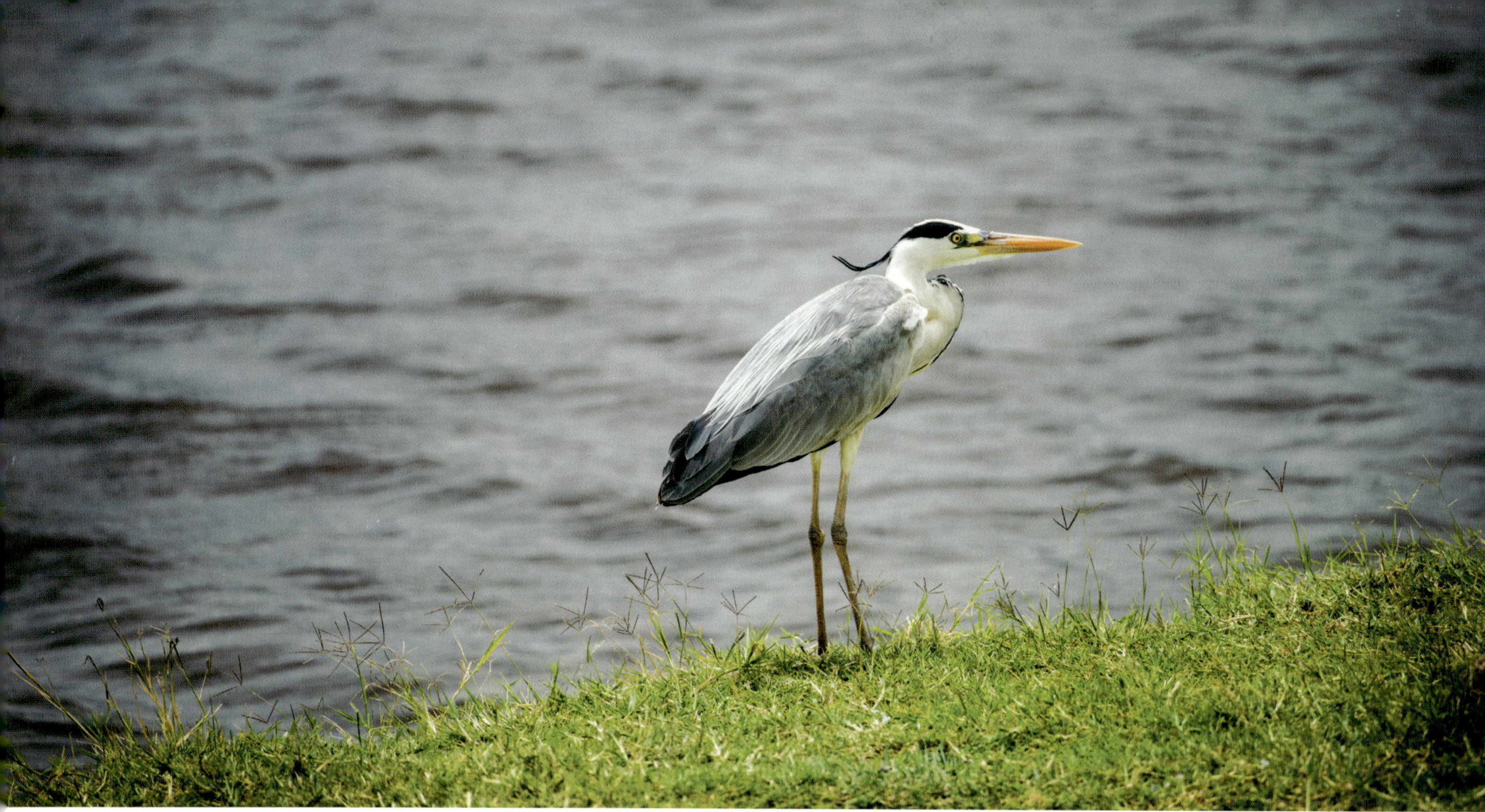

Published by In Touch Ministries, Atlanta, Georgia, 30340

Cover photos by Charles F. Stanley

Dr. Stanley's portrait by Tim Olive

Jacket design by Lisa Dyches

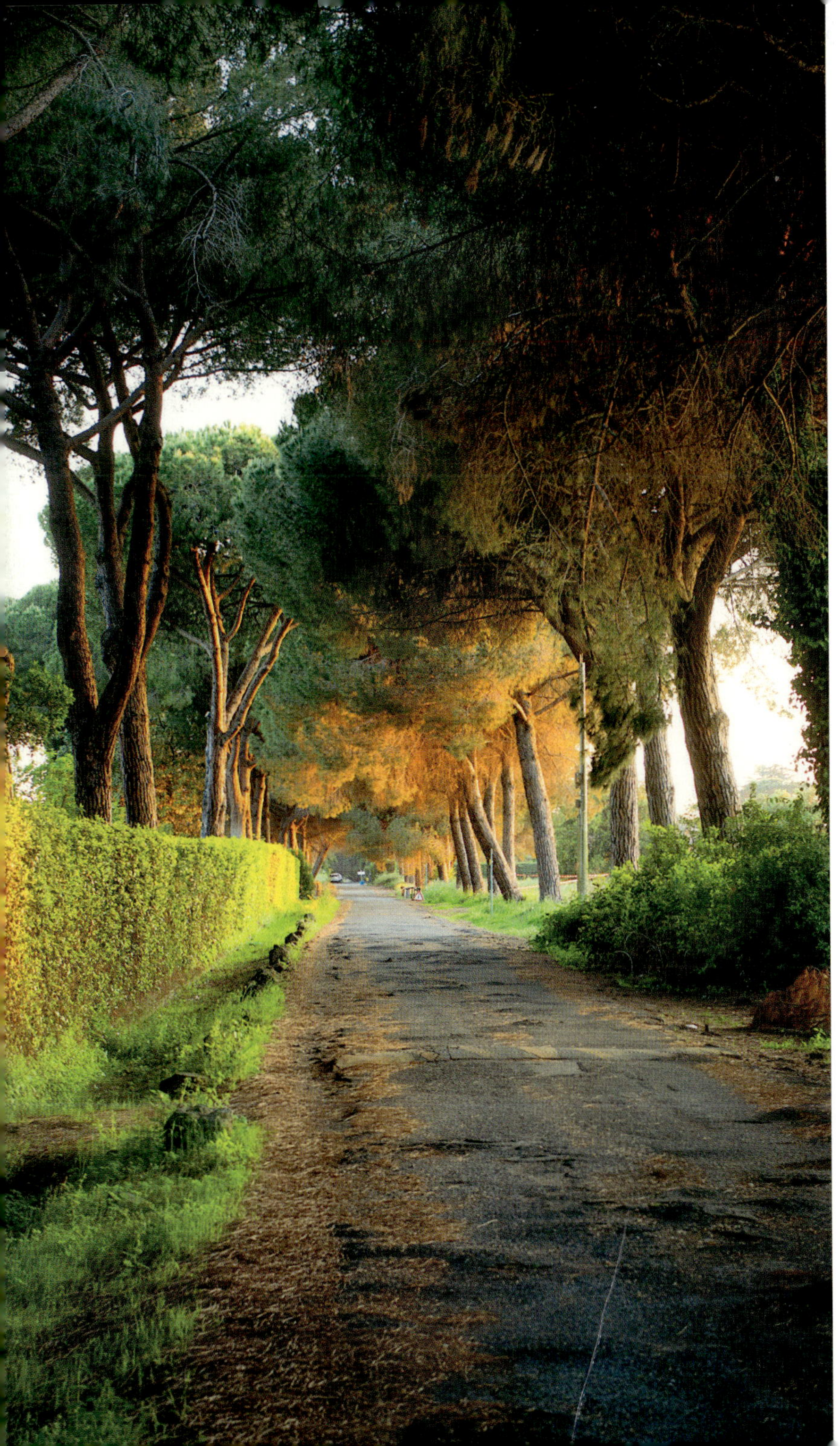

TABLE OF CONTENTS

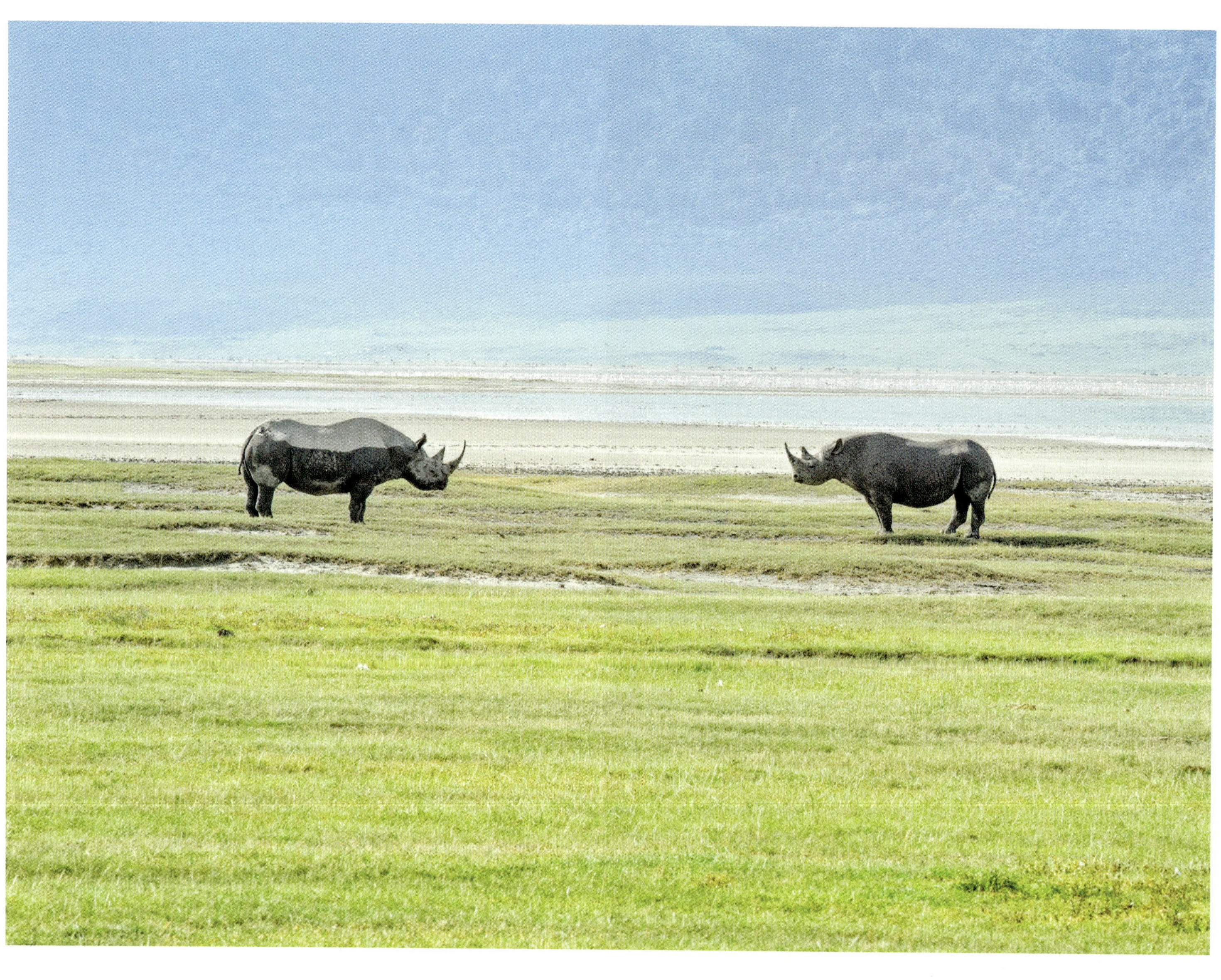

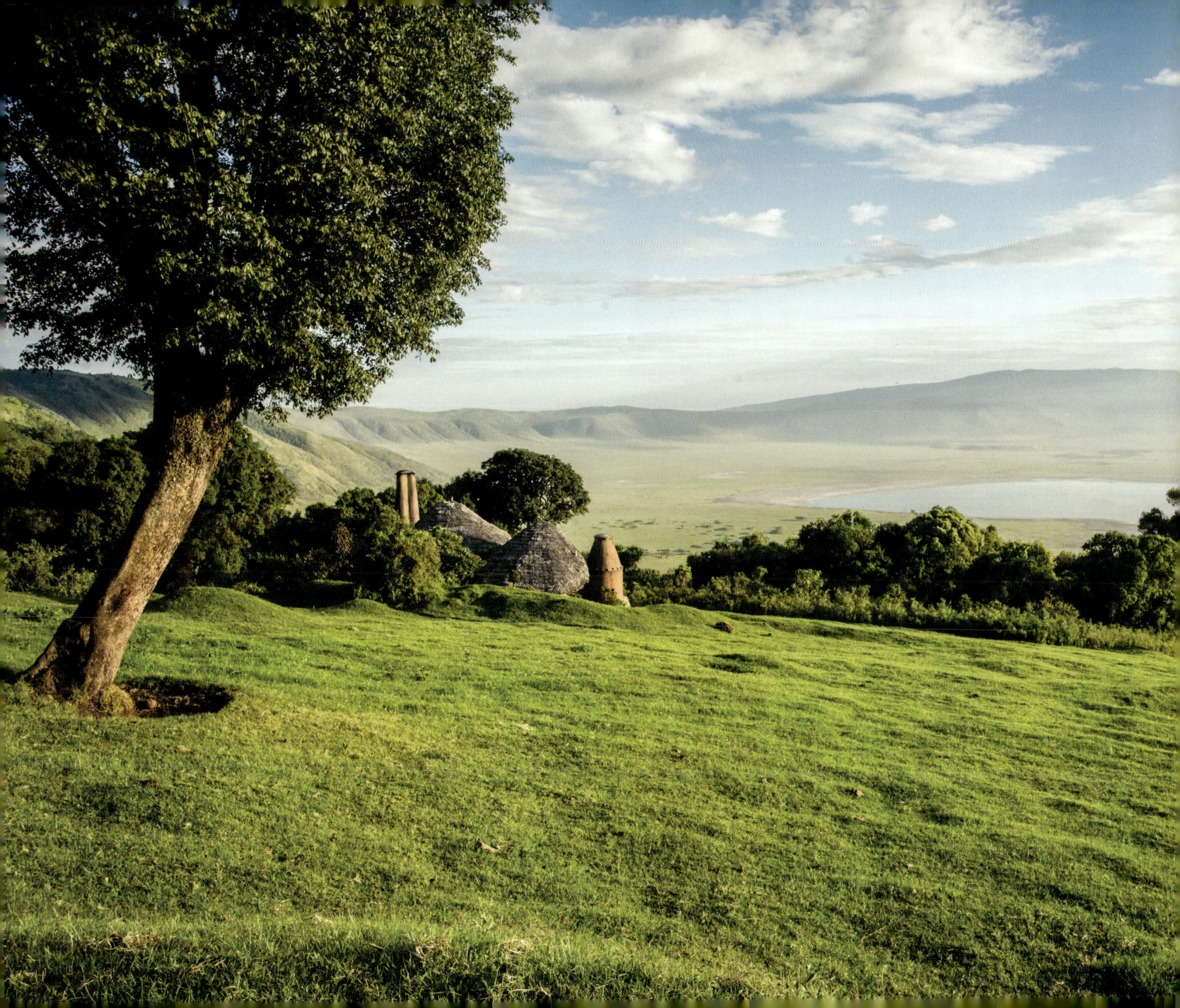

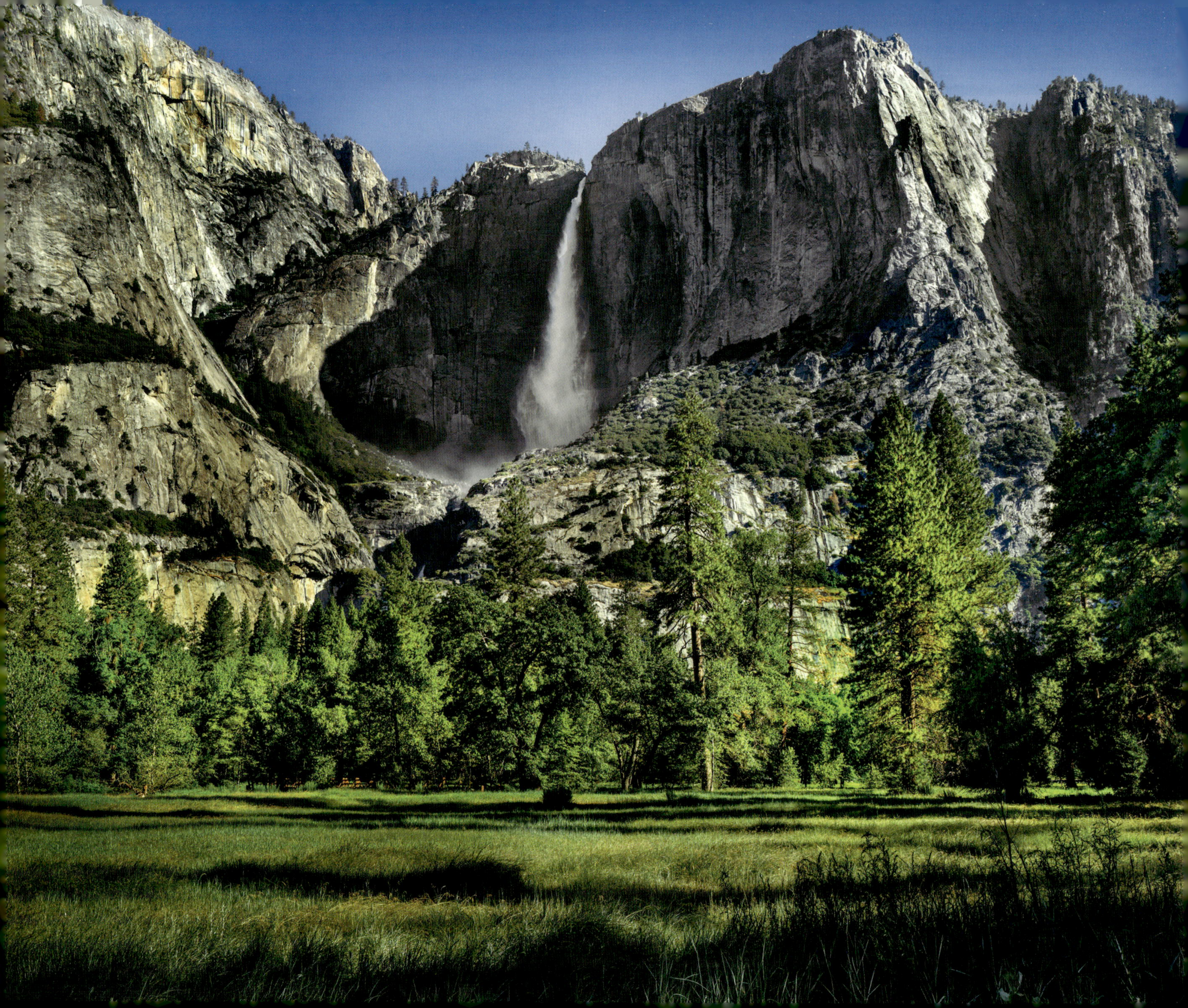

A Note From the Photographer

Dear friend,

Photography has been an important part of my life for many years. As a pastor, I'm always seeking to know God better and help others connect with Him more deeply. Taking photographs of His world is another way He's allowed me to do that. I love to capture the beauty of God's creation with my camera. And I love to share the pictures with others so they can be amazed at His love and power, too, and praise Him.

When we look at all the wonders of nature with an expectant heart, He always rewards us with an awareness of His majesty, His endless creativity, and His tremendous love for us. Oftentimes, I have a sense that He's communicating a special message to me through the scenes I photograph—something to help or encourage me in all the ups and downs of life.

Over the years, God has blessed me with the opportunity to visit many beautiful places all over the world. From Alaska to Africa and old Europe to the American West, I've been able to enjoy His works and everything they reveal about Him. Snowy mountains, quiet lakes, birds in flight—they all display the awesome glory of our God in a powerful way. Psalm 105:1-4 says,

> Oh give thanks to the Lord, call upon His name;
> Make known His deeds among the peoples.
> Sing to Him, sing praises to Him;
> Speak of all His wonders.
> Glory in His holy name;
> Let the heart of those who seek the Lord be glad.
> Seek the Lord and His strength;
> Seek His face continually.

God's handiwork is visible all around us, but His greatest work is our salvation, which He provided for us through the sacrifice of His Son, Jesus. It's only through the blood of Christ that we can draw near to God as our heavenly Father. May these photographs, devotions, and scriptures help you seek Him and enjoy Him more. Listen quietly for whatever He might reveal to you about Himself, His plans for your eternal life in Jesus, and the endless good He has in store for you as His beloved child. Remember, He loves you and He delights to reward those who seek Him.

Prayerfully yours,

Charles F. Stanley

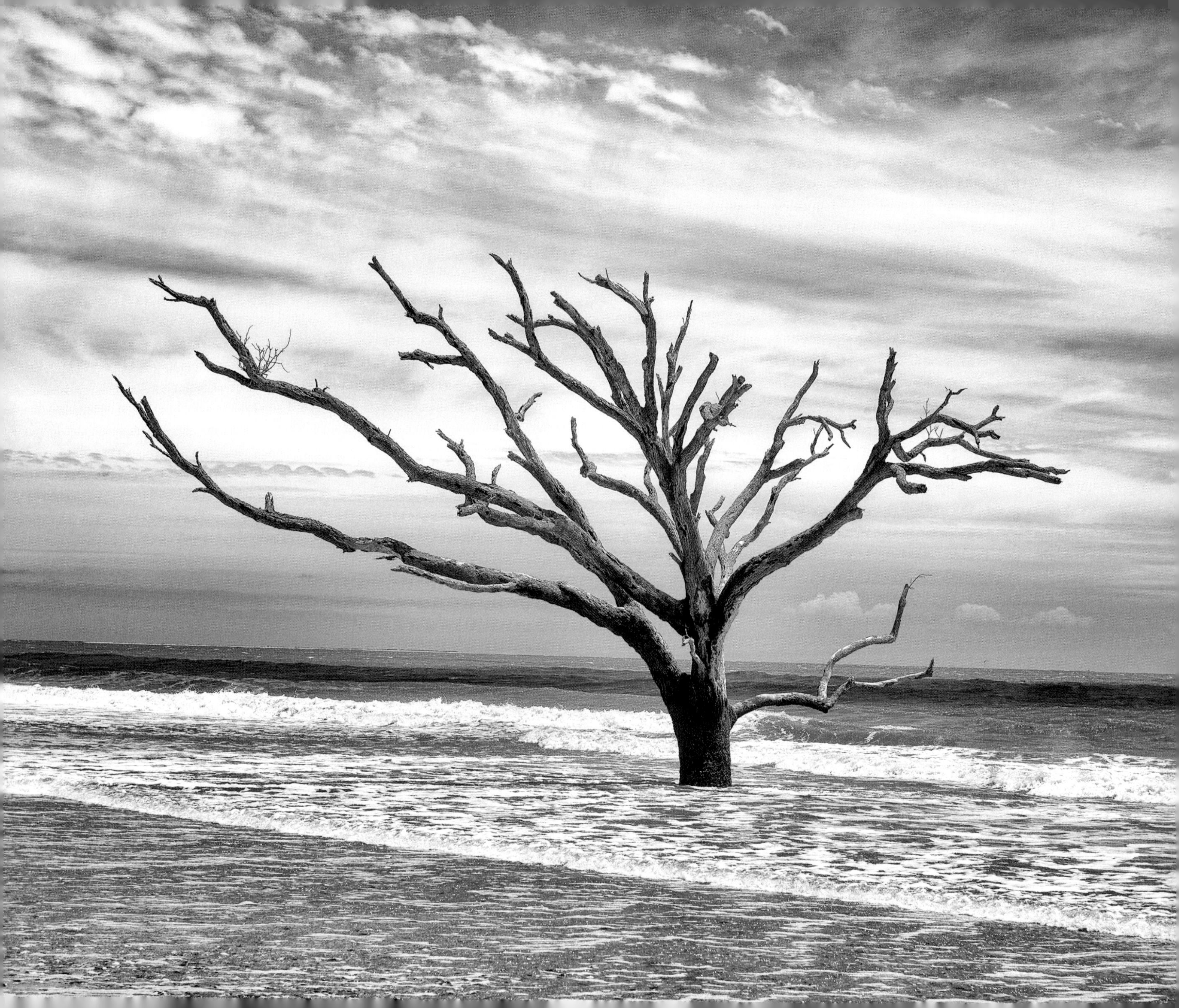

How to Use This Book

God reveals Himself to us in many different ways. One of His primary means of communication is His Word. The Bible contains God's infallible, living, and active voice, and it speaks to us with great power. He also reaches out to us through His created world. In all its complexity and beauty, He shows us His glory and His desire to delight us. We often hear from our Father through the guidance and encouragement of the Holy Spirit, who lives within every believer. Sometimes this comes as a general feeling, or a specific piece of knowledge, or even as silent words that we hear in our souls. And Jesus, as our constant companion, is always communicating with us in special ways that only we might understand.

Our conversation with God is part of our ongoing relationship with Him. We listen for His voice and respond to Him with questions, honesty, and praise. One of the best things we can do to deepen this relationship is to spend time intentionally seeking Him. The book you hold in your hands is meant to be an aid for you in doing that. It is designed to help you focus on the Lord with a listening heart and receive new insights and encouragement from Him, perhaps in a way you never have before.

This book is a visual devotional. It contains many beautiful images of God's created world, taken by Charles F. Stanley. The photographs are accompanied by passages of Scripture, short meditations, and inspiring quotes from Dr. Stanley's lifetime of ministry. The texts create a bridge between God's Word and the photographs of His world. Perhaps you will find one leading to the other and back again as you encounter each page. The chapters tell a story and can be read sequentially, but they may also be enjoyed separately.

We invite you to use this book as an opportunity to contemplate God's love and majesty, the miracle of life in Jesus Christ, and the Christian journey of faith. May you grow in the grace and knowledge of our Lord, be strengthened in your walk with Him, and deepen your relationship with God and the body of Christ on earth as you journey through the book. God bless you!

TIPS FOR READING

As you explore this devotional, try to do so in an unhurried manner. Here are some tips to help you get started:

1. Open your heart to the Lord and ask Him to speak to you. Pray for the Holy Spirit to be your guide as you look through the book.
2. Read the chapter introduction, which sets the stage for the visual and scriptural experience you are about to encounter.
3. Enjoy the photographs that follow, letting your heart respond to their expression of God's love and majesty.
4. When you come to a page of text within the chapter, you will find two different elements: a brief meditation on a spiritual theme, and a verse from Scripture for you to reflect on.
5. Let the title draw you in and guide your thoughts.
6. Read the brief meditation and consider how your own experience with the Lord might express similar truths.
7. Reflect on the Scripture verse. Ask the Holy Spirit to grant you fresh insight into God's Word.
8. Spend some time enjoying the surrounding photographs, and listen for whatever God may reveal to you through the beauty of His natural world.
9. Pray often. Savor the insights you receive.
10. Thank God for His gifts and His presence!

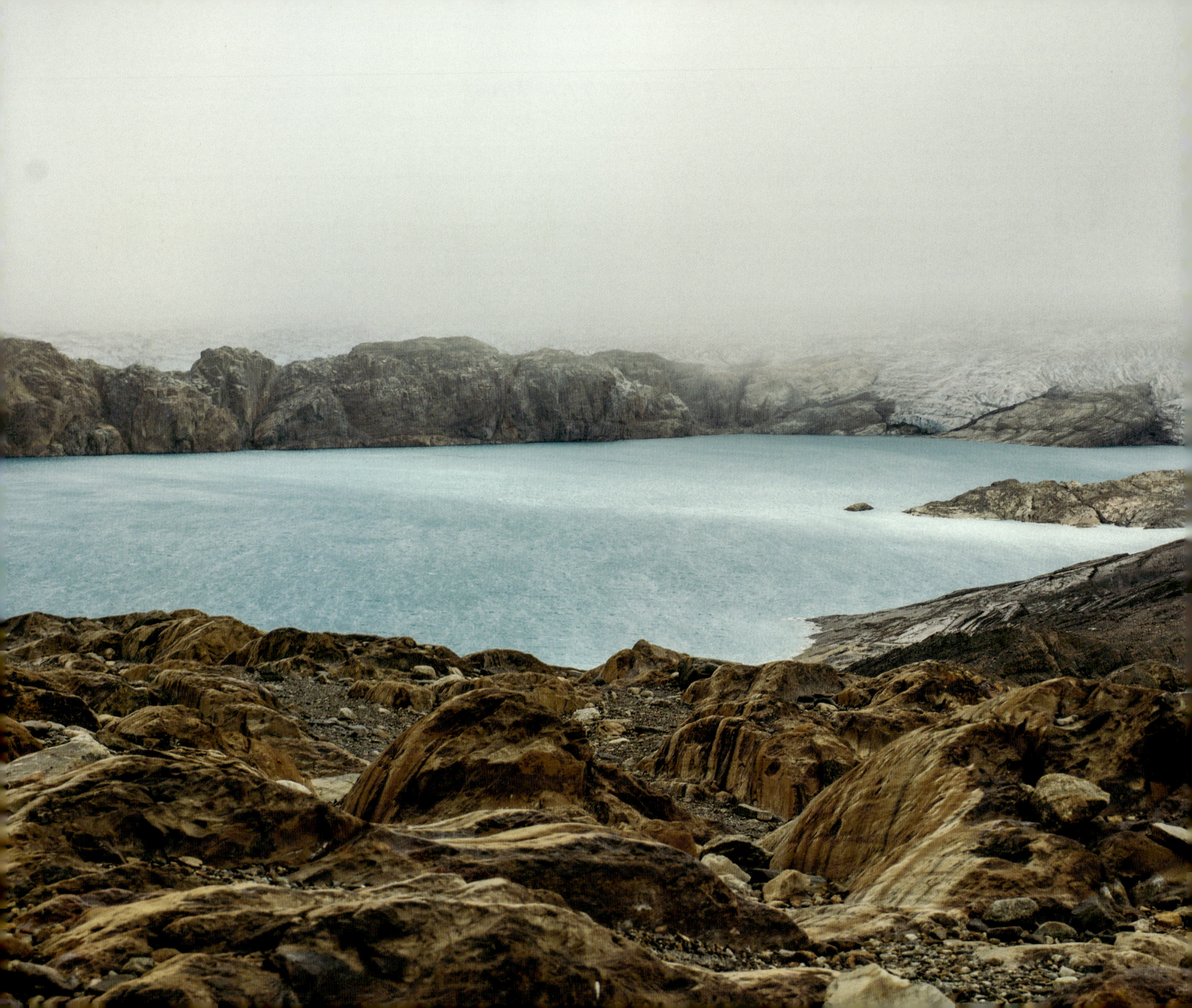

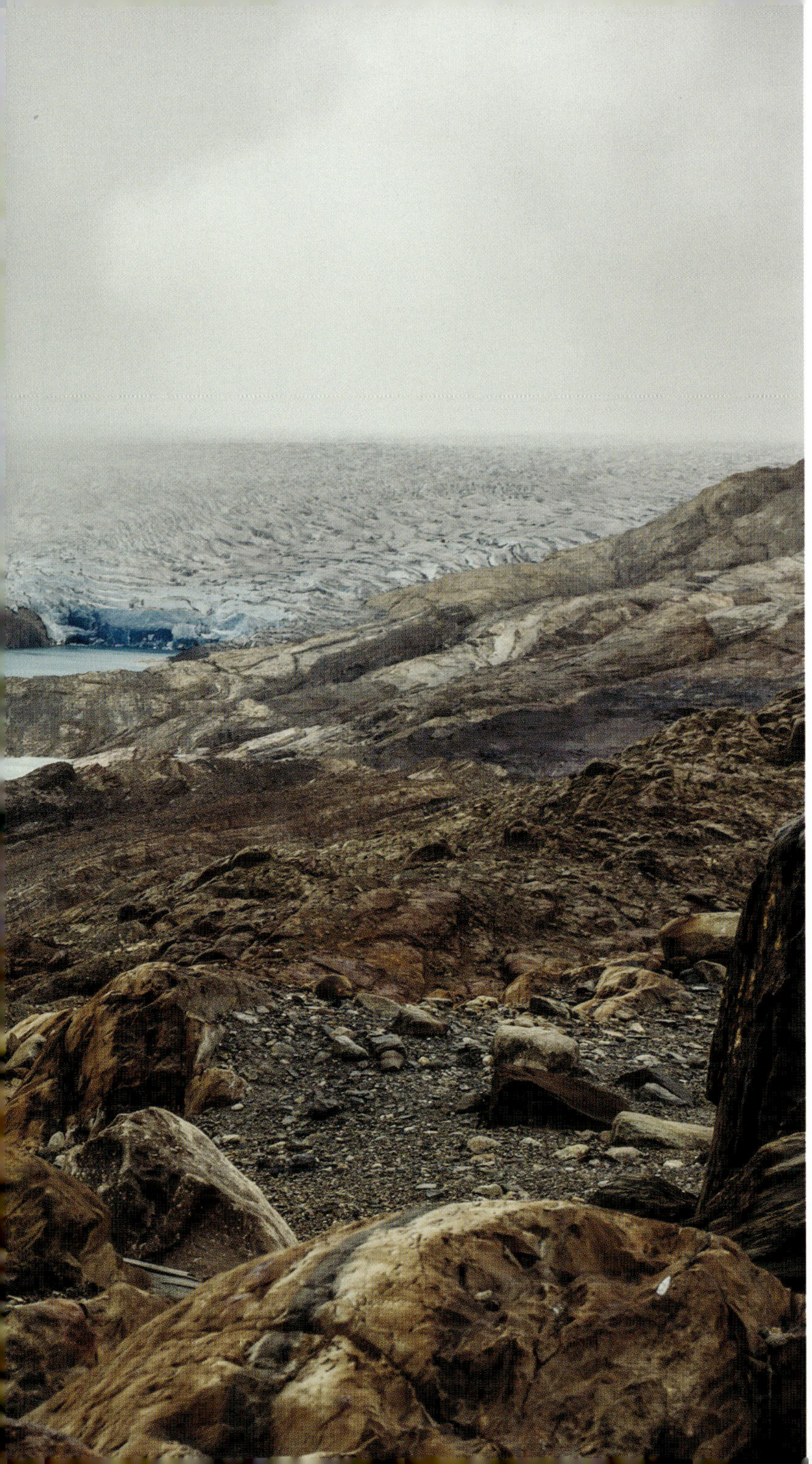

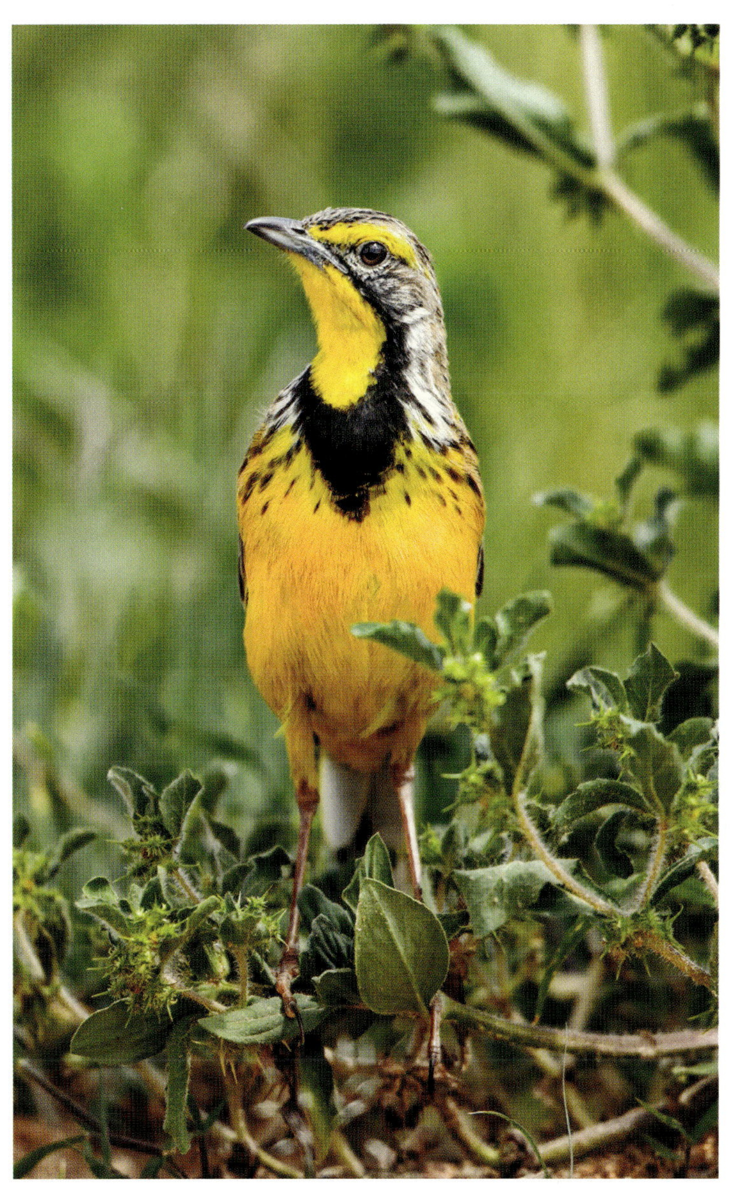

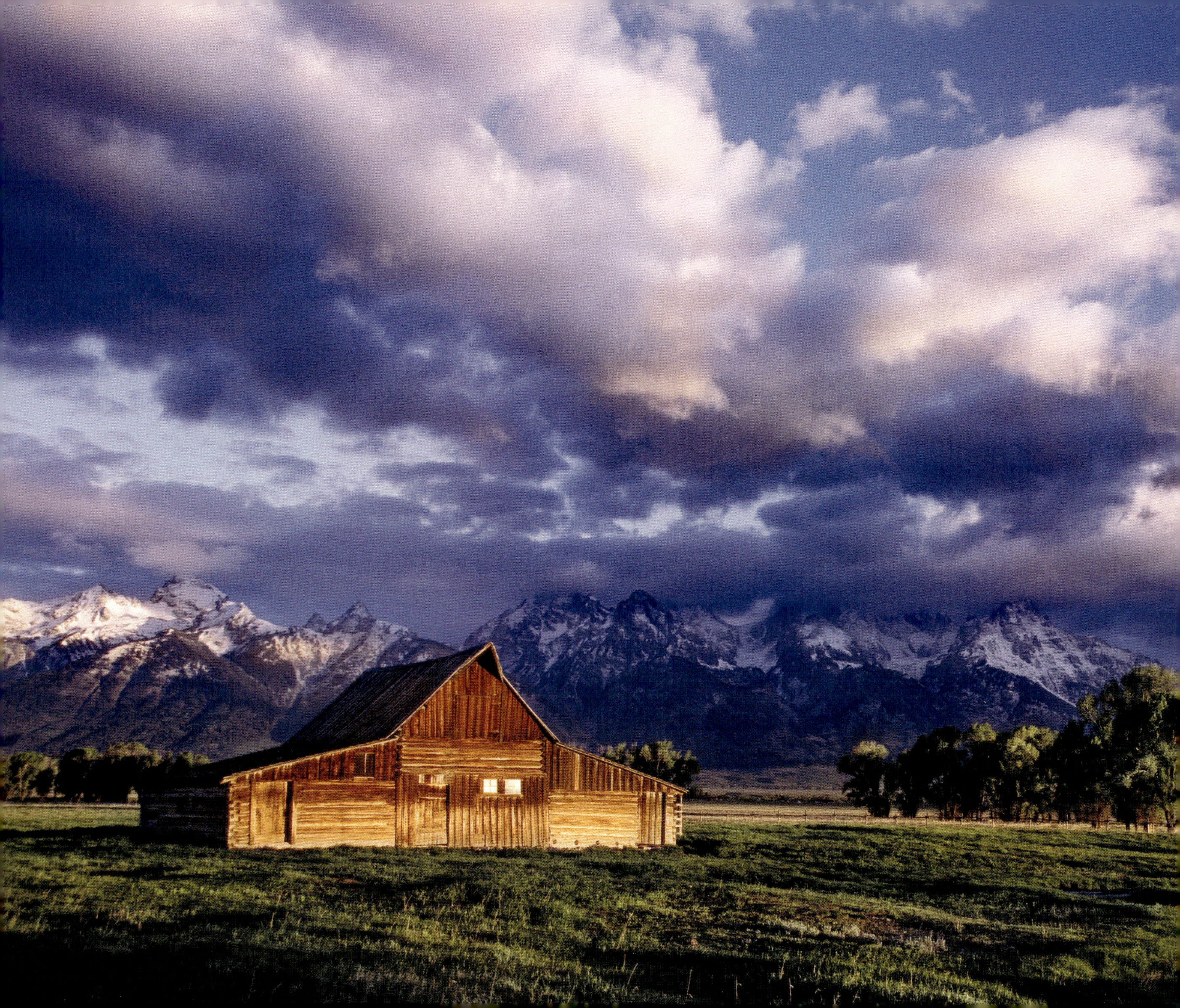

CHAPTER ONE

THE POWER OF GOD'S LOVE

Love spoke the world into being. Scripture tells us that God is love, and by His word, the world sprang into existence. Behind every granite peak and every blade of grass, behind life itself, is the unstoppable and incredible force that is the love of God. This love creates, and it supplies for the needs of all it has created. With wisdom and power, our heavenly Father provides food, water, air, and shelter. He watches over the changing of the seasons and the many processes that ensure continuance of life on earth.

In the world's fallen state, the groans of creation are often felt in destructive natural forces, but life is still upheld. Human history goes on, often in the midst of great beauty. Our God delights to restore, bringing spring on the heels of winter and blossoms in the wake of decay. Though we witness the toll of sin in lack and suffering, God's love is still present, carrying us forward.

Since time began, He has sustained the world, unchanging in His glorious strength even as oceans rise and fall and year turns into year. We can see God's love at work all around us, in towering mountains, colorful sunsets, and flowers bursting into bloom. From the story of life recorded in the knots of an ancient tree, to the dance of surf over rock as it heads toward shore, all creation speaks of the mighty power of God's wonderful and caring heart.

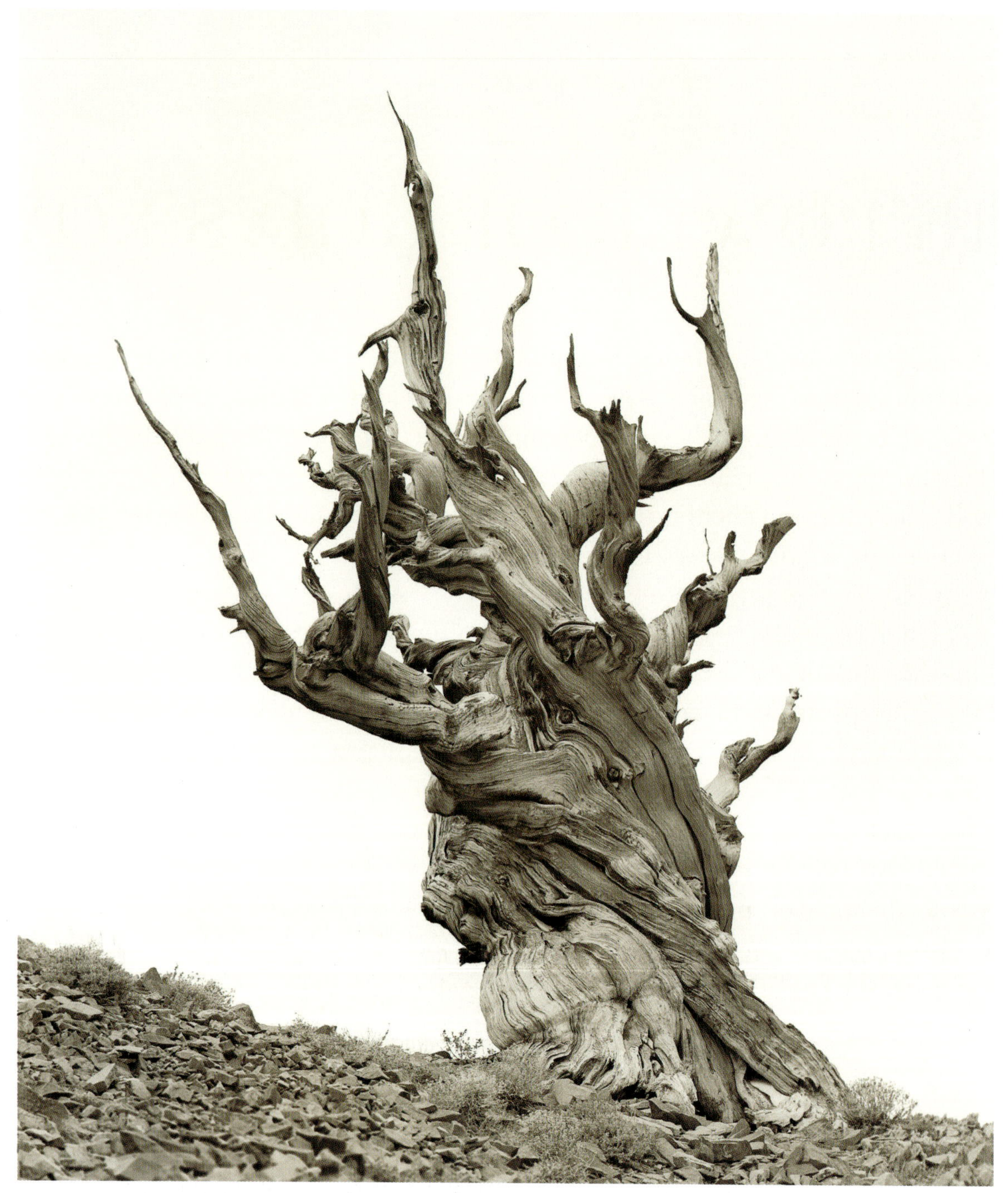

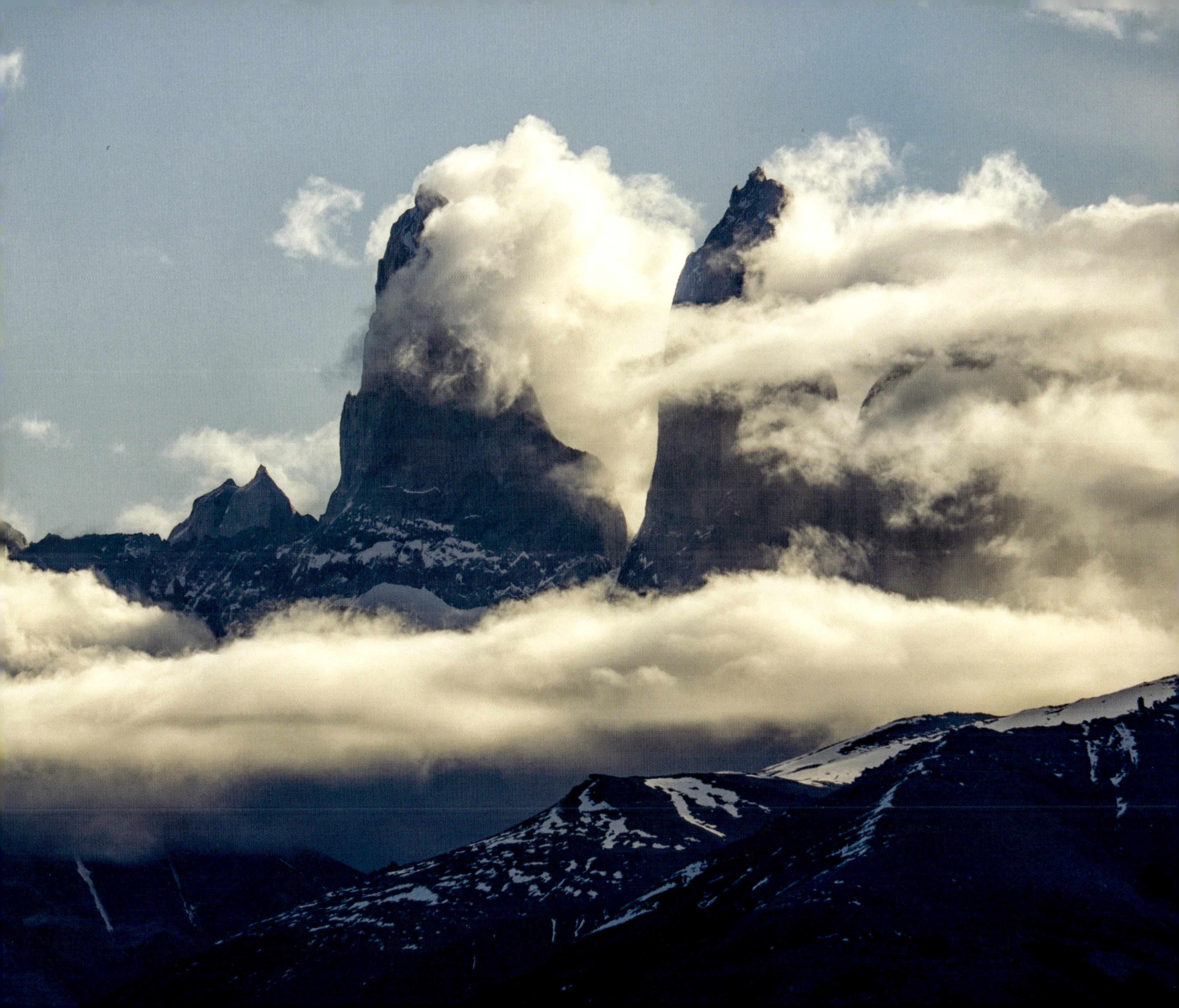

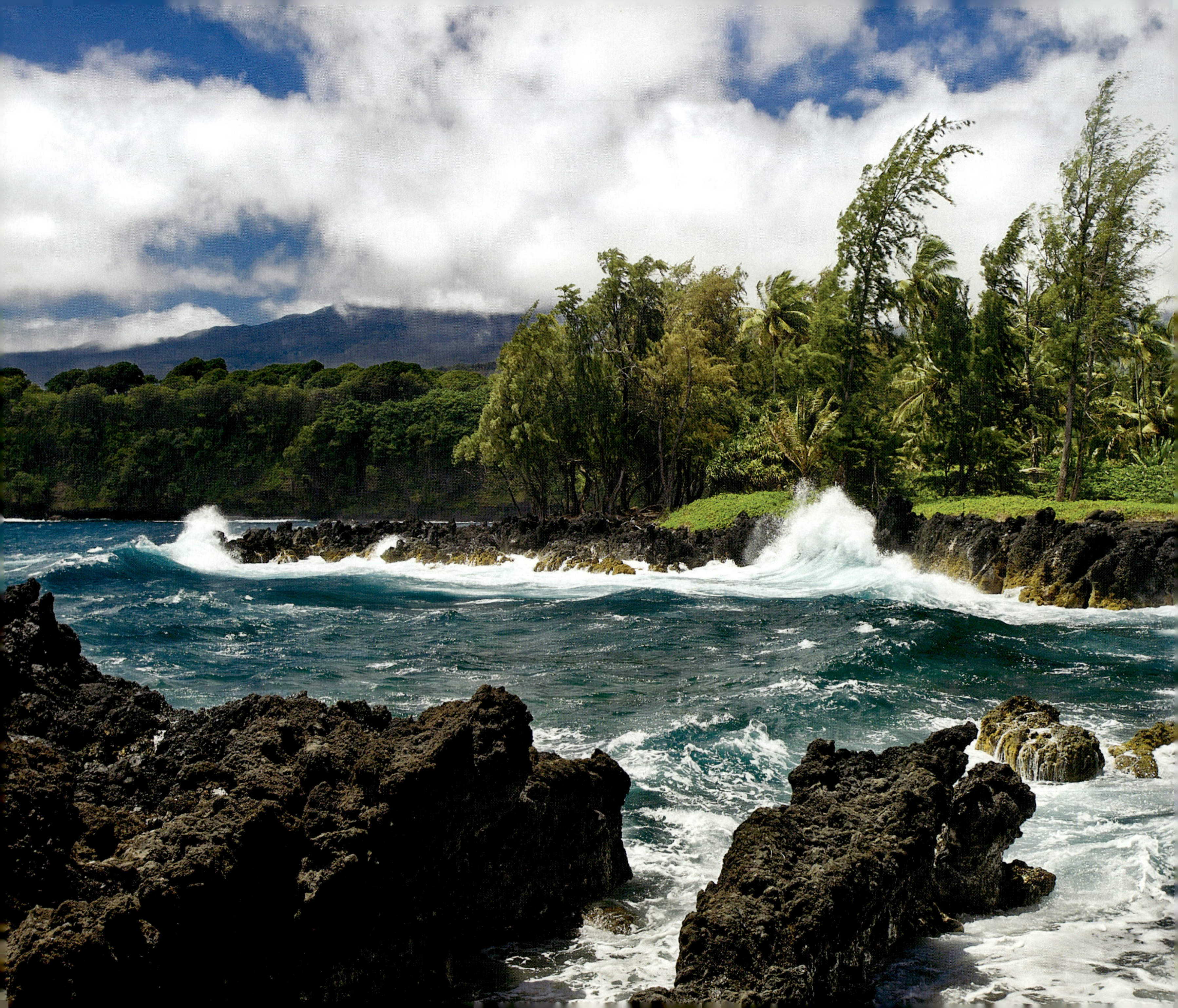

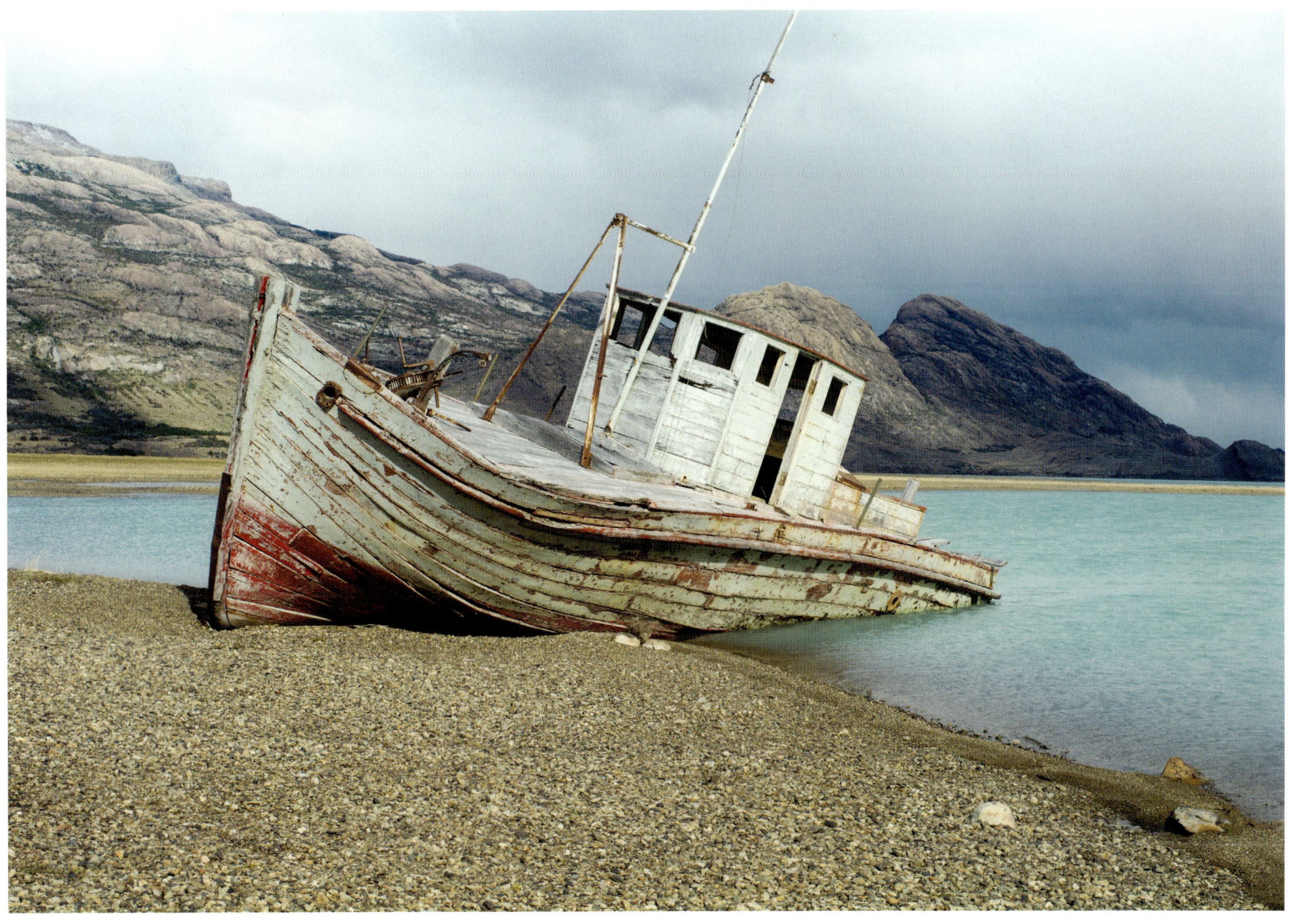

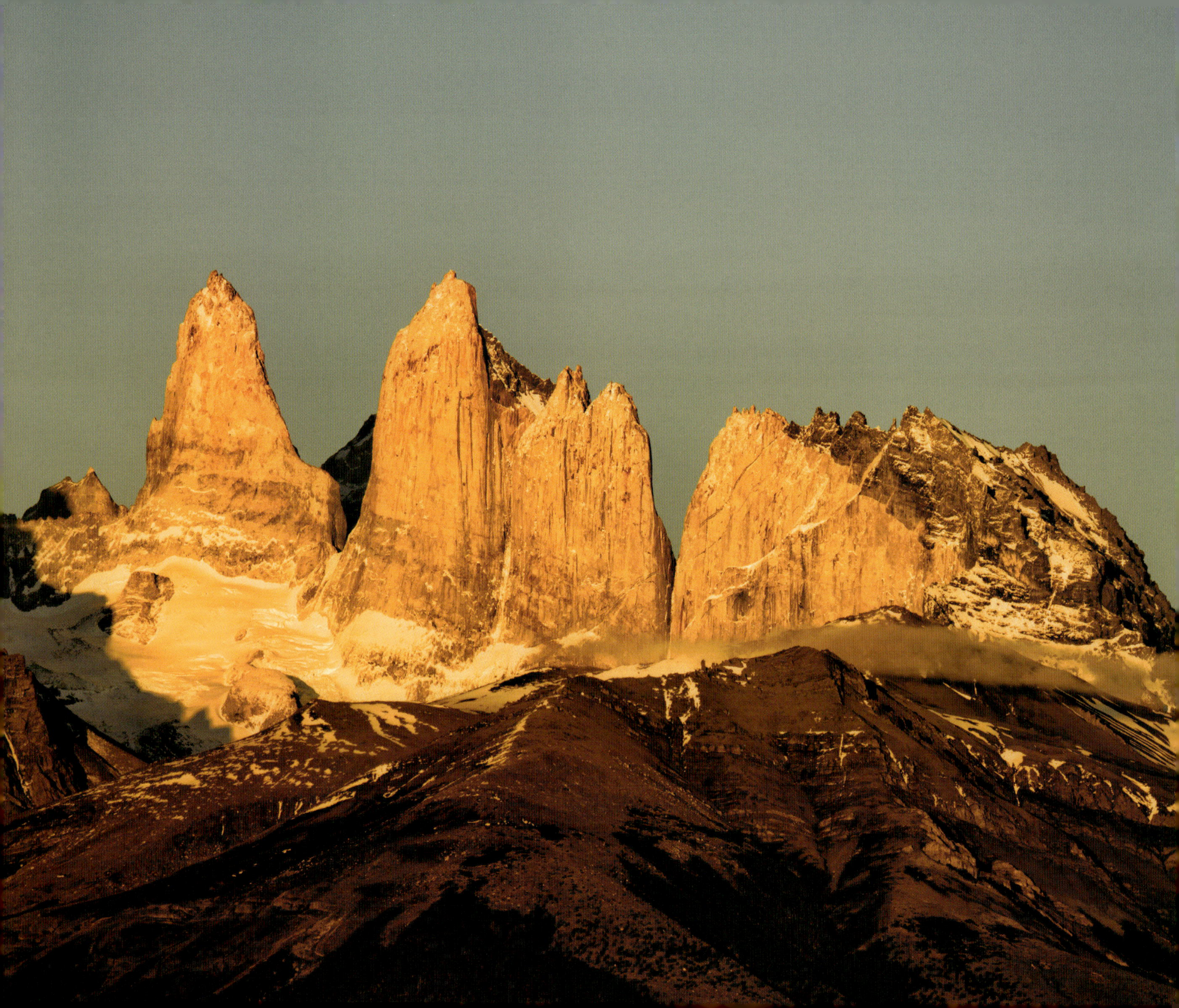

rock, wind, water, star

With tender attention and glorious power, God has filled the world with treasures. He pours out riches to glorify Himself and delight His creatures. Creation is a love letter from the Lord, written in tiny lines with the unique pattern of each snowflake, and in tremendous, swirling script as rivers fall over cliffs. We are surrounded with evidence of His glory and His thoughtfulness toward us. His love is everywhere, both graceful and majestic.

REFLECT

The earth is full of the lovingkindness of the Lord.
By the word of the Lord the heavens were made, and by the breath of His mouth all their host.

PSALM 33:5-6

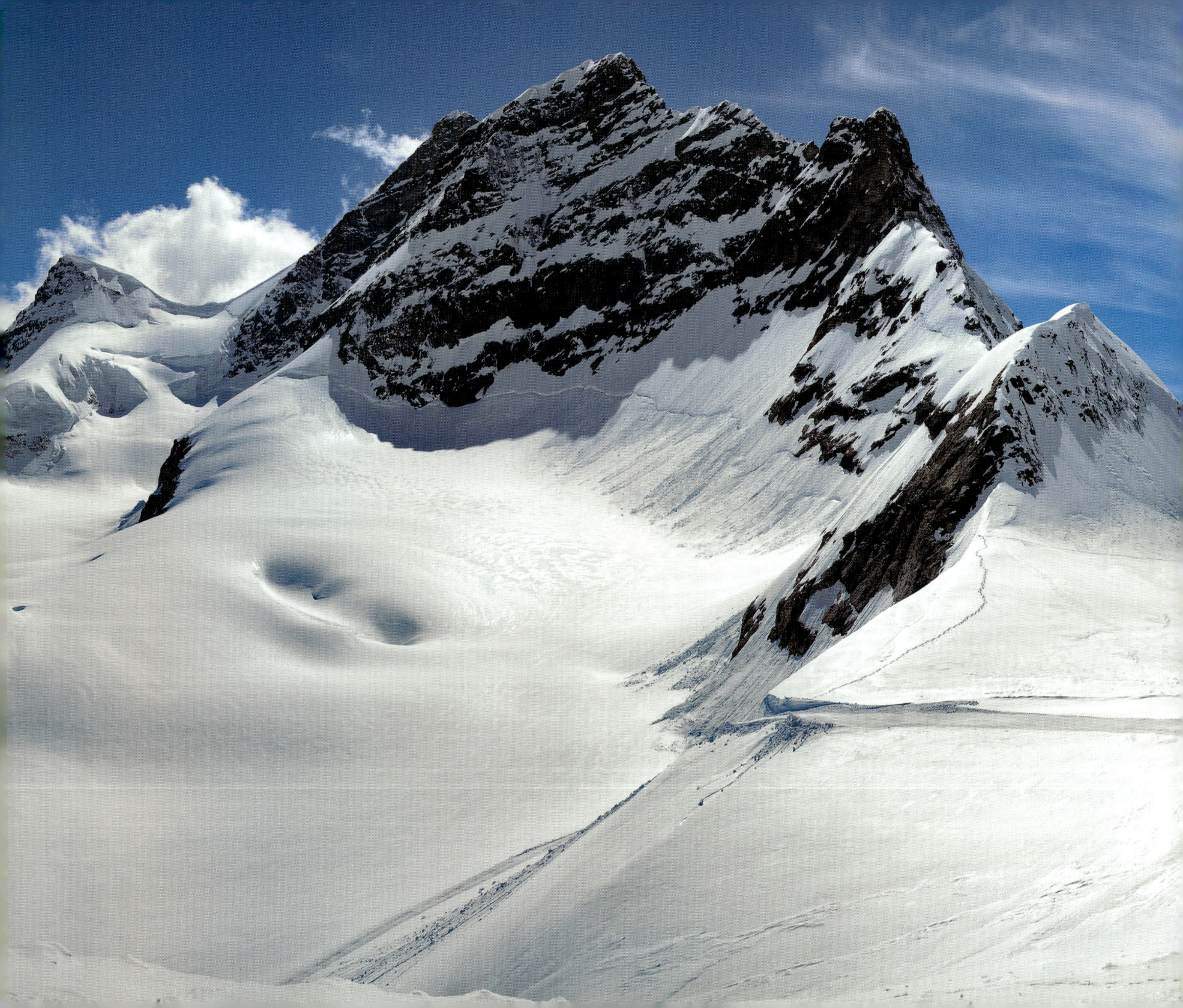

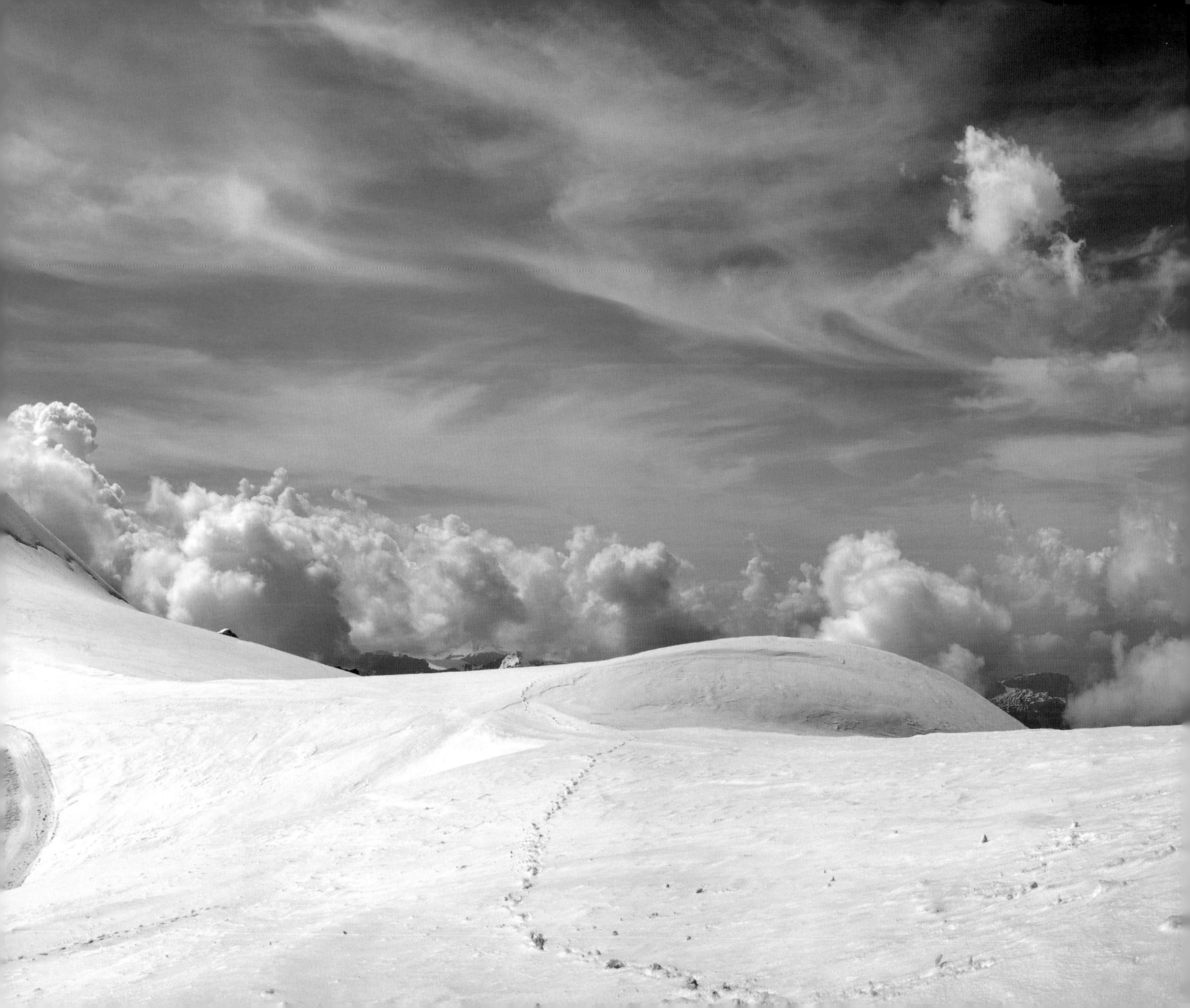

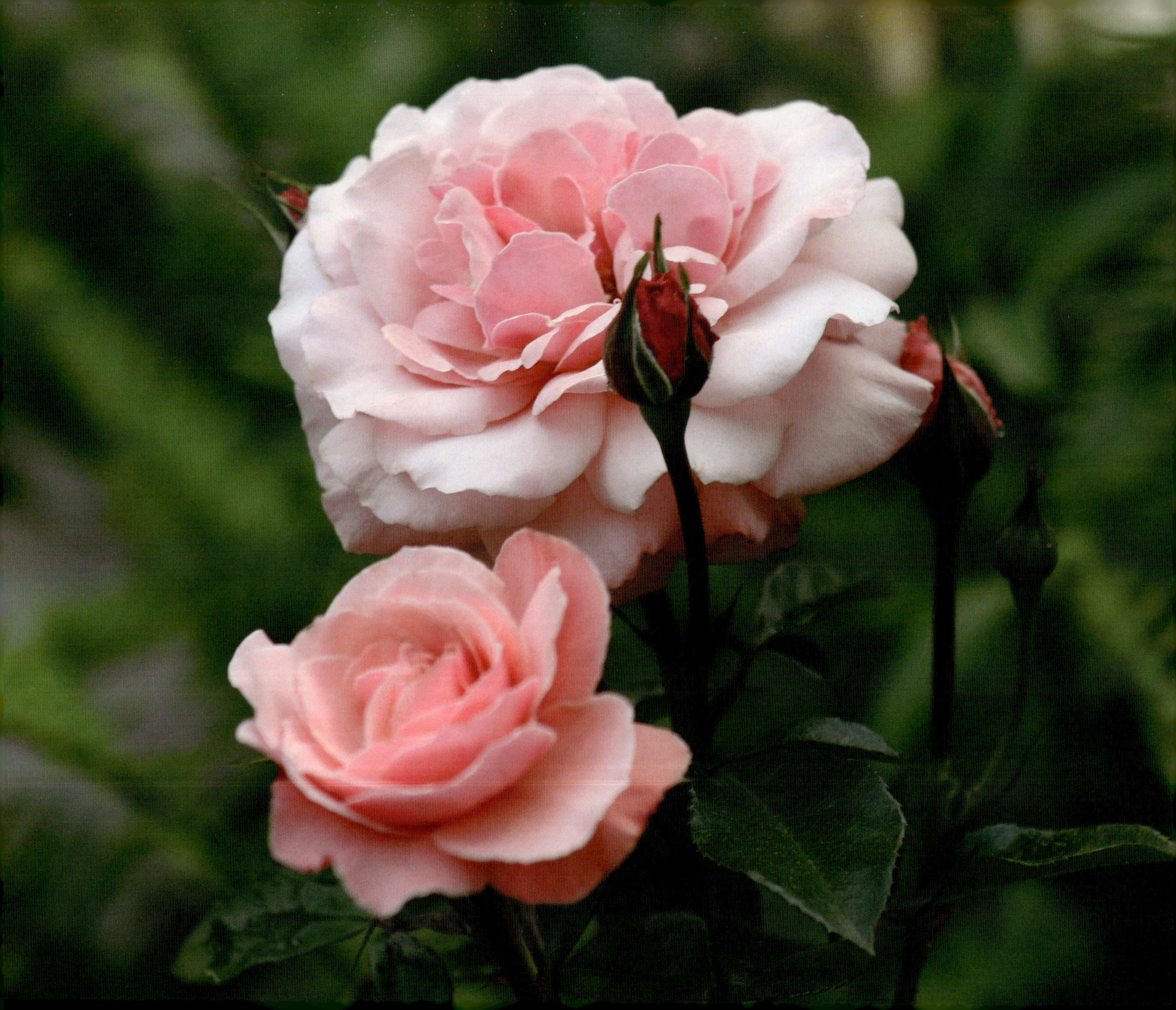

Why is it we can walk up to a red rose and find one fragrance? Why can we walk up to a yellow rose and find another fragrance? Why does a peach have a different aroma altogether? Where do all these beautiful flowers come from? And all of these trees, the birds of the air, and the incredible beauty of creation? God created everything in heaven and on the earth. He created all things visible and invisible. Creation is an expression of God's tremendous power and love. It's a display of His goodness and His concept of beauty. Creation shows us the infinite, divine, supernatural character of God, which is totally beyond our human comprehension.

— DR. CHARLES STANLEY —

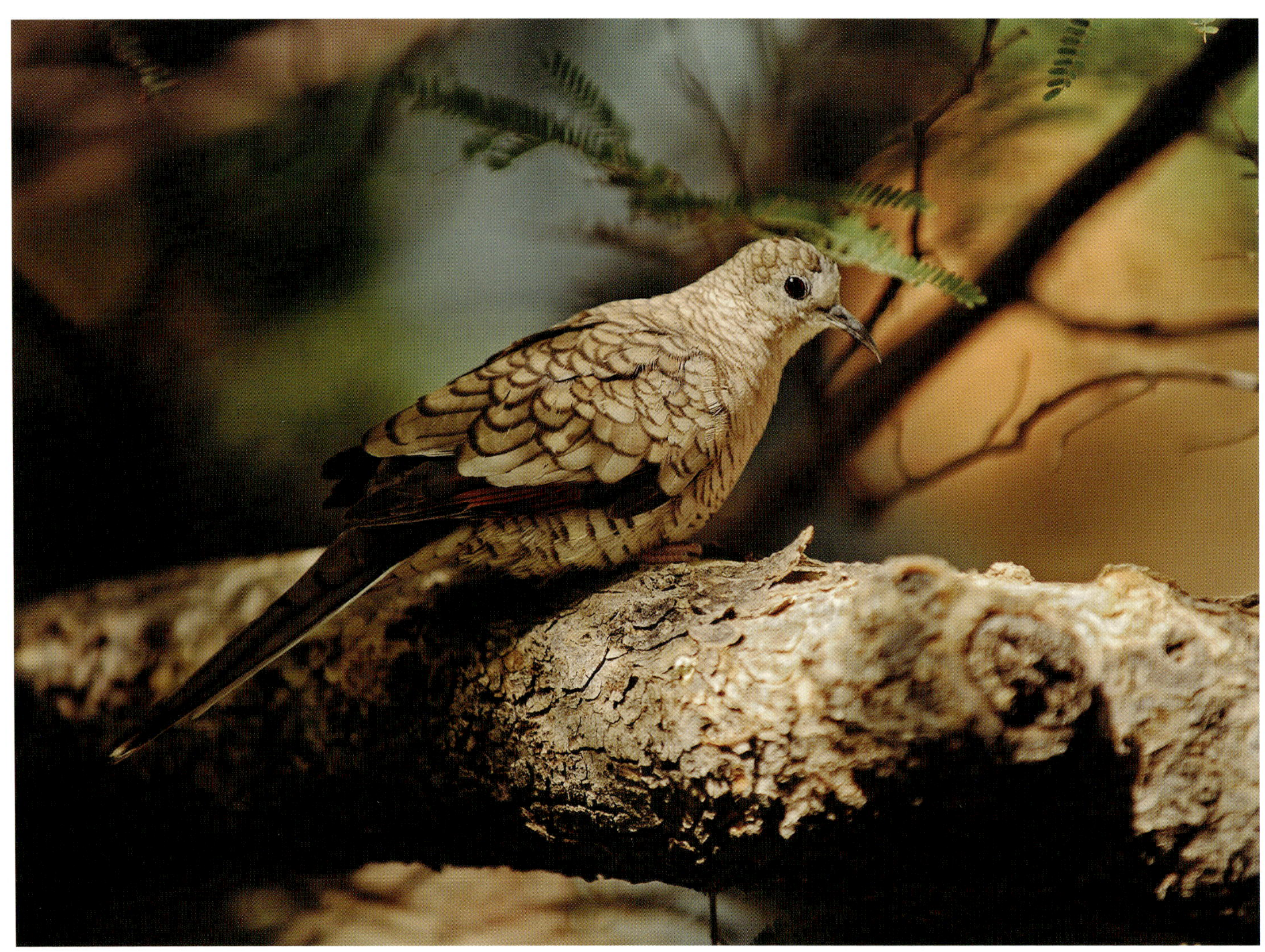

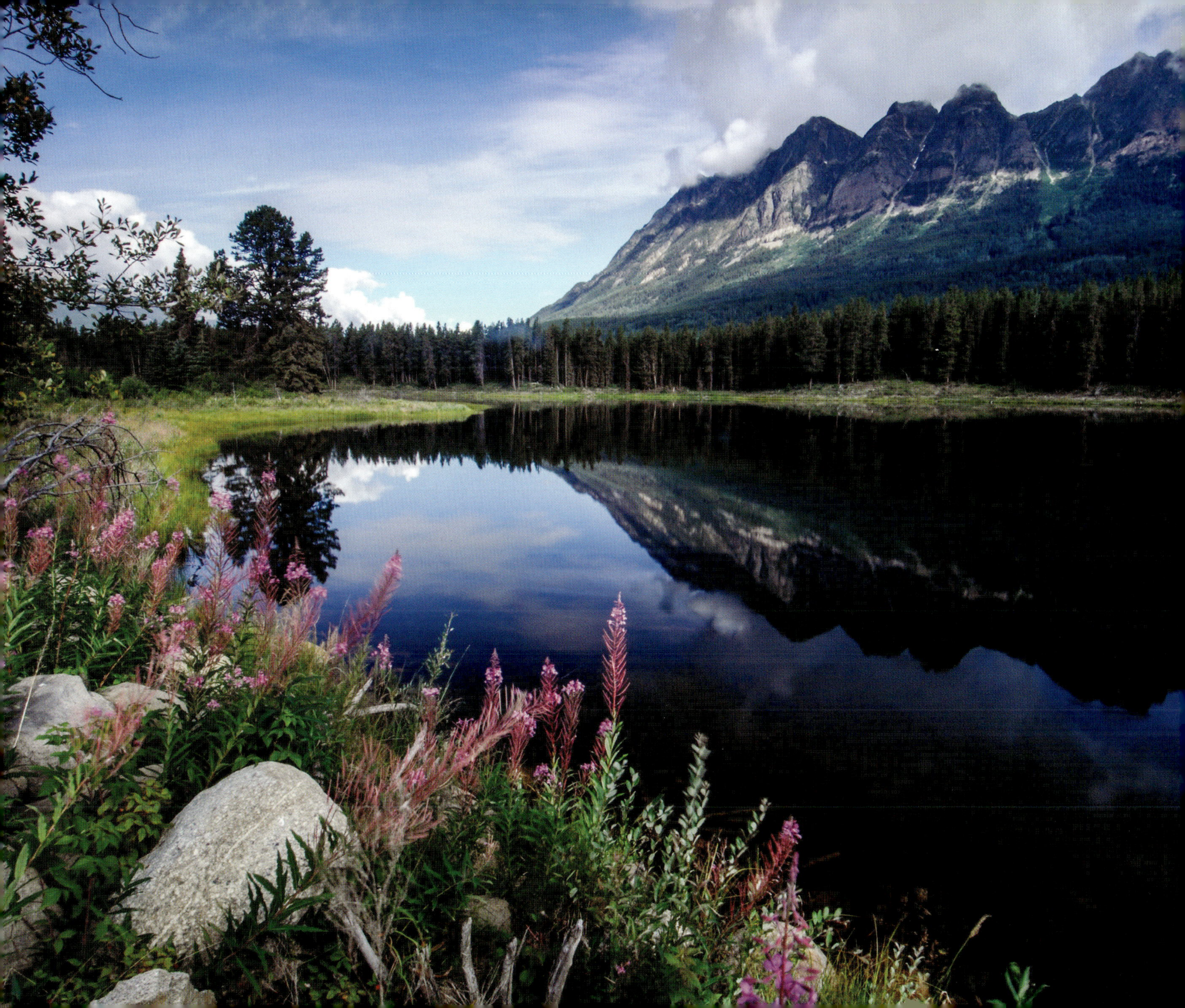

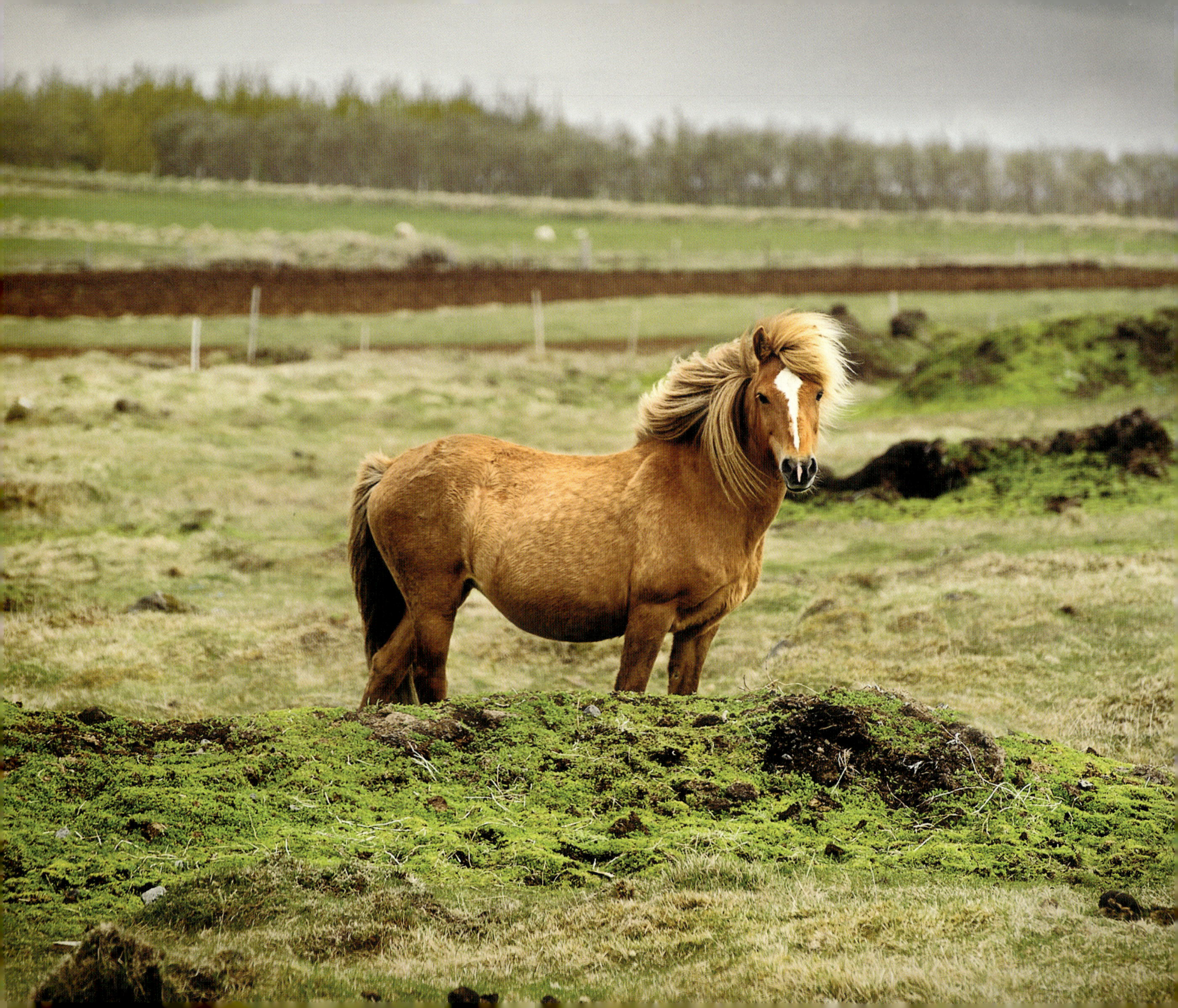

our loving provider

Dependence forms the framework of our most important relationship: We depend on God for everything. Even our next breath is a whisper of love from the Creator. He is the One who grants us air, lungs, and life. What He provides is not always what we expect, but the simplest of meals can be satisfying to a heart that has been humbled. From a moment's rest to a stunning miracle, all creation relies on the generosity of God, who alone provides it all.

REFLECT

The eyes of all look to You, and You give them their food in due time. You open Your hand and satisfy the desire of every living thing. The Lord is righteous in all His ways and kind in all His deeds.

PSALM 145:15-17

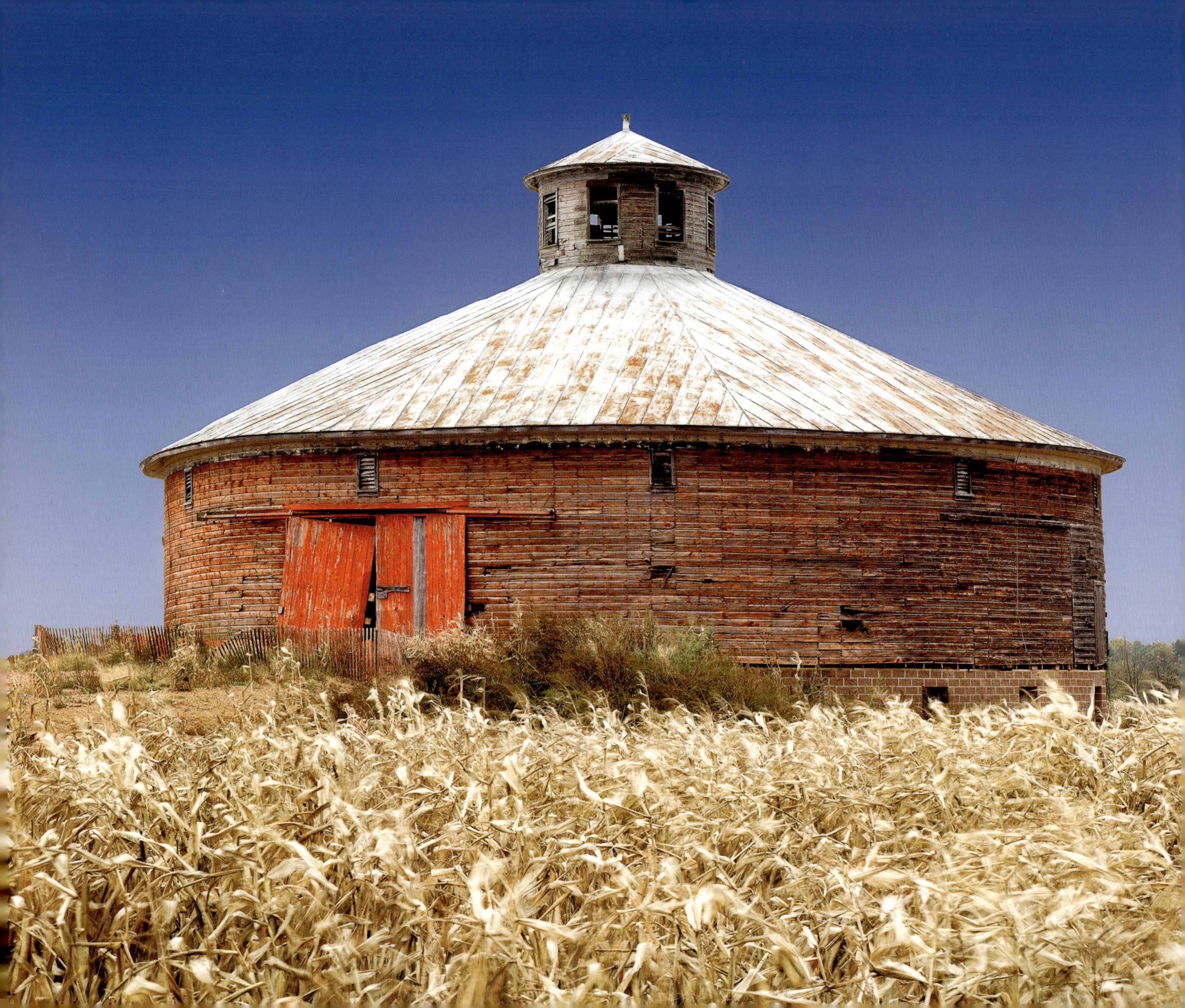

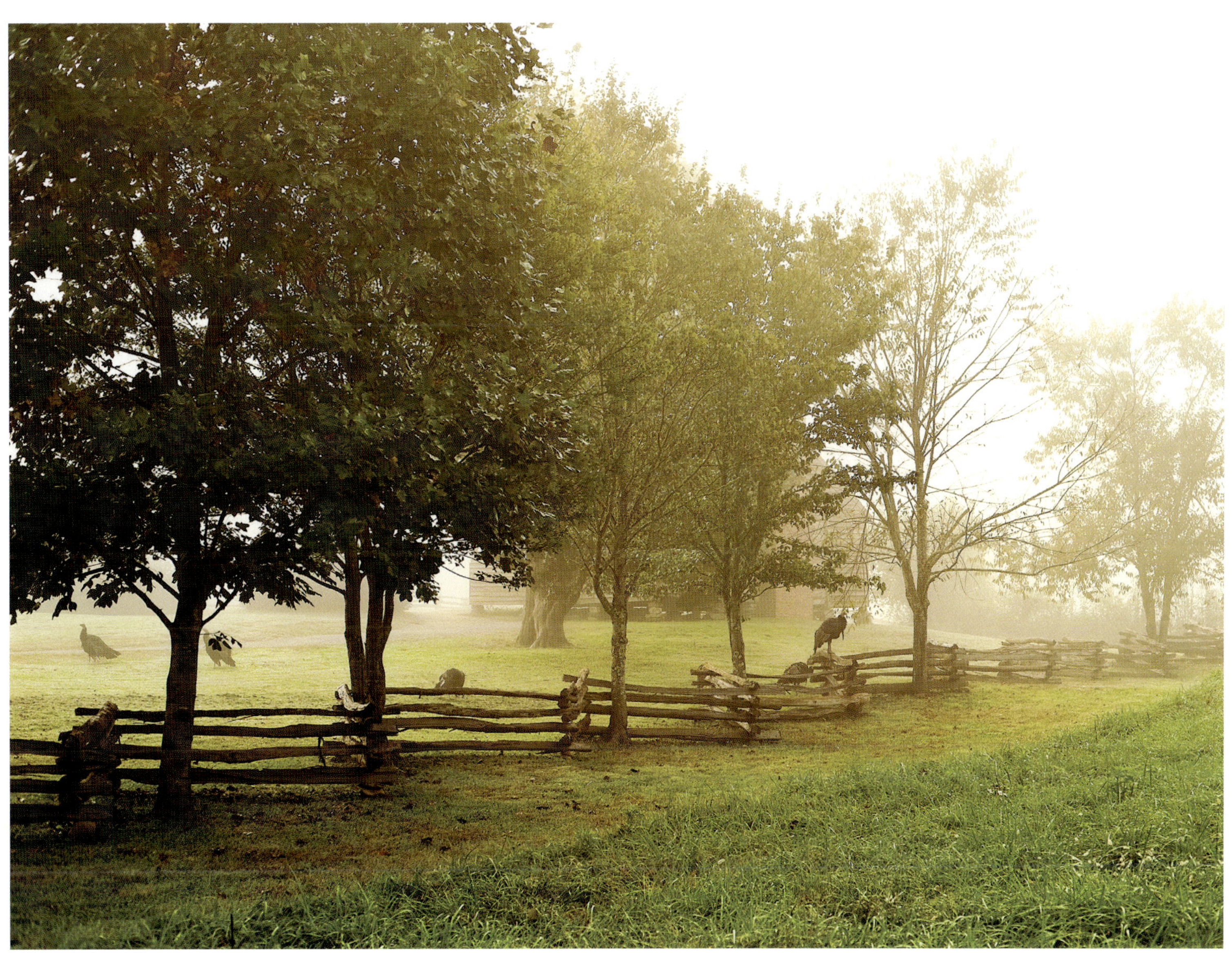

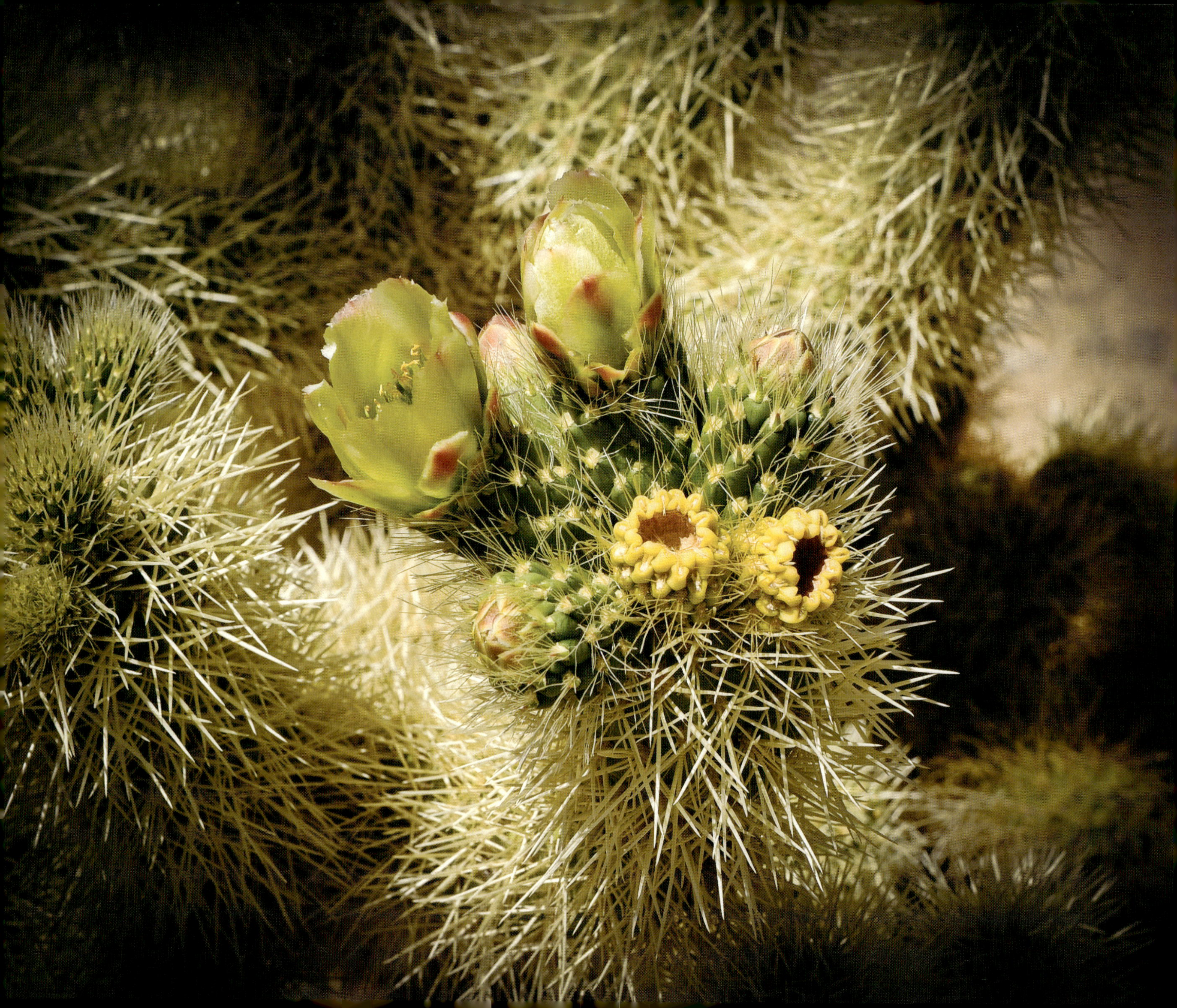

the restoring hand of God

What seems destroyed when cold descends or barrenness claims the land can be made new in moments, seasons, or generations. Through cracked and dry earth, a spiky plant can make its way into the world, and almost unbelievably, yield a cluster of flowers or a crown of berries. A snow-covered field will show its grass again in the golden light of summer. For our souls God does no less. He heals our wounds and tends to our traumas, and one day, He will make all things new. It is the nature of His love to restore.

REFLECT

The desert and the parched land will be glad;
the wilderness will rejoice and blossom. Like the crocus,
it will burst into bloom; it will rejoice greatly
and shout for joy.

ISAIAH 35:1-2 (NIV)

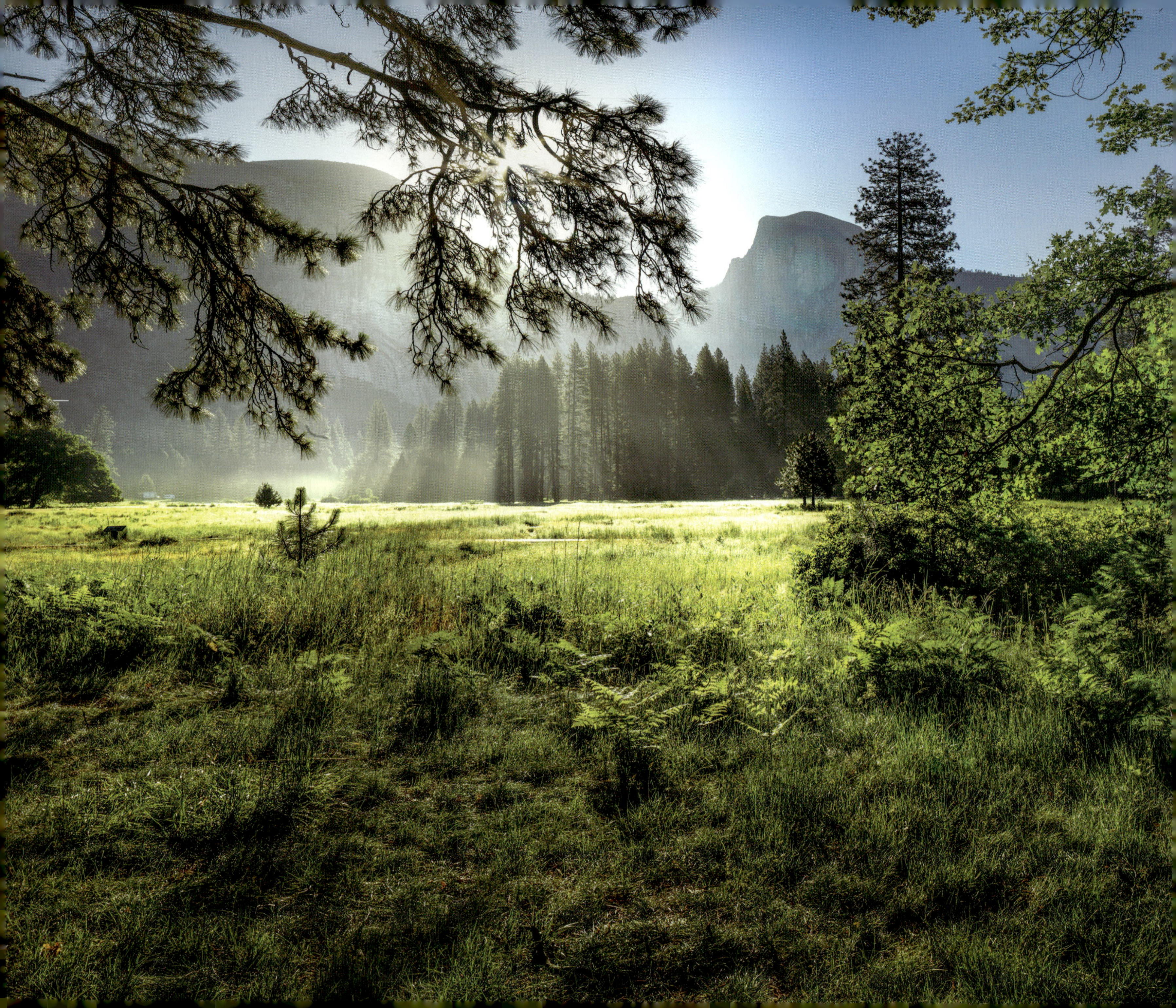

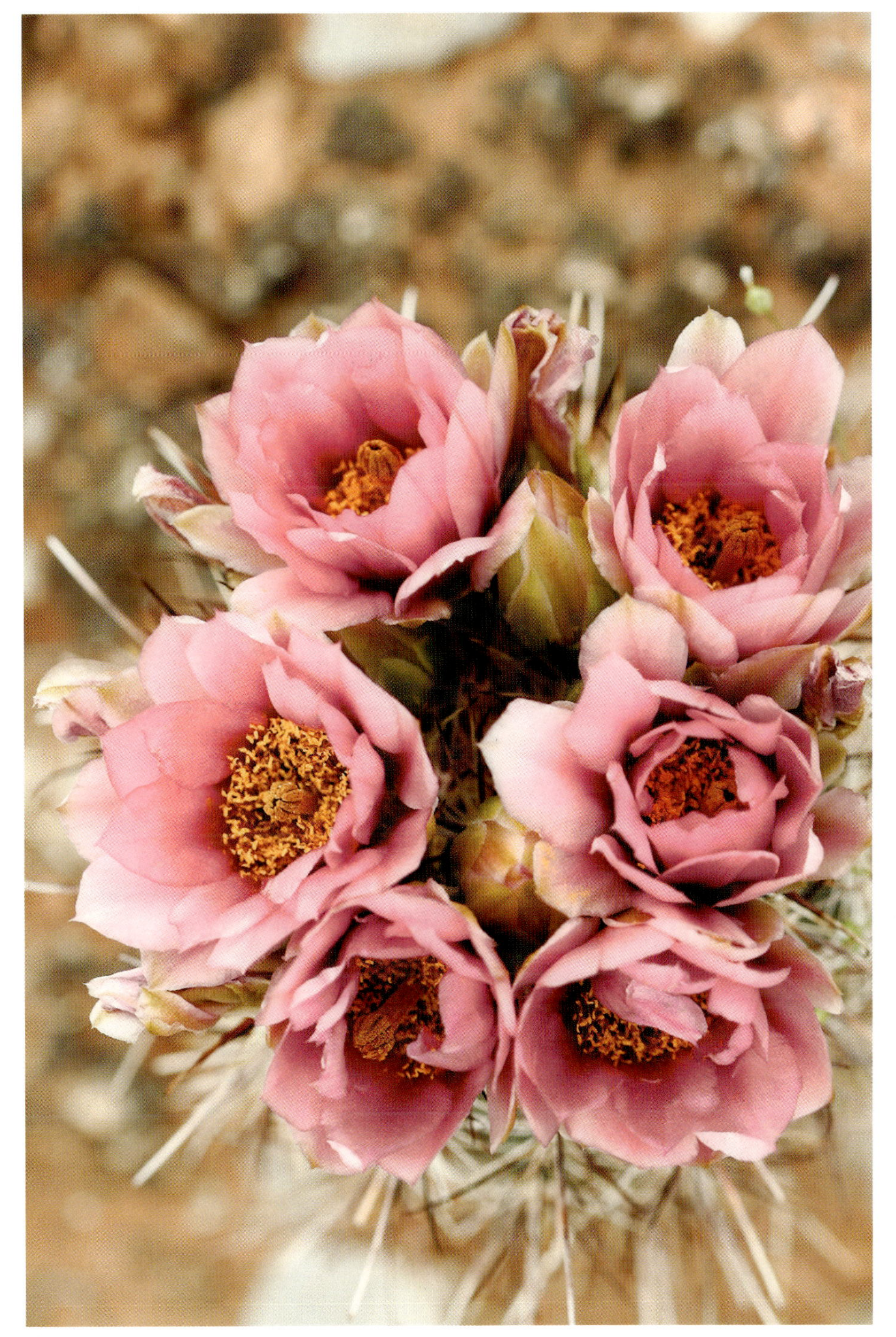

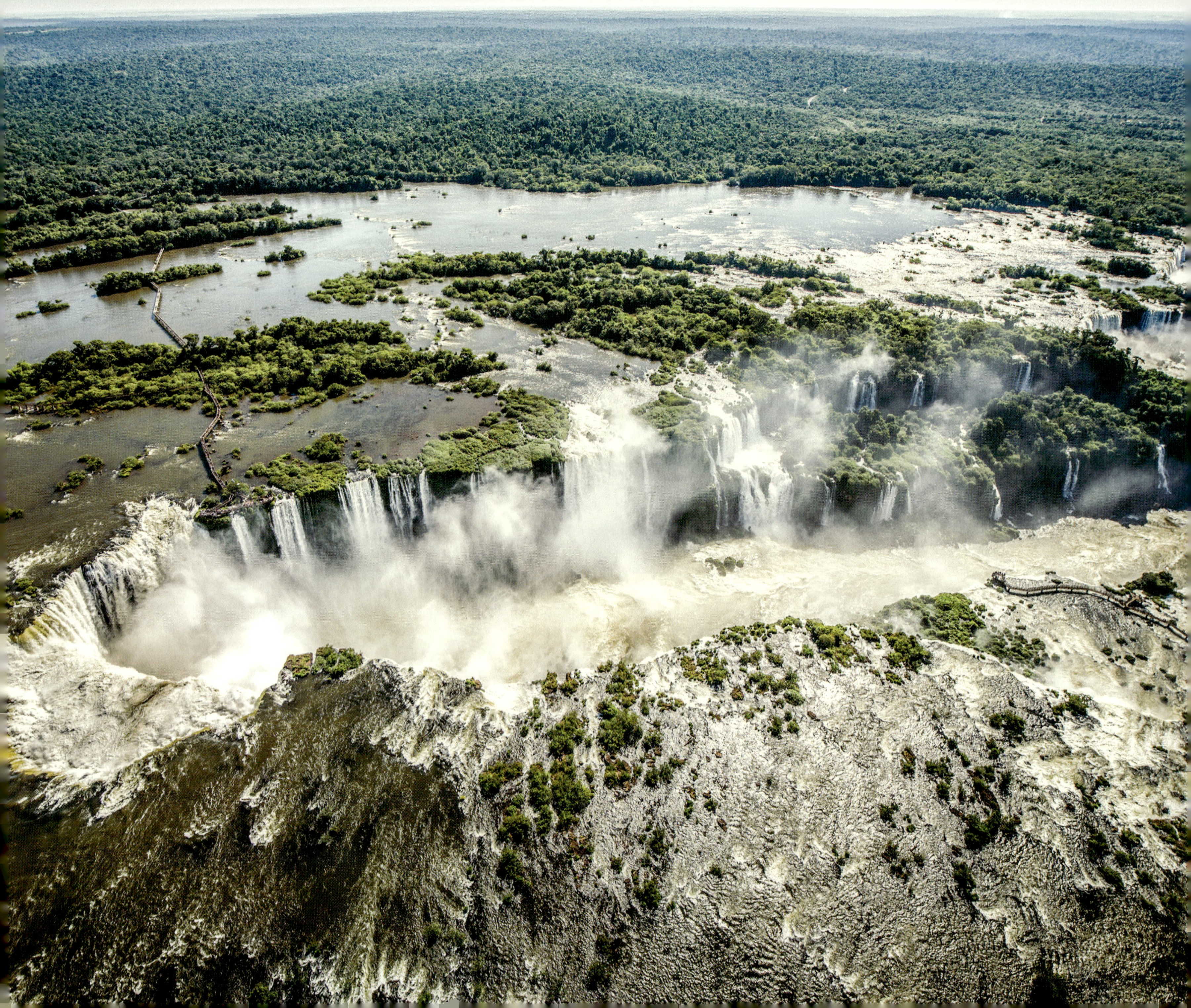

His love is endless

From moment to moment and from age to age, the love of God is certain. Mountains will crumble, rivers will flood their banks, but behind it all is the steady care of a God who remains constant. He calls to us over and over with the news of His great faithfulness. Like the rings of a tree that tell of its endurance in every season, the Word testifies of His unfailing love to His people. Over time, He inscribes the same record on our hearts.

REFLECT

Give thanks to Him, bless His name. For the LORD is good; His lovingkindness is everlasting and His faithfulness to all generations.

PSALM 100:4-5

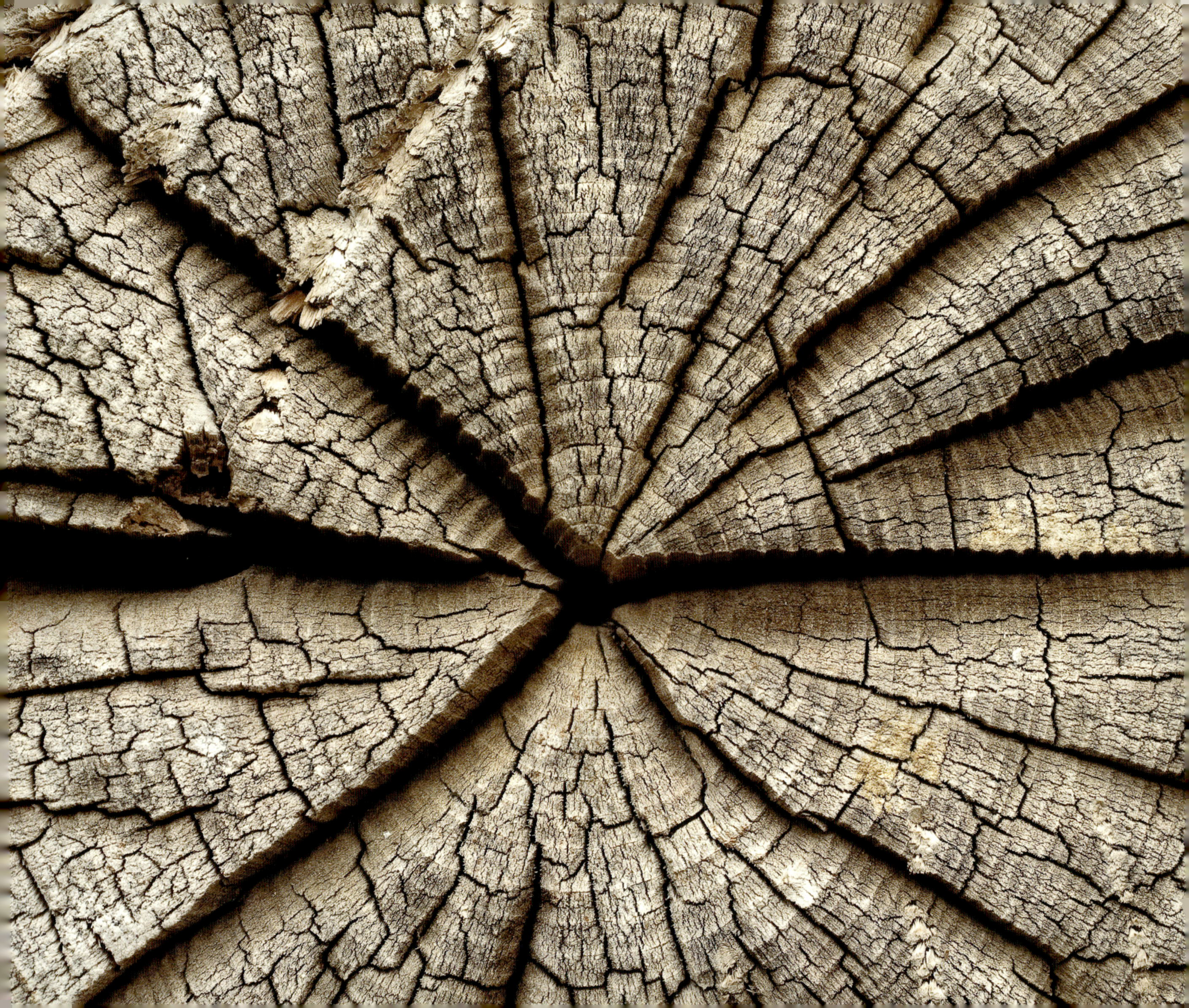

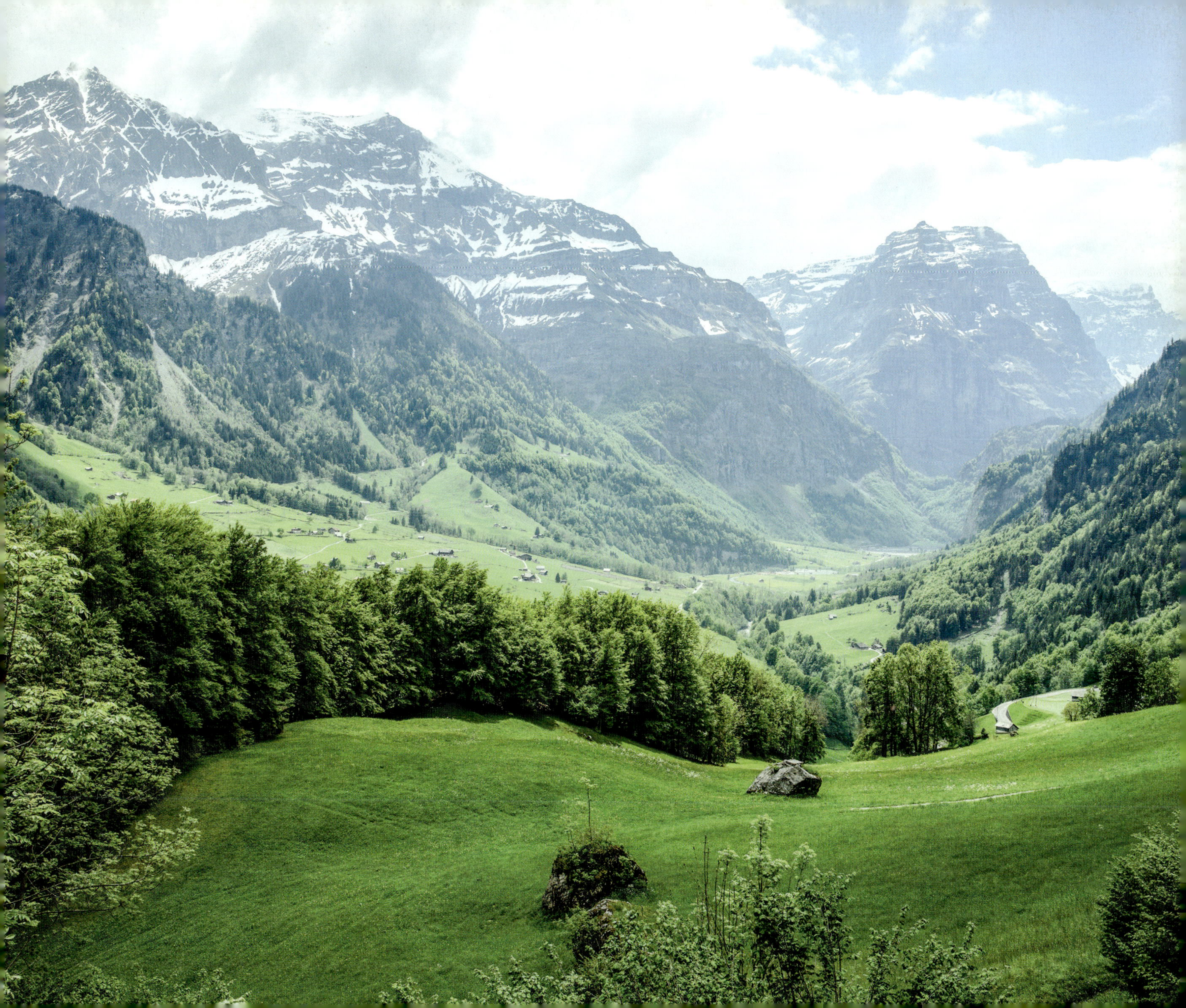

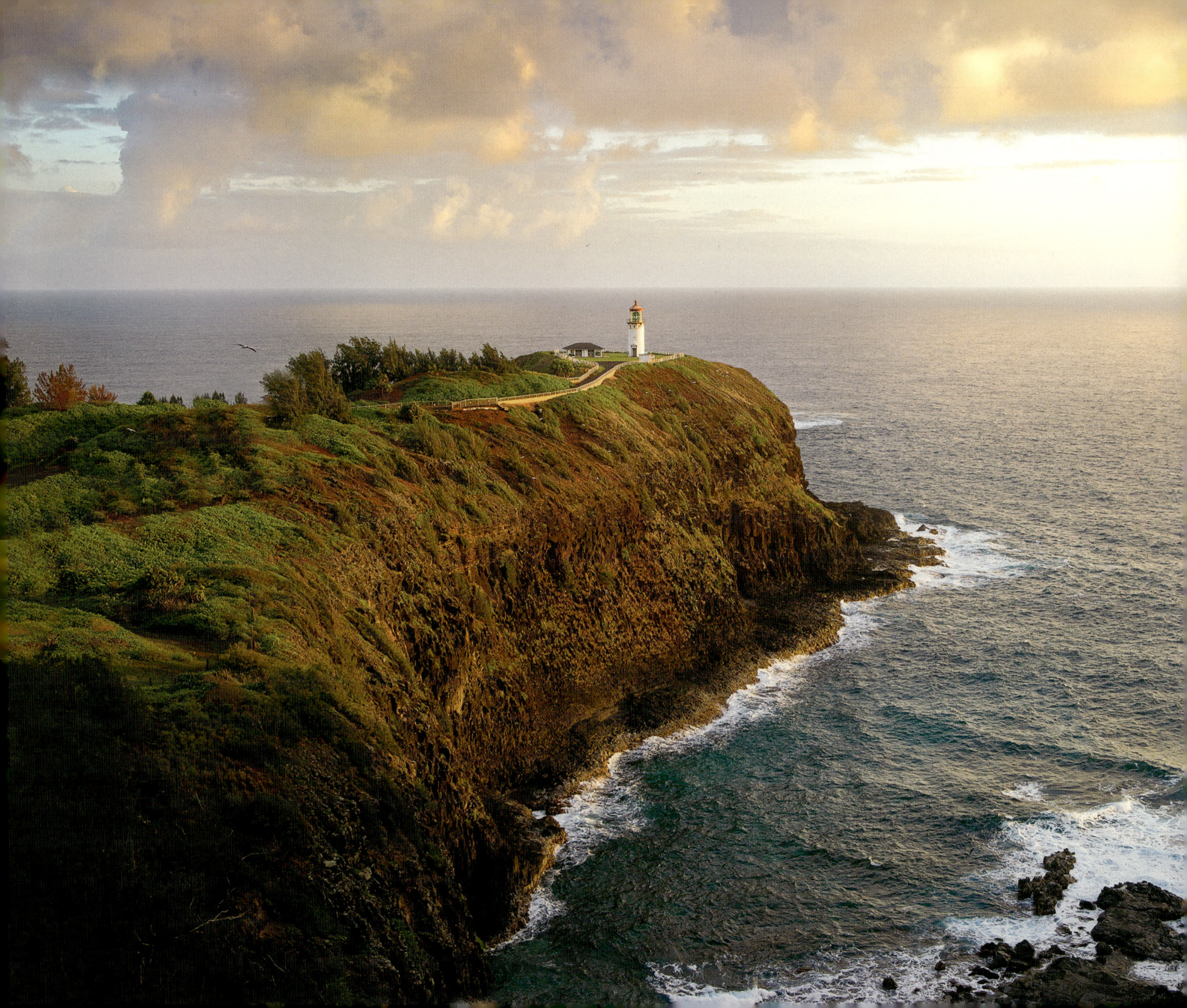

REFLECT

O come, let us sing for joy to the Lord ...
Let us shout joyfully to Him with psalms.
For the Lord is a great God
And a great King above all gods,
In whose hand are the depths of the earth,
The peaks of the mountains are His also.
The sea is His, for it was He who made it,
And His hands formed the dry land.
Come, let us worship and bow down,
Let us kneel before the Lord our Maker.
For He is our God,
And we are the people of His pasture
and the sheep of His hand.

PSALM 95:1-7

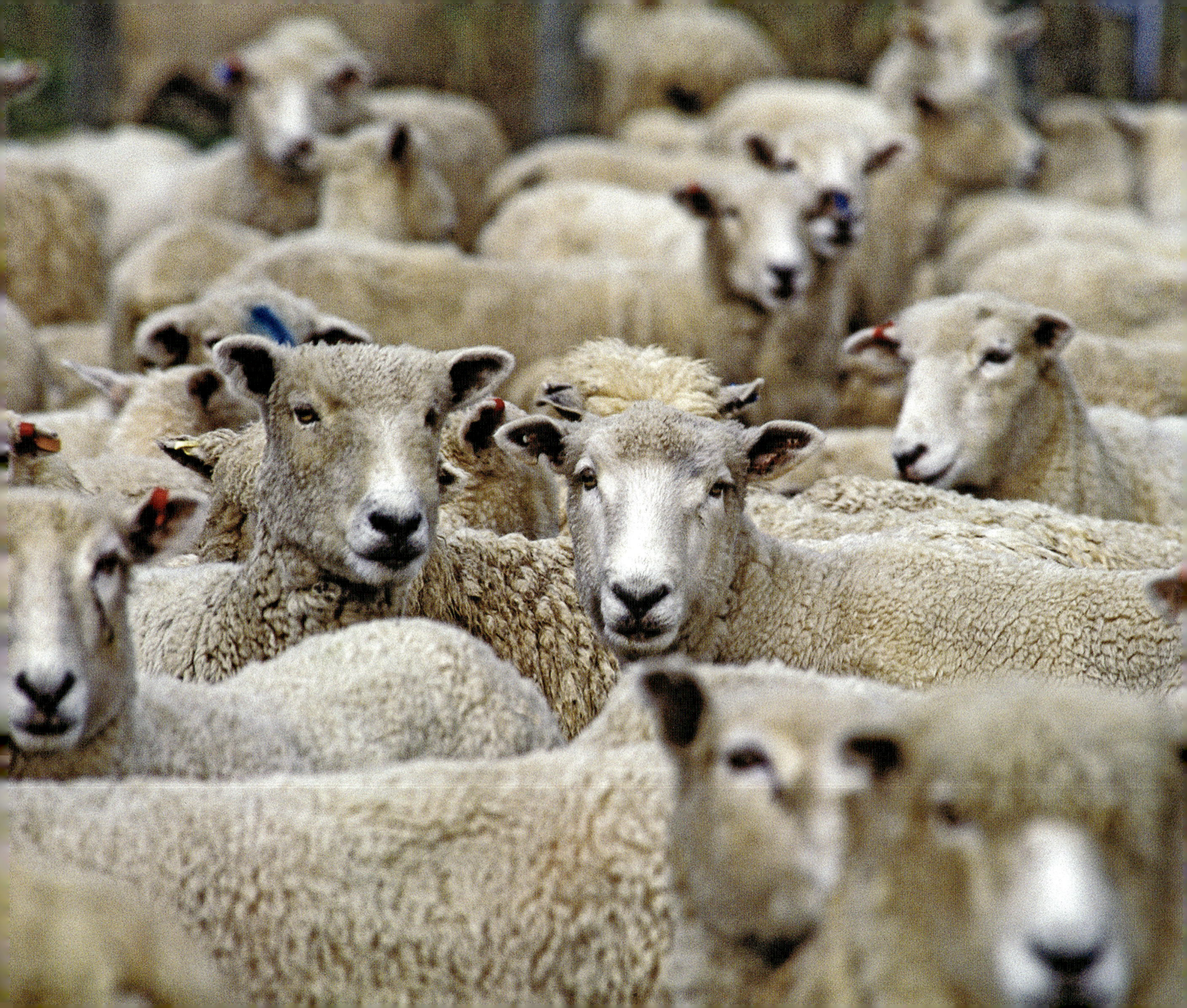

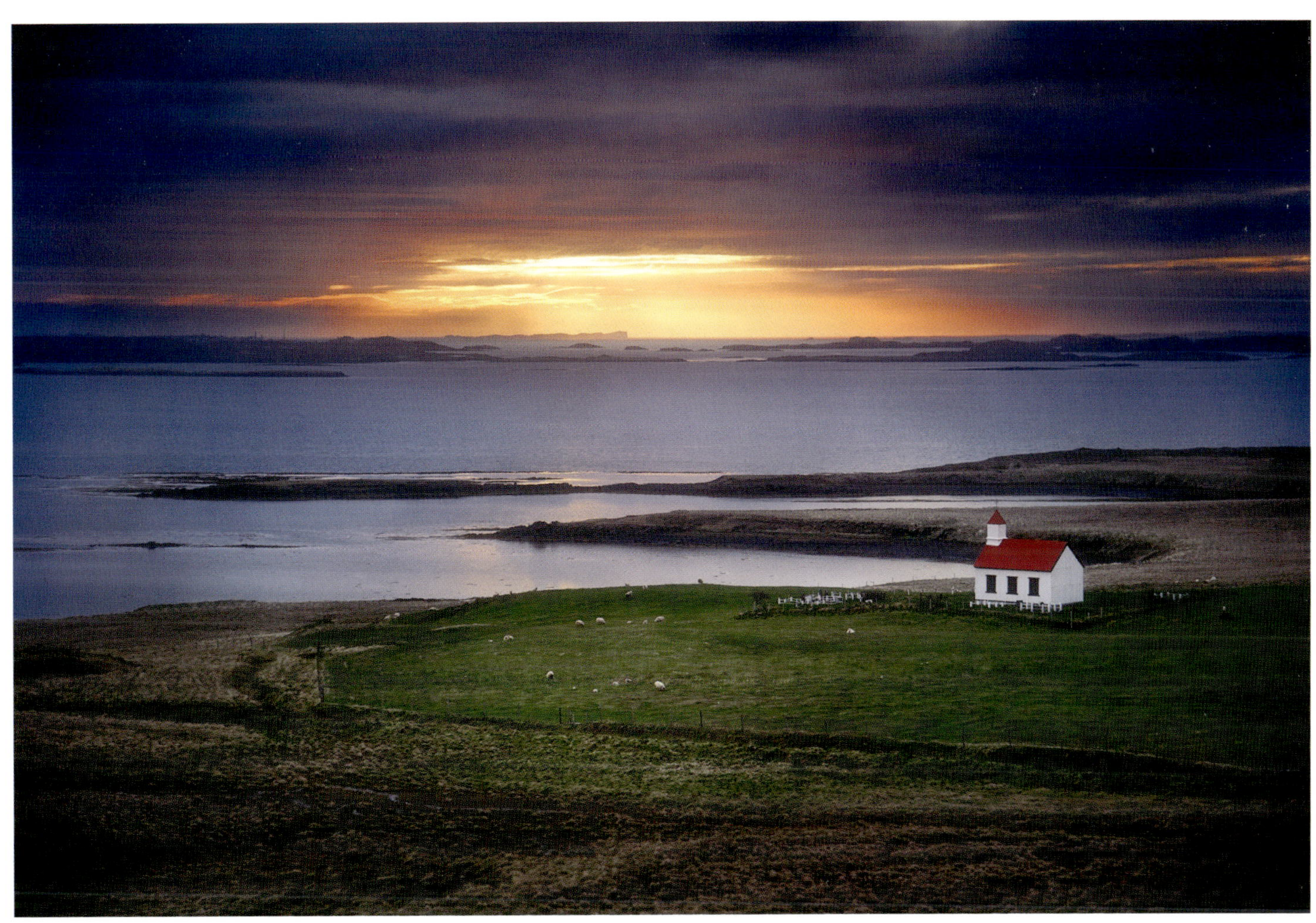

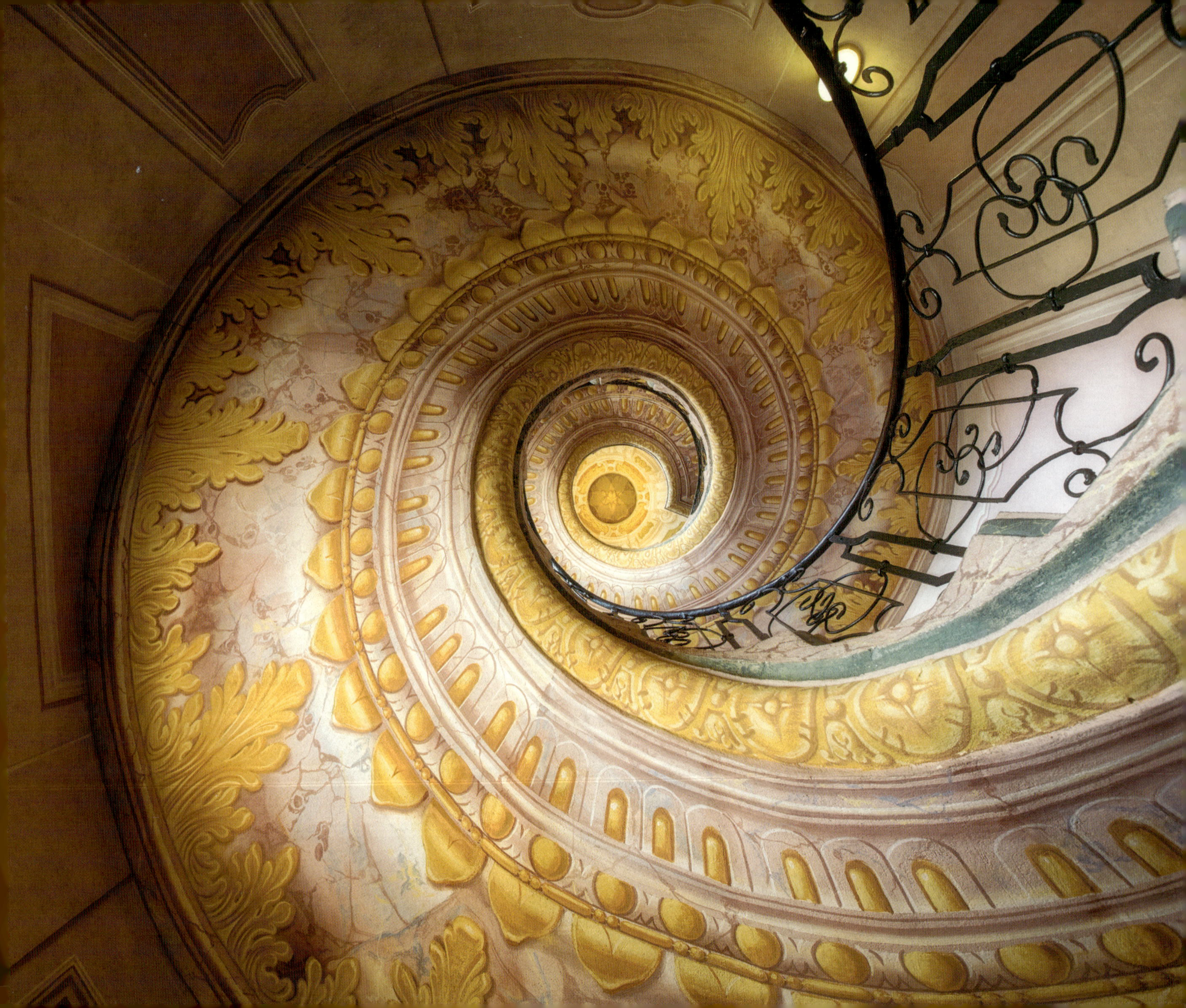

CHAPTER TWO

THE MYSTERY OF THE SON

One night in Bethlehem, God opened the door and entered His creation. The One who could not be contained allowed Himself to be concealed in the womb of a woman, and to come forth in human flesh as the Son of God.

He donned clothing, took up tools, and pressed the dirt with the mark of His heels. Sunlight warmed His face. He celebrated, wept, and ate. He loved His friends. The streams of the earth ran their hands over His, bringing the world into an incredible encounter with its Creator. With a man's ears He heard the sound of birds singing, catching echoes of what His own words had set in motion thousands of years before, as together with God the Father and the Holy Spirit, He brought the world into being.

Jesus, as God in the flesh, became the entry point of eternity into time, and time into eternity. What a mysterious confluence between His timeless deity and the limits in which we live. Rocky hills and cool riverbeds met the Christ in human form, but on Calvary the veil was torn. Through the death and resurrection of His physical body, every believer down through the ages would one day meet the exalted Christ as brother, friend, and Savior, and begin a relationship that lasts forever.

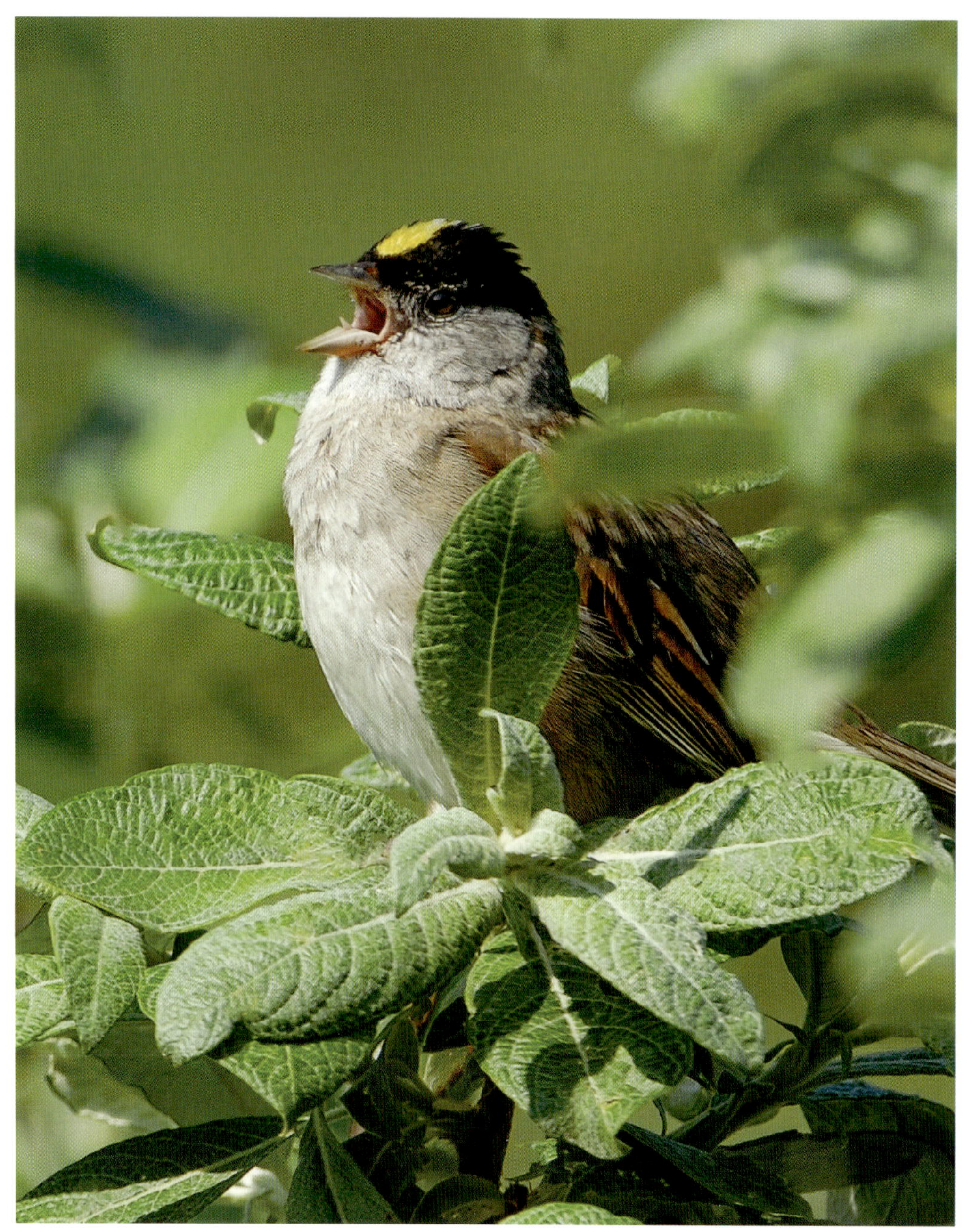

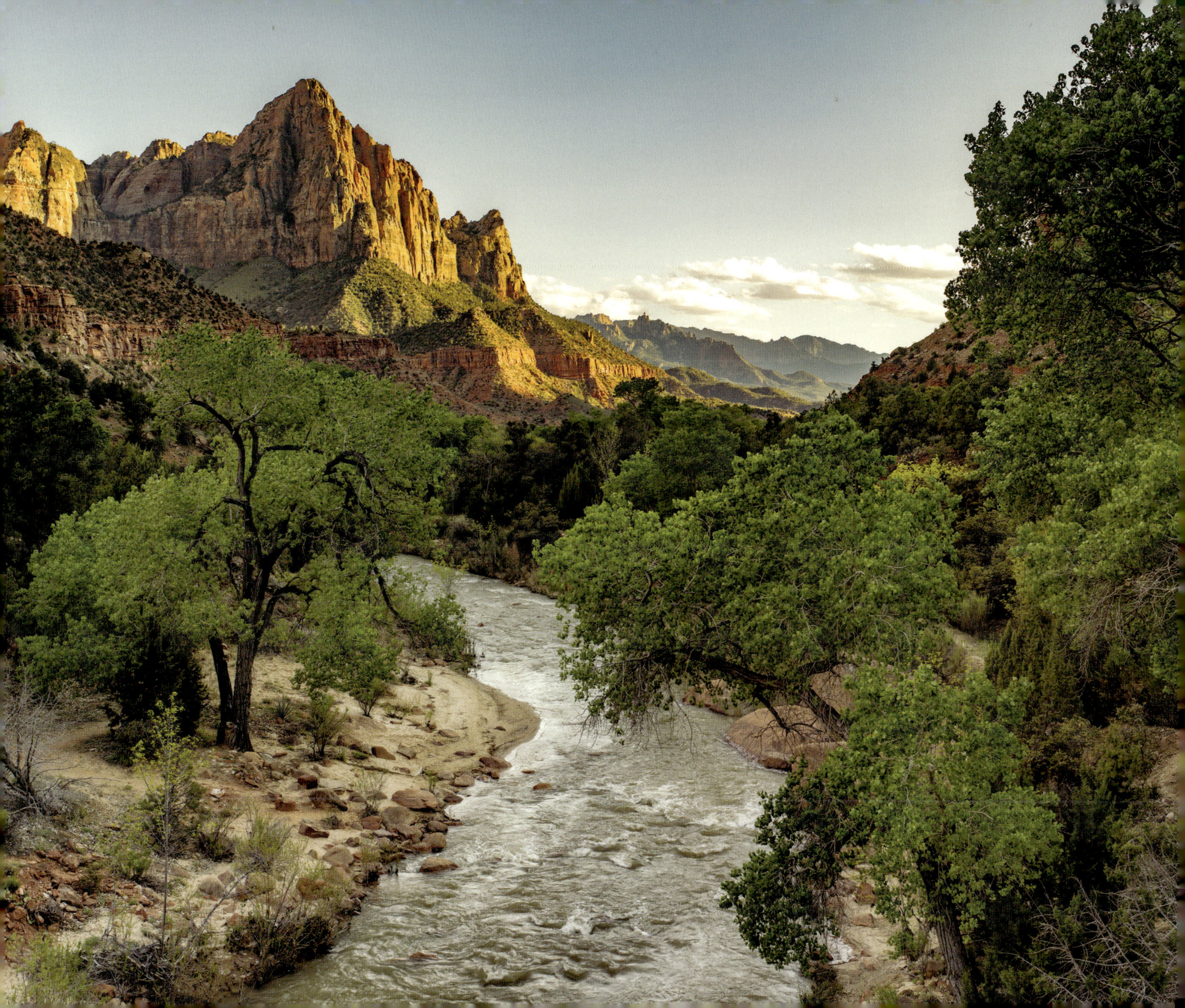

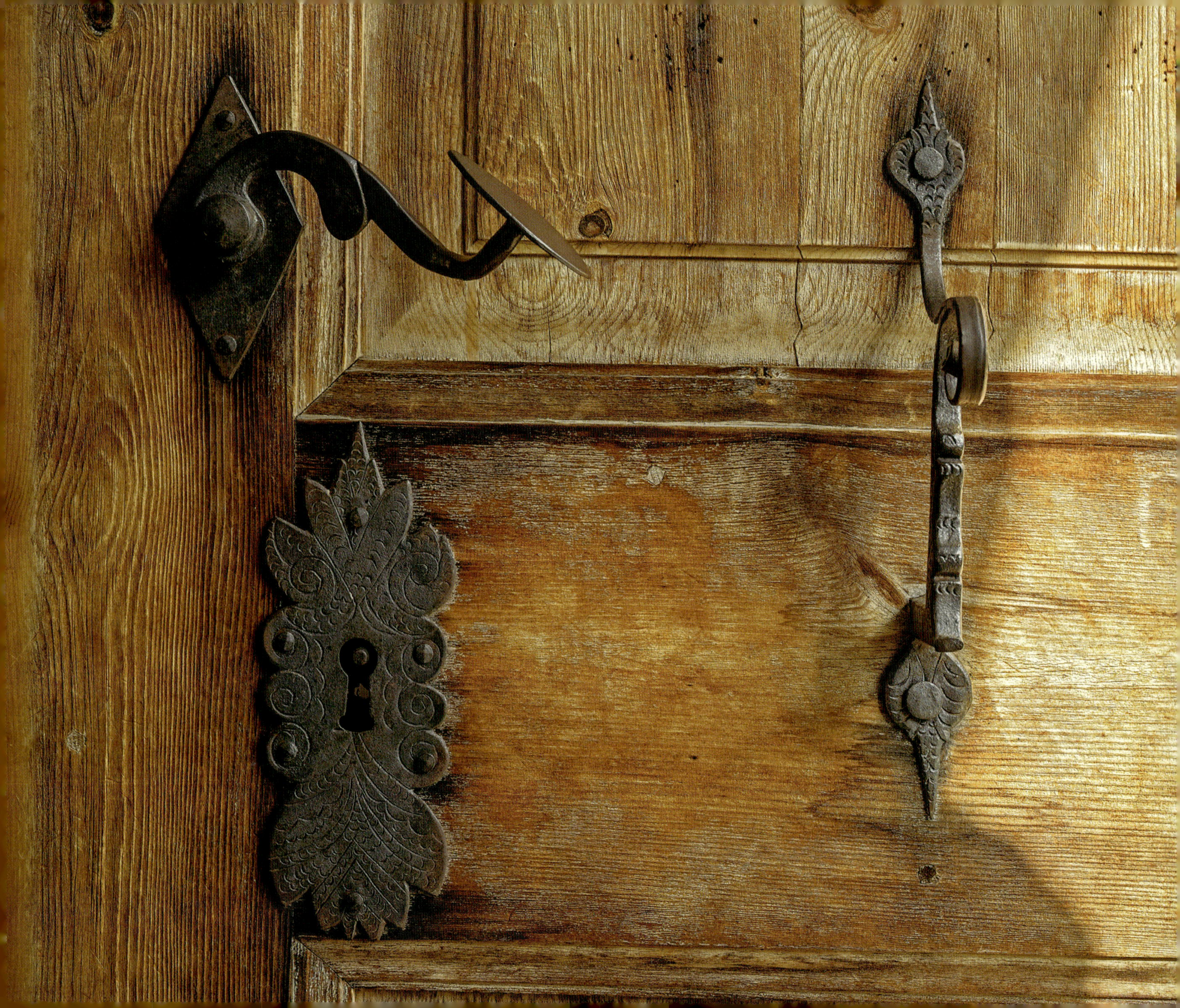

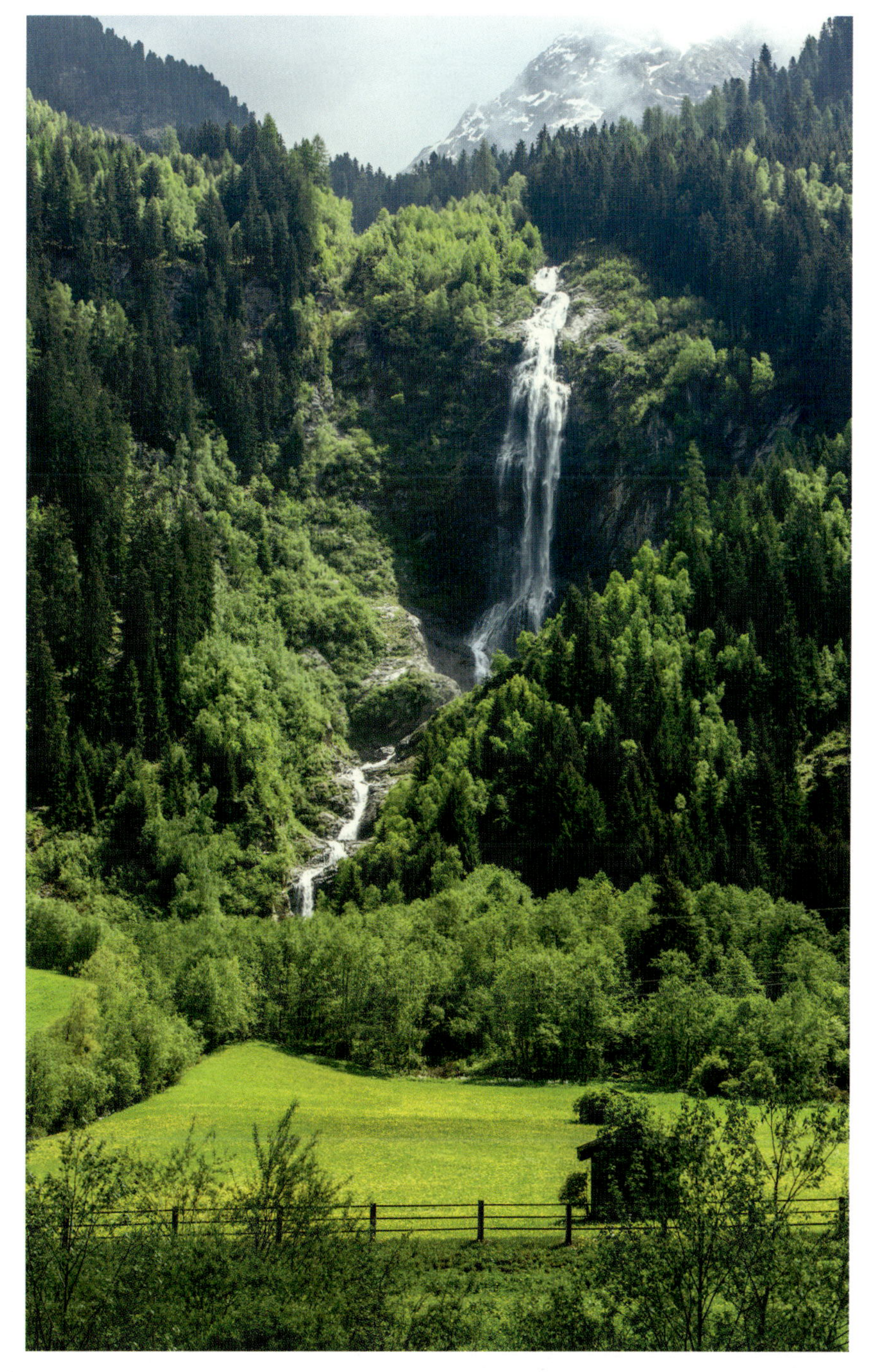

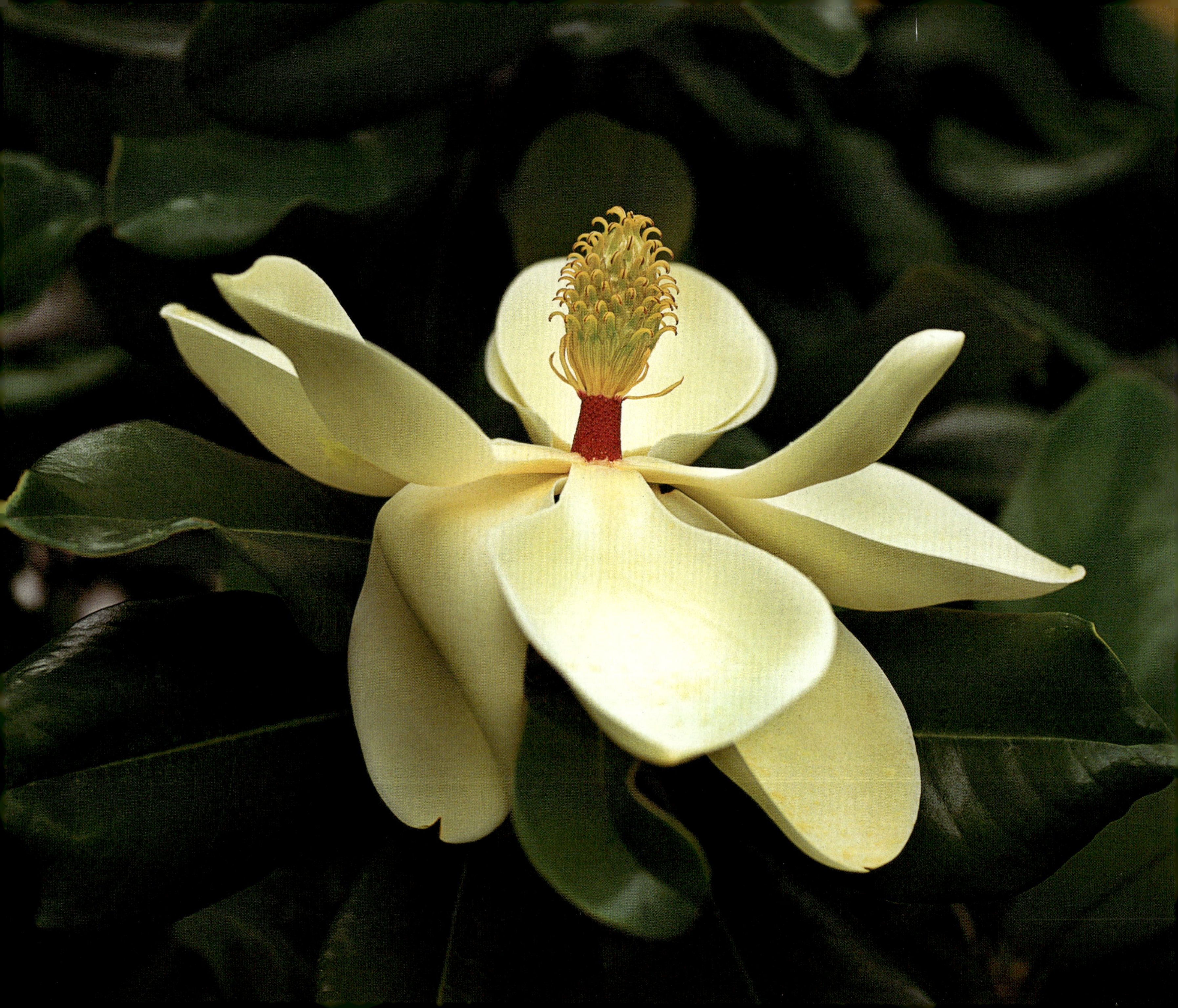

the Word made flesh

When Jesus was born, the walls of this world parted to reveal perfect love, like soil making way for a flower. He was radiant with the glory of the highest heaven, yet close enough that the hem of His robe was in reach. The idea of divinity in human form, walking the earth in sandals, brings us face to face with a great mystery: God consented to live like me, and die for me, so I could be reconciled to Him.

REFLECT

So the Word became human and made his home among us. He was full of unfailing love and faithfulness. And we have seen his glory, the glory of the Father's one and only Son. John testified about him when he shouted to the crowds, "This is the one I was talking about when I said, 'Someone is coming after me who is far greater than I am, for he existed long before me.'" From his abundance we have all received one gracious blessing after another.

JOHN 1:14-16 (NLT)

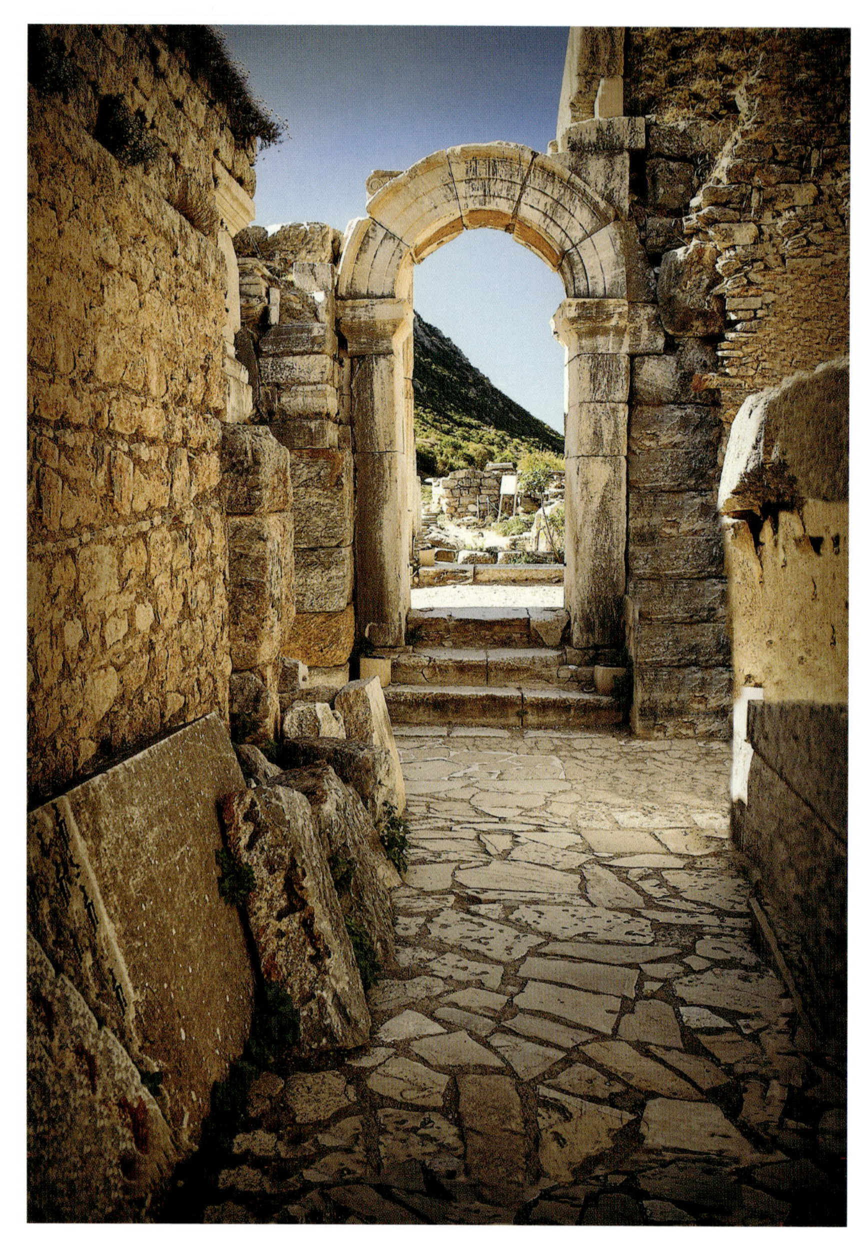

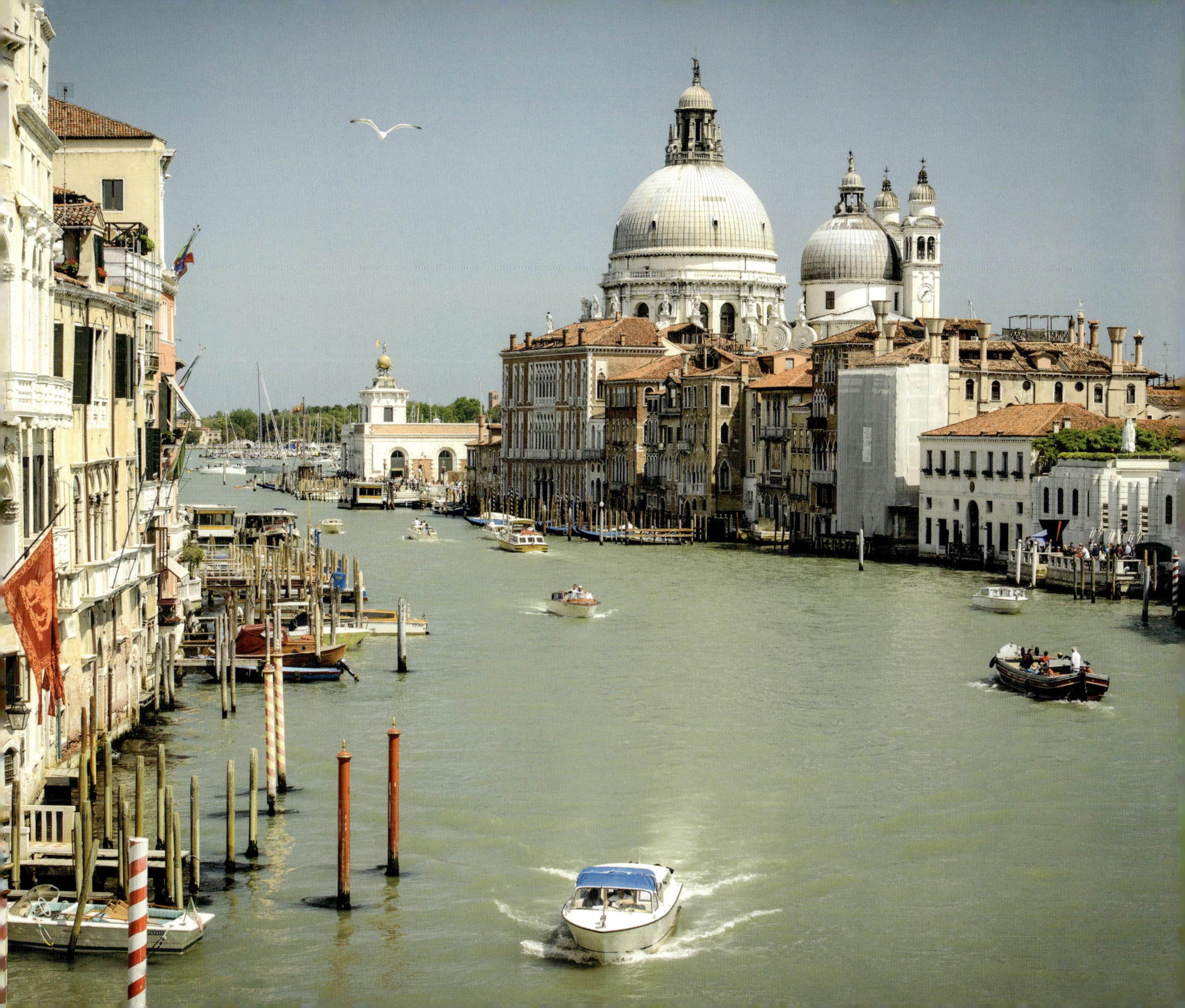

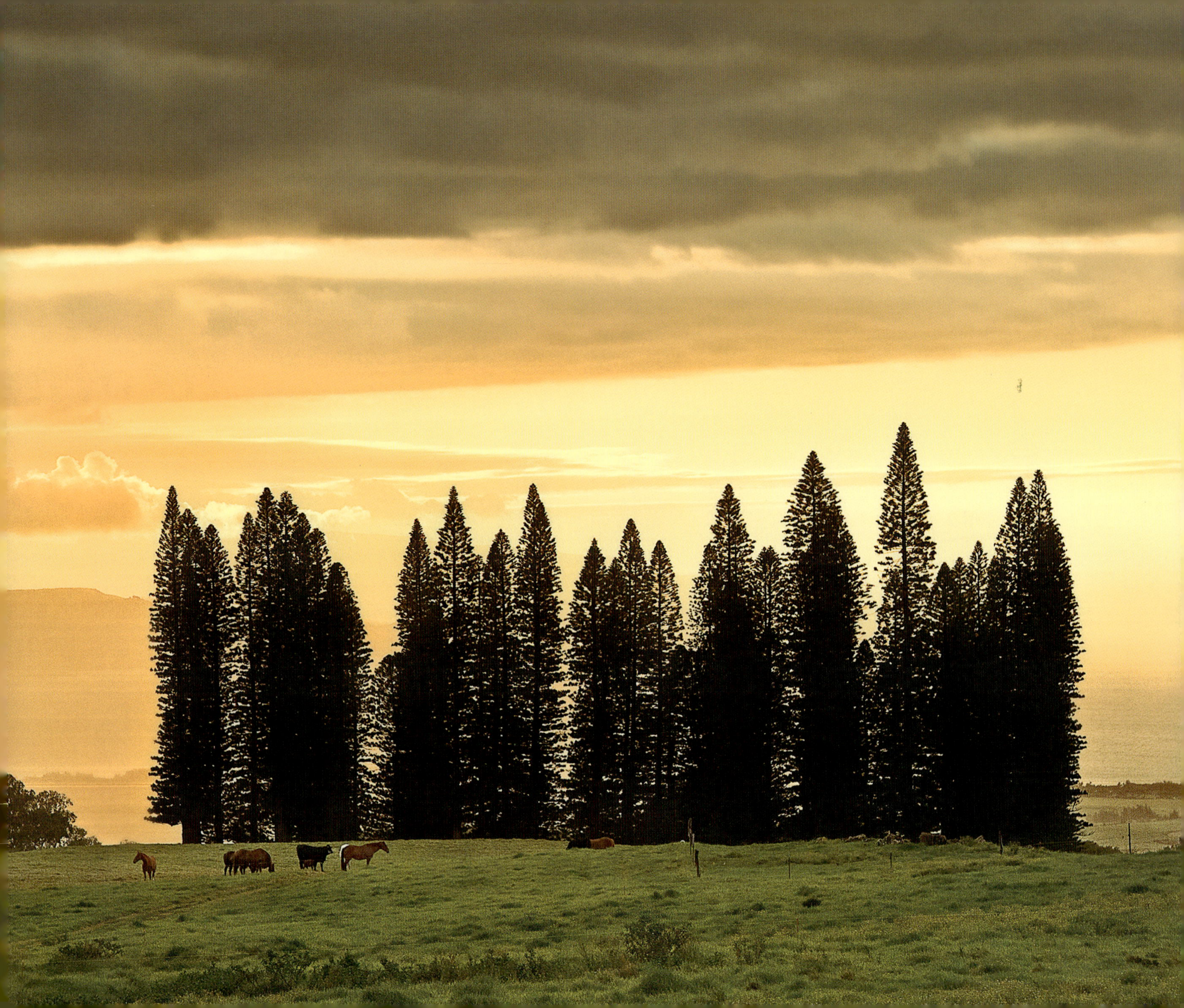

When you look into that cradle, what do you see? It looks like a little Jewish baby. But who is this? This is God, wrapped up in those clothes. The sovereign of the universe, born into the world He created. That cradle was made of wood, and filled with straw. But the One lying there is the One who said, "Let the earth bring forth grass, seeds, and trees." And the earth, at His command, brought forth plants and trees of all types. Whether it's a giant redwood or a little clover, He created them all. And here He is, resting on that straw, splitting time in half, with the most powerful name in all the earth, having existed before any of this was here. This is God incarnate. This is God coming on the scene. This is God breaking into human history.

— DR. CHARLES STANLEY —

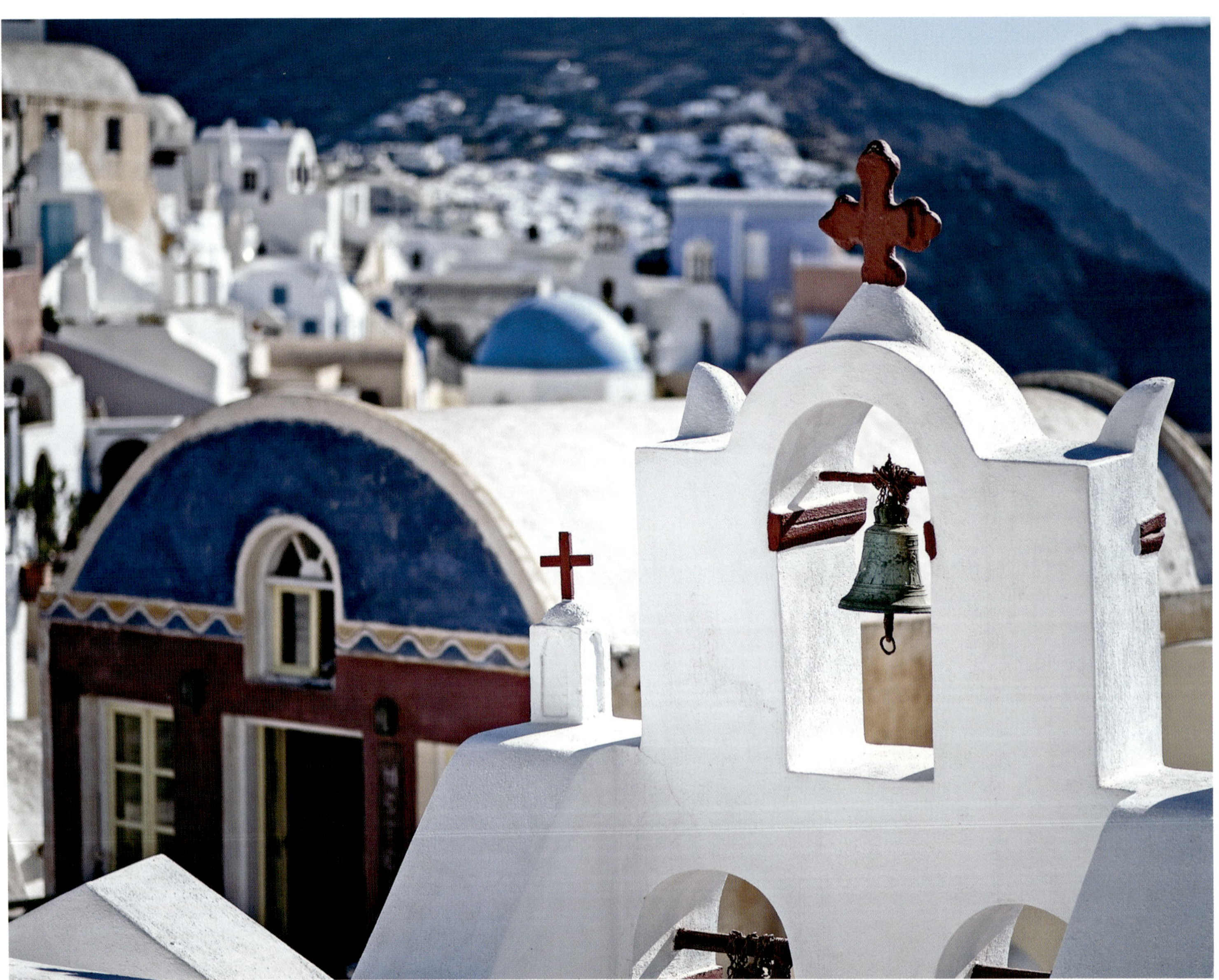

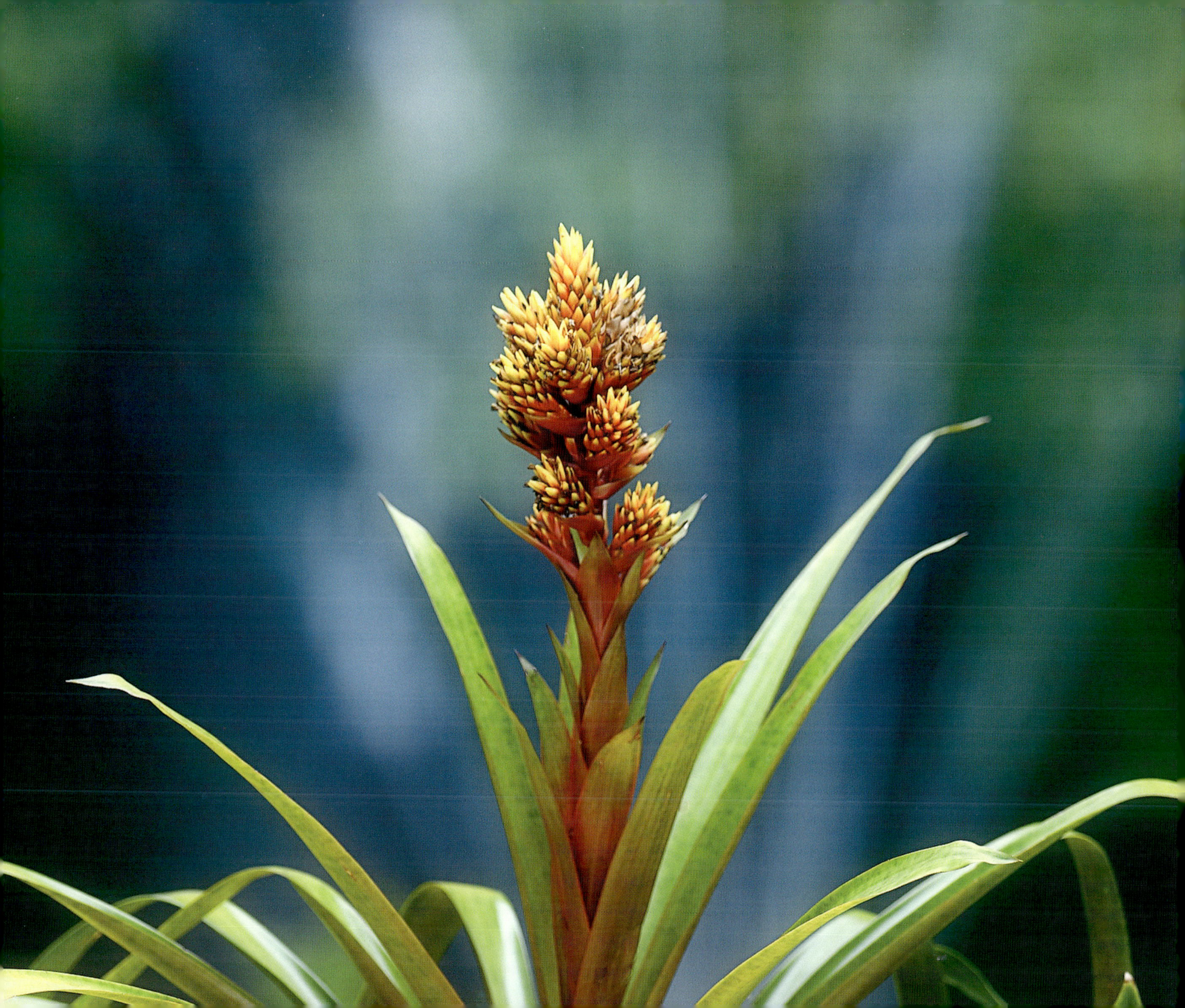

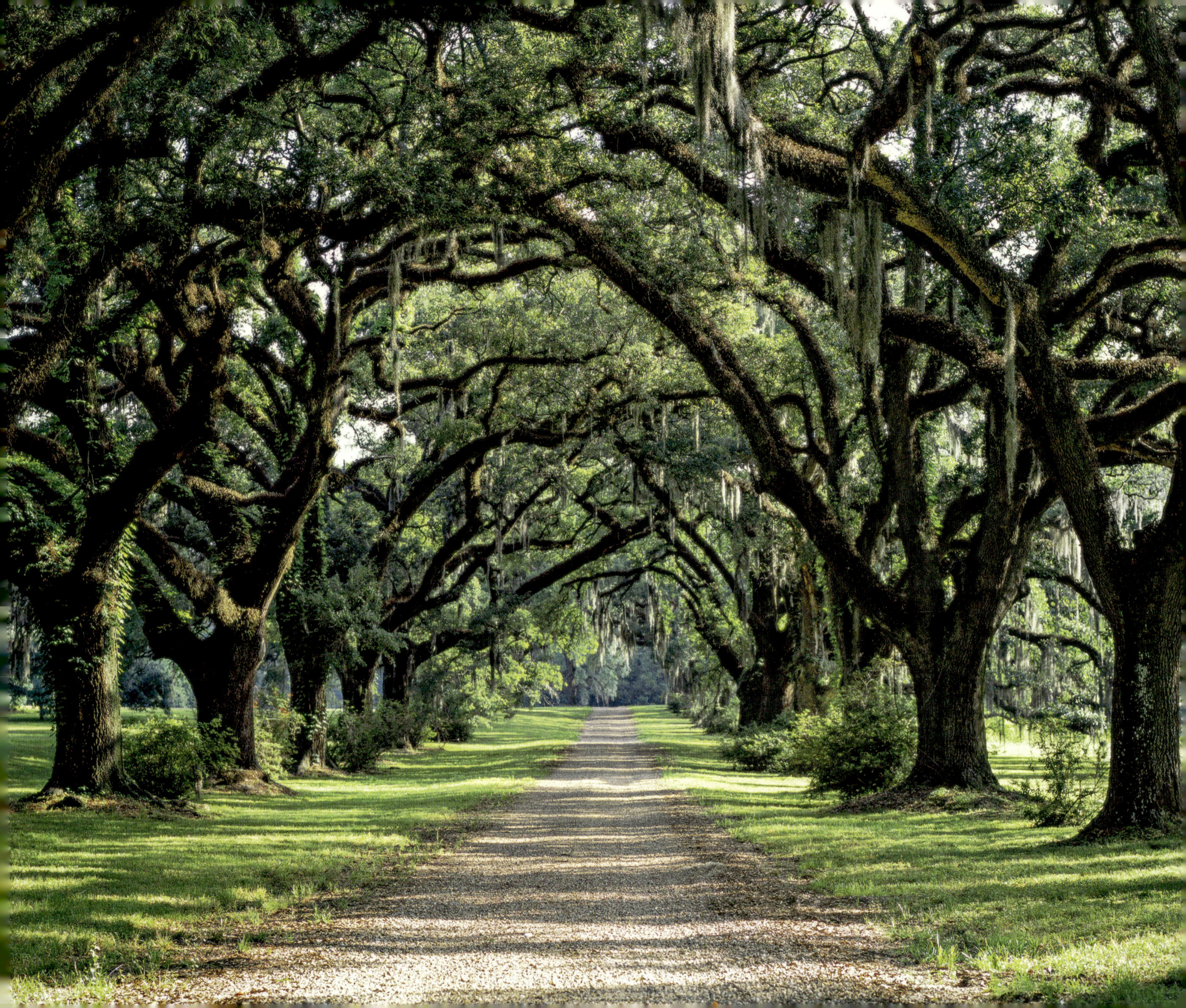

friends with God

To relate to Jesus in His humanity requires trust. He is no longer a distant God, but One who walks on the path right next to us, speaking frankly as a caring friend. As we release ourselves into the closeness of this relationship, our trust begins to grow. Yes, He sees everything, and His eyes are frighteningly honest. But His love, through it all, is unceasing and fiercely loyal. He is indeed the perfect Friend.

REFLECT

"I no longer call you servants, because a servant does not know his master's business. Instead, I have called you friends, for everything that I learned from my Father I have made known to you."

JOHN 15:15 (NIV)

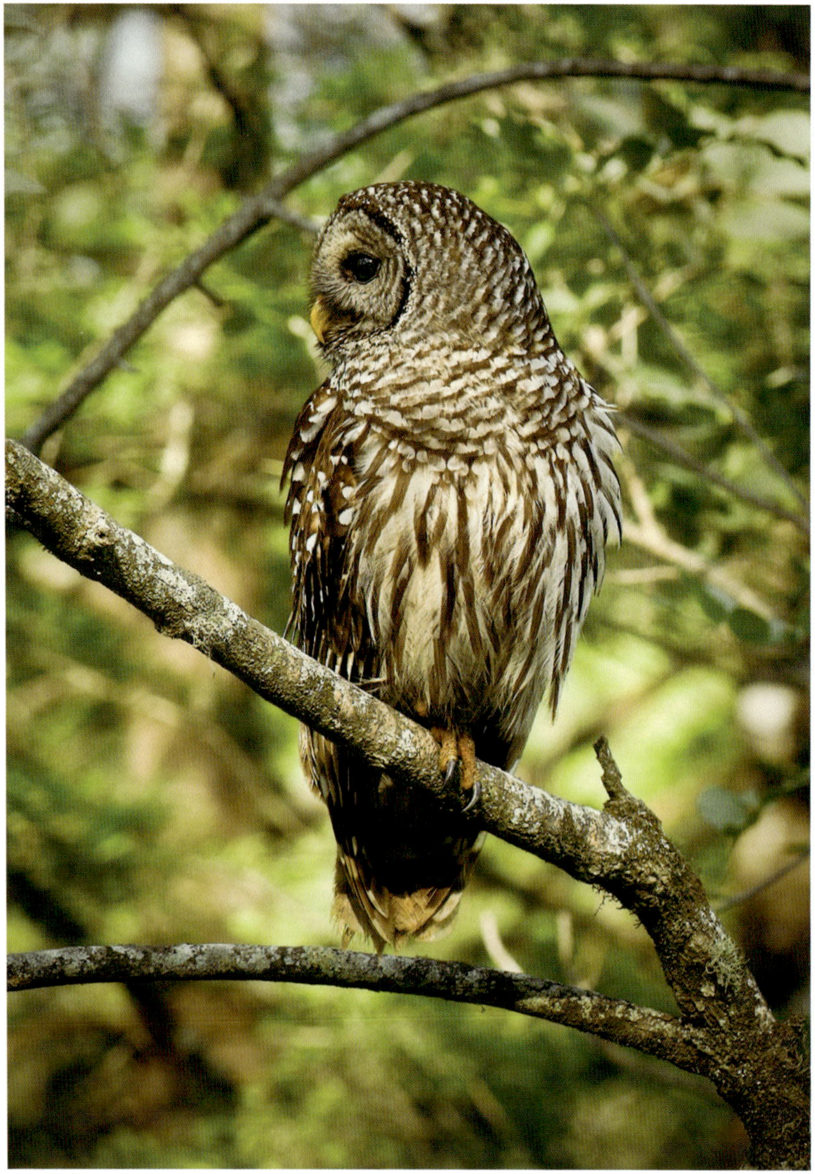

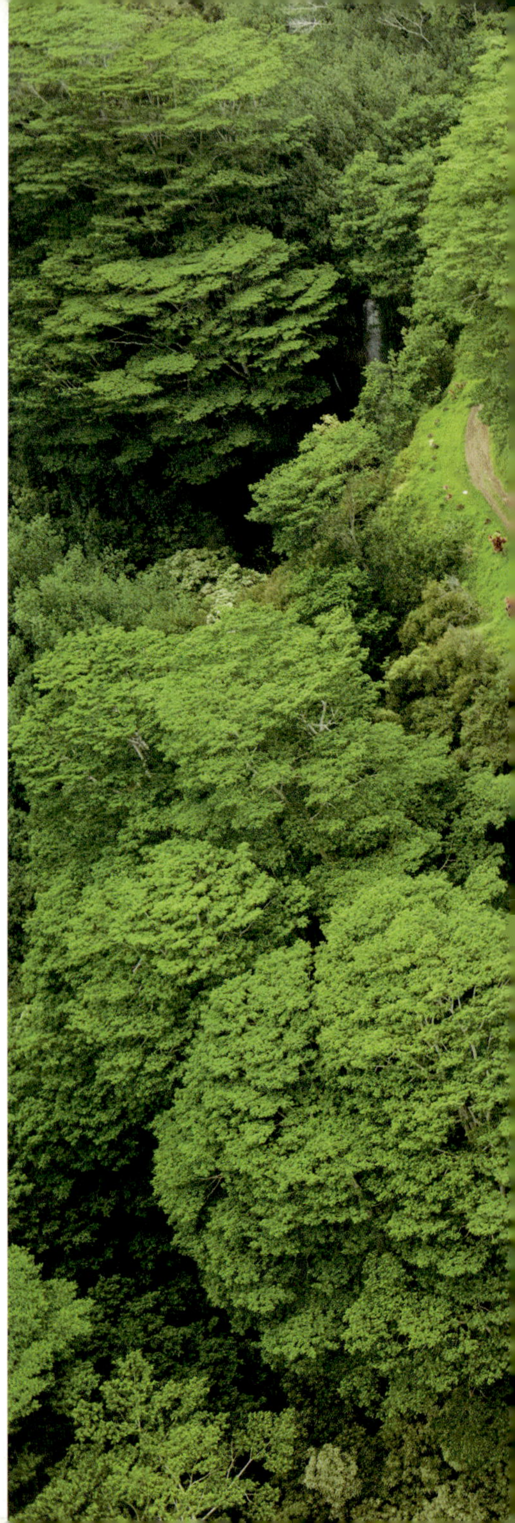

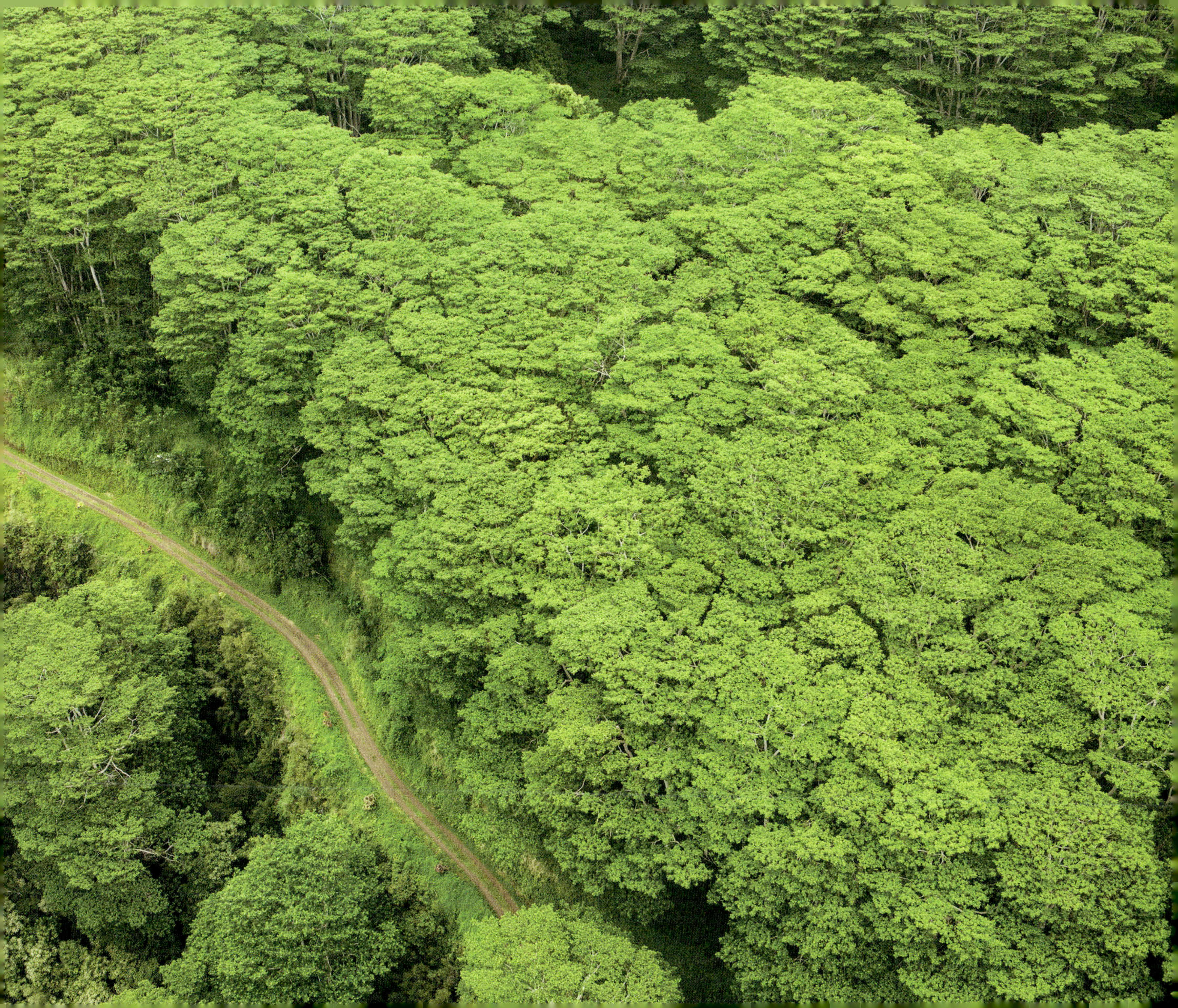

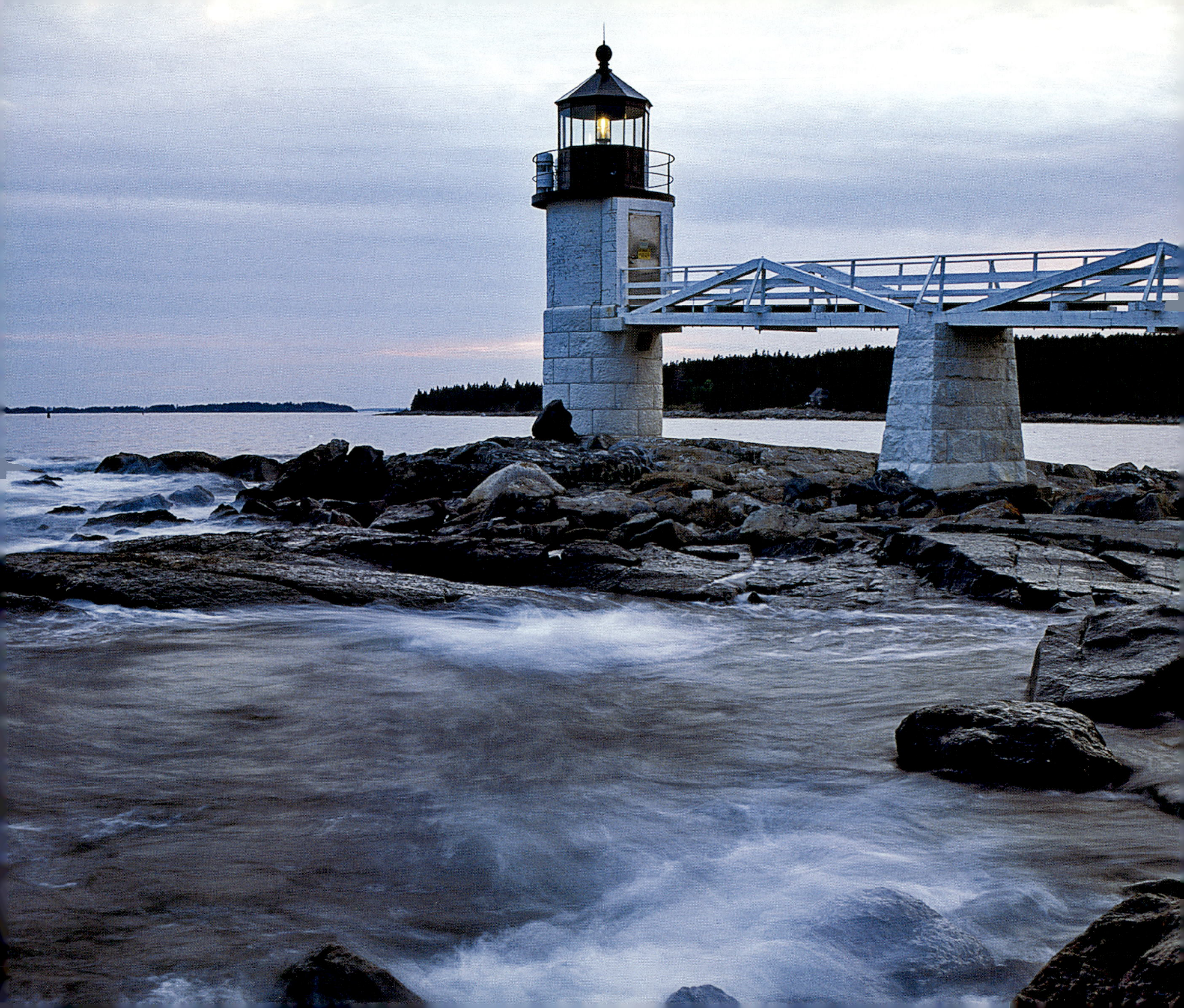

redirection

With His incarnation, Jesus planted Himself like a lighthouse at the crossroads of time. A world that had been falling ever further into ruin received the greatest news imaginable—the Savior had arrived. And just as He turned the course of human history from darkness to light and hope, He redirects our individual lives into a new path: from death to life, despair to eternal comfort, shame to peace, and from ashes to joy.

REFLECT

"As one whom his mother comforts, so I will comfort you; and you will be comforted in Jerusalem."

ISAIAH 66:13

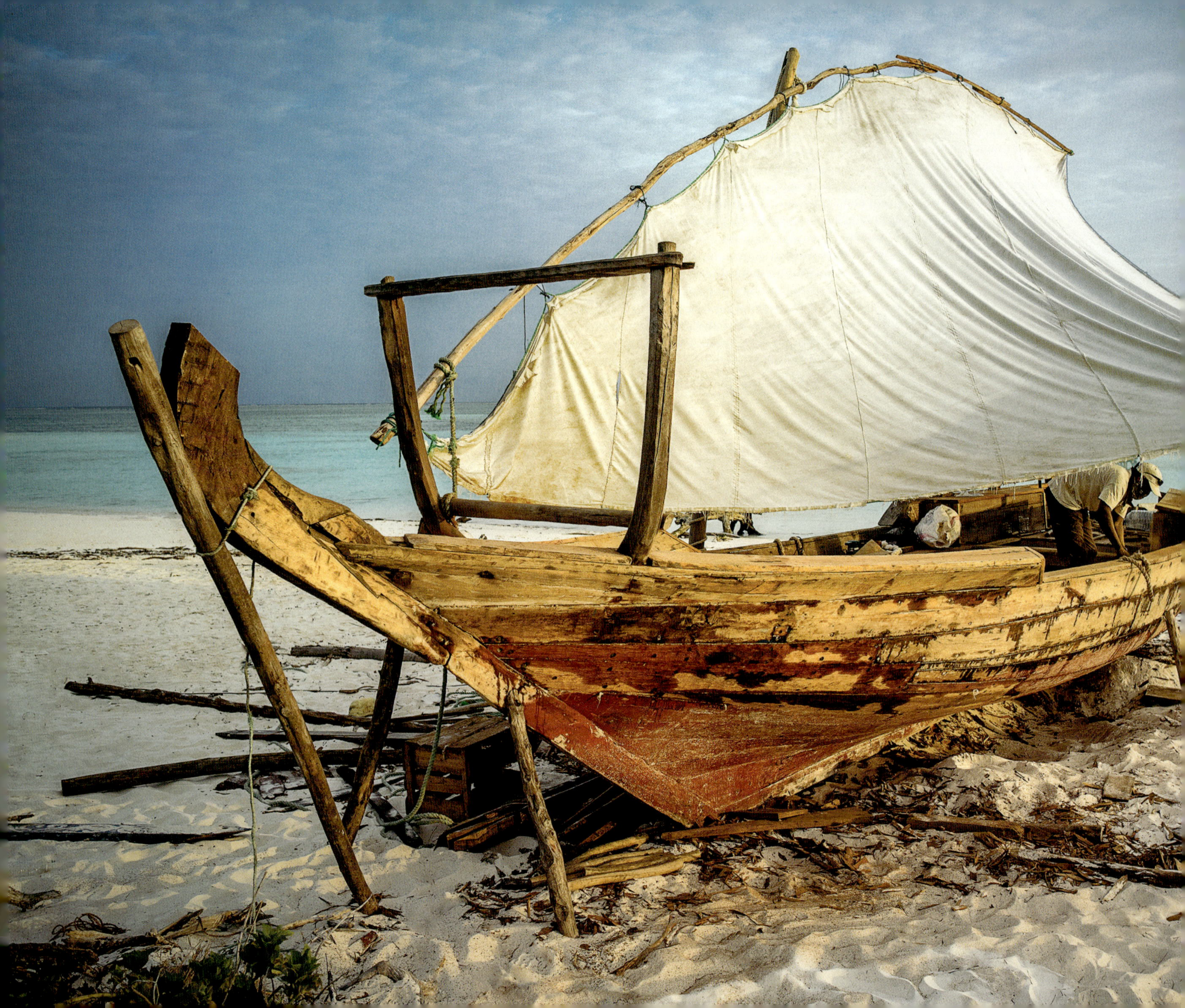

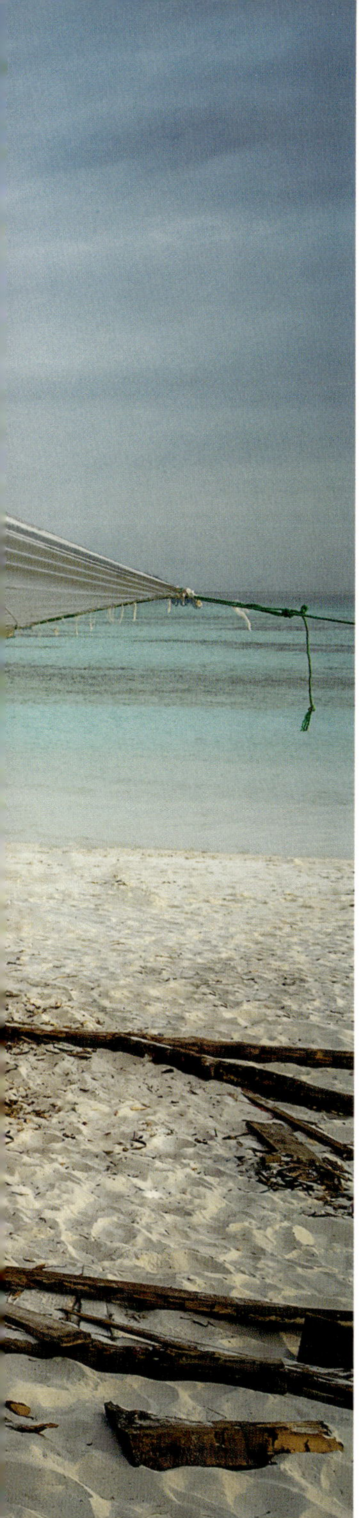

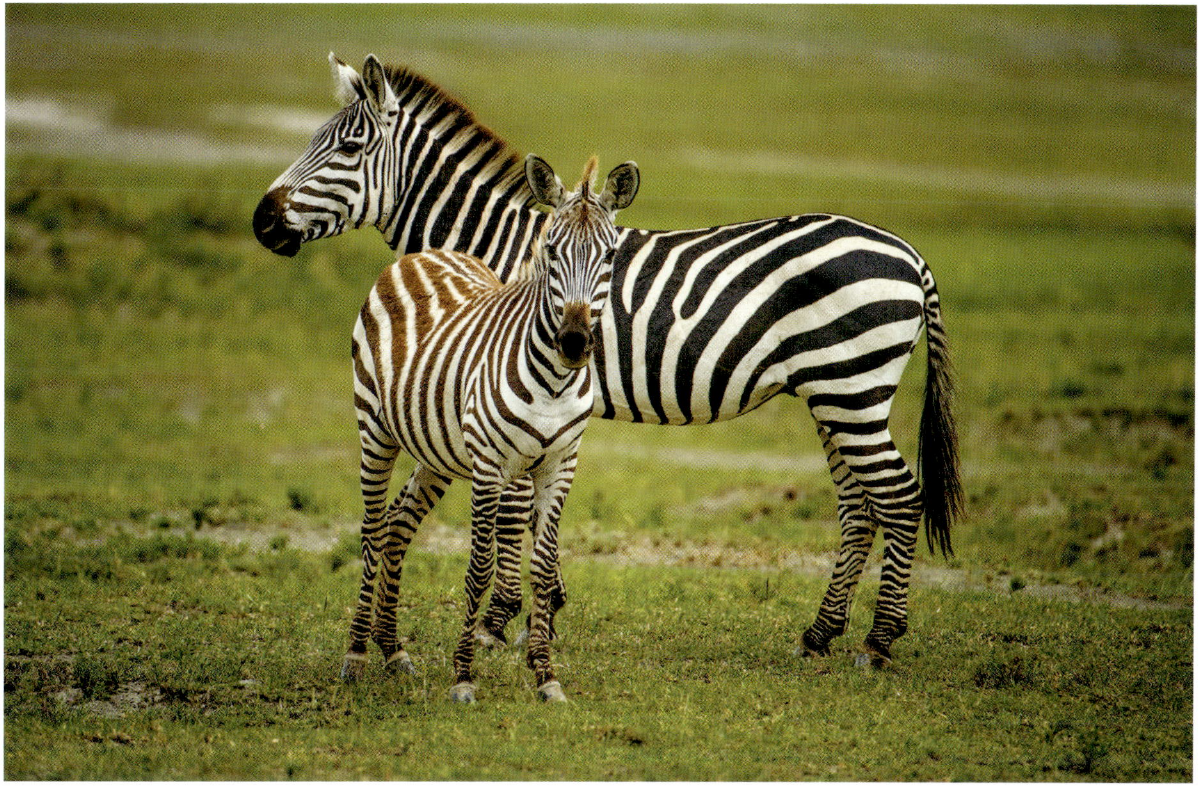

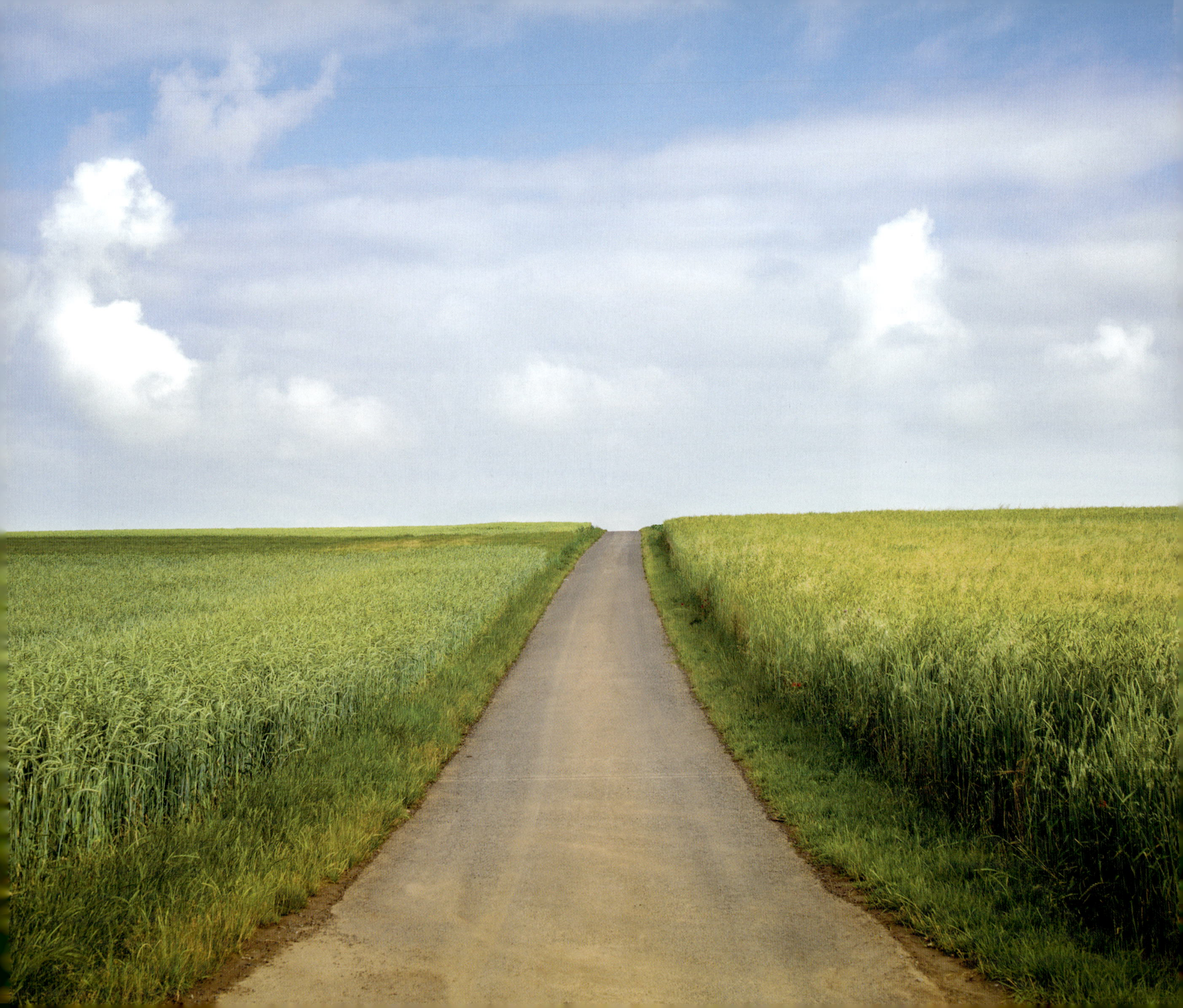

Jesus, the door to eternity

When love hung on the cross at Calvary, the barrier to our Father was done away with forever. Jesus takes us to the place we all long to go, with a longing deeper than any other—the place of communion with God. The green pastures He has for us are eternal. We can scarcely comprehend that we will be with Him forever, that there will be no end to our joy, no end to our peace, no end to our praise, and no end to His presence. Salvation by the blood of Jesus is the end of the end—and the beginning of endless life.

REFLECT

"I tell you the truth, those who listen to my message and believe in God who sent me have eternal life. They will never be condemned for their sins, but they have already passed from death into life."

JOHN 5:24 (NLT)

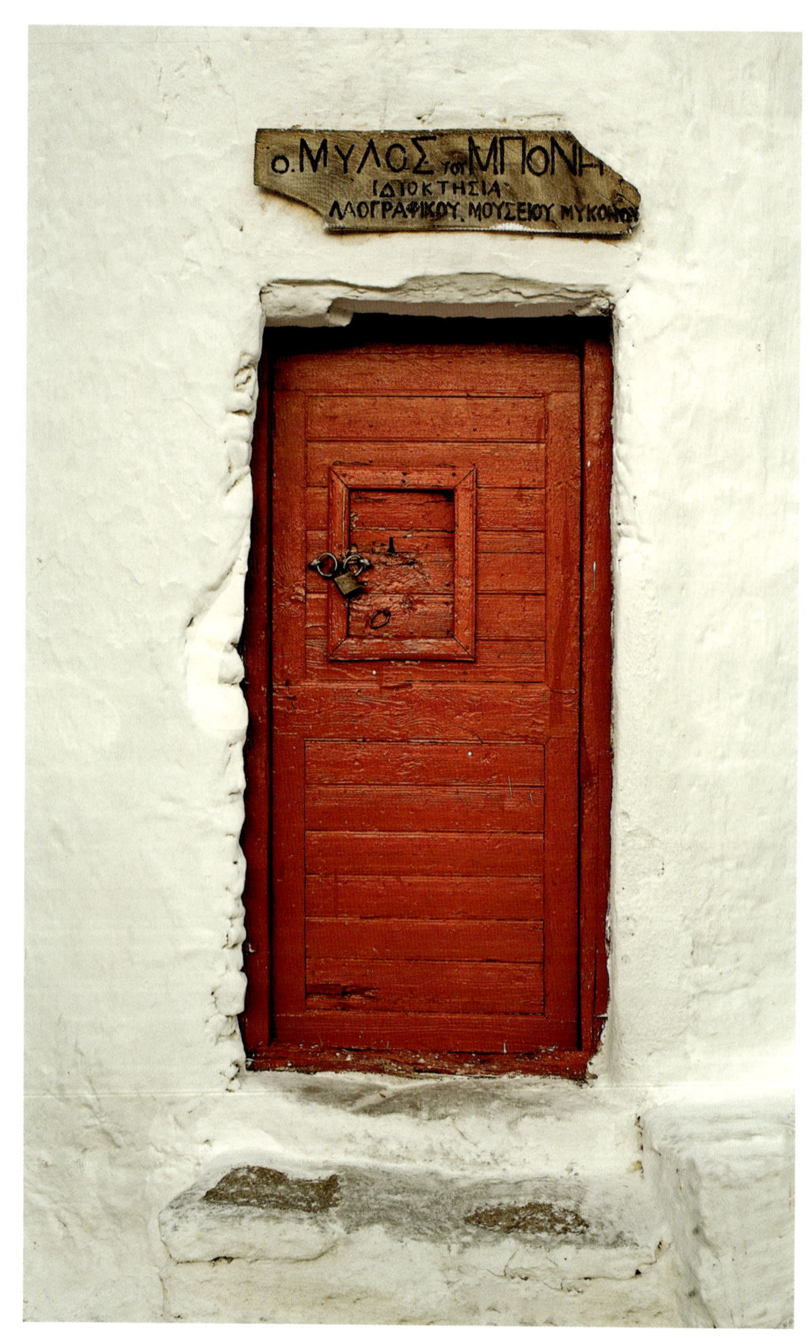
ο. ΜΥΛΟΣ του ΜΠΟΝΗ
ΙΔΙΟΚΤΗΣΙΑ
ΛΑΟΓΡΑΦΙΚΟΥ ΜΟΥΣΕΙΟΥ

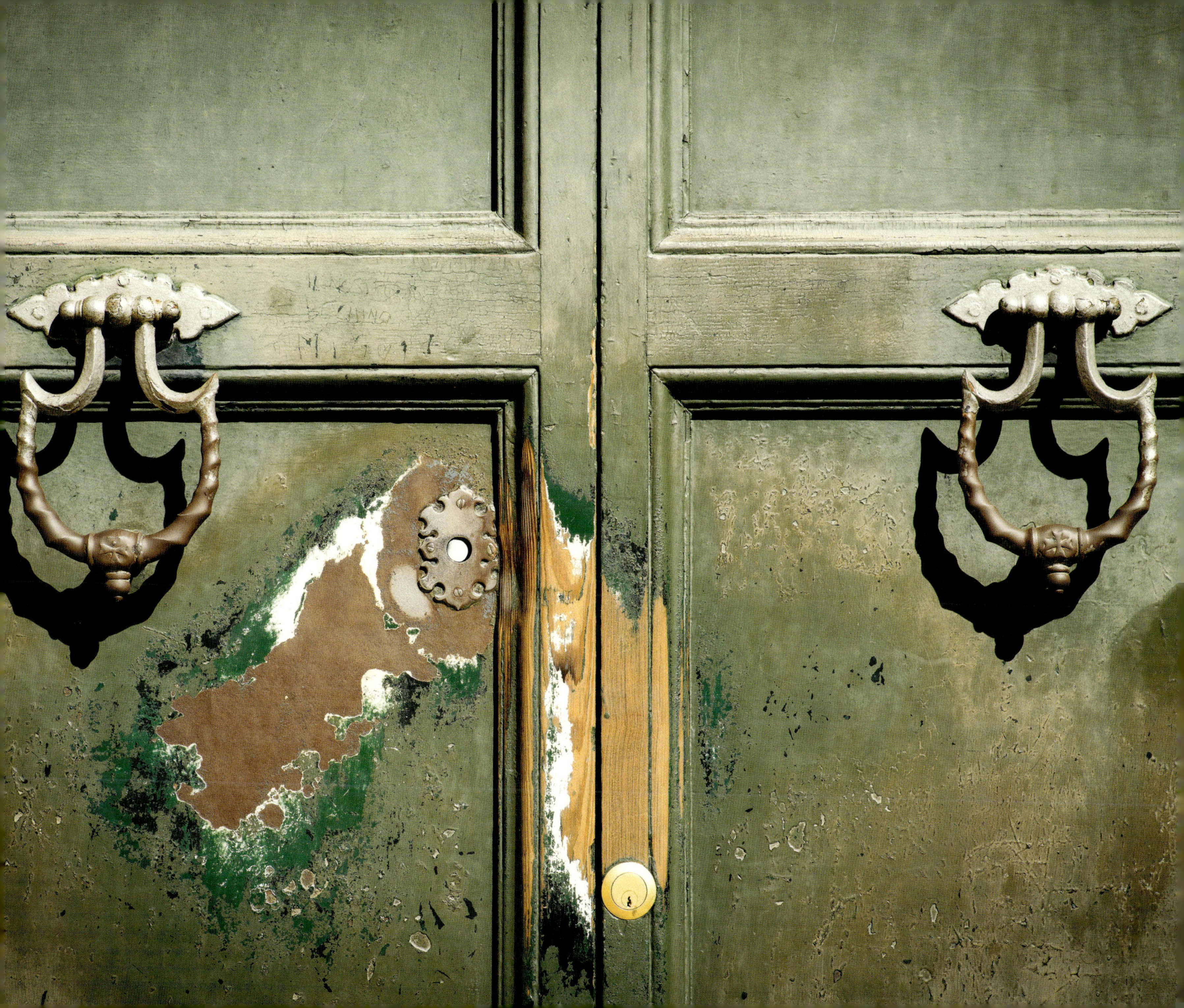

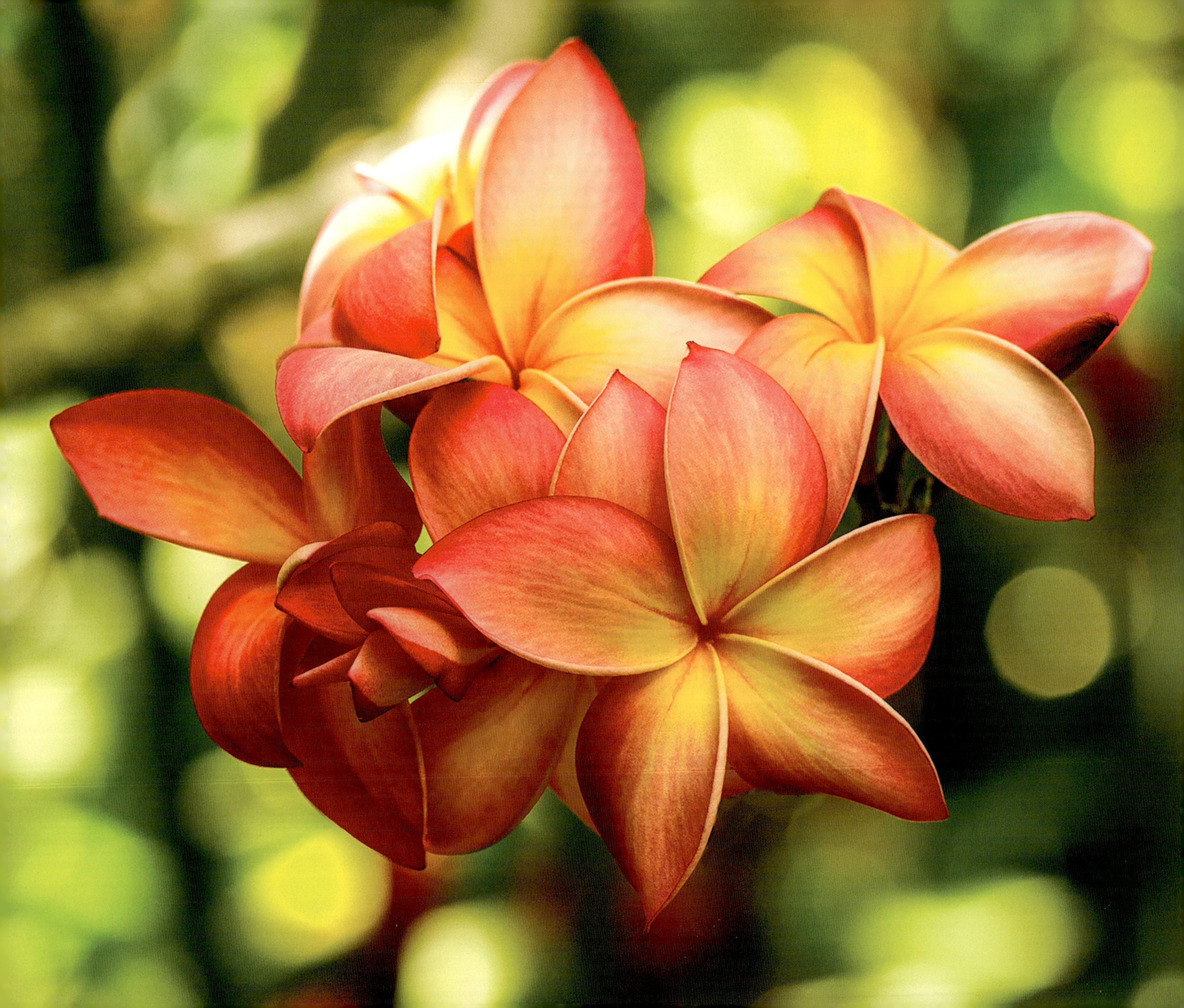

REFLECT

And He who sits on the throne said,
"Behold, I am making all things new…
I am the Alpha and the Omega,
the beginning and the end. I will give to
the one who thirsts from the spring of
the water of life without cost."

REVELATION 21:5-6

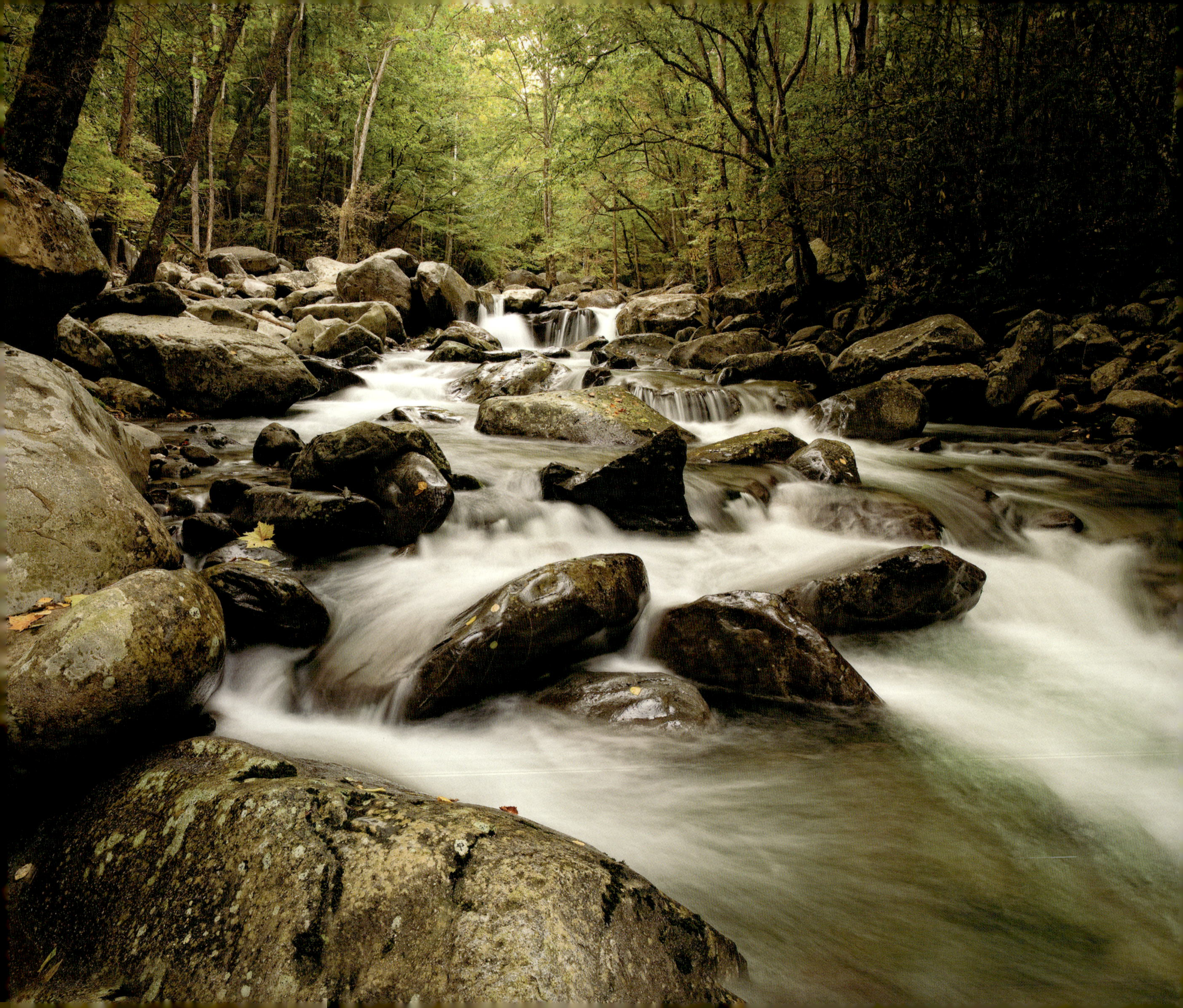

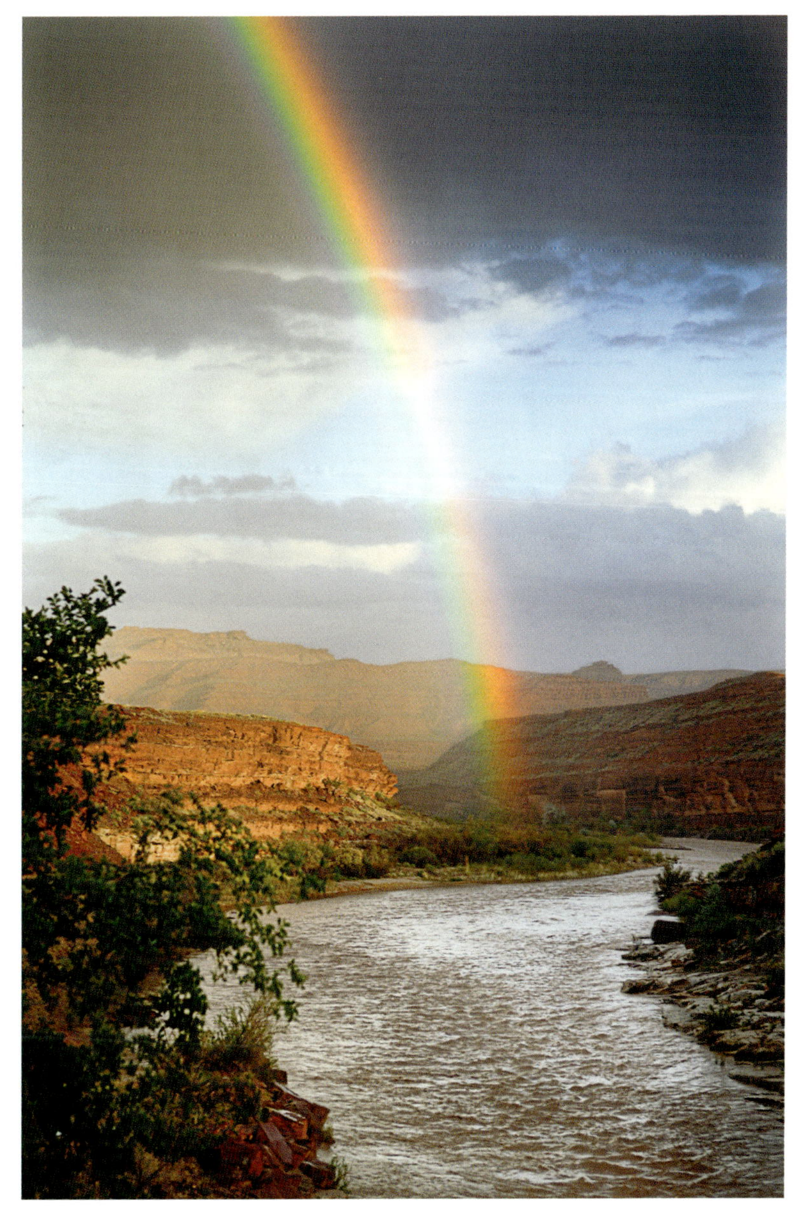

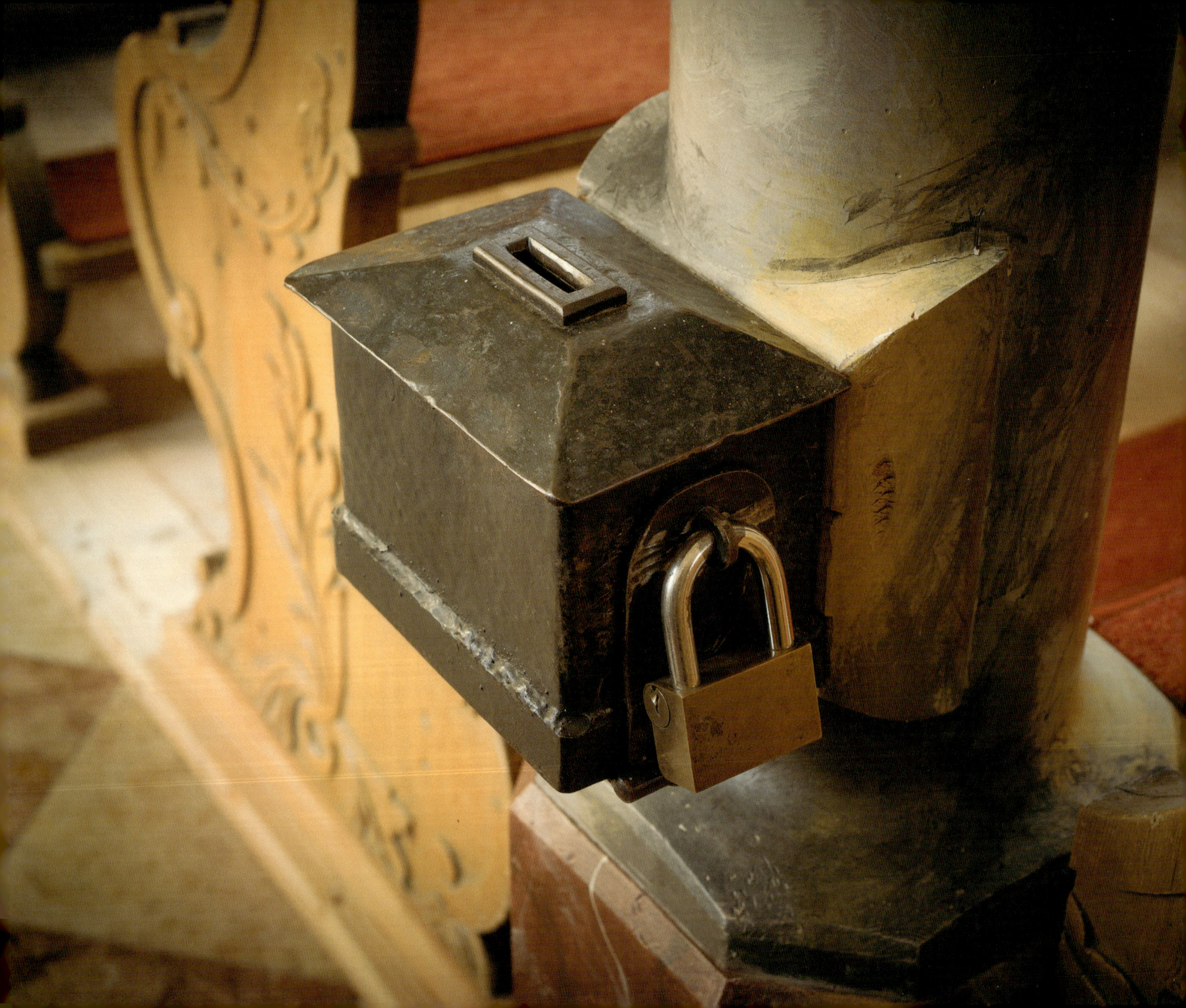

CHAPTER THREE

THE WONDER OF GOD'S PLAN

When we put our faith in Jesus, a strange miracle occurs. God places us in Christ, who, at the same time, comes to live within us. This mysterious intertwining is what Scripture calls union with Christ. We become inseparable. He seals us into Himself as behind the strongest of locks, and simultaneously fills us with Himself like a lantern being lit with a flame. His love begins to burn in us with a warmth we could never produce ourselves. We come to life for the first time.

Under the cover of His grace, God then conforms us more and more into the image of His Son, who works His life through us steadily, day by day. Though the process often causes deep pain and struggle, God leads us deftly to a place where love triumphs. Just as a smooth mountain lake reflects the surrounding peaks, we reflect the marvelous attributes of Jesus our Lord as we fix our gaze on Him in trust. The more we submit our lives to the beauty of the Savior, the more we express to the world His sacrificial love, compassion, and humility.

Yet even as our lives on earth push forward to meet His perfection, we are already justified before God, since we are hidden in Jesus before Him. This is the wonder of God's plan—to bring us, clothed in the righteousness of Christ, to heaven one day; to see His glory unveiled in all its holy brilliance and to rejoice in Him forever.

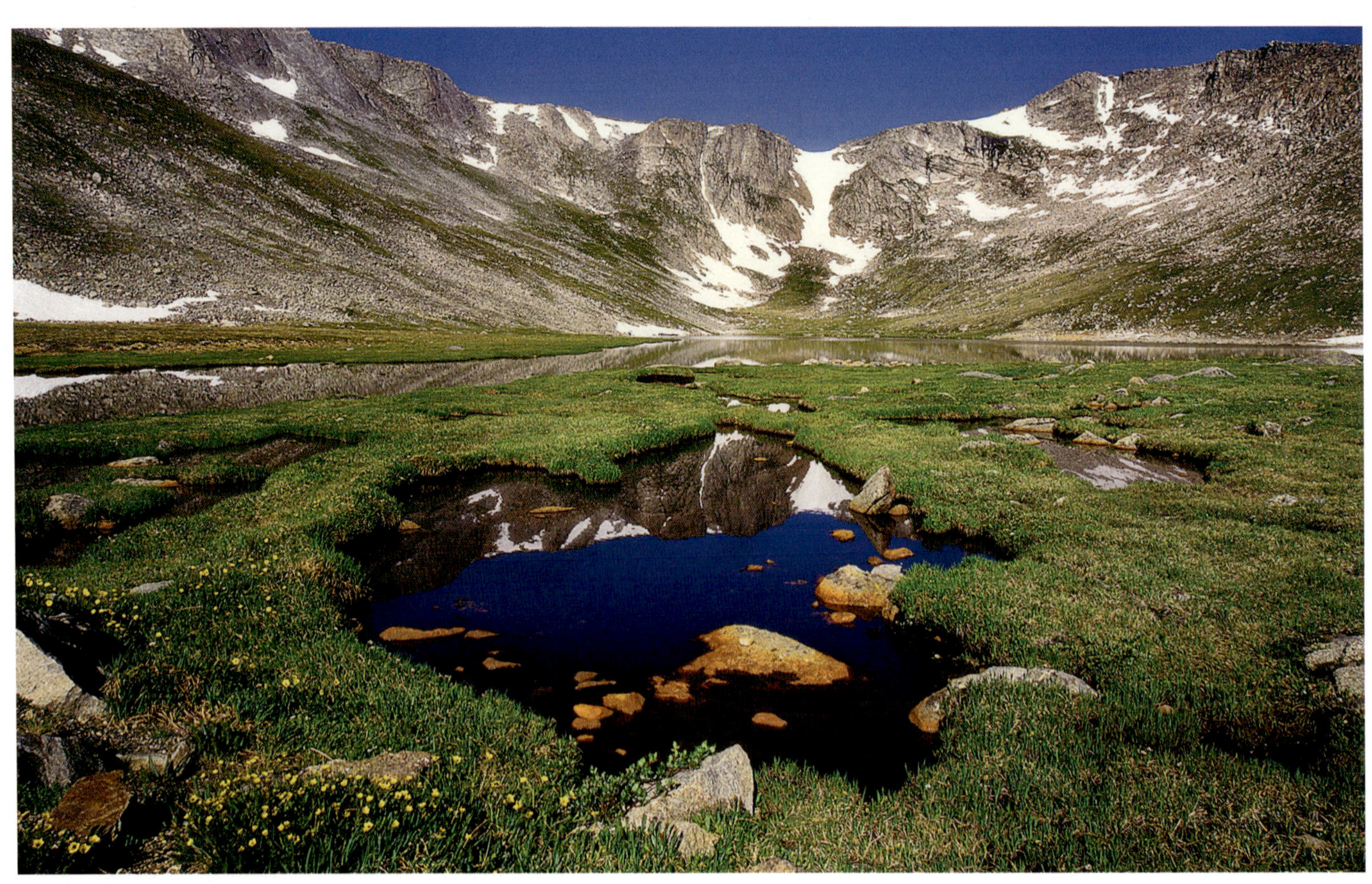

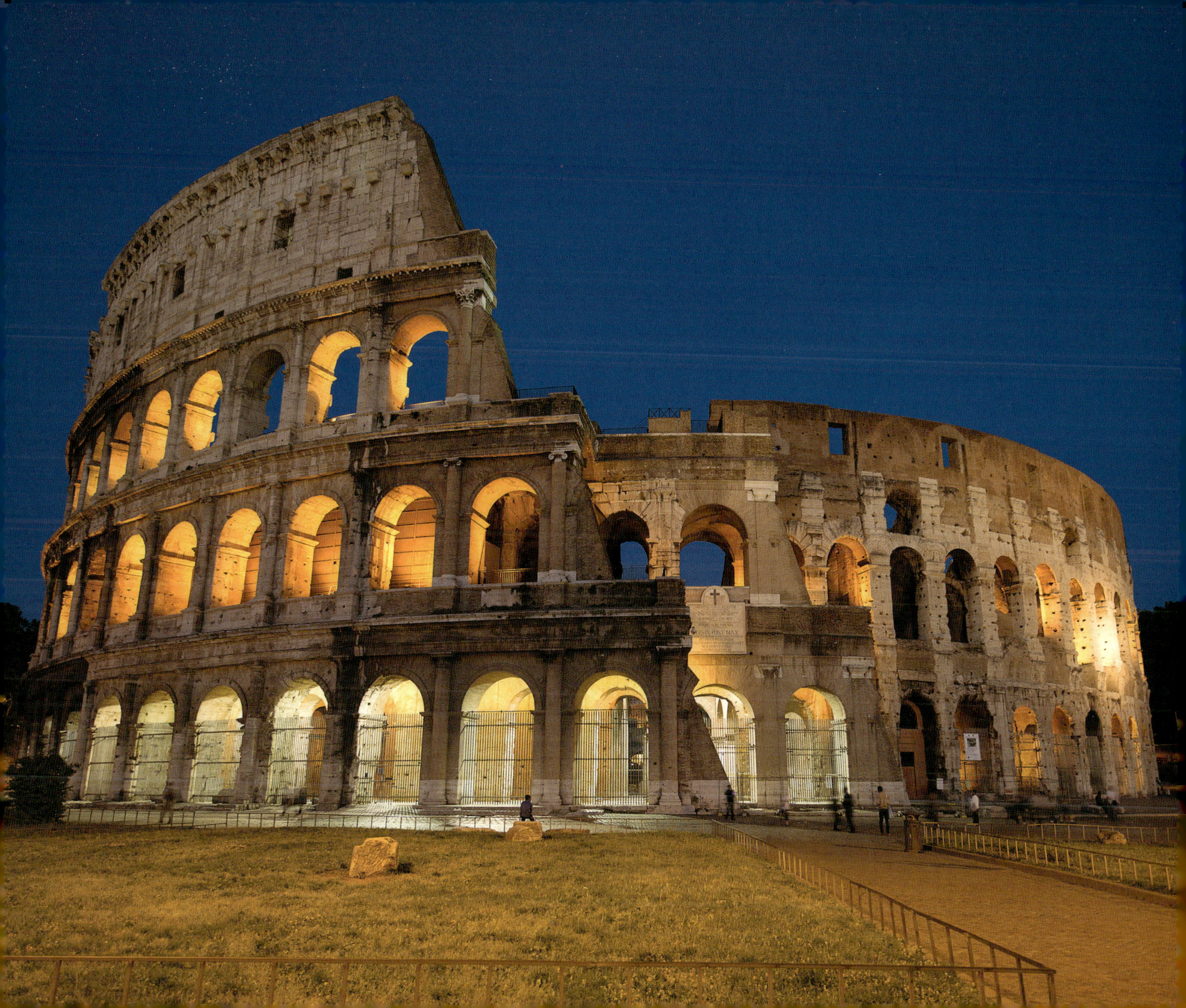

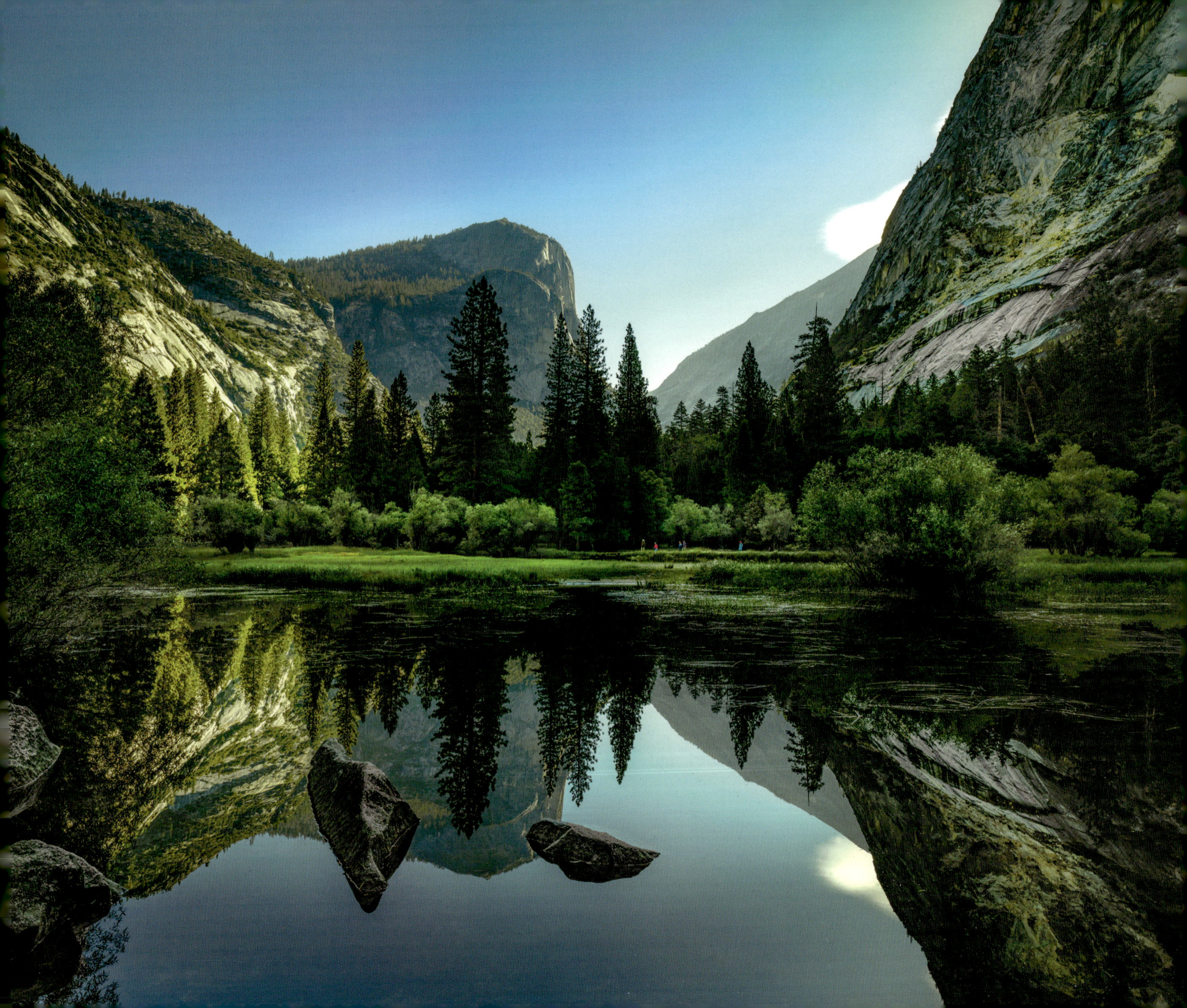

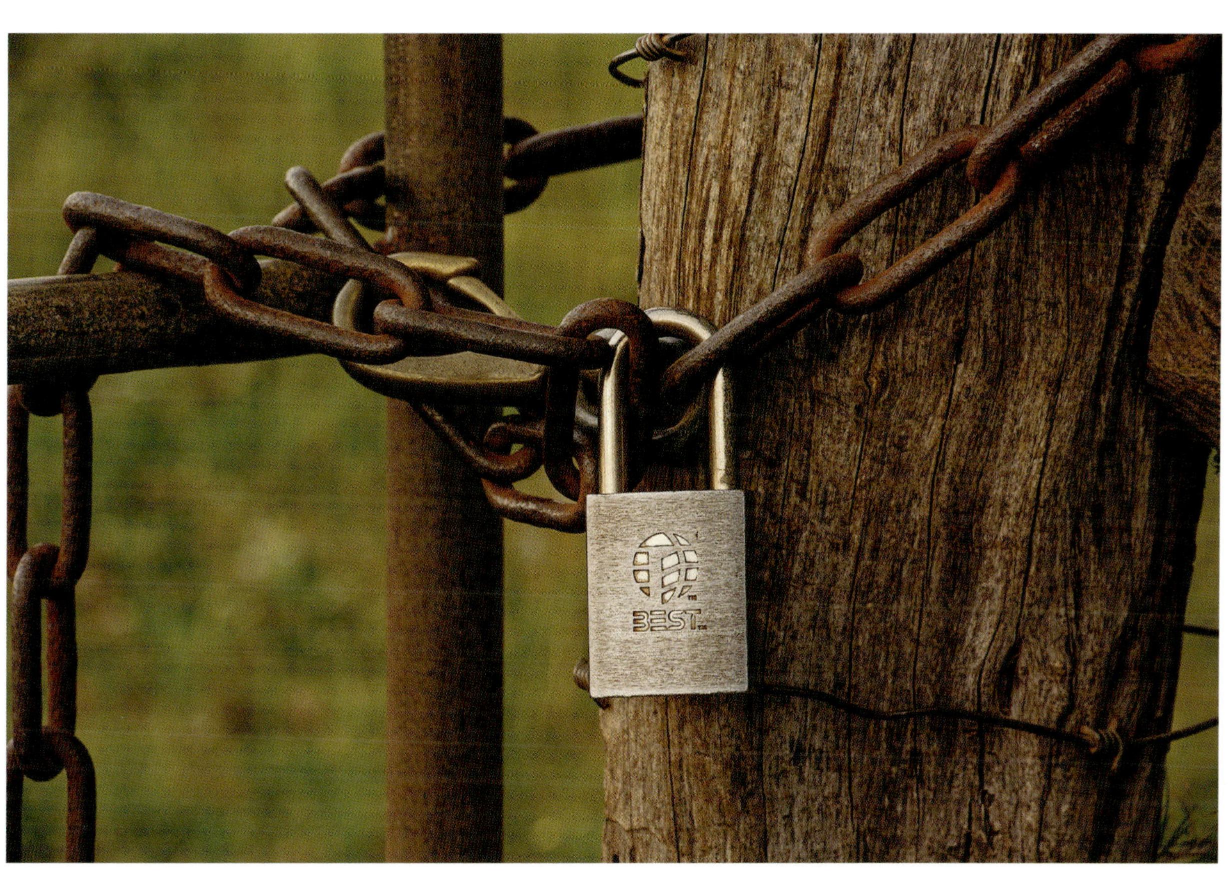
BEST

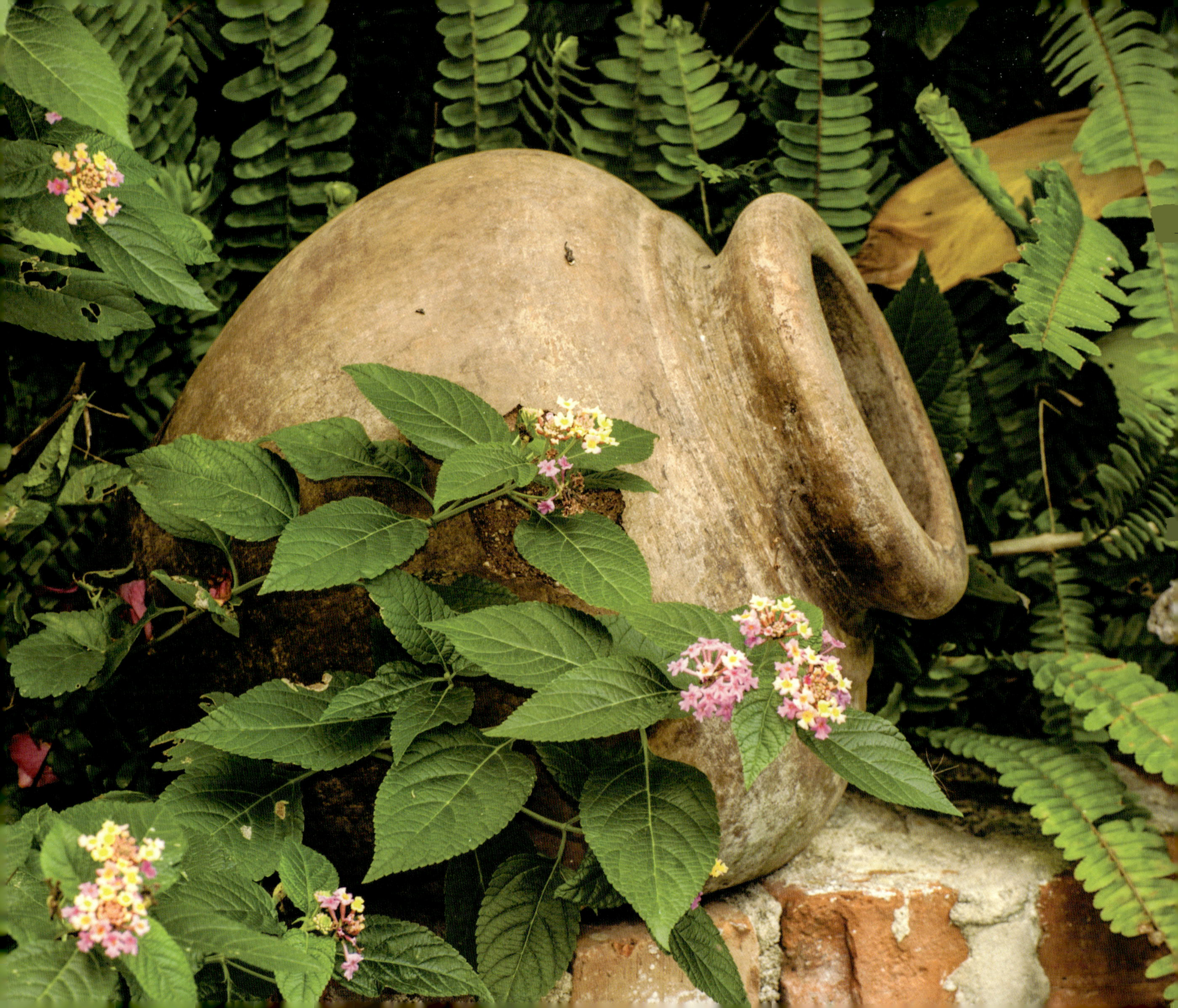

the light within us

The light of God shining within us is an otherworldly experience. How amazing—it is so unlike the weakness of our humanity, in which we house this astonishing presence. As we are strengthened in our union with Christ, His light in us grows brighter and brighter, outshining our flawed natures and drawing attention to His love. A priceless pearl in an imperfect person is soon noticed, but remains puzzling. There is no explanation but God.

REFLECT

For God, who said, "Light shall shine out of darkness," is the One who has shone in our hearts to give the Light of the knowledge of the glory of God in the face of Christ. But we have this treasure in earthen vessels, so that the surpassing greatness of the power will be of God and not from ourselves.

2 CORINTHIANS 4:6-7

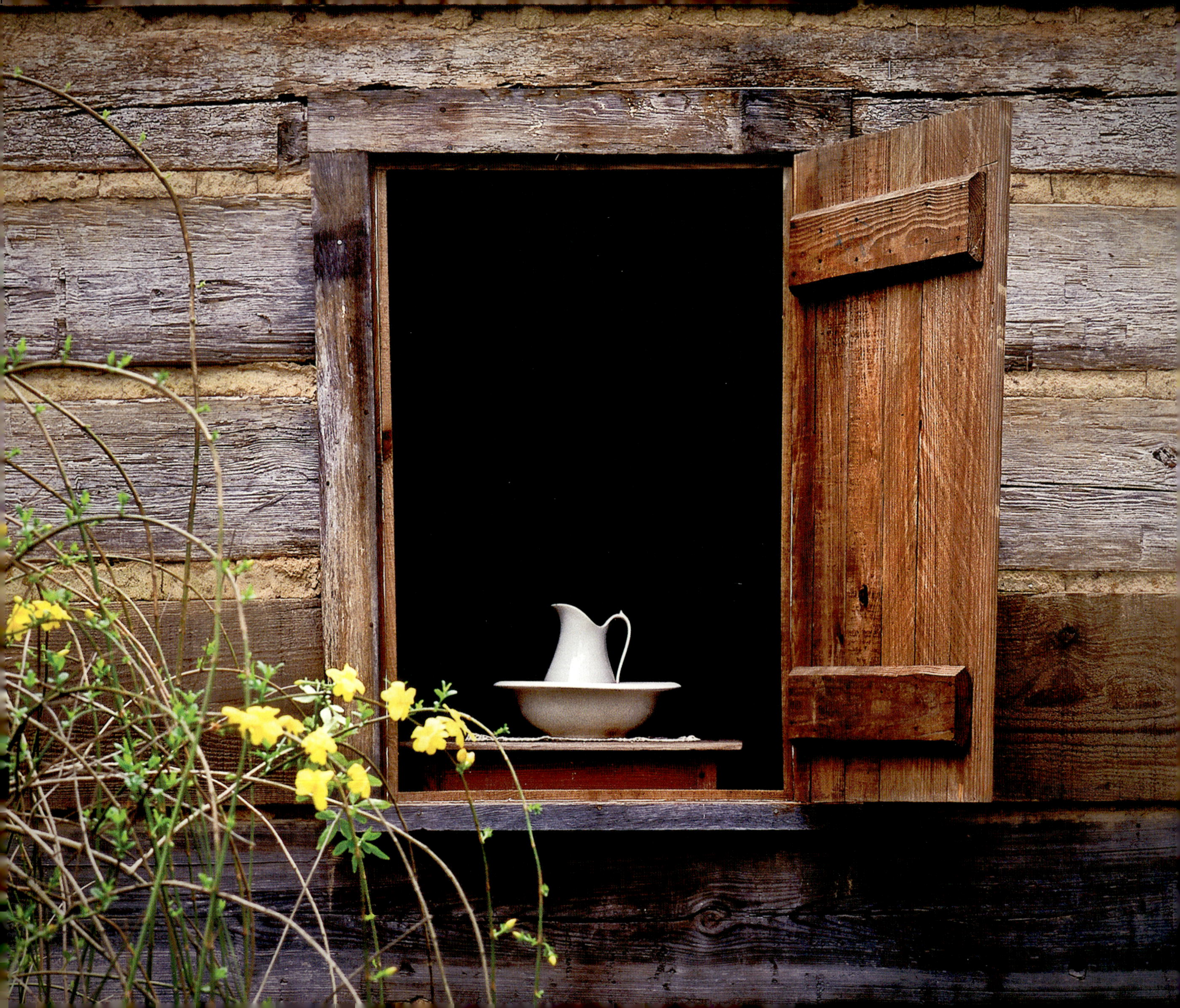

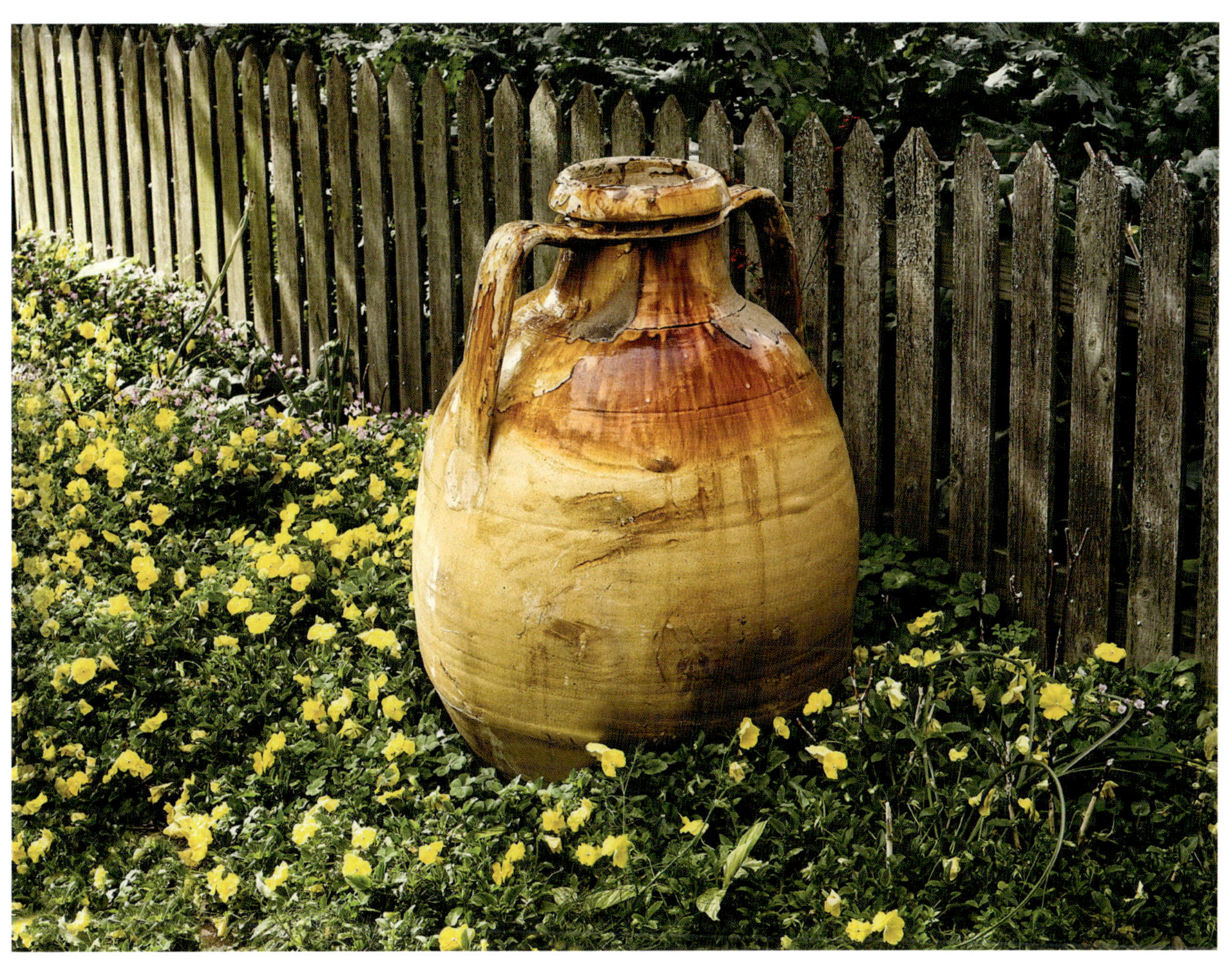

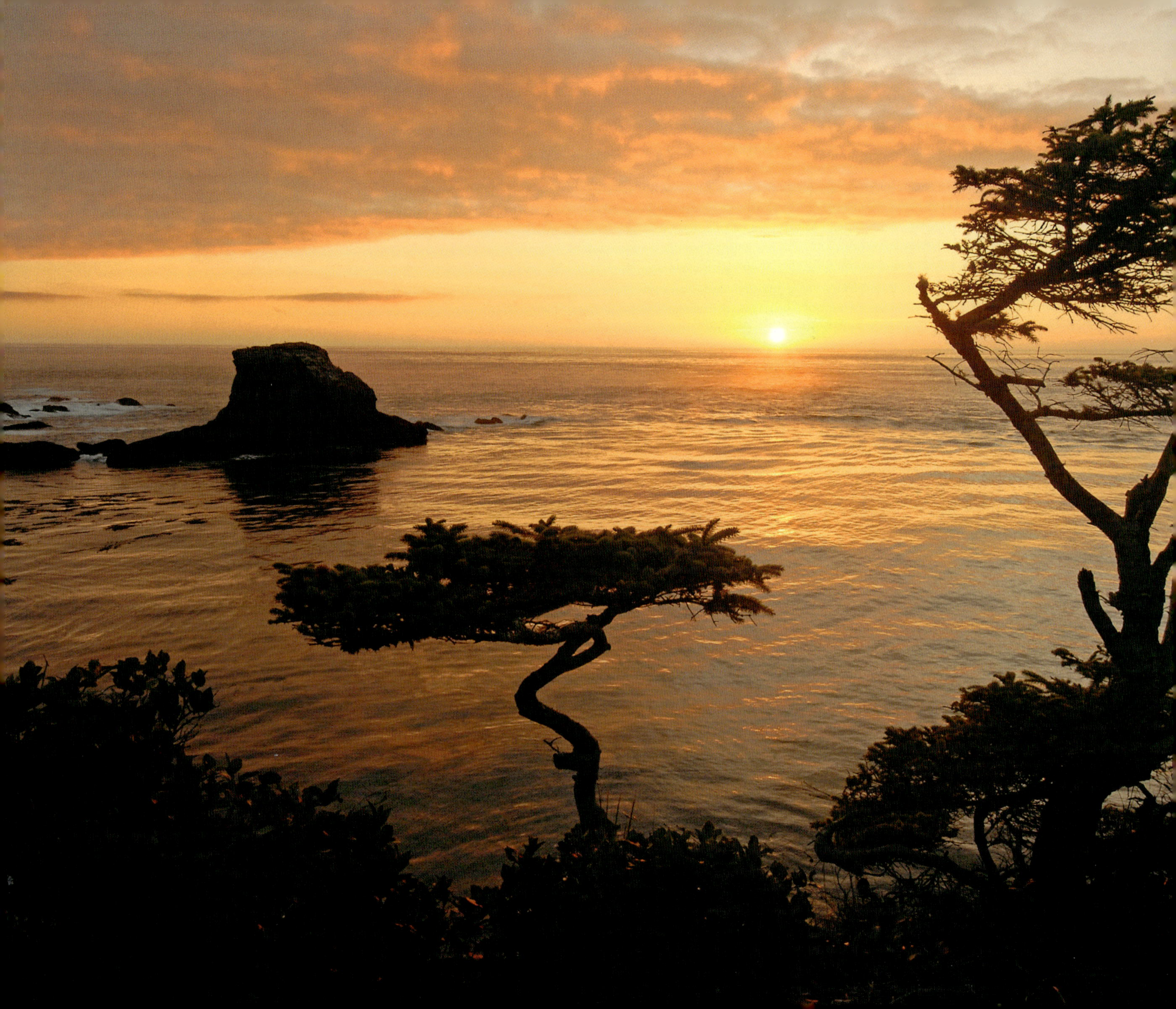

When you were saved, you received an assignment: Shine! Purity of heart, purity of purpose, purity of motivation, and purity of life make it possible for Jesus Christ, who is indwelling you, to shine. That's why He left you here. That's your purpose as a child of God.

— DR. CHARLES STANLEY —

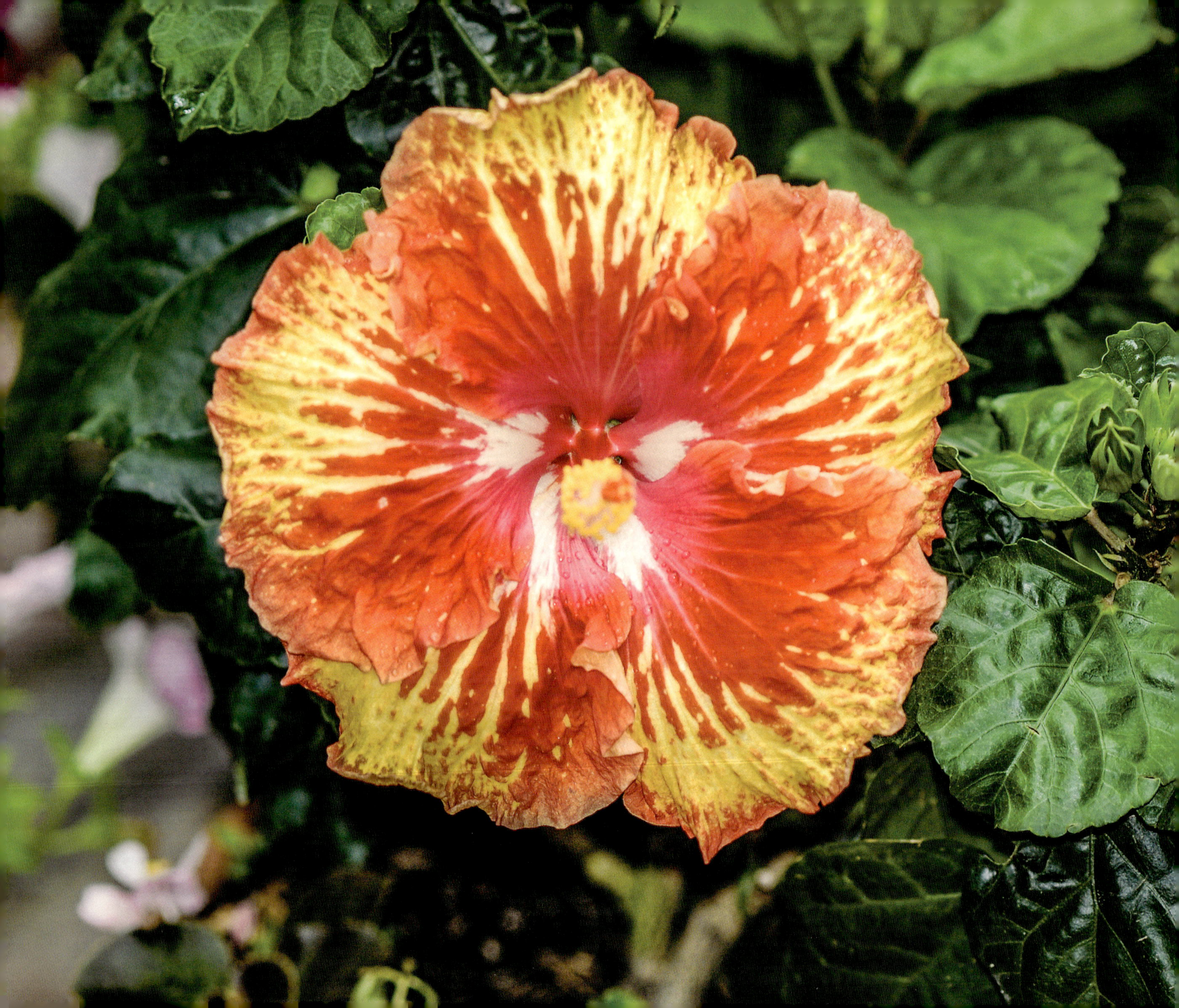

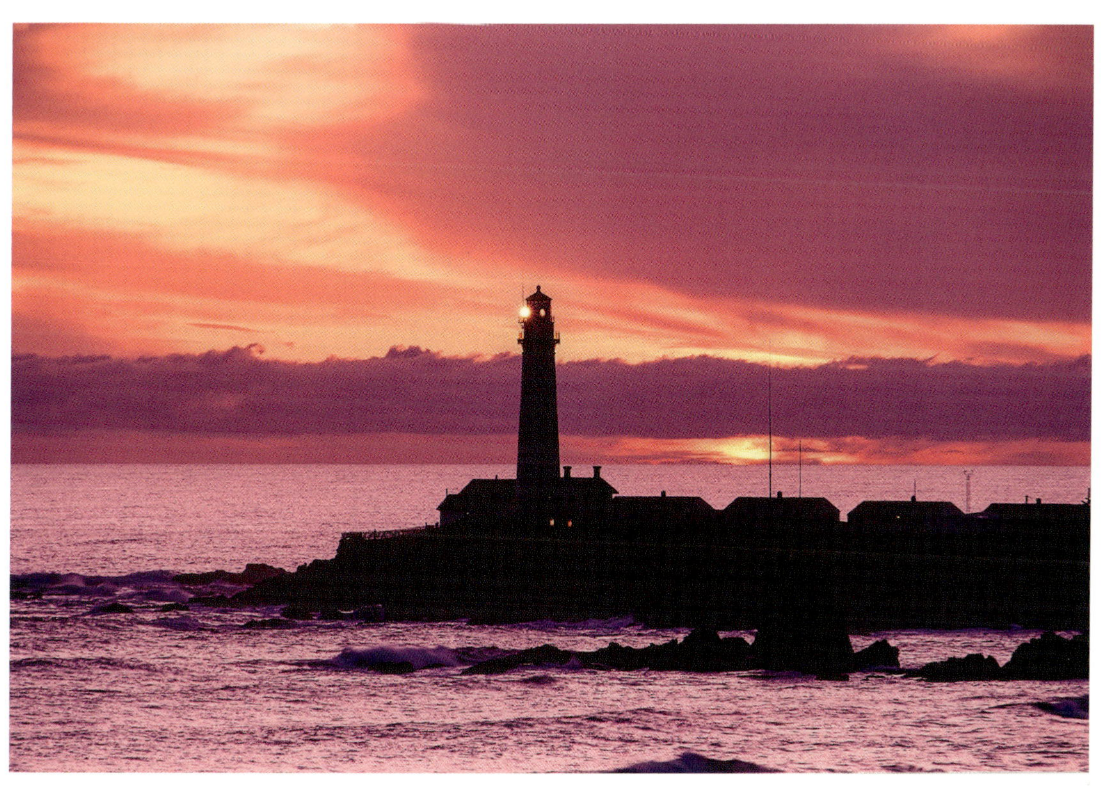

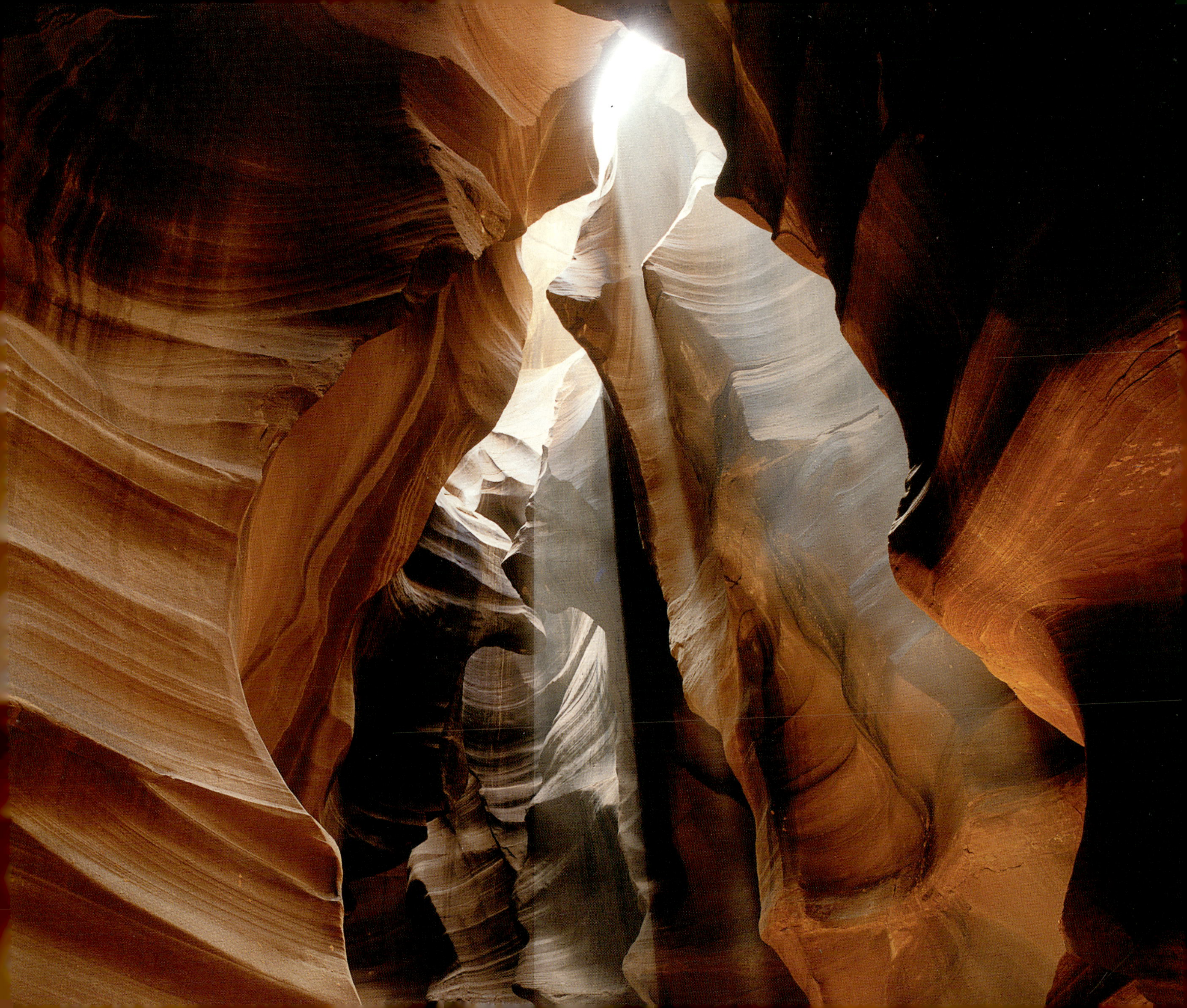

hidden in Him

There is no safer haven, no stronger fortress, than the place we dwell—with the One who saved us. He is a shelter in the storm and a tower in every siege. In the refuge of His grace, He protects and sustains us. Our true identity is kept for us there, like a blossoming garden behind a high wall. As we rest more and more in our dwelling place in Christ, this garden becomes evident in our lives. We give ourselves up as we enter His fortress, only to find our real selves for the first time.

REFLECT

For you have died and your life is hidden with Christ in God.

COLOSSIANS 3:3

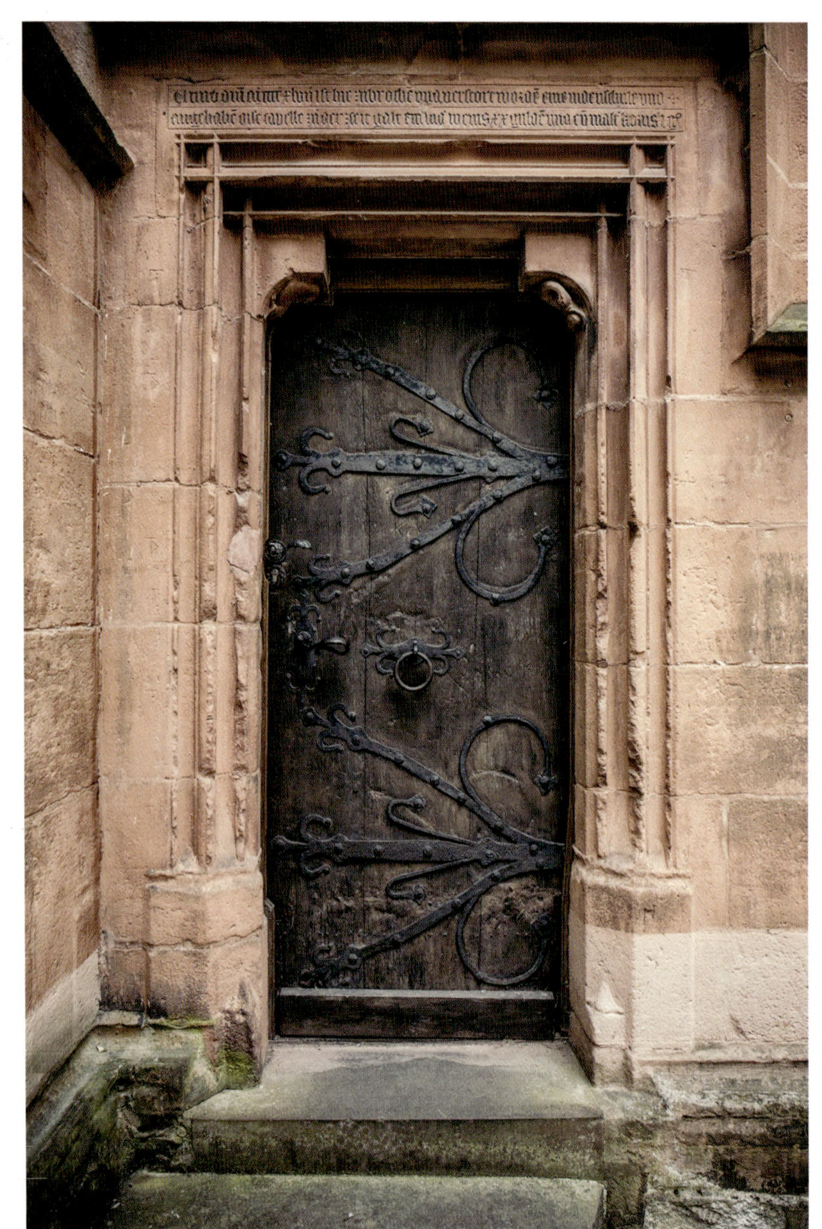

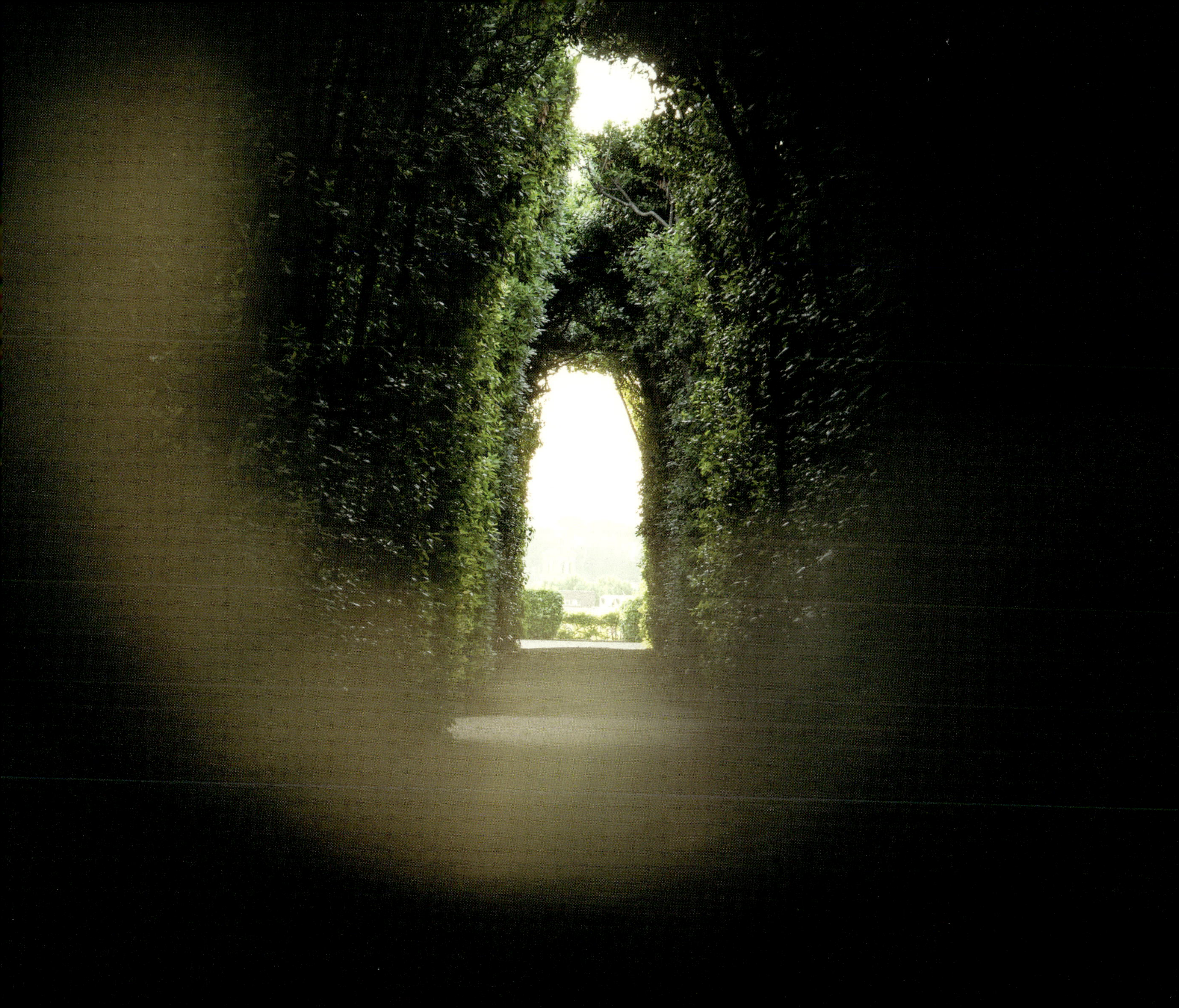

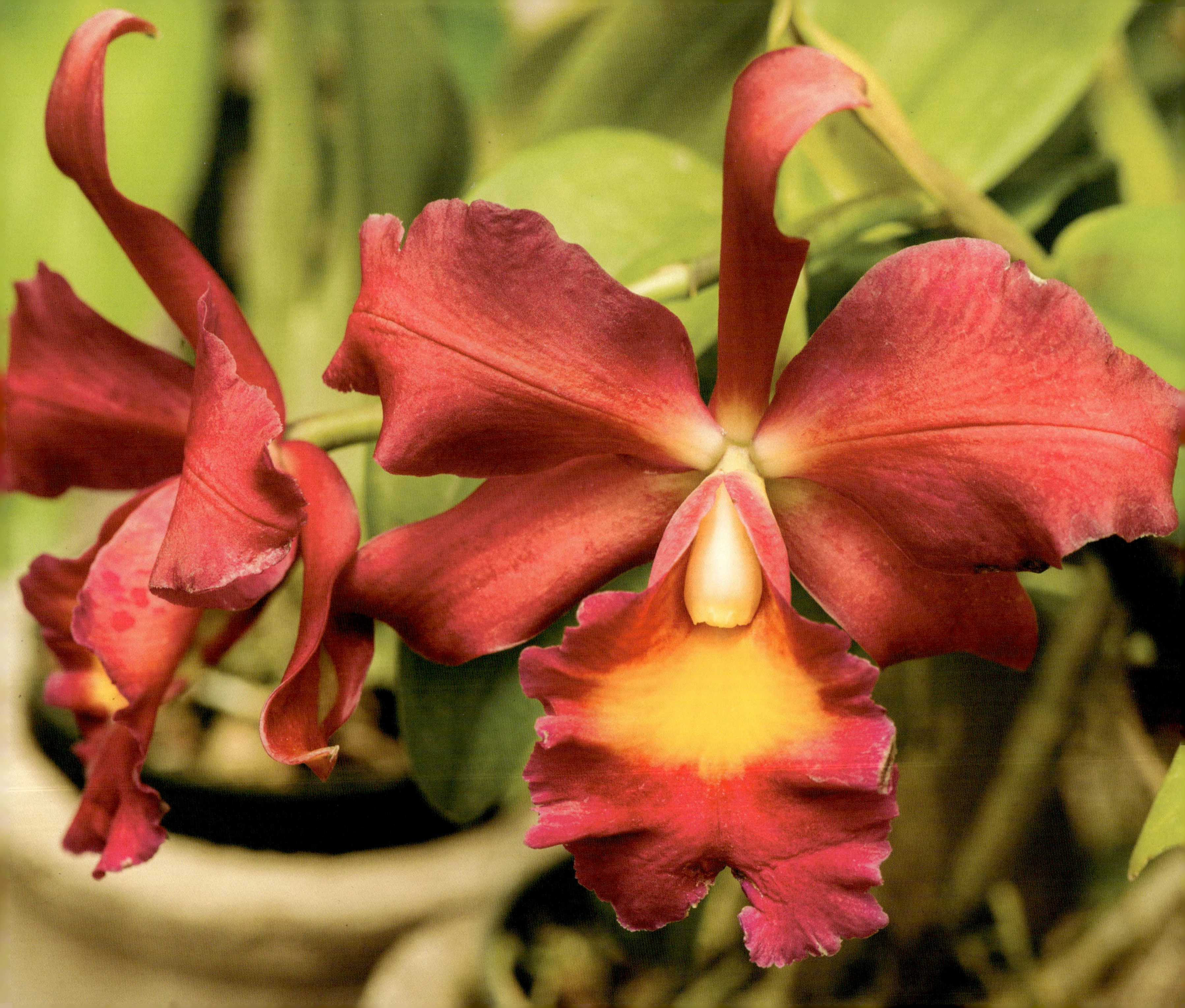

make us like You, Lord

What an honor it is to be shaped into the likeness of Jesus! As we behold Him in our hearts and learn to worship and adore Him, we become more like our Savior every day. God Himself begins to sand and smooth us, washing away flaws and polishing our best qualities. His plans are always perfect and His promise firm: He will carry them on to completion. With time, we become the very person He meant us to be from the start.

REFLECT

But we all, with unveiled face, beholding
as in a mirror the glory of the Lord, are being
transformed into the same image from glory to glory,
just as from the Lord, the Spirit.

2 CORINTHIANS 3:18

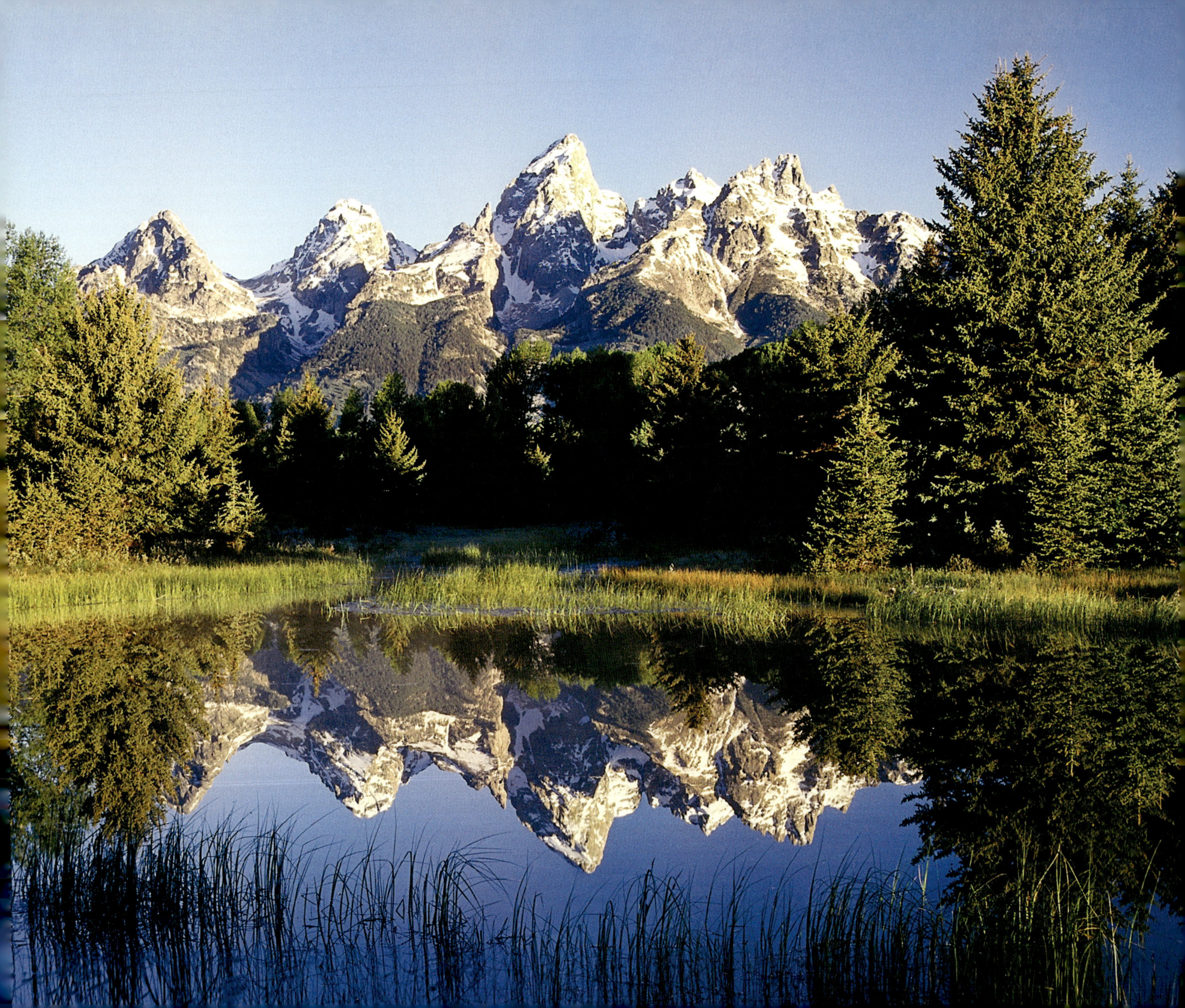

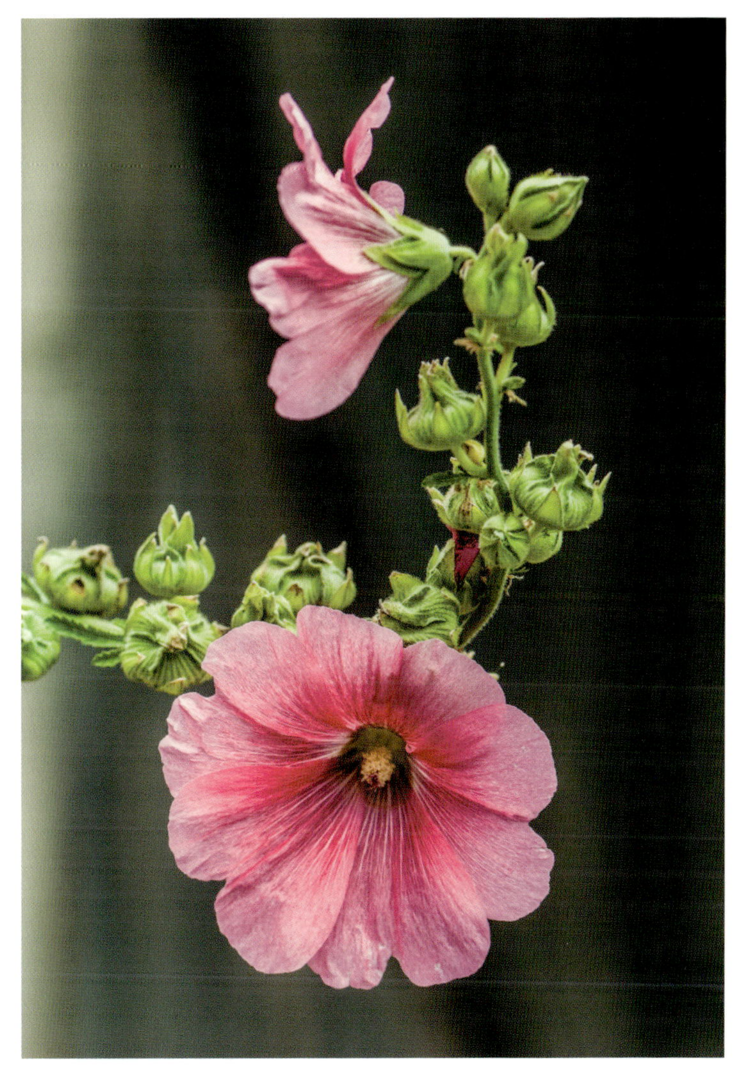

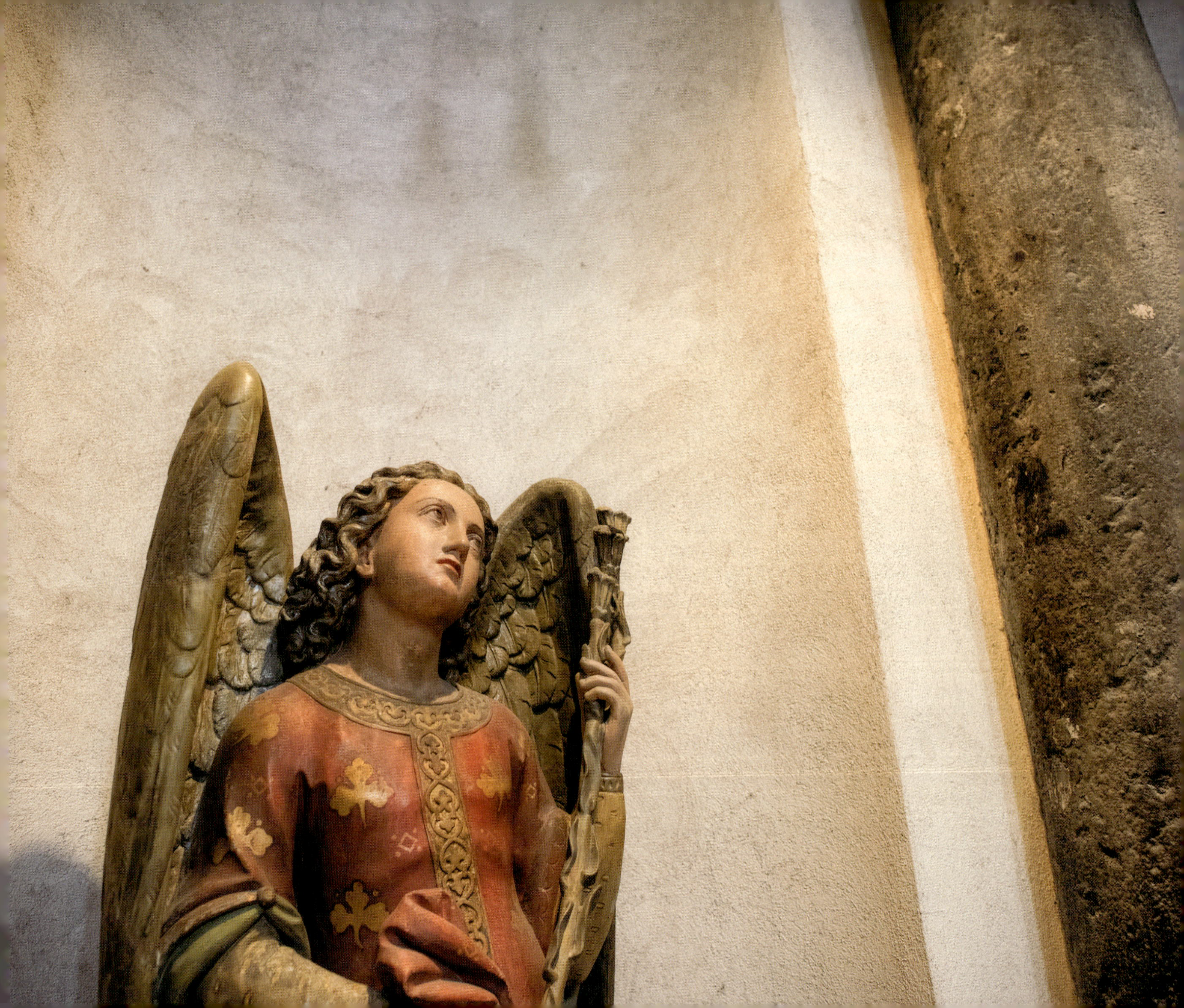

the hope of heaven

This is the great anticipation of the children of God: We have the hope of being in heaven one day, to sing eternal praises to our King and enjoy His presence forever. Until then, even our most beautiful offerings will only hint at the hope our hearts treasure, the splendor of the magnificent domain where our Lord Jesus Christ awaits us.

REFLECT

But you have come to Mount Zion and to the city of the living God, the heavenly Jerusalem, and to myriads of angels, to the general assembly and church of the firstborn who are enrolled in heaven.

HEBREWS 12:22-23

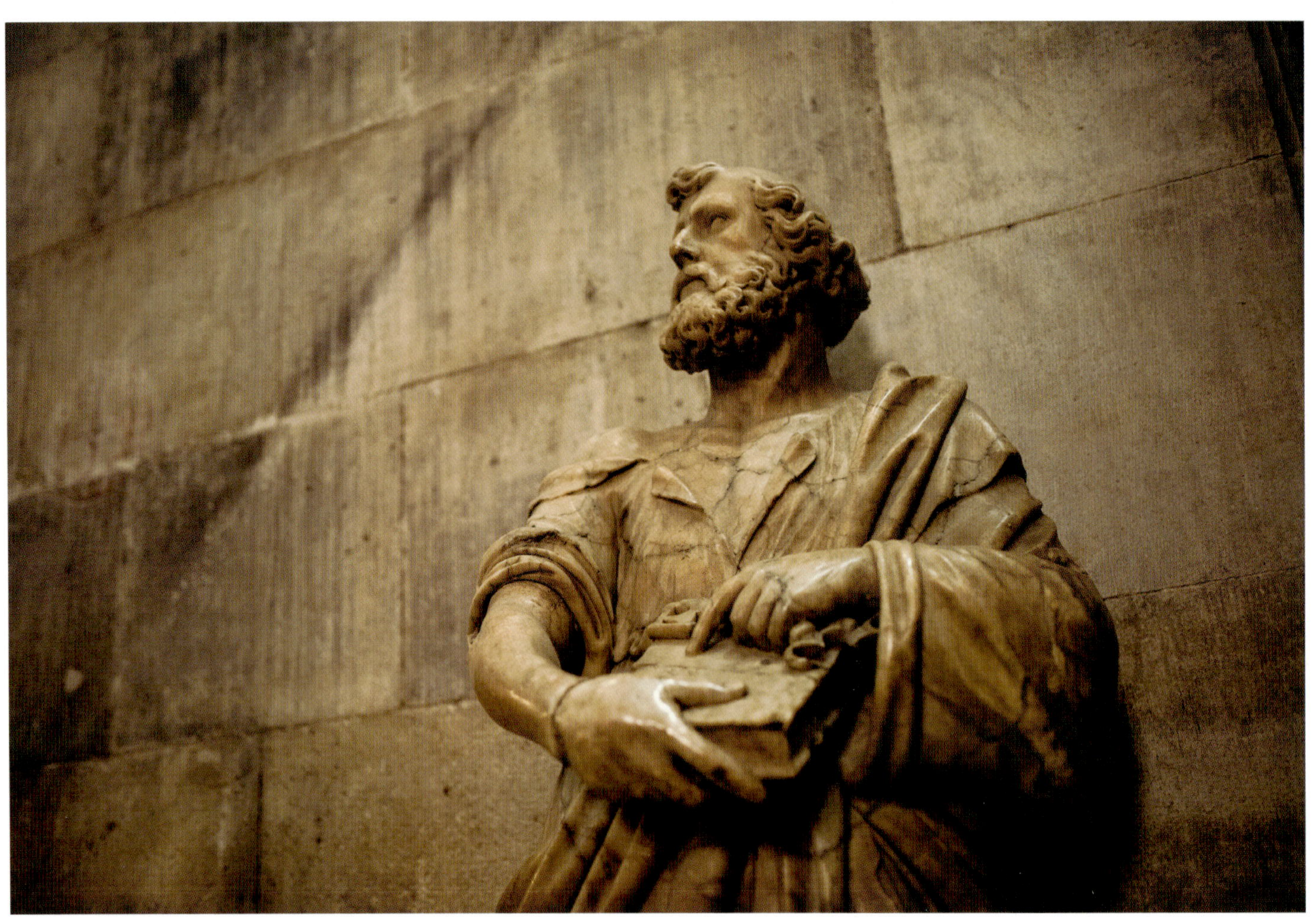

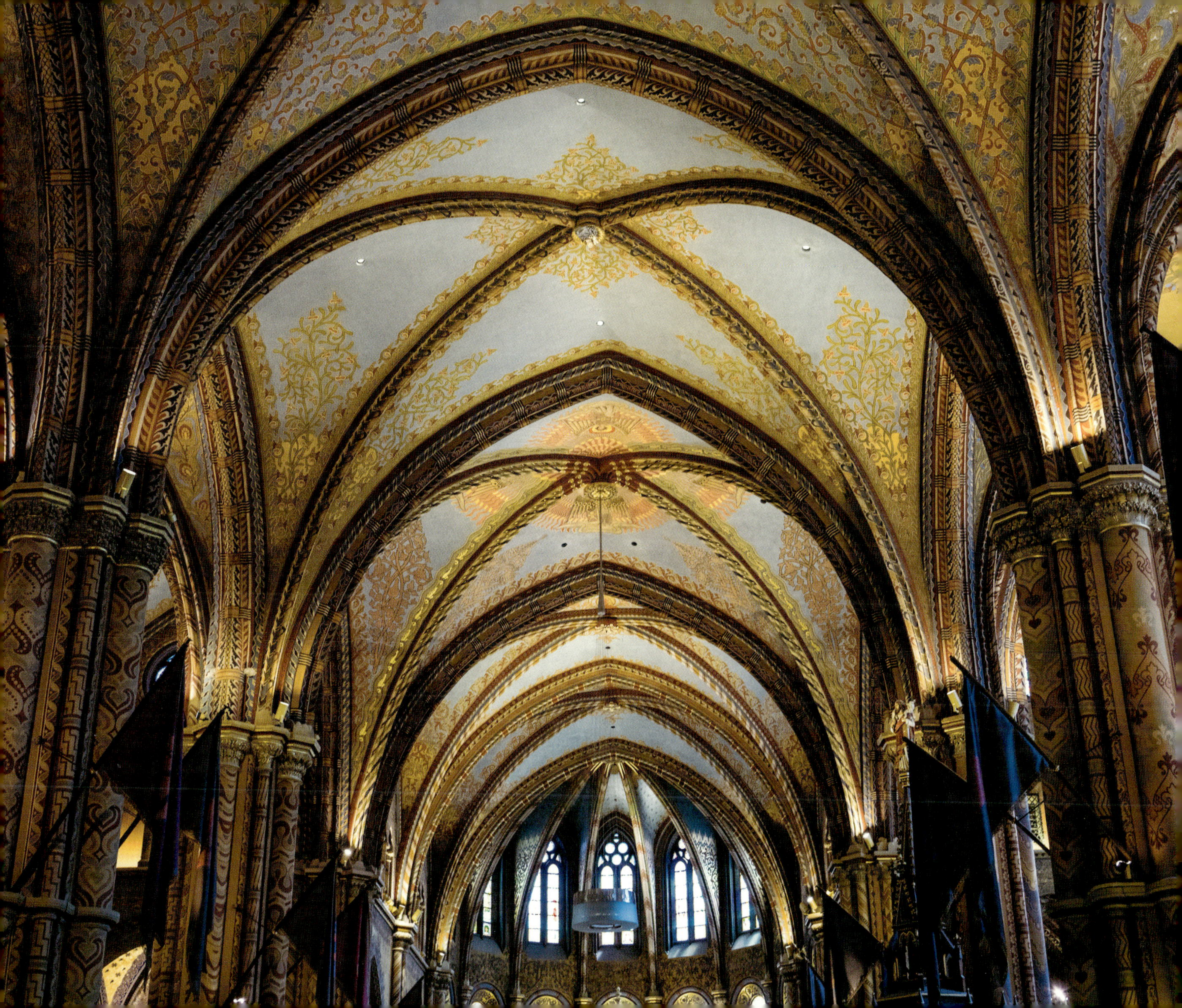

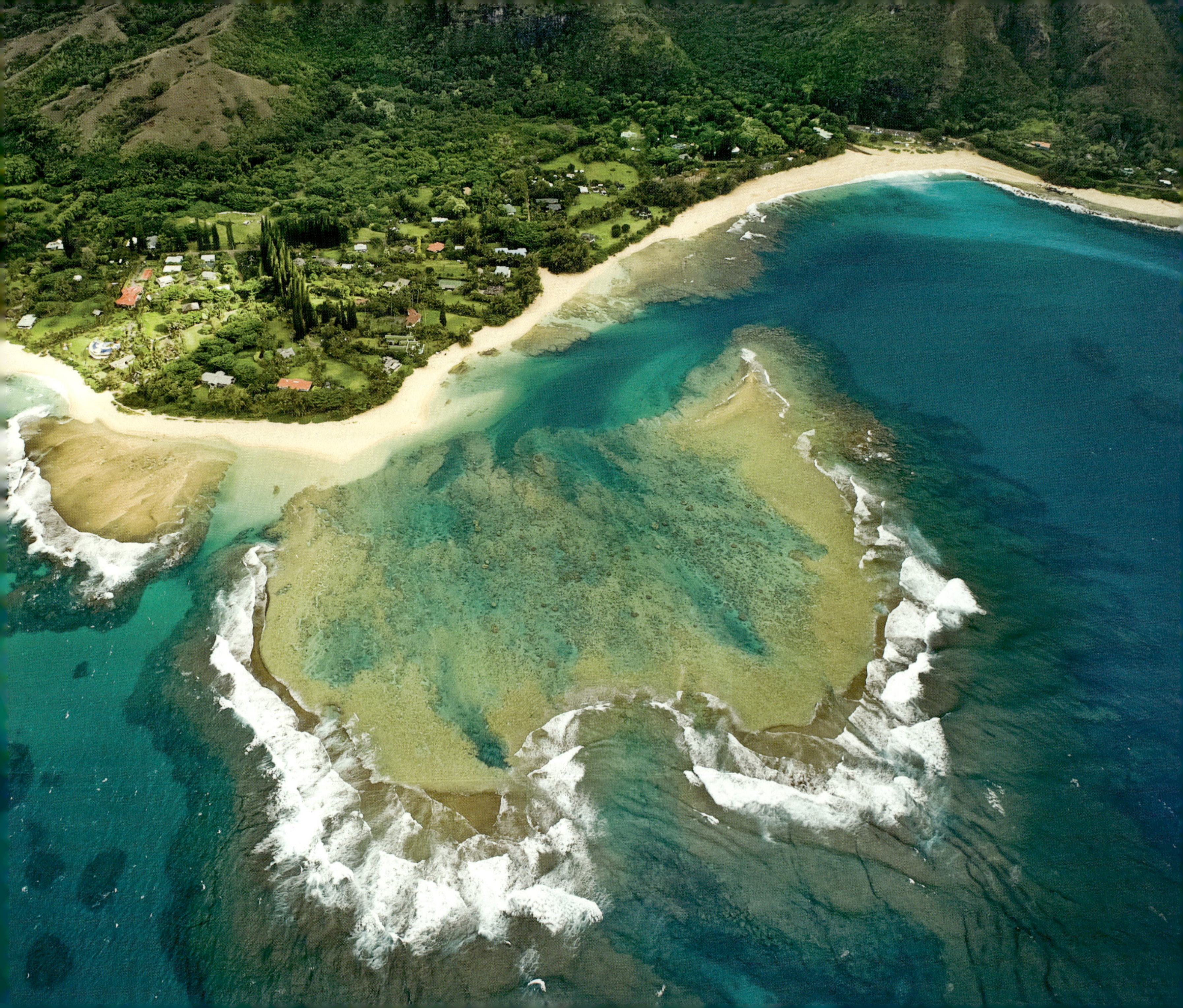

REFLECT

I pray that out of his glorious riches he may strengthen you with power through his Spirit in your inner being, so that Christ may dwell in your hearts through faith. And I pray that you, being rooted and established in love, may have power, together with all the Lord's holy people, to grasp how wide and long and high and deep is the love of Christ, and to know this love that surpasses knowledge—that you may be filled to the measure of all the fullness of God.

EPHESIANS 3:16-19 (NIV)

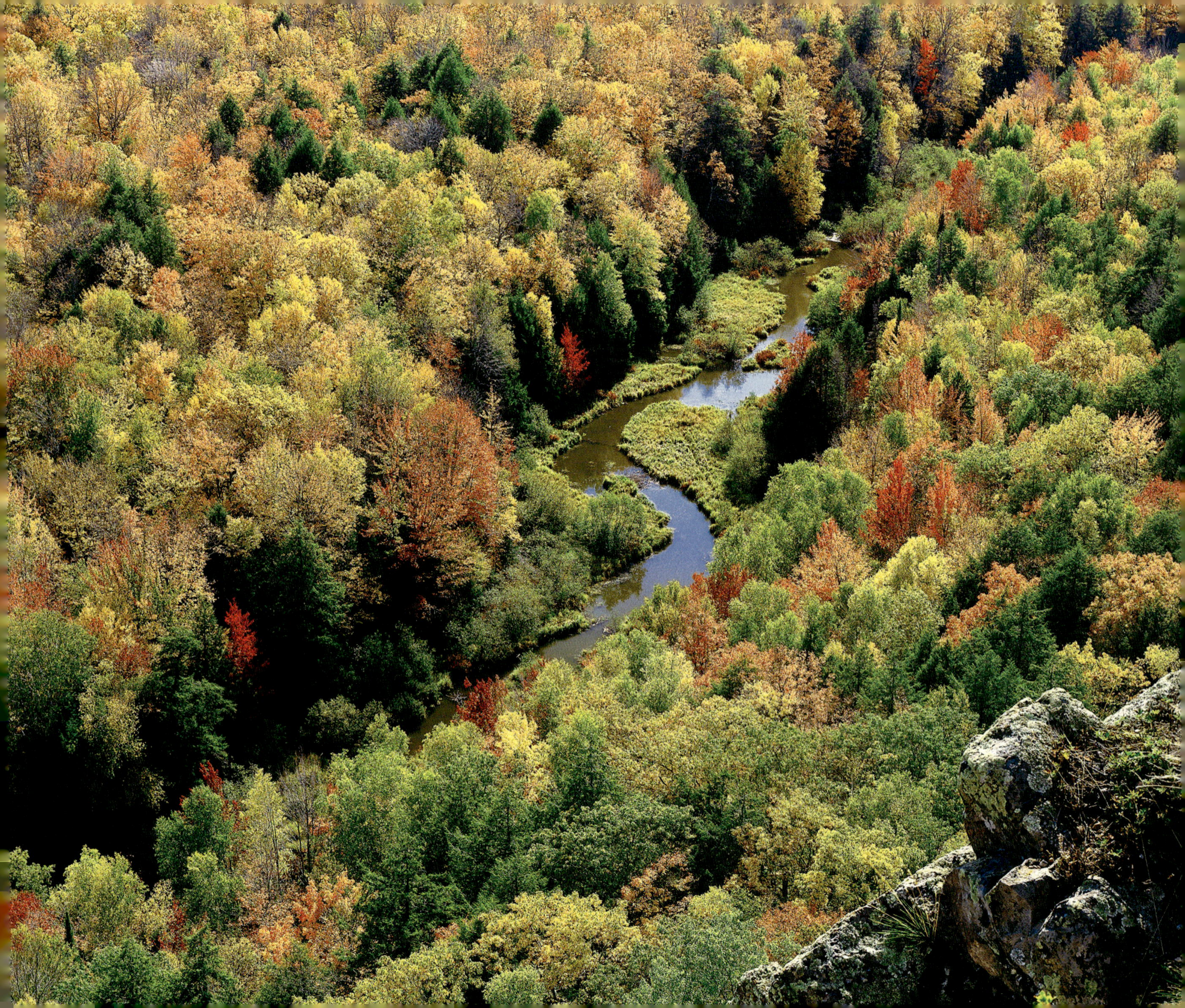

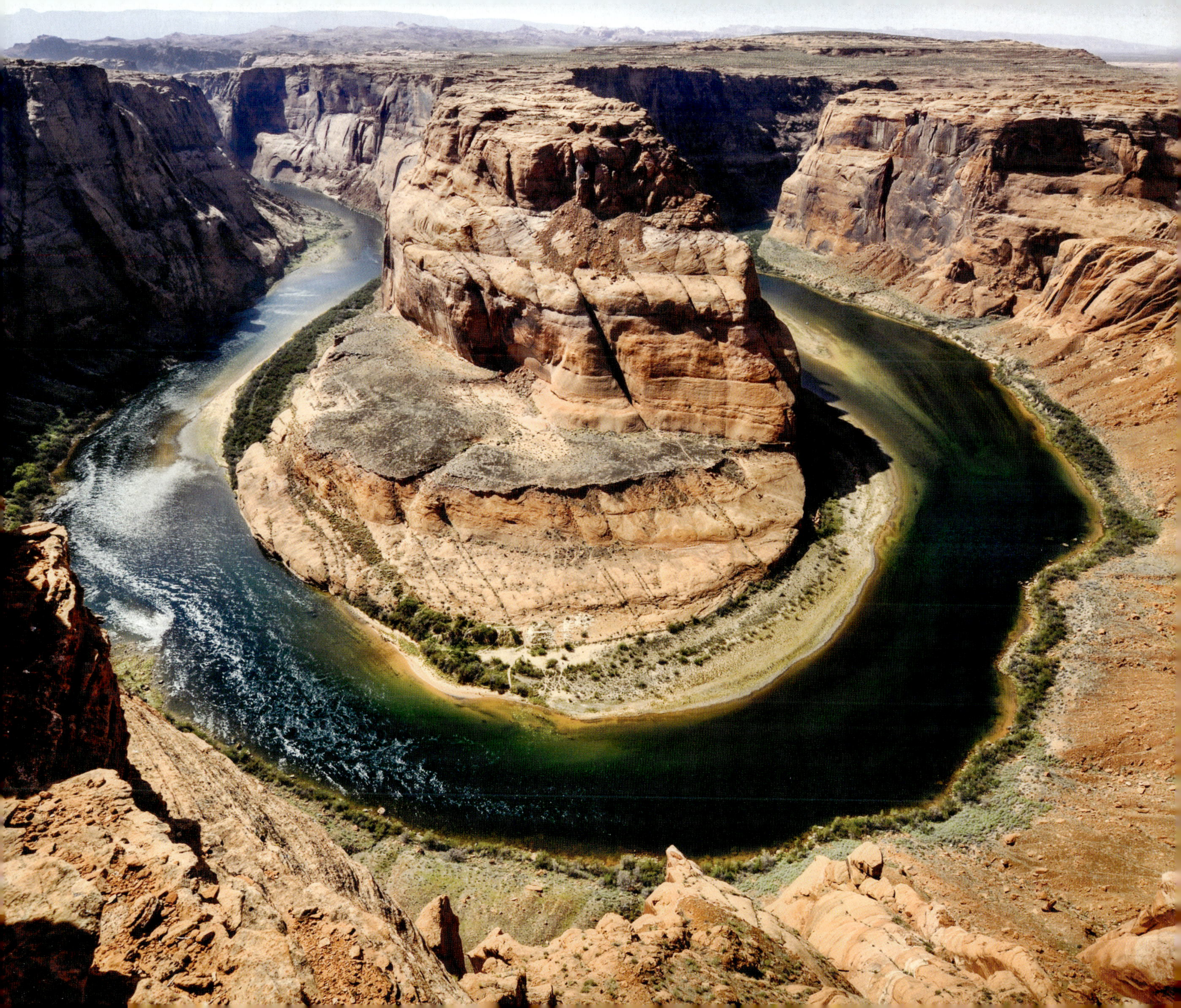

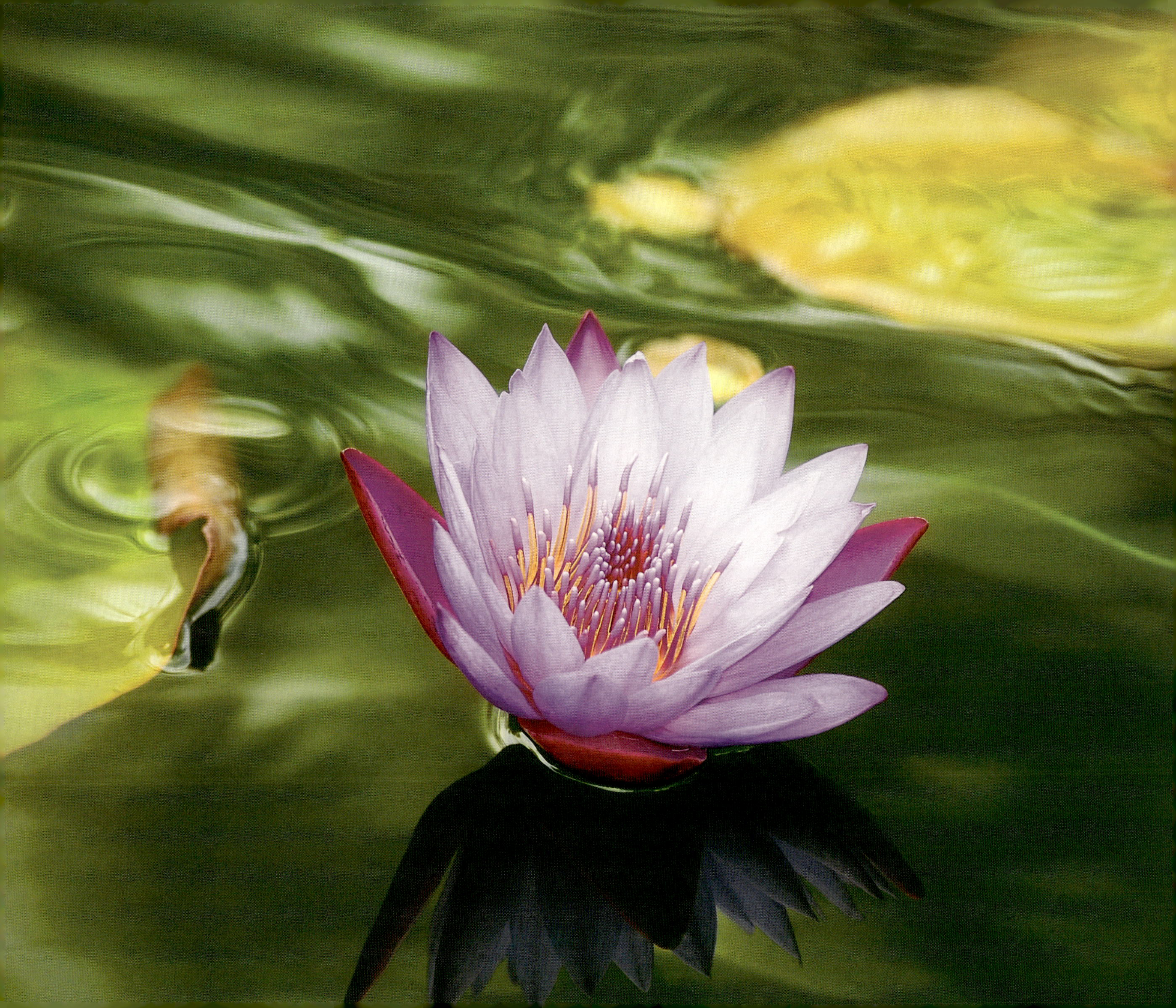

CHAPTER FOUR

THE PEACE OF GOD'S PRESENCE

To find oneself daily in the presence of the Lord is to find rest for the soul. Worn out from seeking solace in the world or trying to build our own righteousness, we come at last to the only source of true peace: the One who redeems us from the hand of darkness, washes away our sins, gives us eternal life, and works through us with grace and strength. Only the blood of Jesus can defeat the soul's gnawing sense of unrest and deliver us from guilt and shame—this is the primary peace, from which all others flow.

Jesus, as our Savior, is our peace. Walking with Him quiets the mind and casts out anxious thoughts. With our eyes fixed on Him in trust, muddied channels begin to flow like clear and unimpeded streams. His presence brings clarity and light to our minds, and stability to the very ground on which we walk. Amid such life-giving conditions we can grow in a healthy way, encouraged by His grace and compassion.

We discover a power that is not of ourselves. In Jesus we are freed from the burden of self-reliance, and rest instead in something far greater: the power of the Son of God Himself. In return for our trust in Him, He grants us peace, as we see Him working in all things on our behalf—and accomplishing more through us than we, in our weakness, could ever imagine.

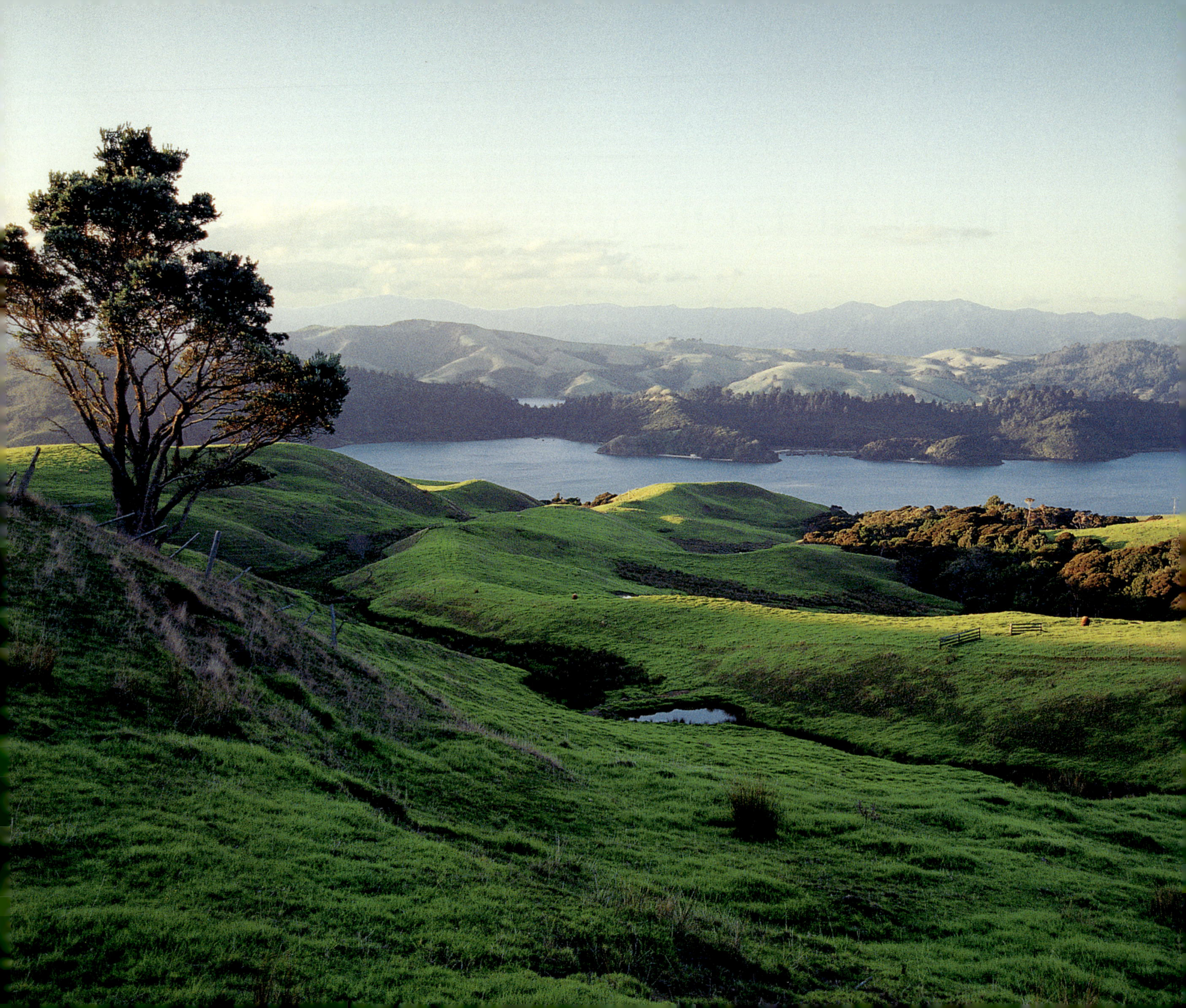

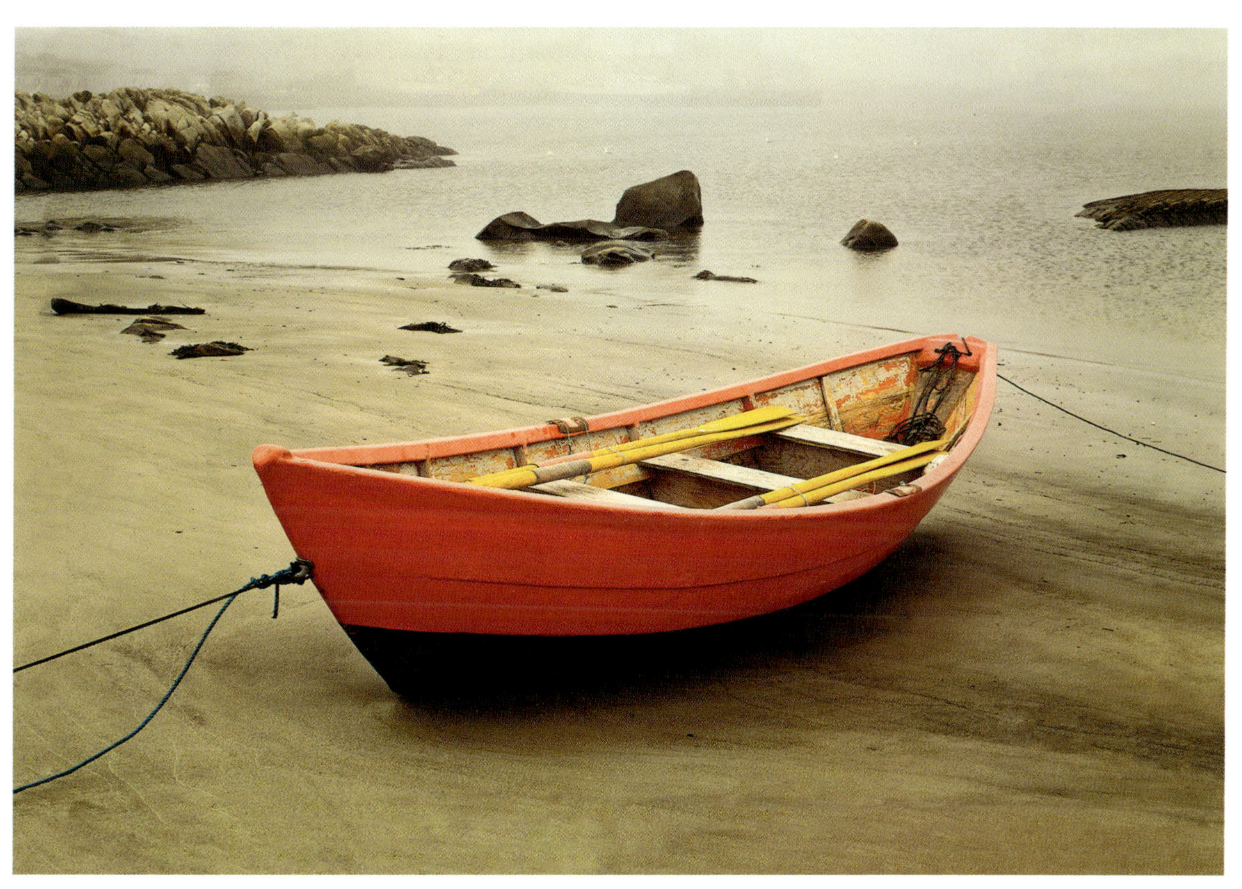

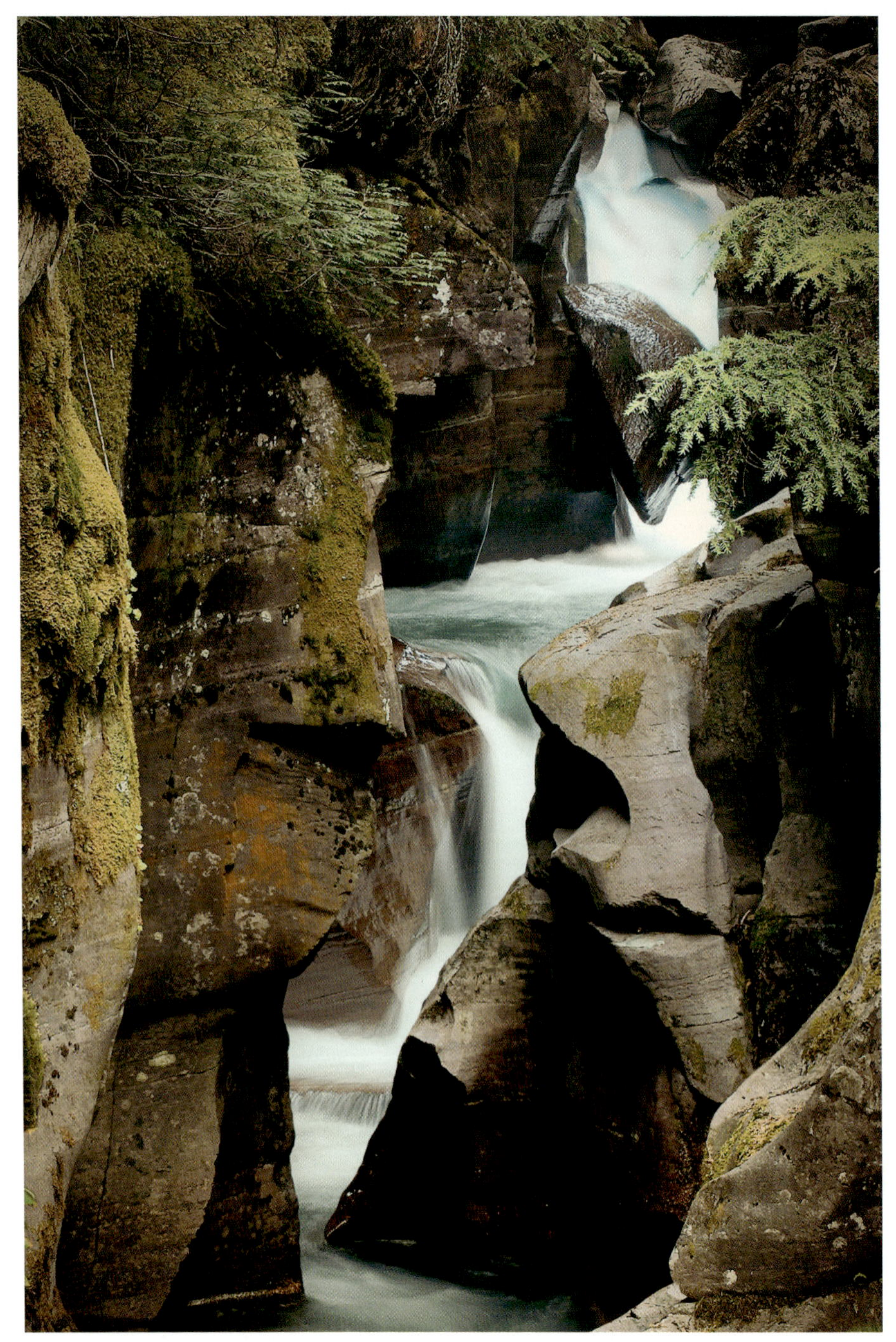

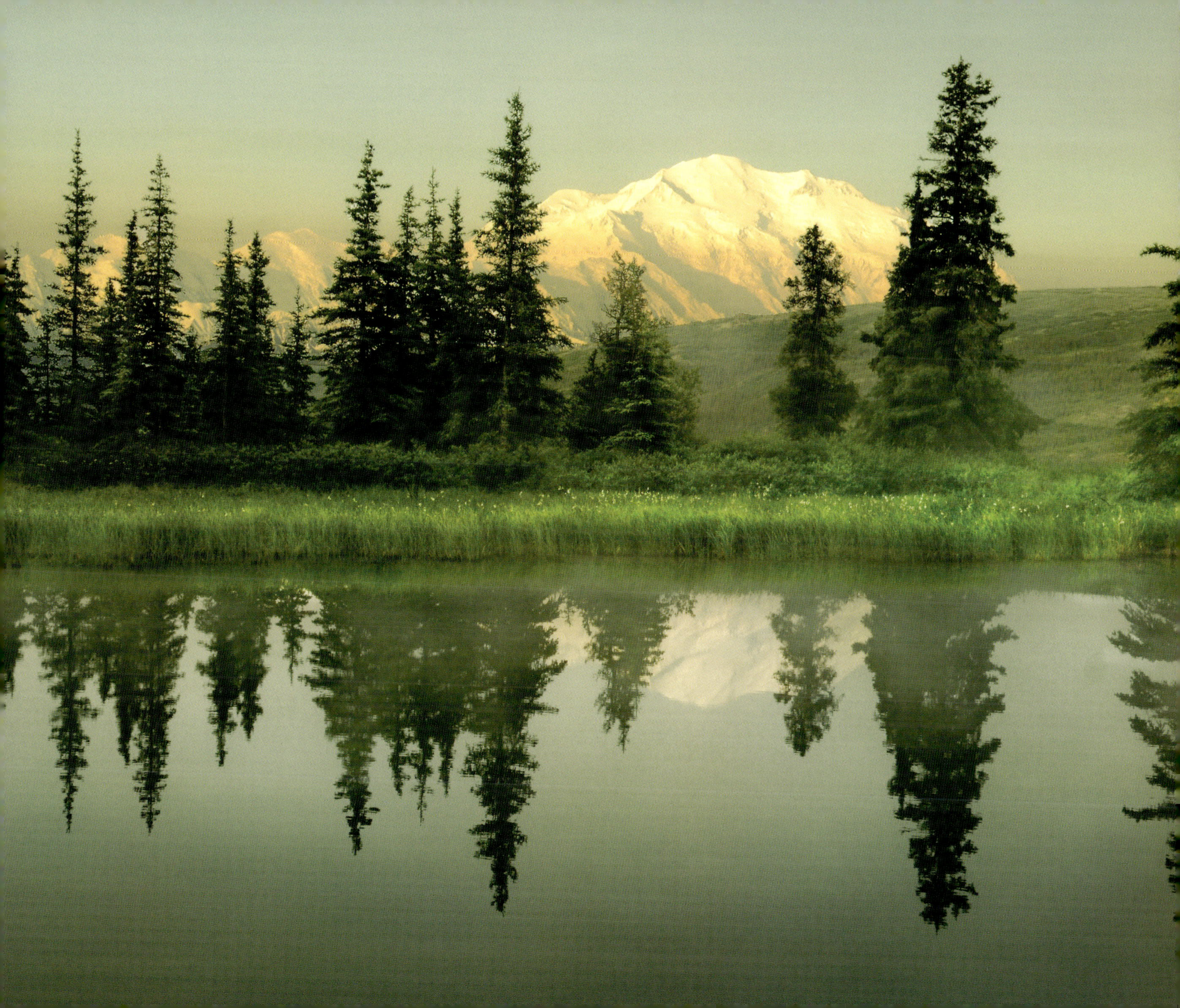

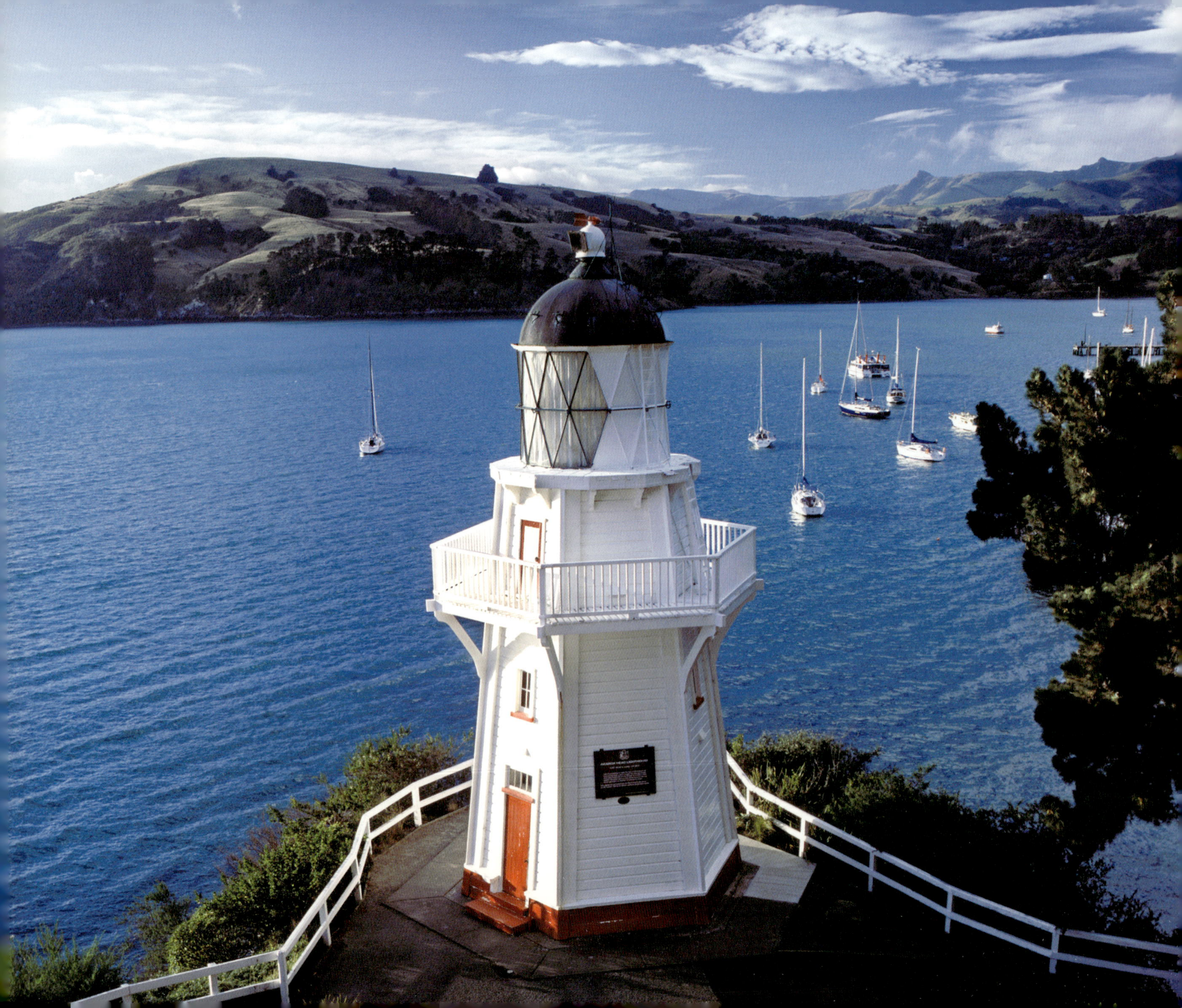

a heart calmed

United with Christ through faith, we enter the peace of the divine exchange: He took our sins upon Himself, canceled them, and gave us His righteousness in return. Though we must continue to put to death our unholy inclinations, another part of us already rests in the harbor of forgiveness carved for us by the Son of God. Sheltered from the storm of its great and terrible problem, the heart grows calm, at anchor in the quiet waters of grace.

REFLECT

In Him we have redemption through His blood,
the forgiveness of our trespasses, according to the
riches of His grace which He lavished on us.

EPHESIANS 1:7-8

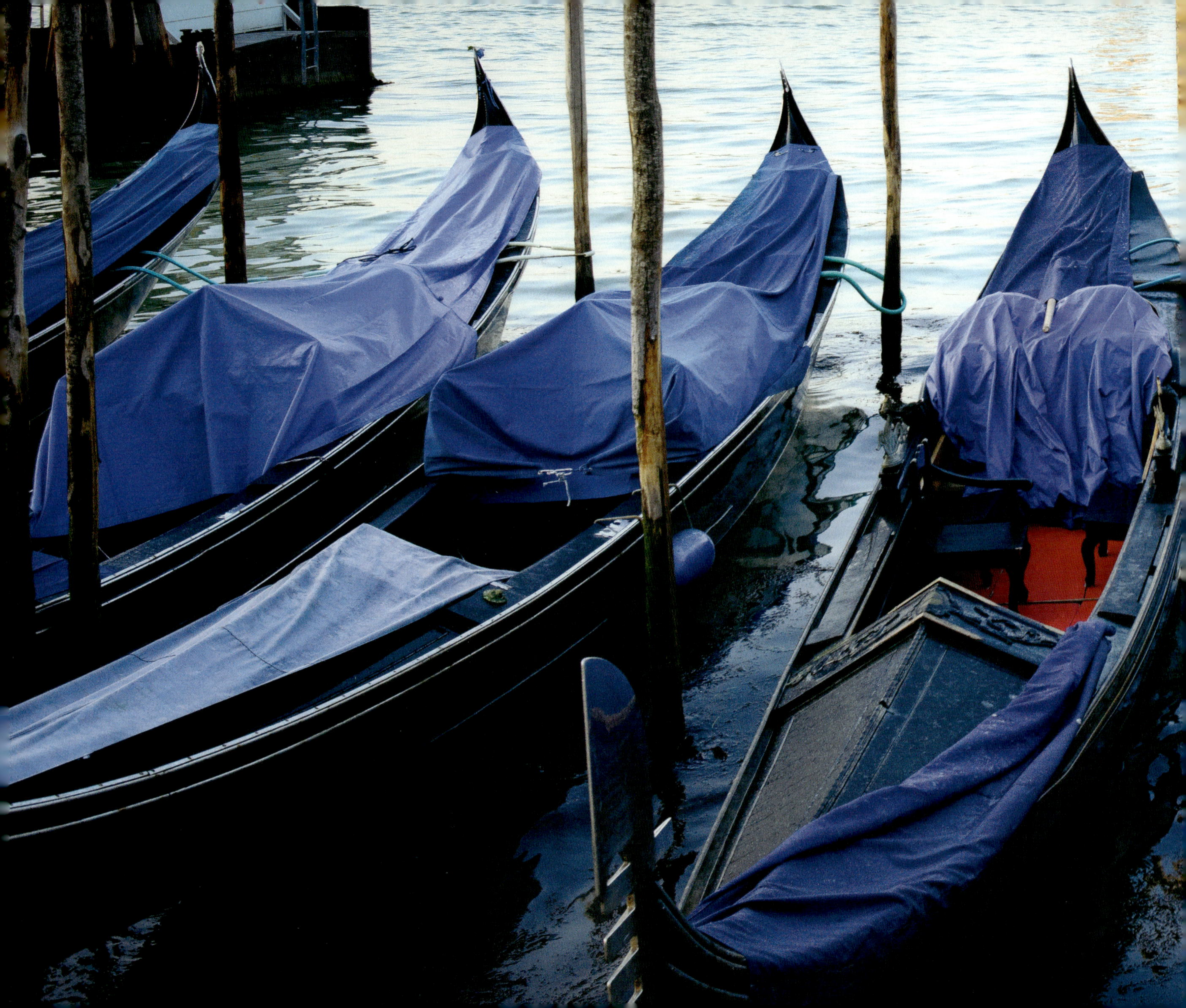

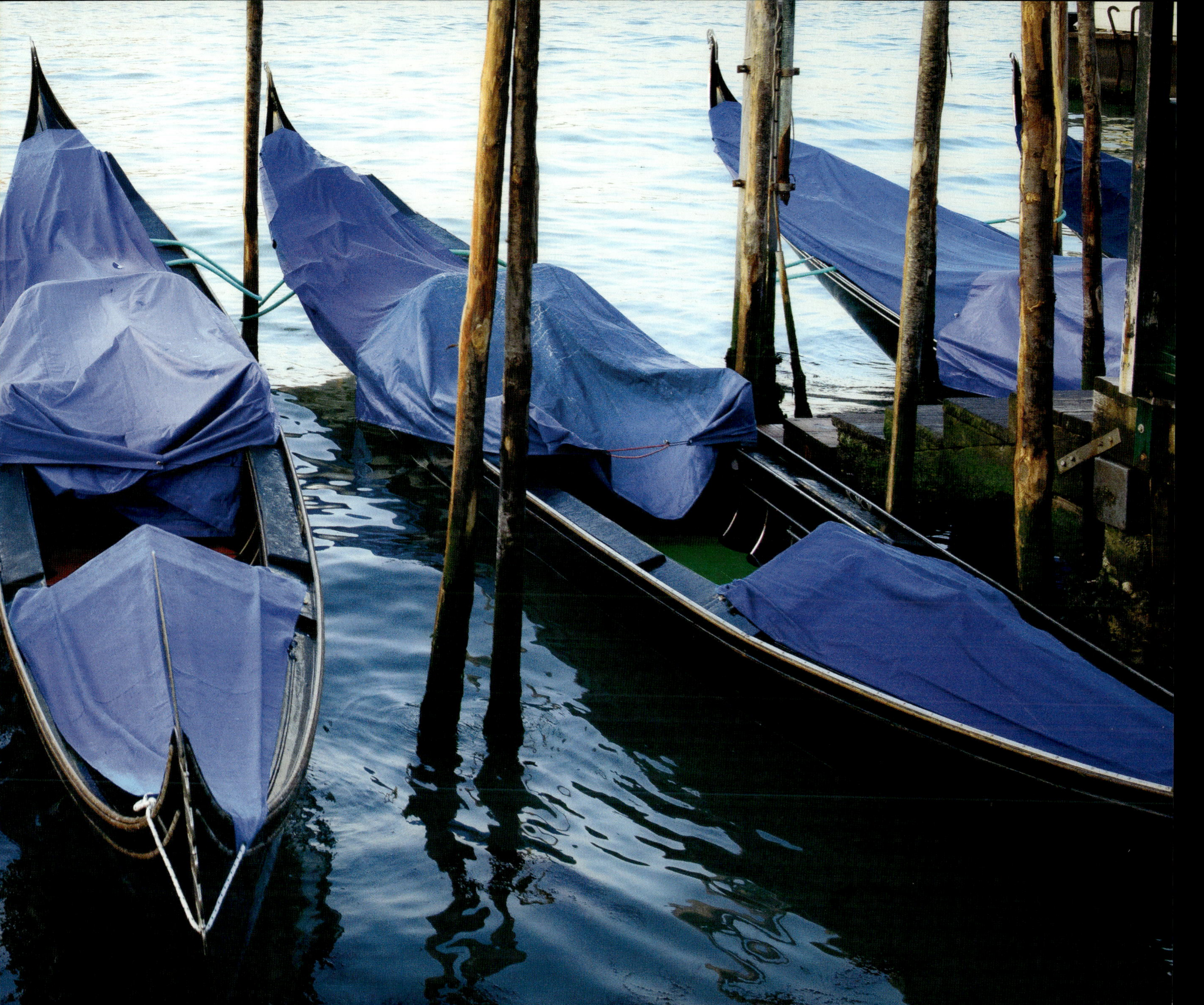

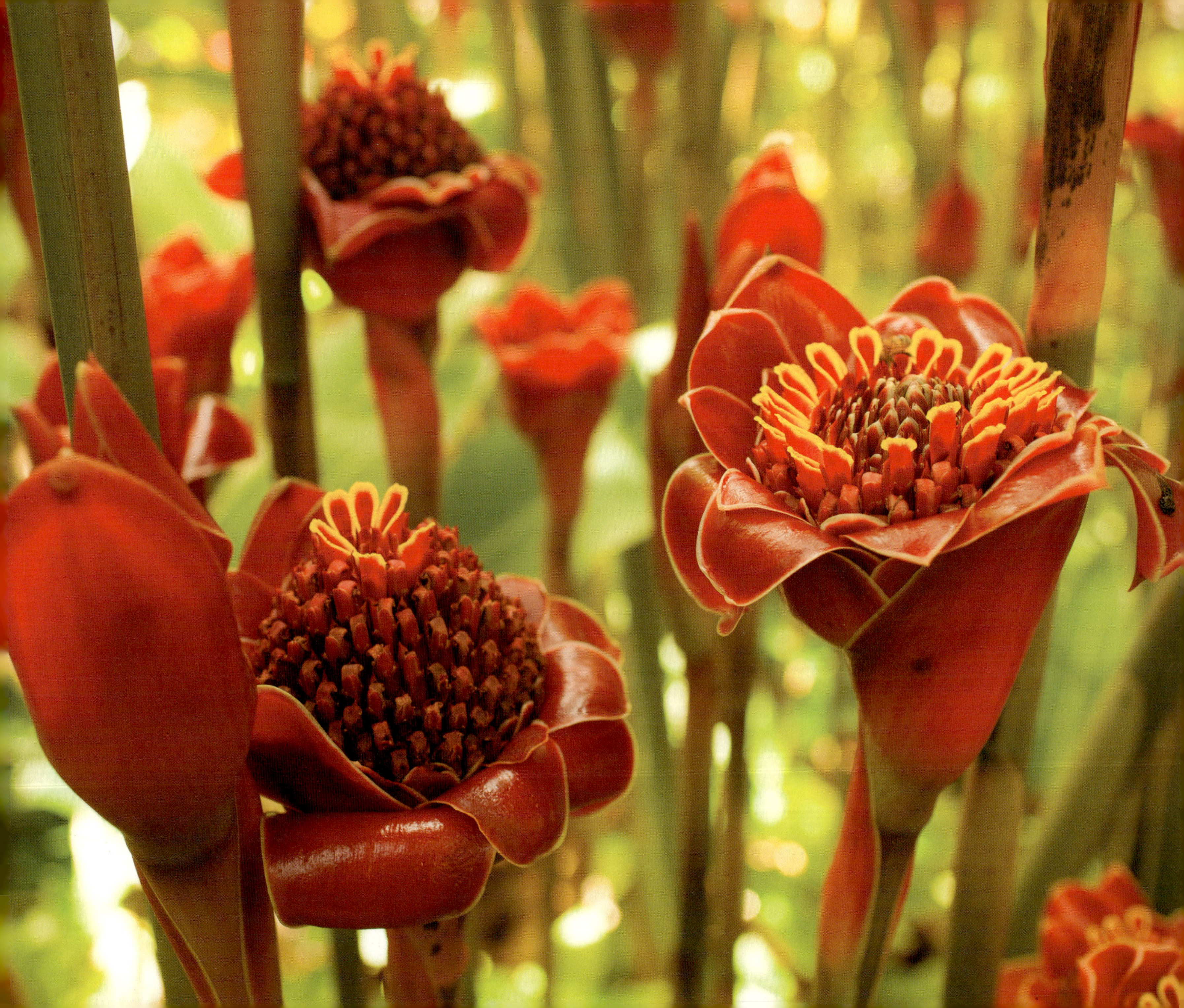

You're in Christ; Christ is in you. He is your life. He's living on the inside of you. As you begin responding to life according to that awareness, here's what happens. You begin to experience a love that cannot be fathomed, a life that can never die, a righteousness that cannot be tarnished, a peace that cannot ever be understood, a rest that cannot be disturbed, a joy that cannot be diminished, a hope that cannot be disappointed, a light that cannot be darkened, a happiness that cannot be interrupted, a strength that cannot be enfeebled, a purity that cannot be defiled, a beauty that cannot be marred, a wisdom that cannot be baffled, and resources that cannot be exhausted.

— DR. CHARLES STANLEY —

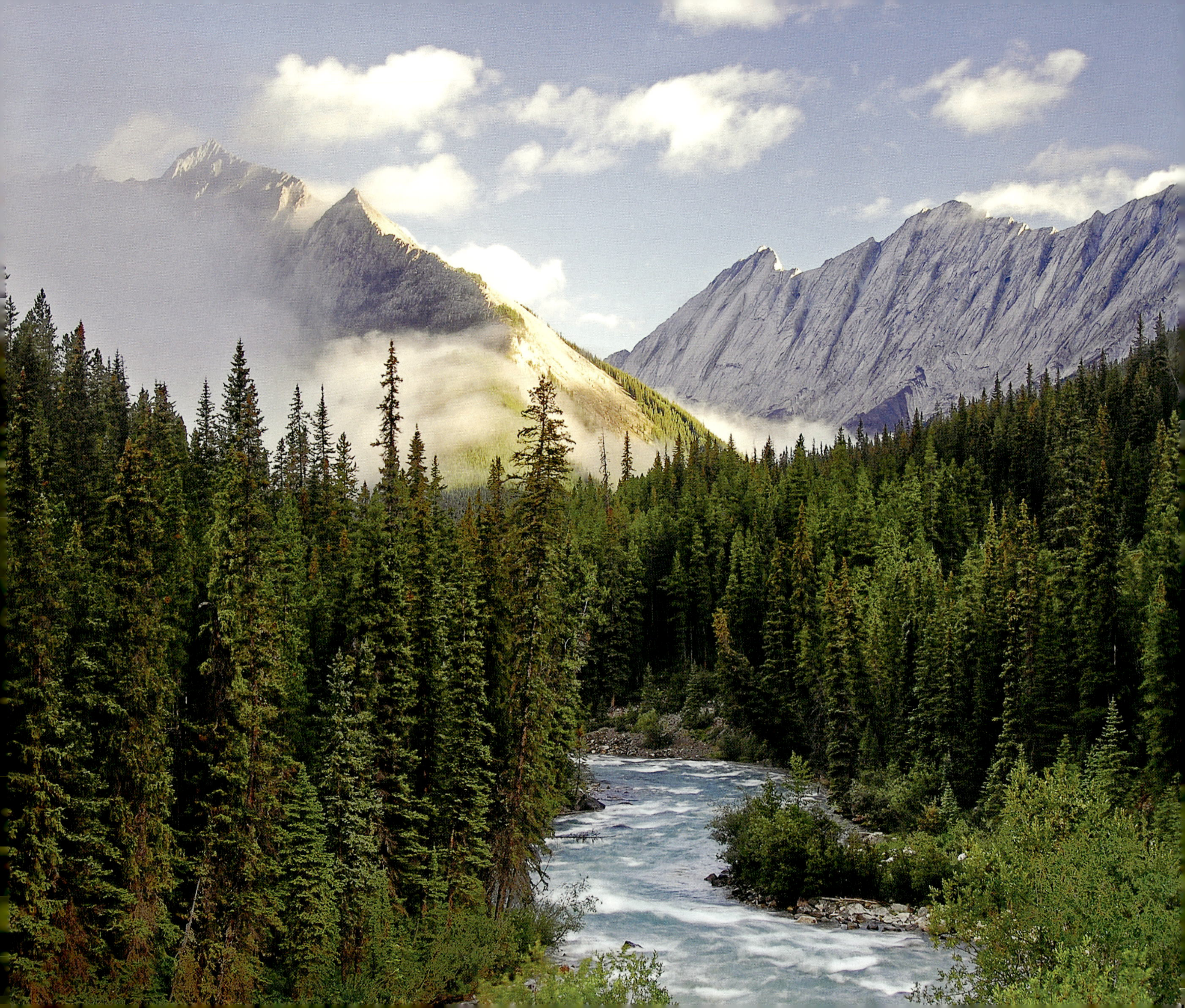

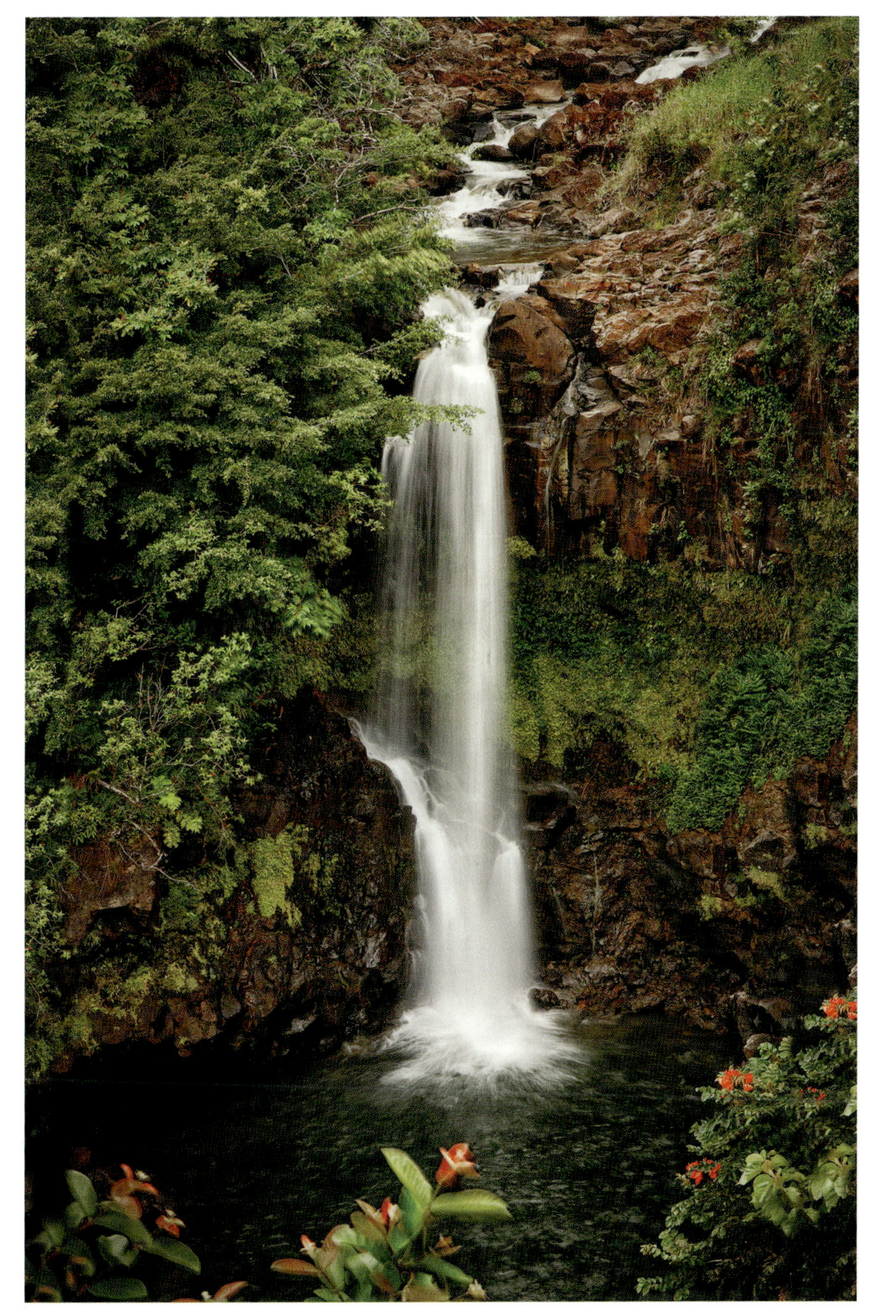

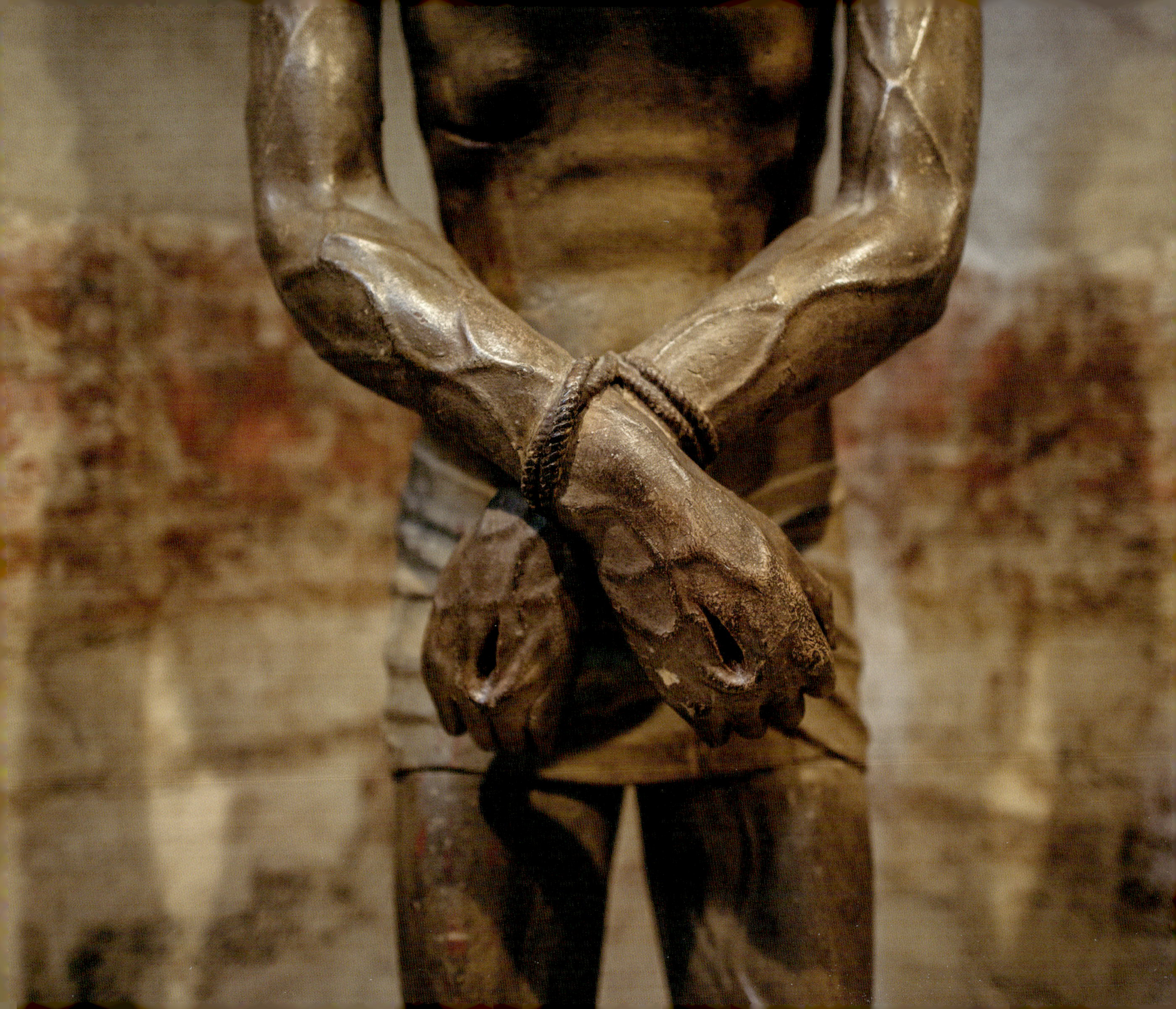

how lovely You are, Jesus

To consider the Person of Jesus is to behold purity, strength, true kingliness, and welcoming love. In a world stained with sin and disfigured by brokenness, His perfection captivates and soothes. As His presence permeates our lives, we come to dwell naturally on the sweeter aspects of the world around us: a bird's voice, a building's careful lines, a hand of friendship. Order, beauty, sincerity, compassion—thoughts of Christ, and all that reflects Him, make a gracious and peaceful mind.

REFLECT

Finally, brothers and sisters, whatever is true,
whatever is noble, whatever is right,
whatever is pure, whatever is lovely, whatever
is admirable—if anything is excellent or
praiseworthy—think about such things.

PHILIPPIANS 4:8 (NIV)

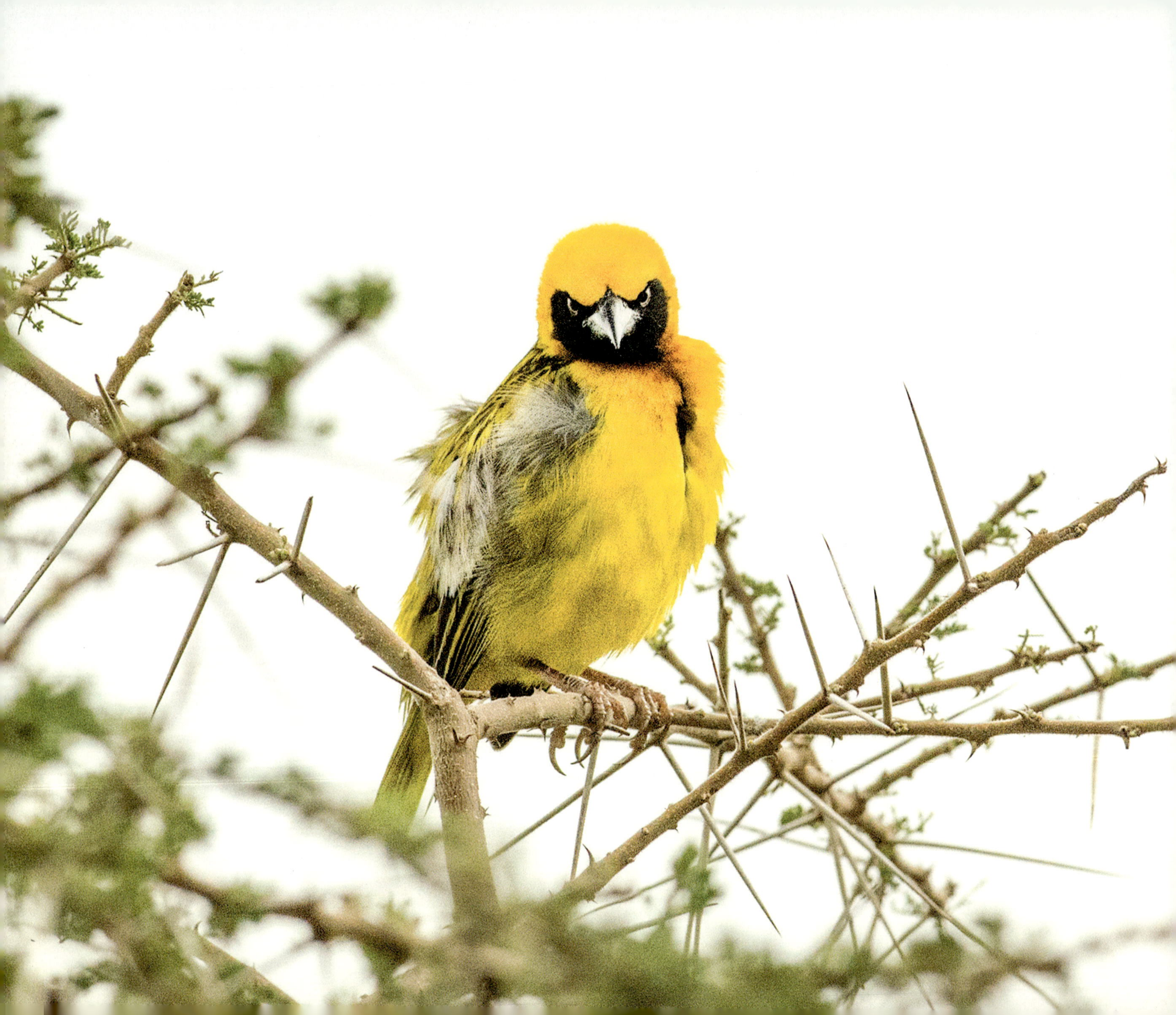

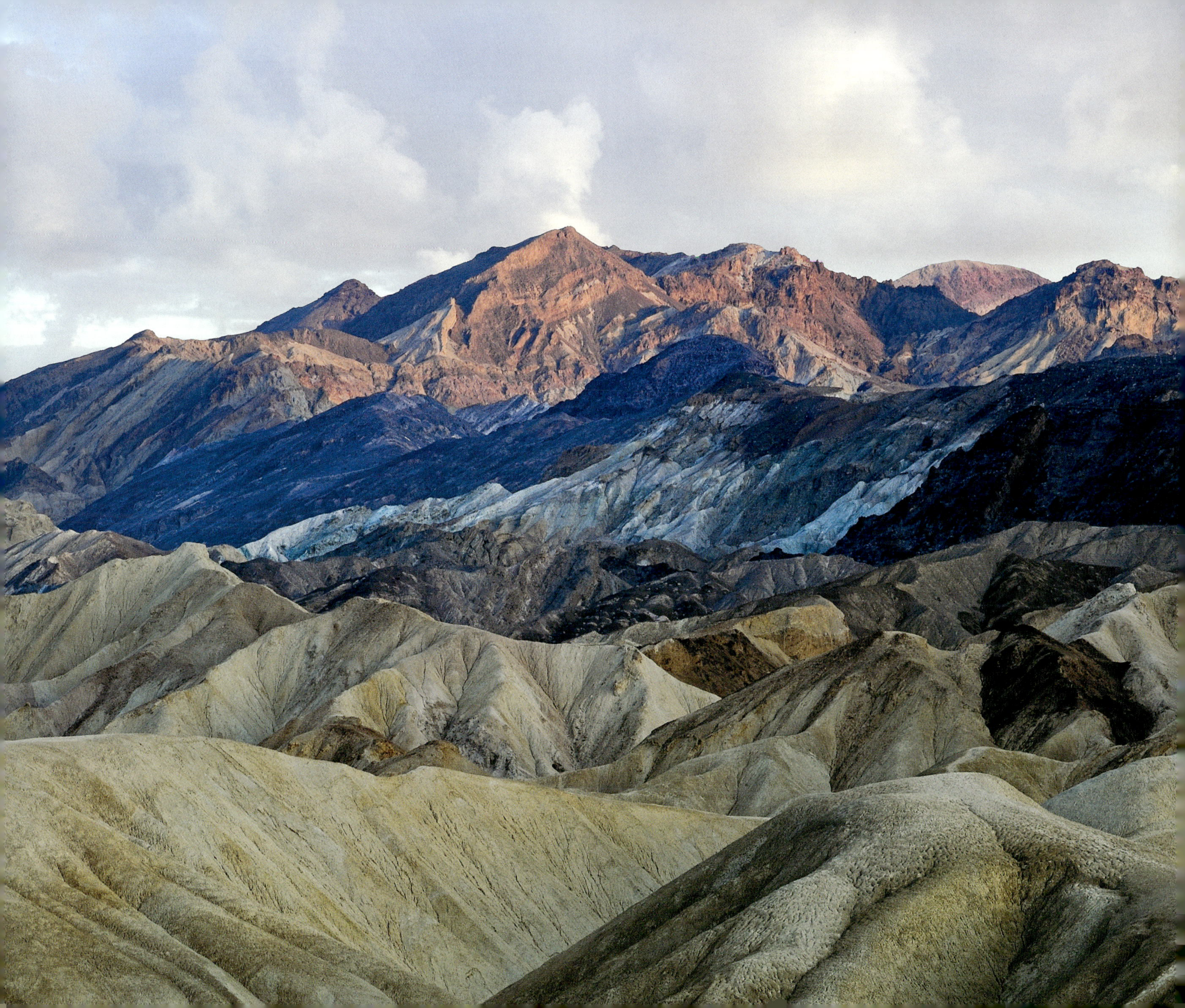

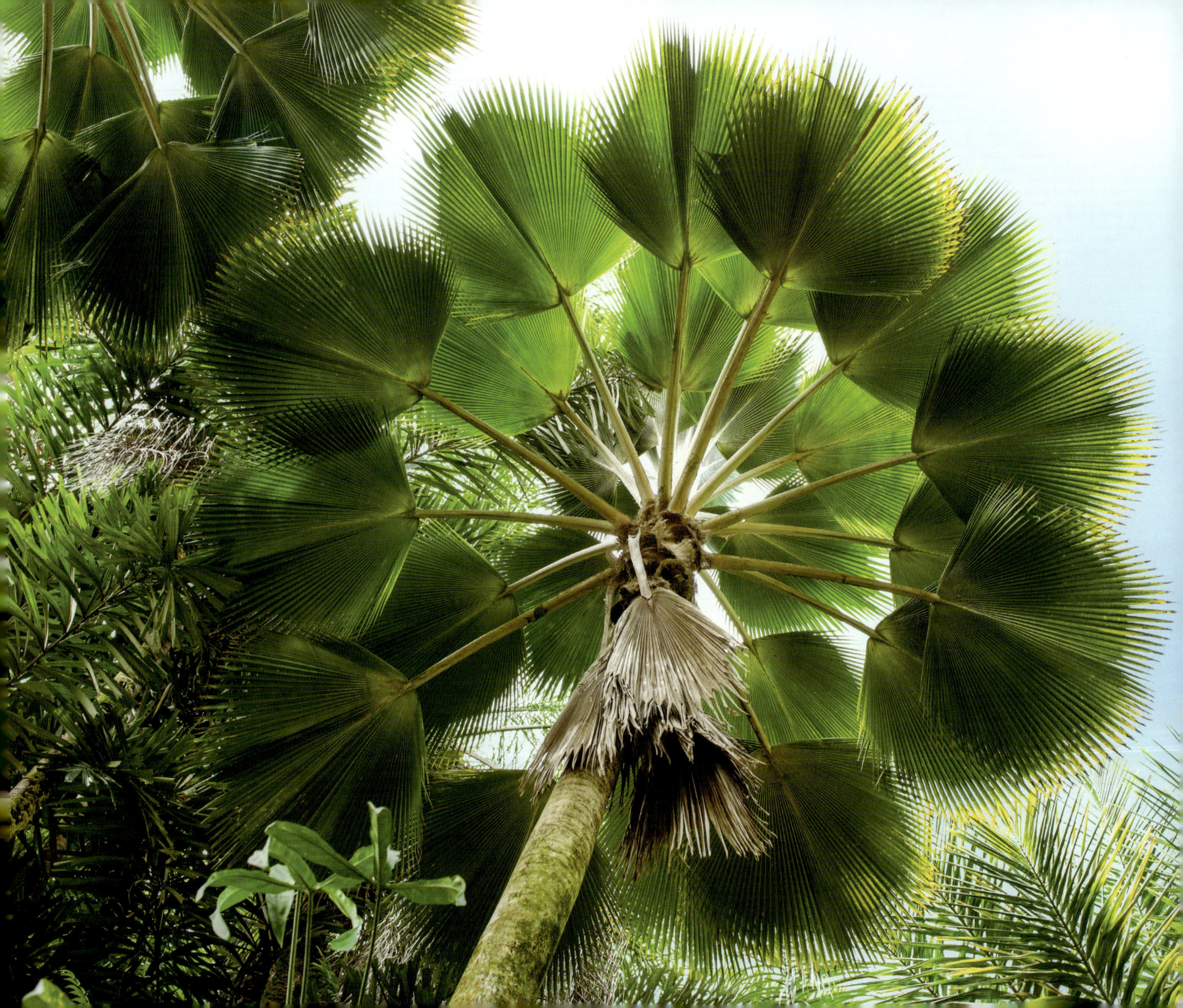

ever upward

To grow in Christ is to advance steadily in noble stature and the greatness of humility. We may see bumps, turns, and adjustments as we negotiate the trials and smaller defeats of life, but the larger picture is one of steadfast and peaceful incline, a tree reaching ever higher into the warmth and light above. As God uses every stumble to His good purpose in us, we perceive the unfolding of His plan, and glorify Him in our hearts.

REFLECT

And we know that God causes all things to work together for good to those who love God, to those who are called according to His purpose. For those whom He foreknew, He also predestined to become conformed to the image of His Son.

ROMANS 8:28–29

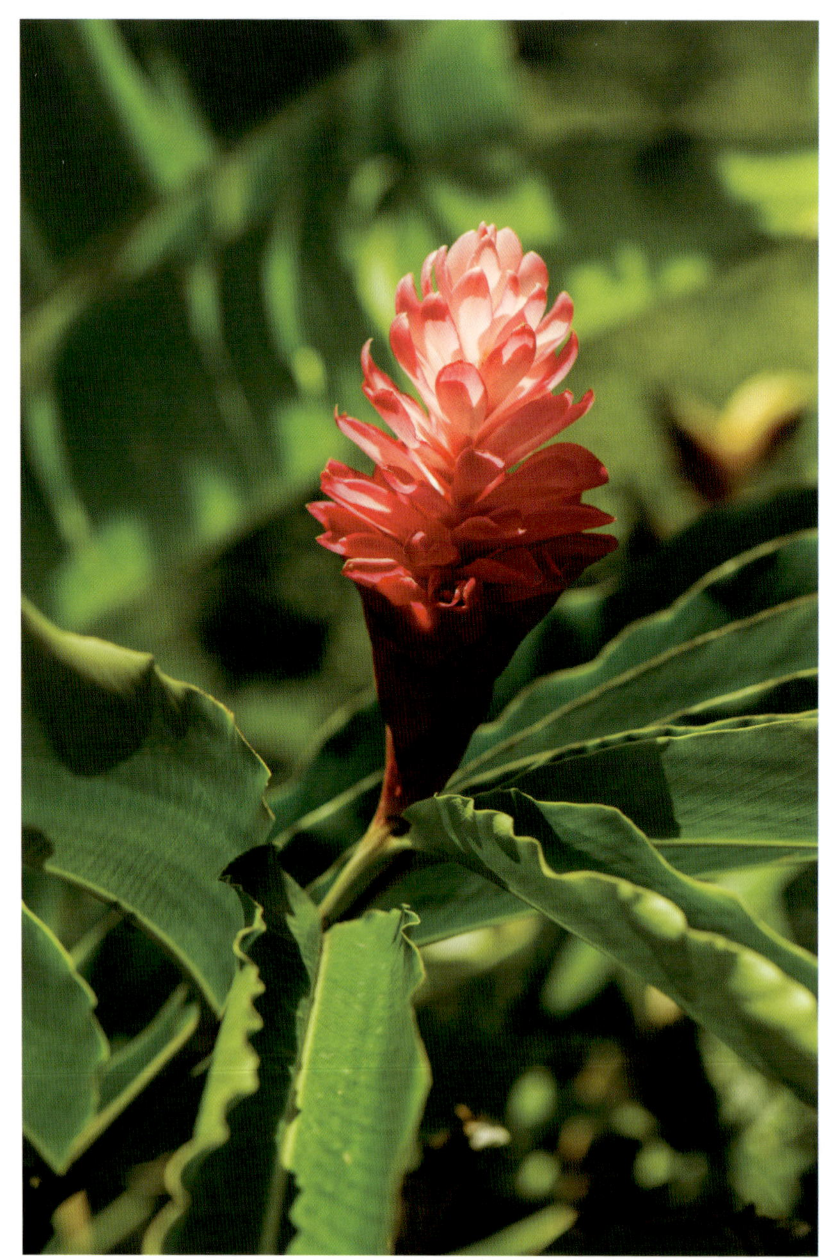

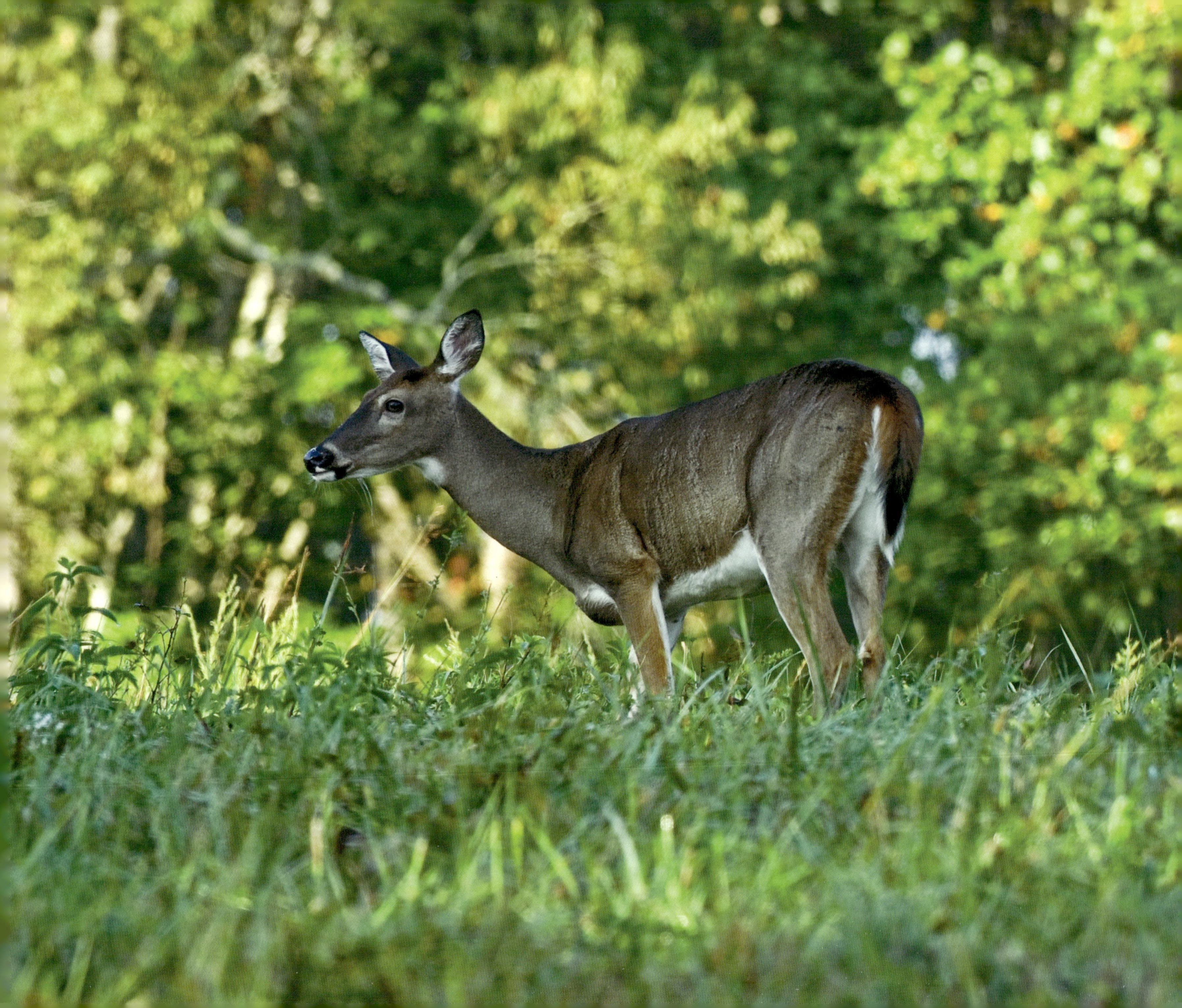

yielding gratefully

The power at work in us is no longer our own. In surrendering to our Savior, we yield to the One who holds the universe together and allow Him free reign in our lives. Our inadequacy becomes a source of happiness, because it serves as a stage for the amazing sufficiency of our Lord, who always surprises us with what He can accomplish when we let Him. Our hearts can be tender, our glance simple, our footsteps light when the true power comes from Him. In relief, we put fear aside and receive peace.

REFLECT

But he said to me, "My grace is sufficient for you,
for my power is made perfect in weakness." Therefore
I will boast all the more gladly about my weaknesses,
so that Christ's power may rest on me.

2 CORINTHIANS 12:9 (NIV)

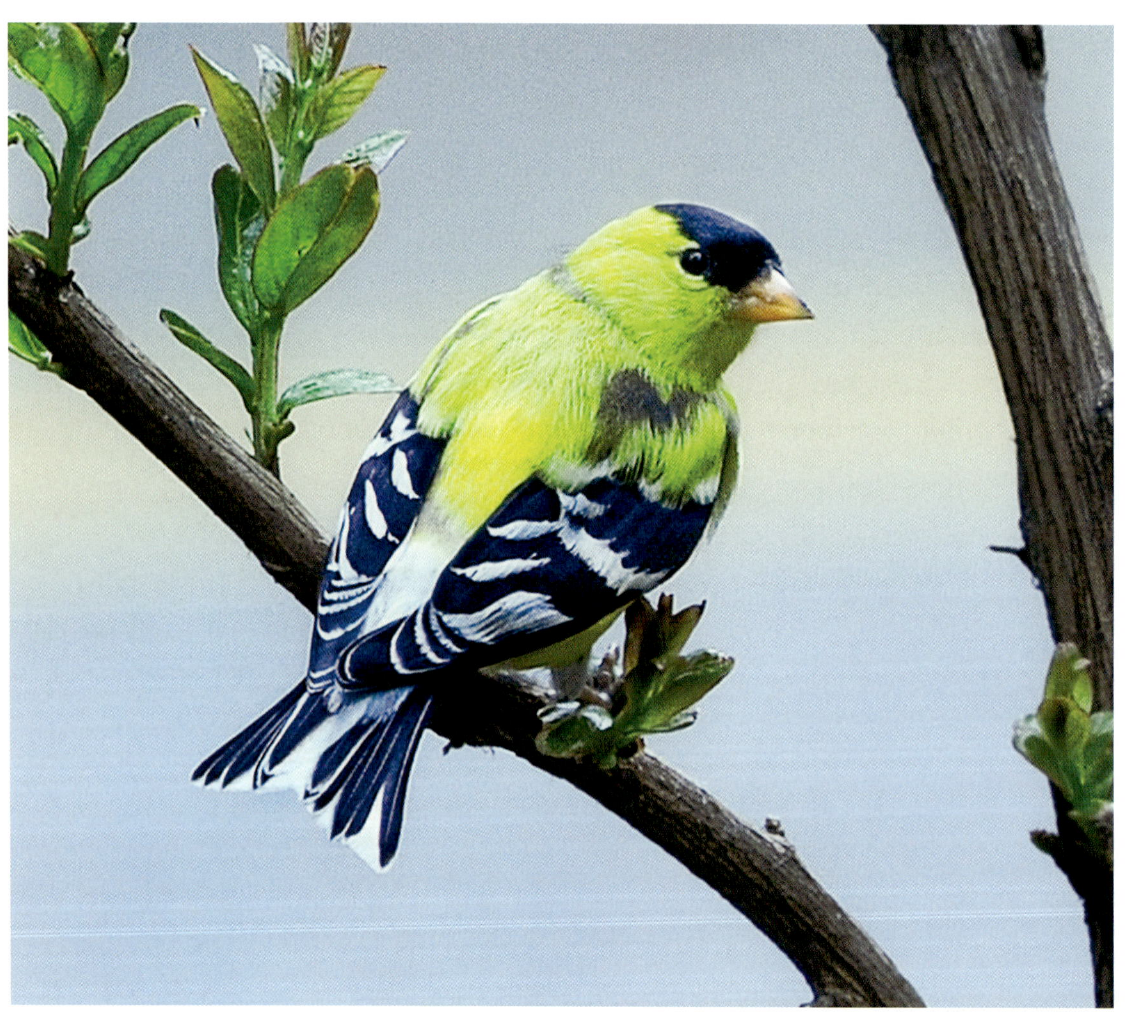

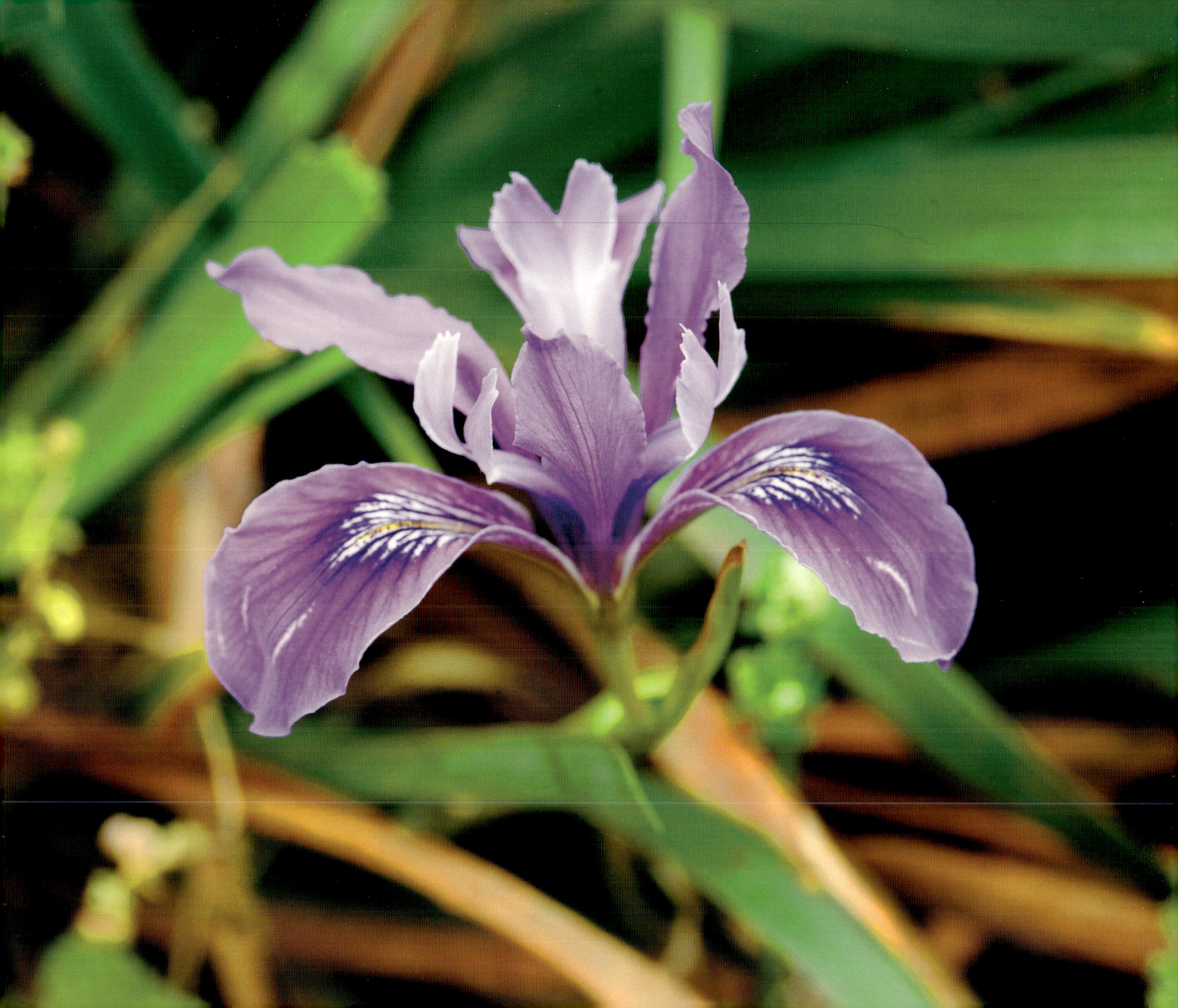

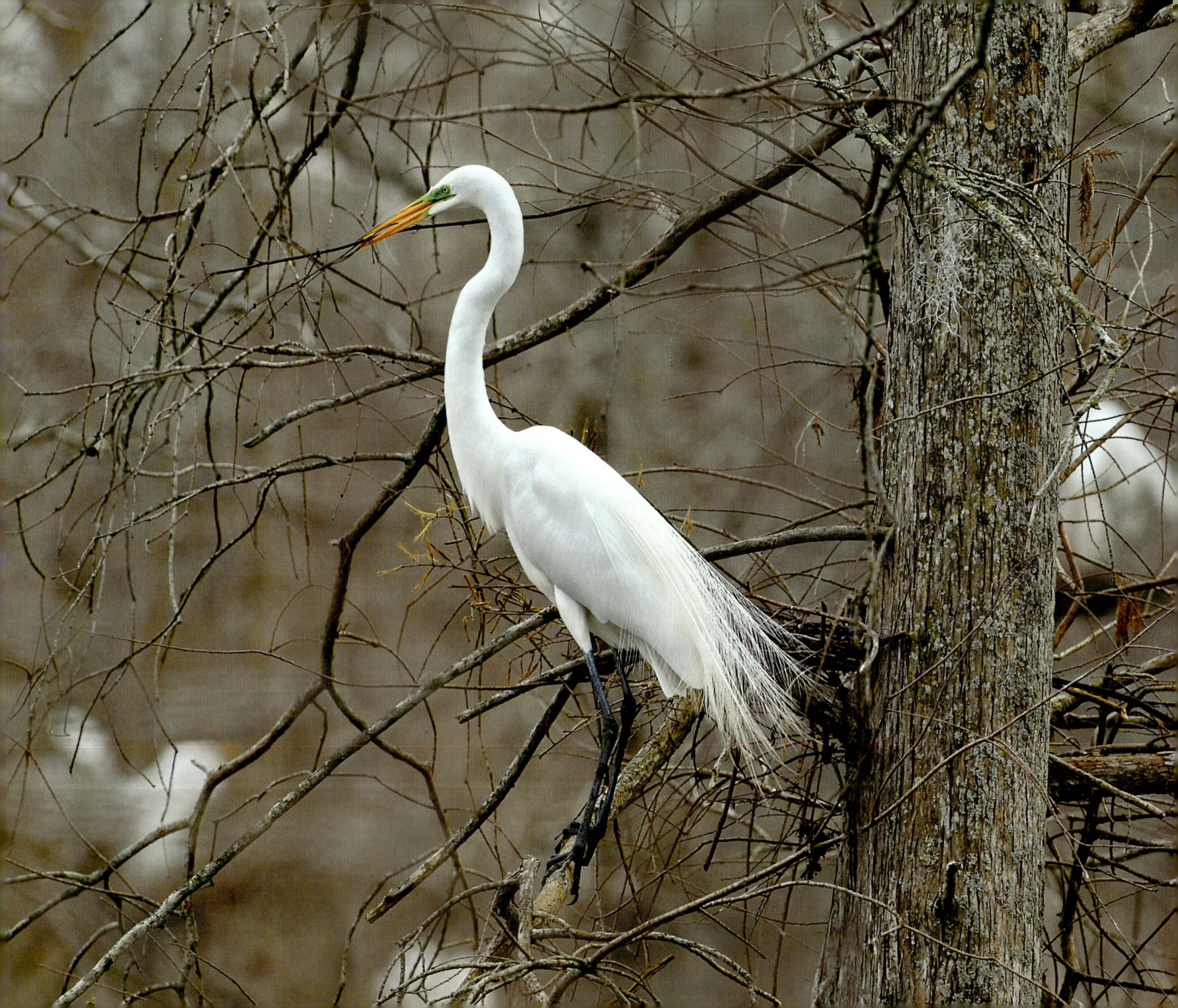

REFLECT

You will keep in perfect peace
all who trust in you,
all whose thoughts
are fixed on you!

ISAIAH 26:3 (NLT)

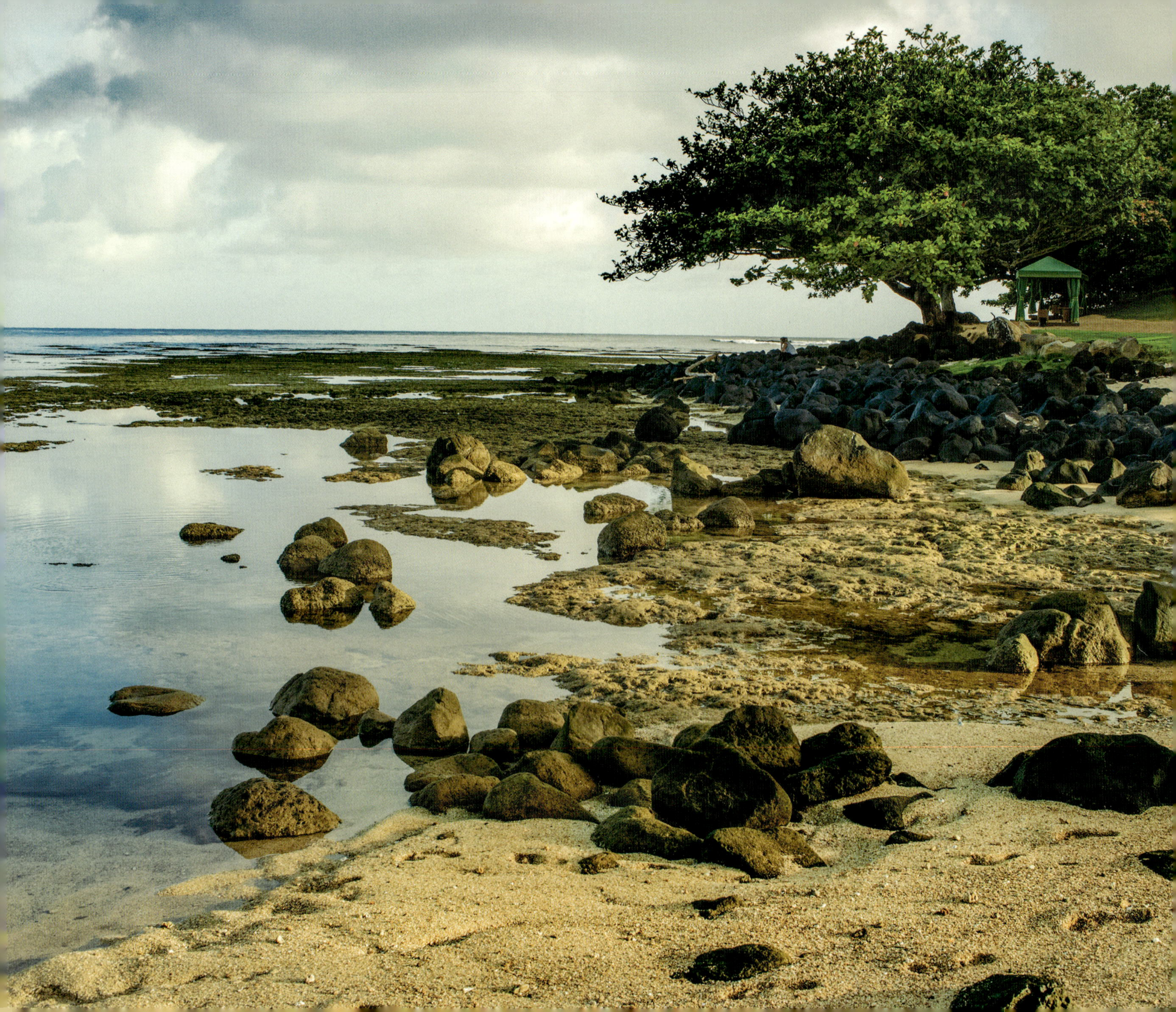

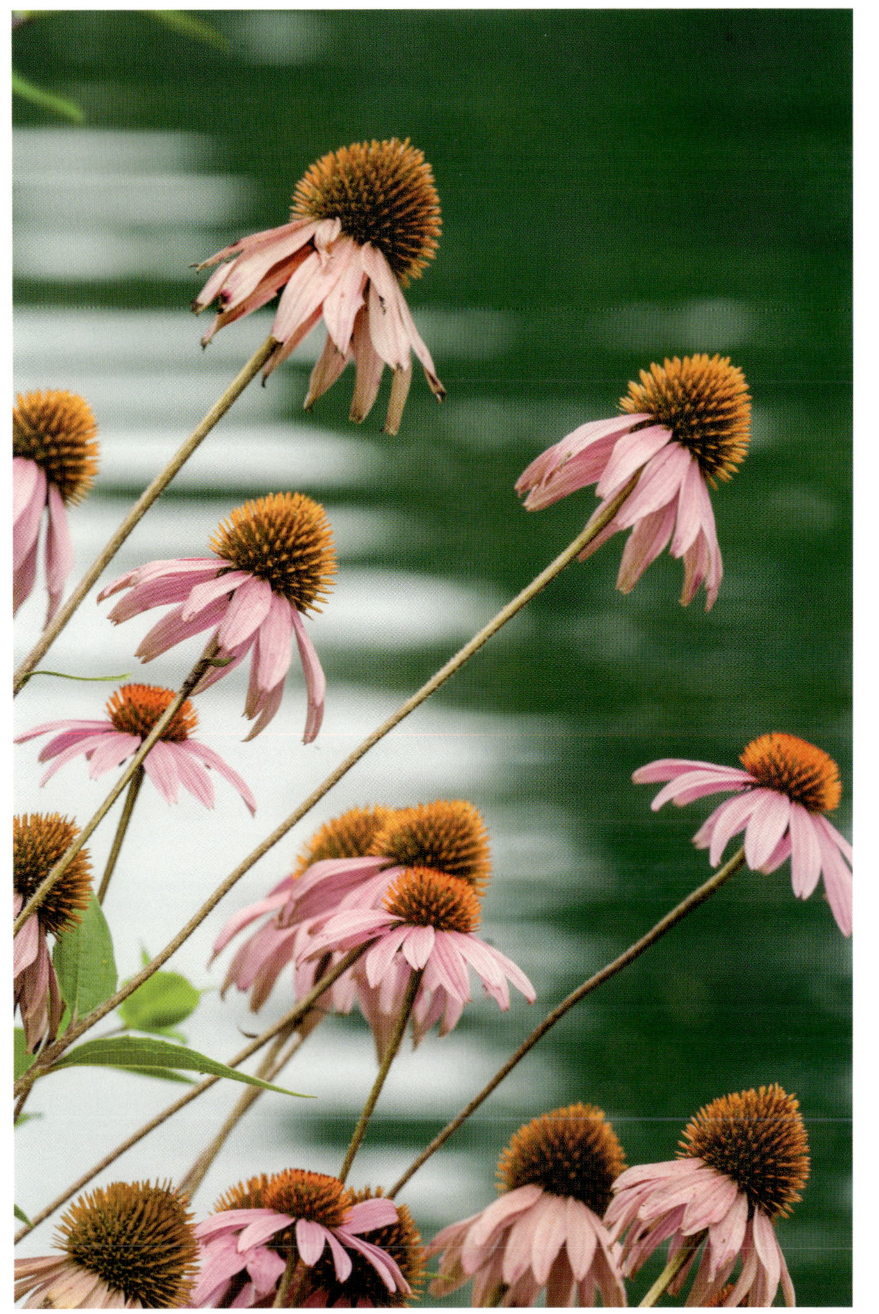

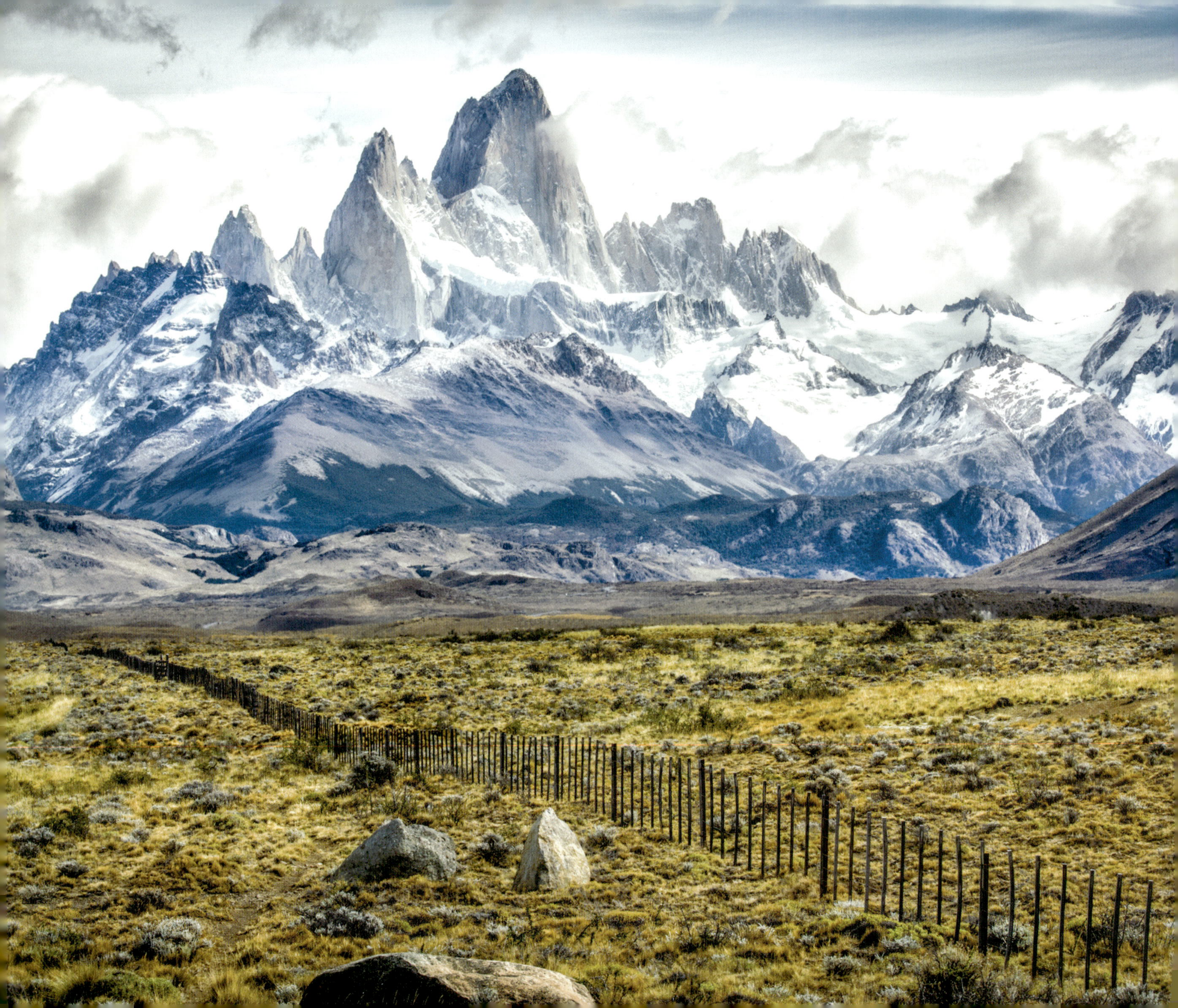

CHAPTER FIVE

THE JOY OF GOD'S SPIRIT

When the life of Christ wells up within us, we experience sheer joy. Thoughts of God's grace and mercy, His rescue of our souls, and the happiness that awaits us in heaven fill us with this previously unknown joy. Our hearts magnify and exalt the Lord as we contemplate what He has done.

No earthly circumstance can quench a joy that springs from the presence of Jesus and our faith in Him, which somehow holds us aloft through every trial, tragedy, and trauma. Our sins have been forgiven. We have been set free from bondage to the law, and can grow daily in the righteousness and purity that are the longing of every redeemed soul. This is true freedom, the treasure of every blood-bought child of God.

Hope replaces the dead ends and empty pursuits of a life without Christ. Our lives take on a momentum not their own, as we are lifted ever higher in the skies of His grace. Though we still face cliffs of challenge and valleys of intense struggle, we have the promise that in all these things, we are more than conquerors through Him who loved us. Because the joy that comes from Jesus is our strength, we can do things we never thought possible. In Him, we can move mountains, climb heights, and cross oceans. His victories are very real—and He rejoices with us over every one.

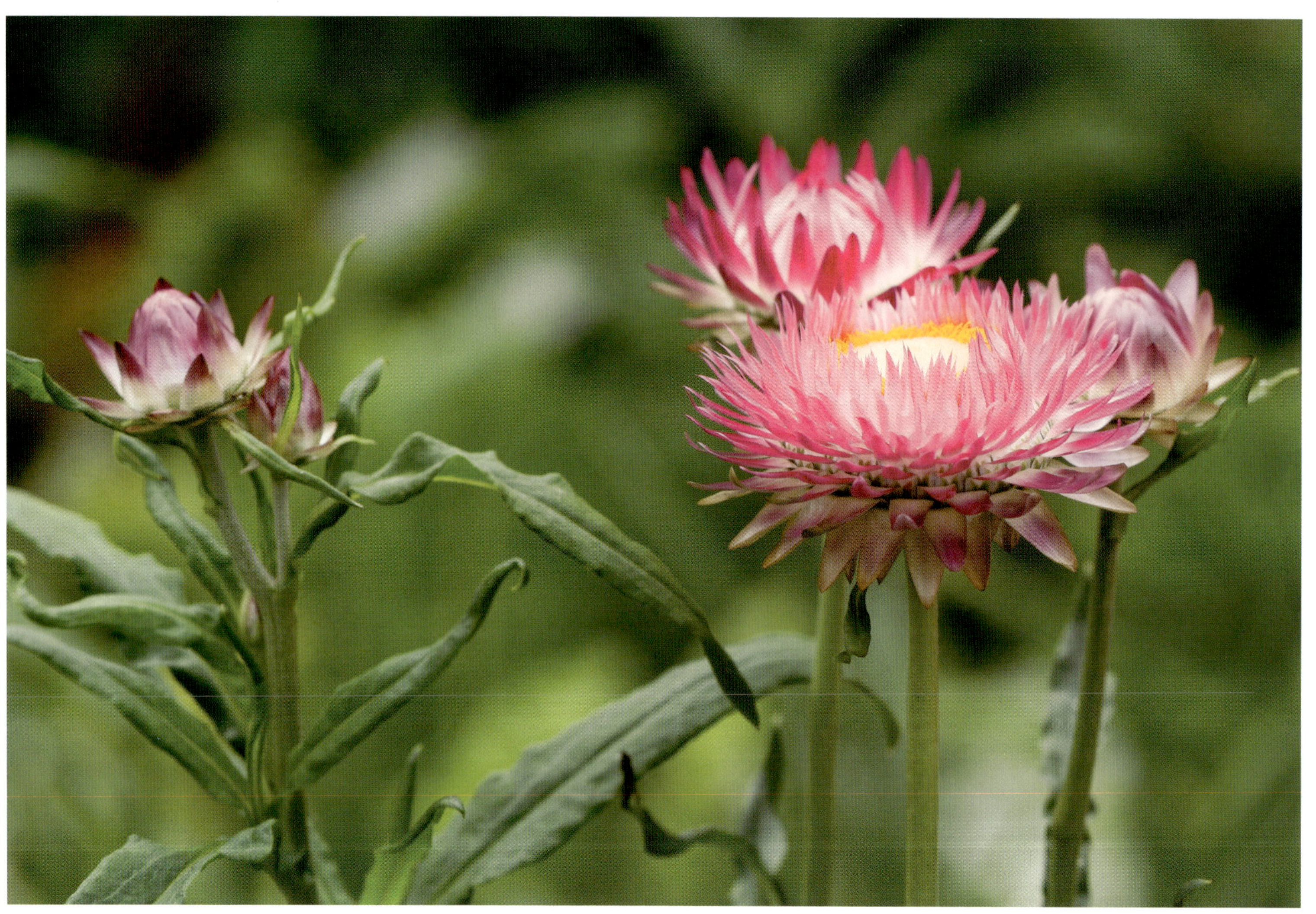

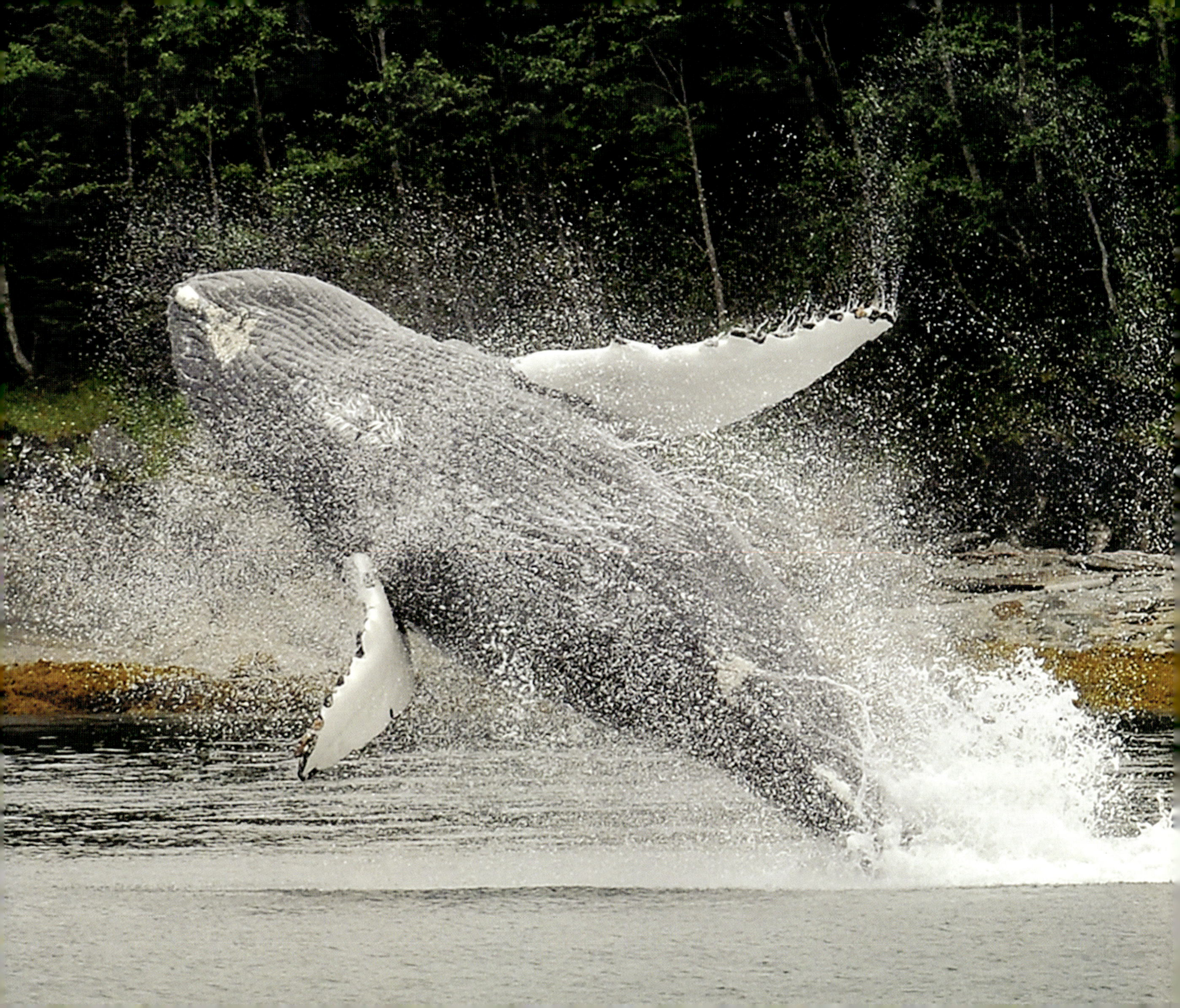

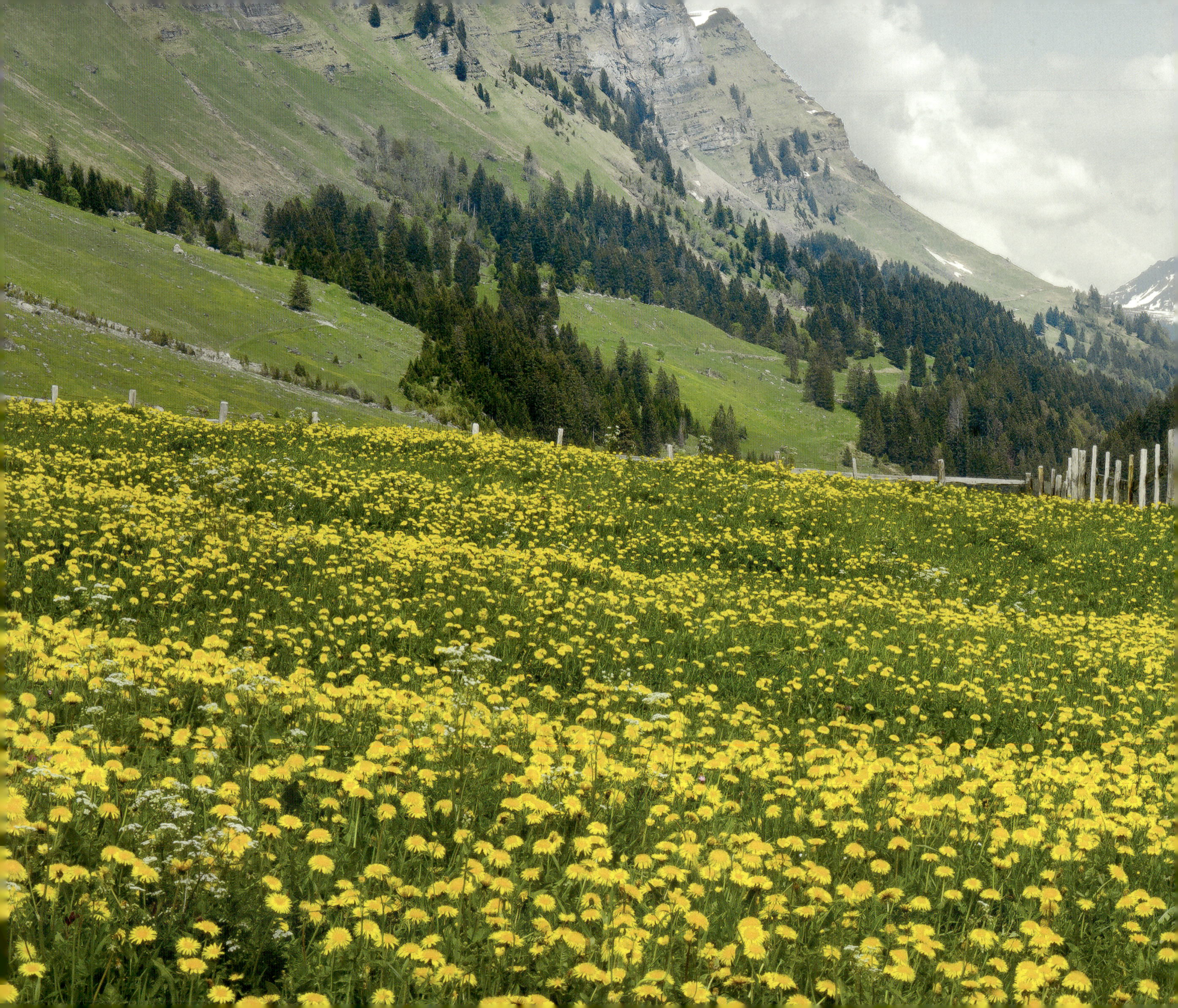

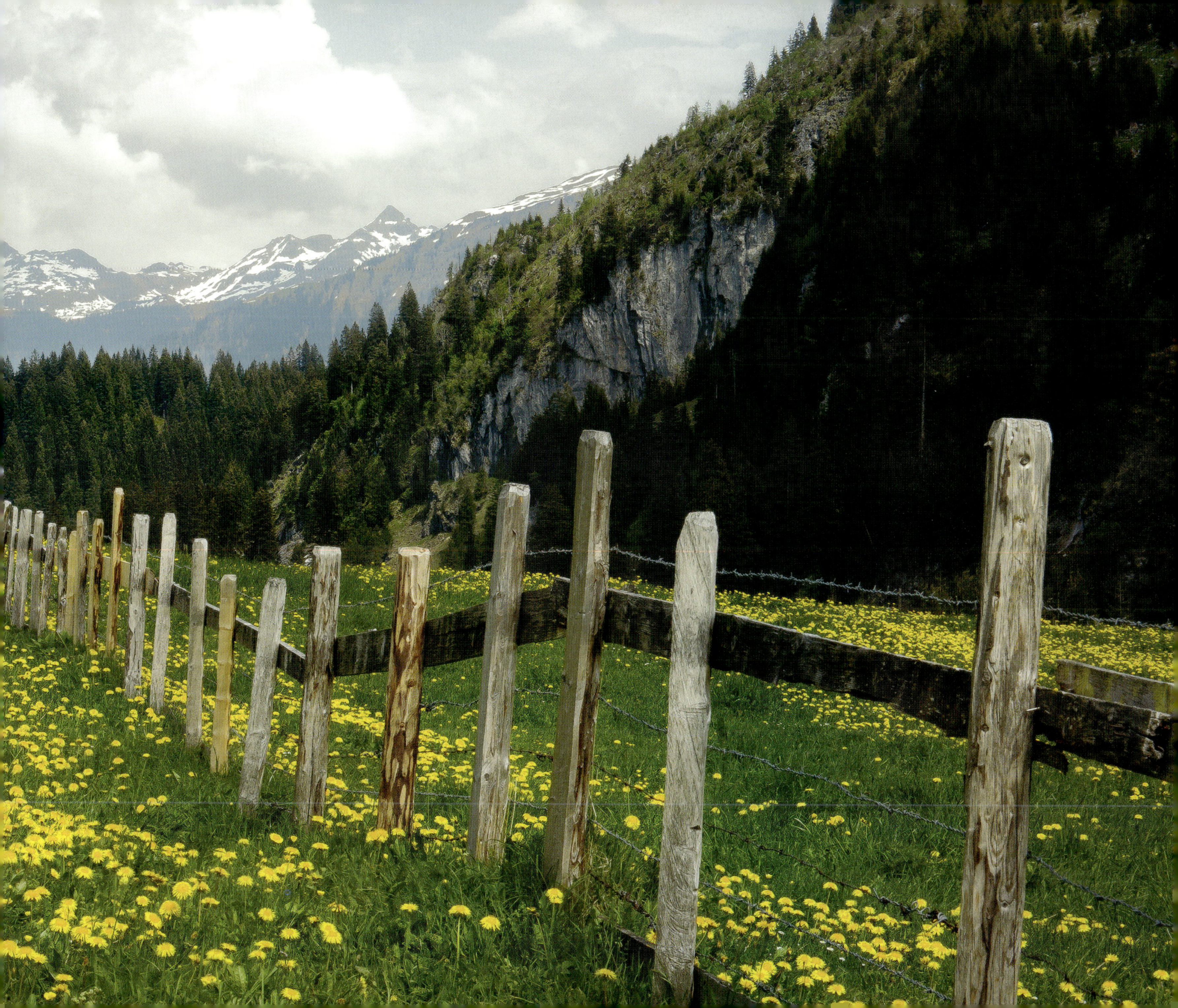

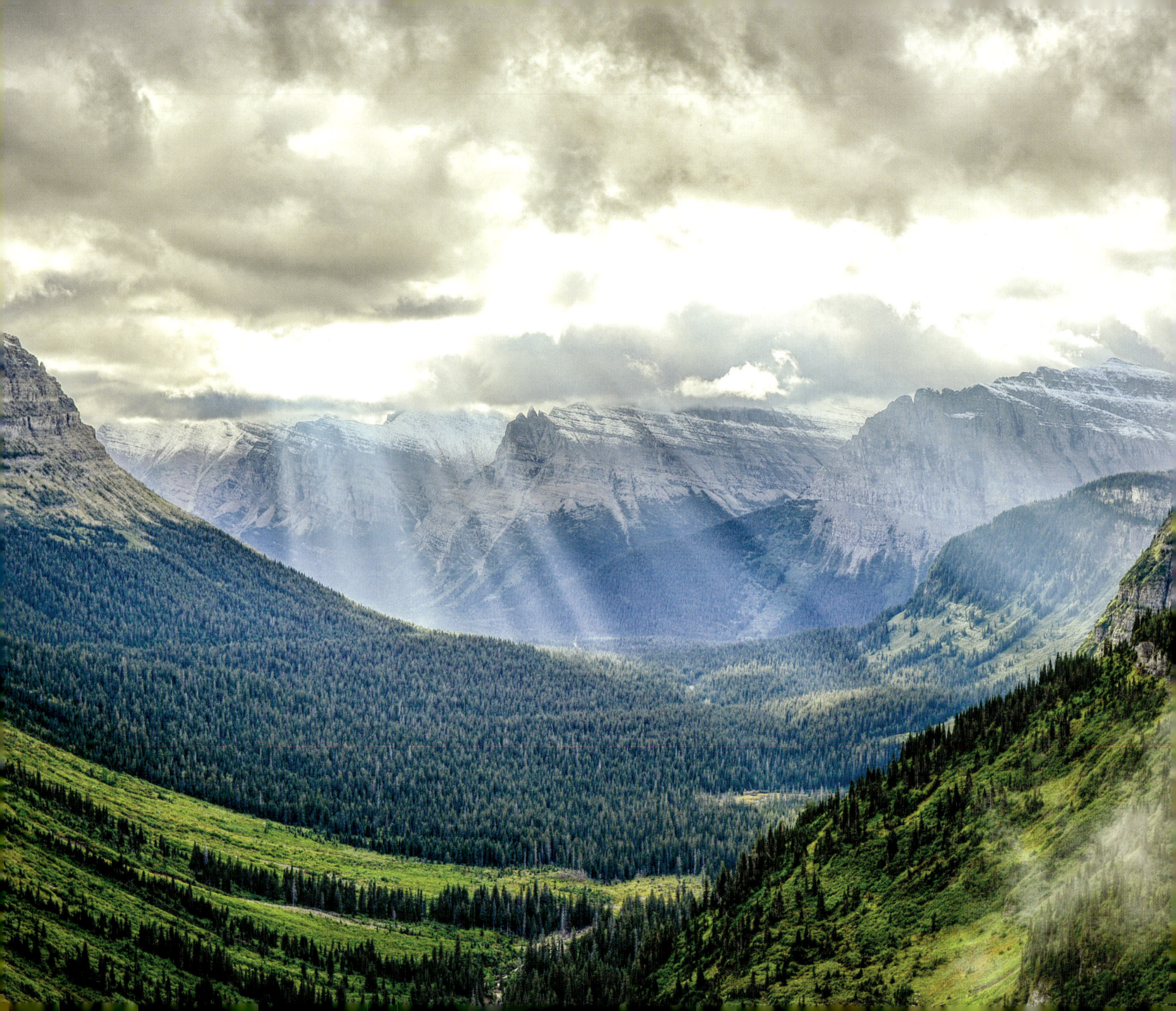

what happiness in my heart!

Few emotions are as beyond words as the joy we experience through our faith in Jesus. Scripture itself calls this joy "unspeakable." It is a shout in the heart, a bubbling, endless spring, a face turned radiant to the Lord in celebration. When this joy reigns in us, it seems even the sun laughs, the hills dance, and the mundane objects of life rejoice. Every trace of shame flees. God delights in us, and we in Him.

REFLECT

O sing to the Lord a new song, for He has done wonderful things ... The Lord has made known His salvation ... Shout joyfully to the Lord, all the earth; break forth and sing for joy and sing praises.

PSALM 98:1-2, 4

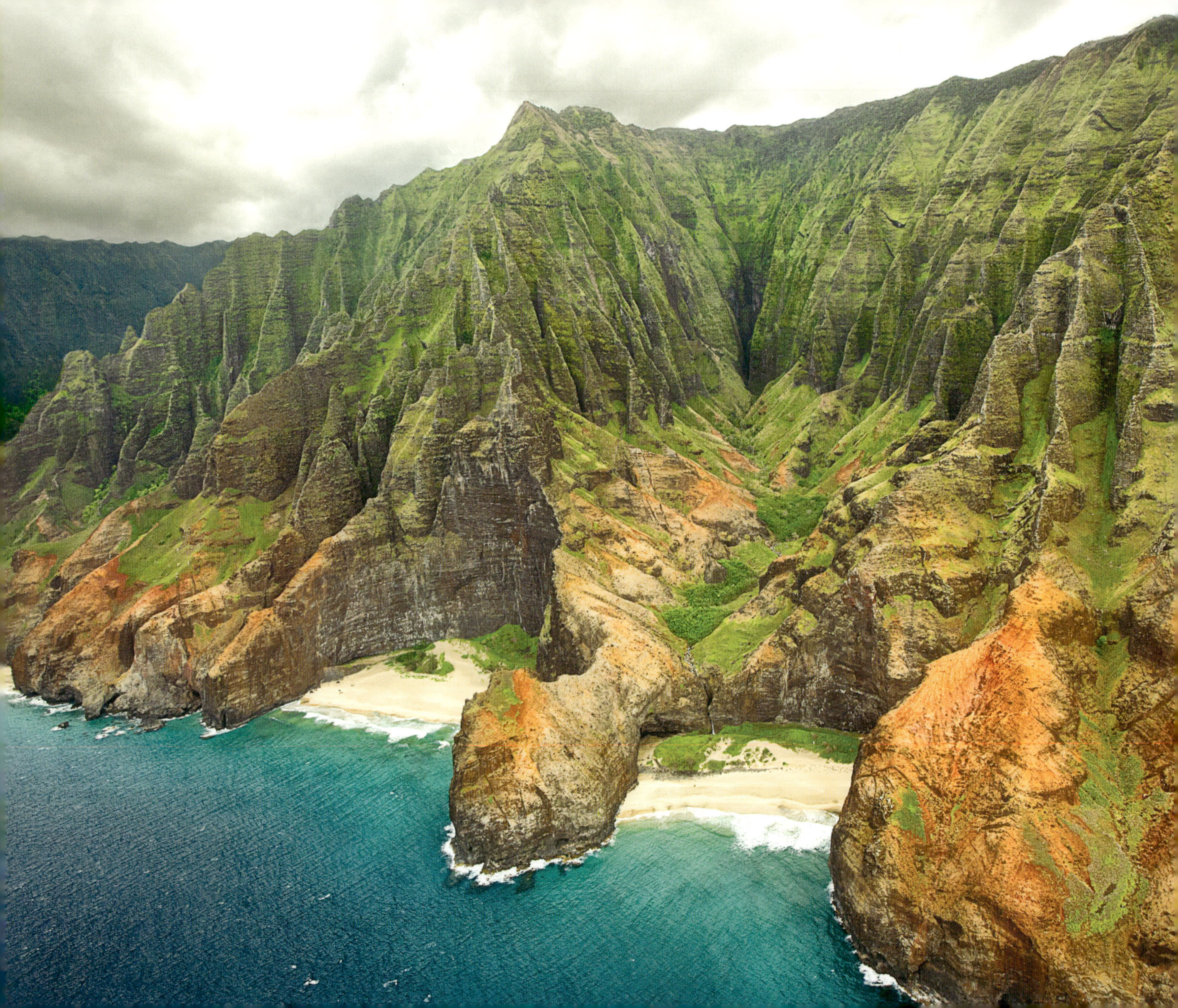

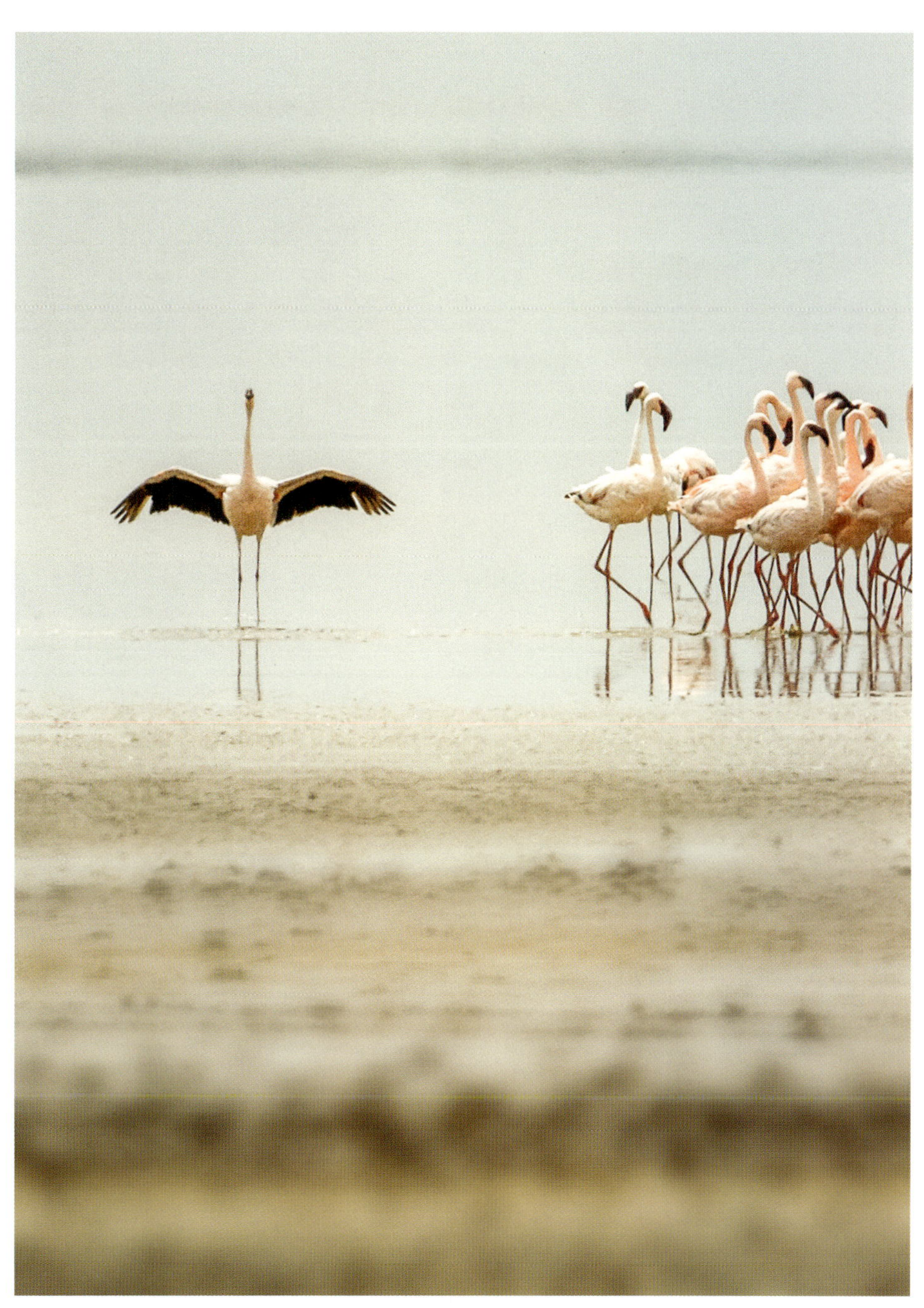

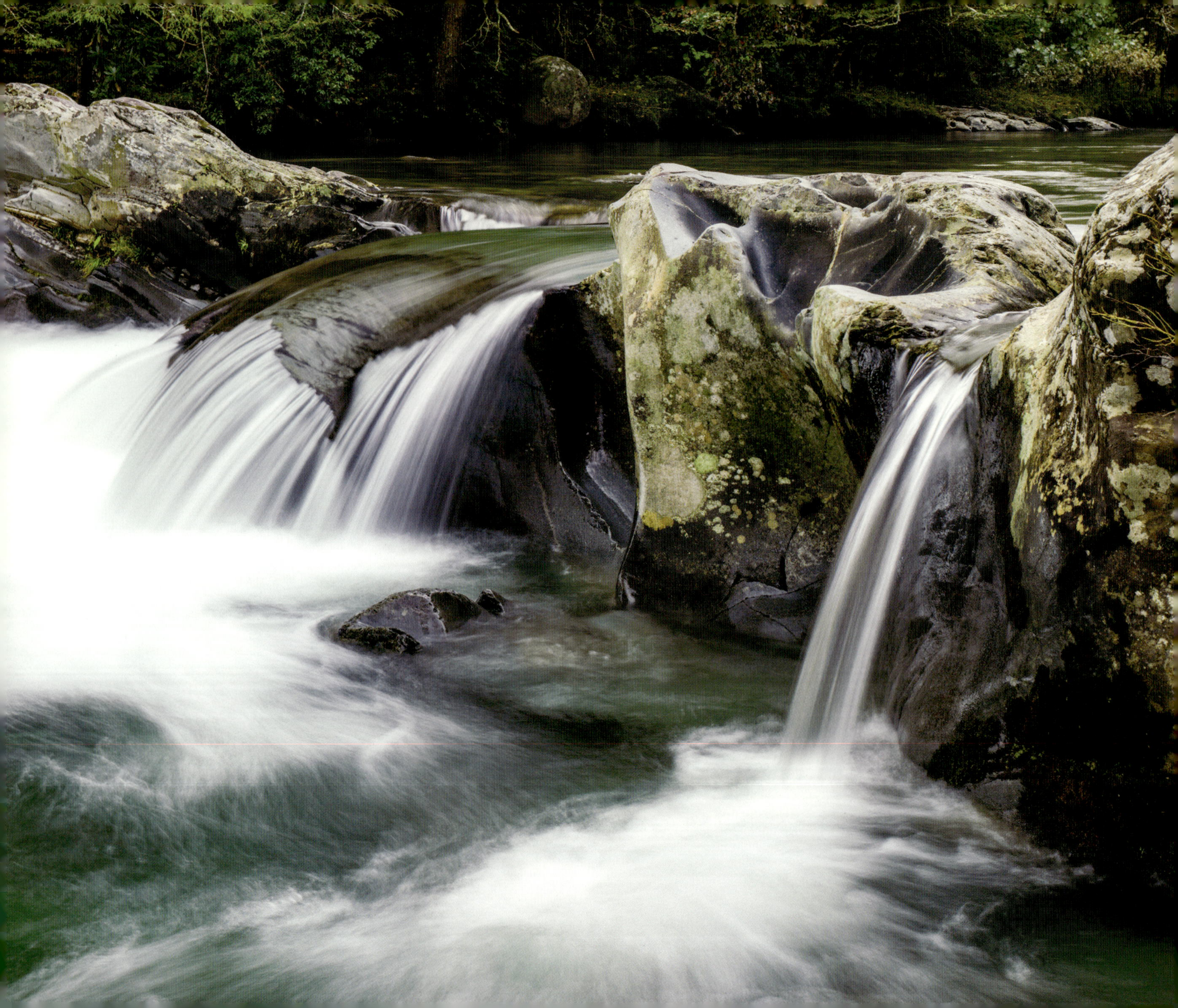

When you're in love with someone, you are excited about the relationship and time spent together. Likewise, when you're in love with Jesus, you can't keep to yourself the joy that comes from knowing Him—it just spills over, bearing witness and strengthening other believers. In fact, as you give testimony of who God is and how He's working in your life, it makes no difference whether you speak quietly or with great exuberance. In their spirit, others will pick up on the deep, genuine gladness in your heart that goes beyond natural happiness. As you allow the Holy Spirit to increasingly express His life and power through you, contagious joy will be the fruit of His indwelling presence.

— DR. CHARLES STANLEY —

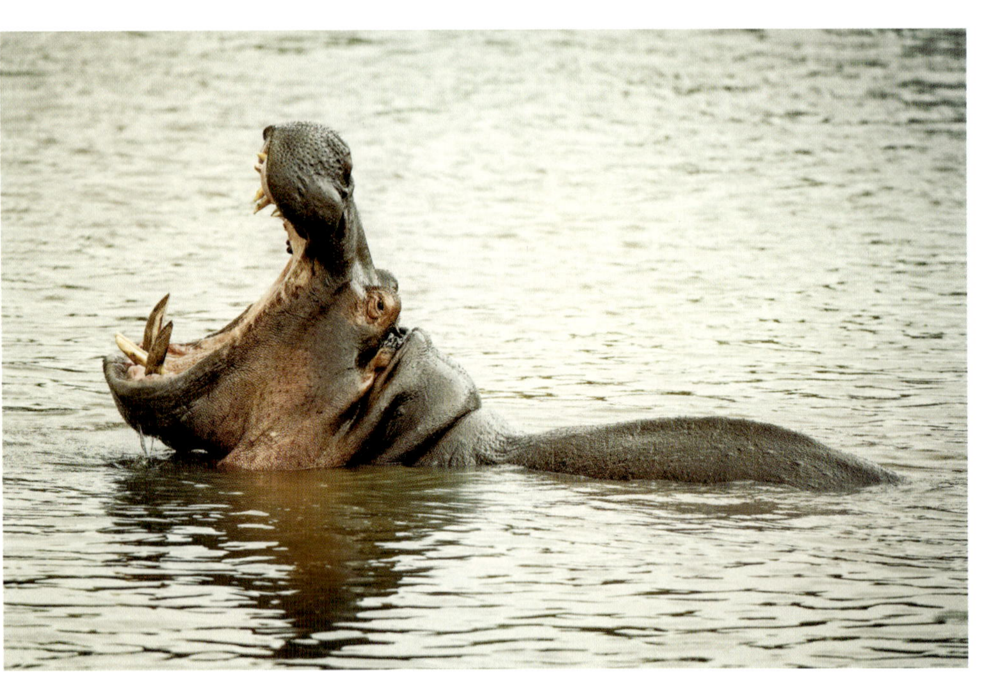

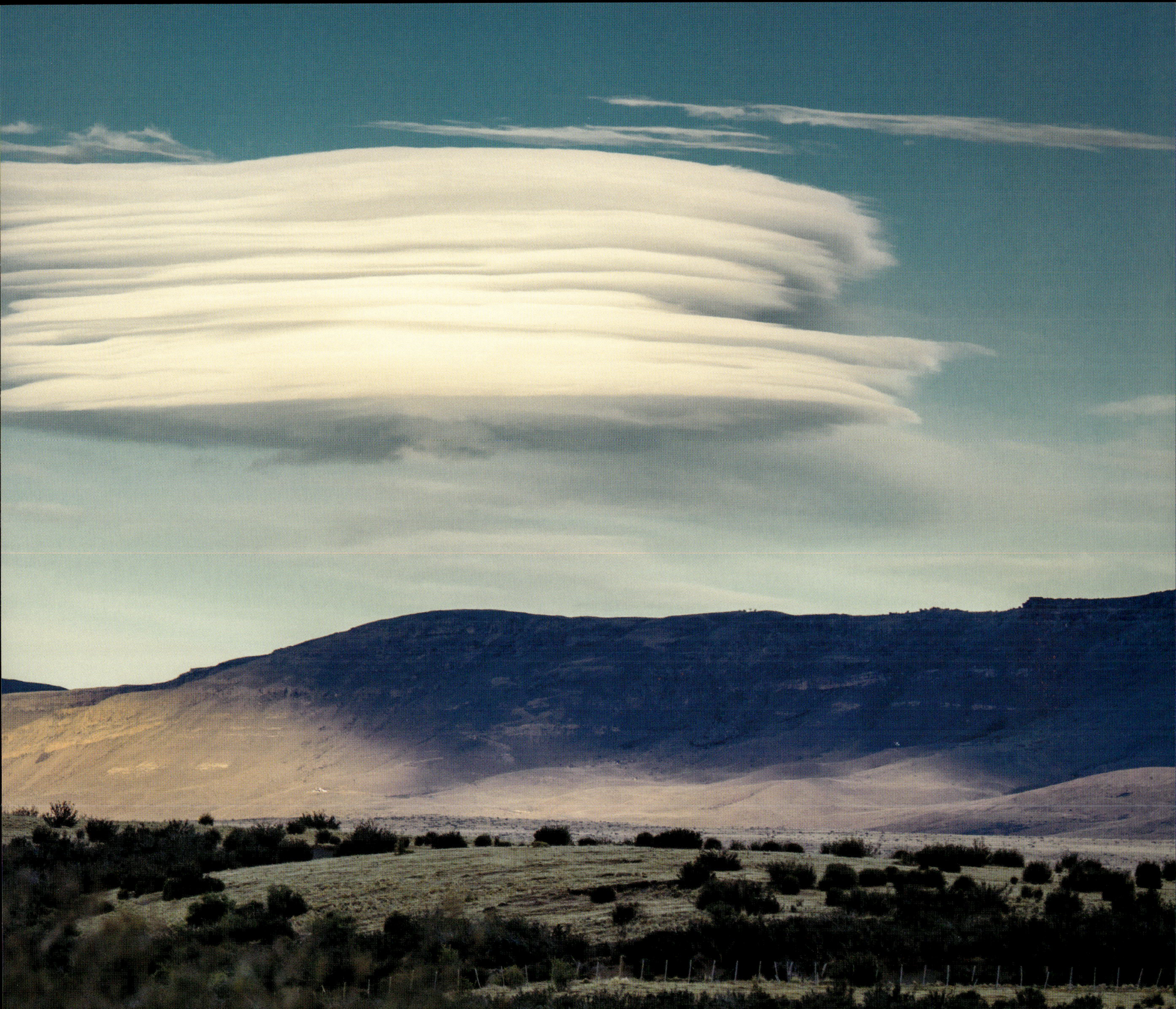

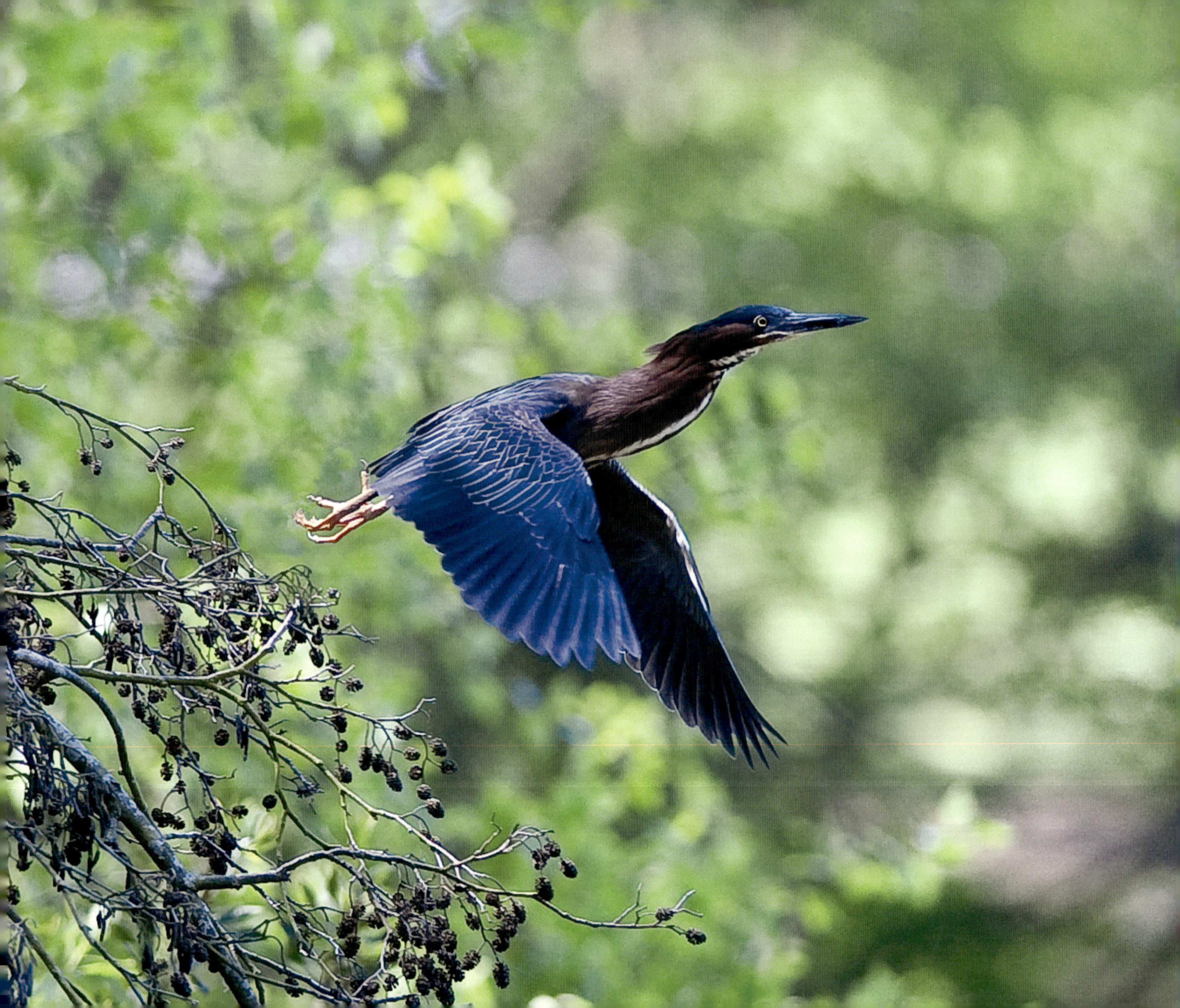

free and full of joy

Where once there was bondage, now there is liberty. Where once there was guilt and condemnation, now there is acquittal and acceptance. Where once there was misery, now there is love. Where once there was impossible striving, now there is power to live for God and walk in obedience. When judgment is replaced by grace, the shackles on our souls fall away and our hearts can celebrate. We are free in Christ, and freedom brings joy.

REFLECT

Therefore there is now no condemnation for those who are in Christ Jesus. For the law of the Spirit of life in Christ Jesus has set you free from the law of sin and of death.

ROMANS 8:1-2

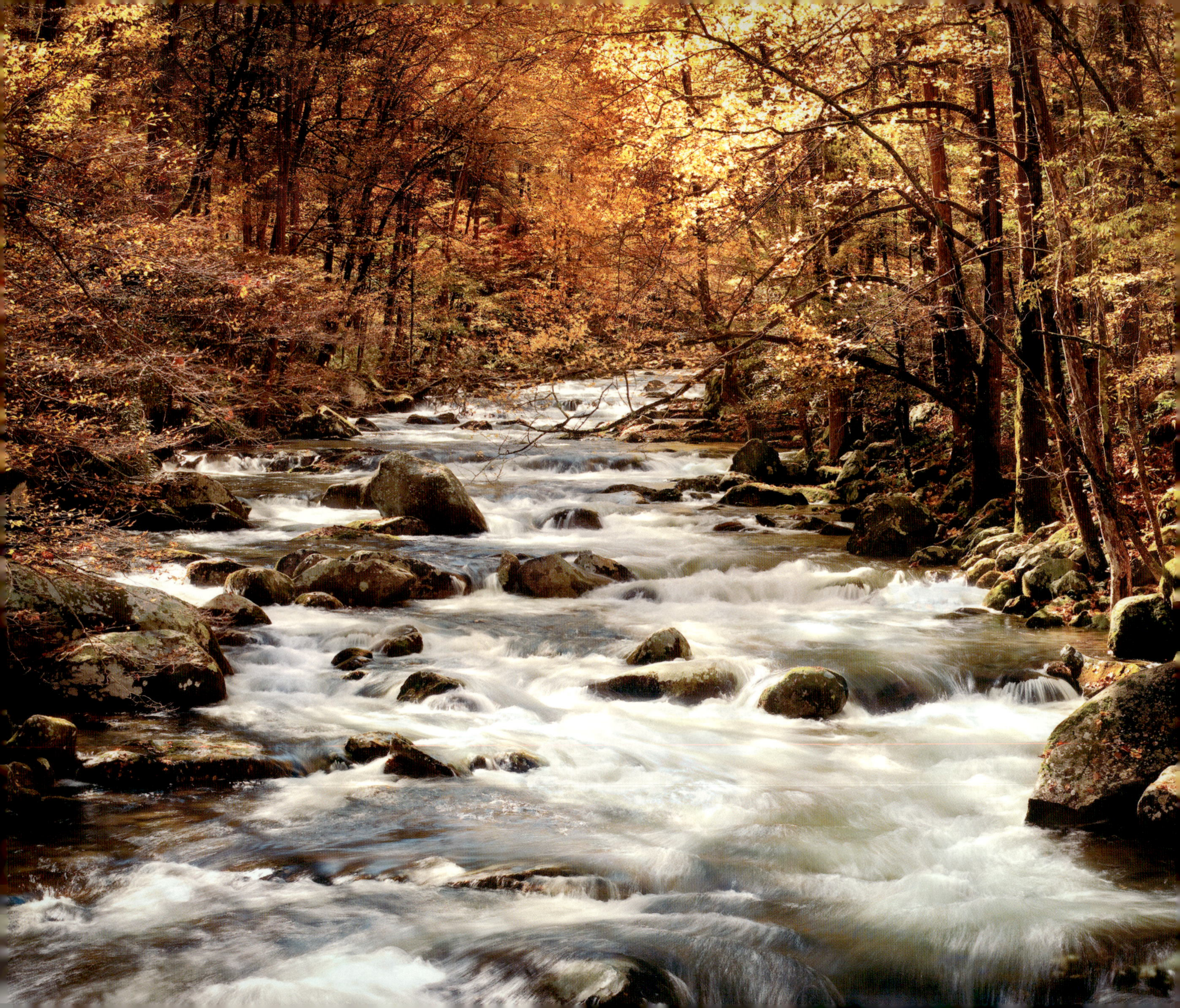

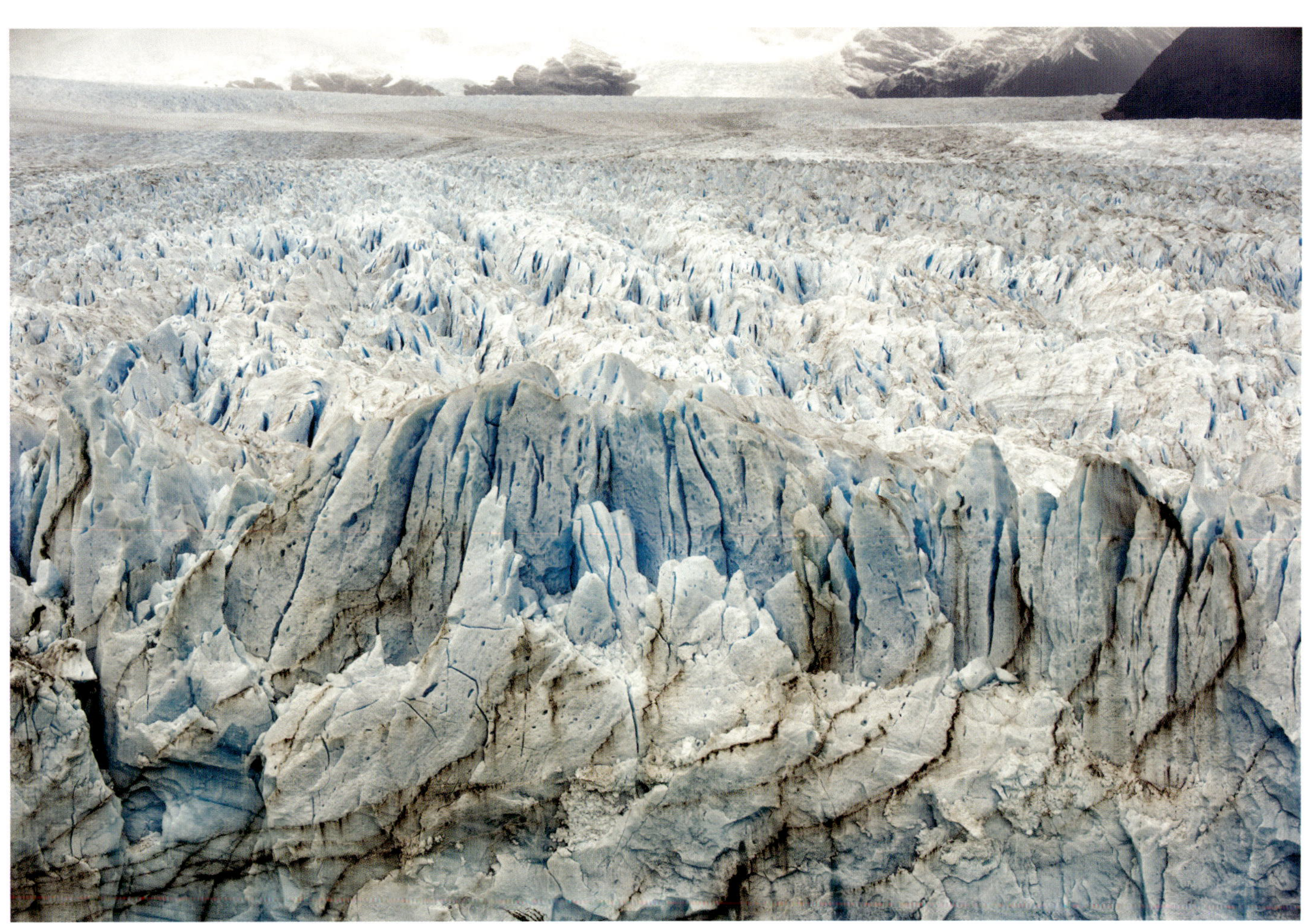

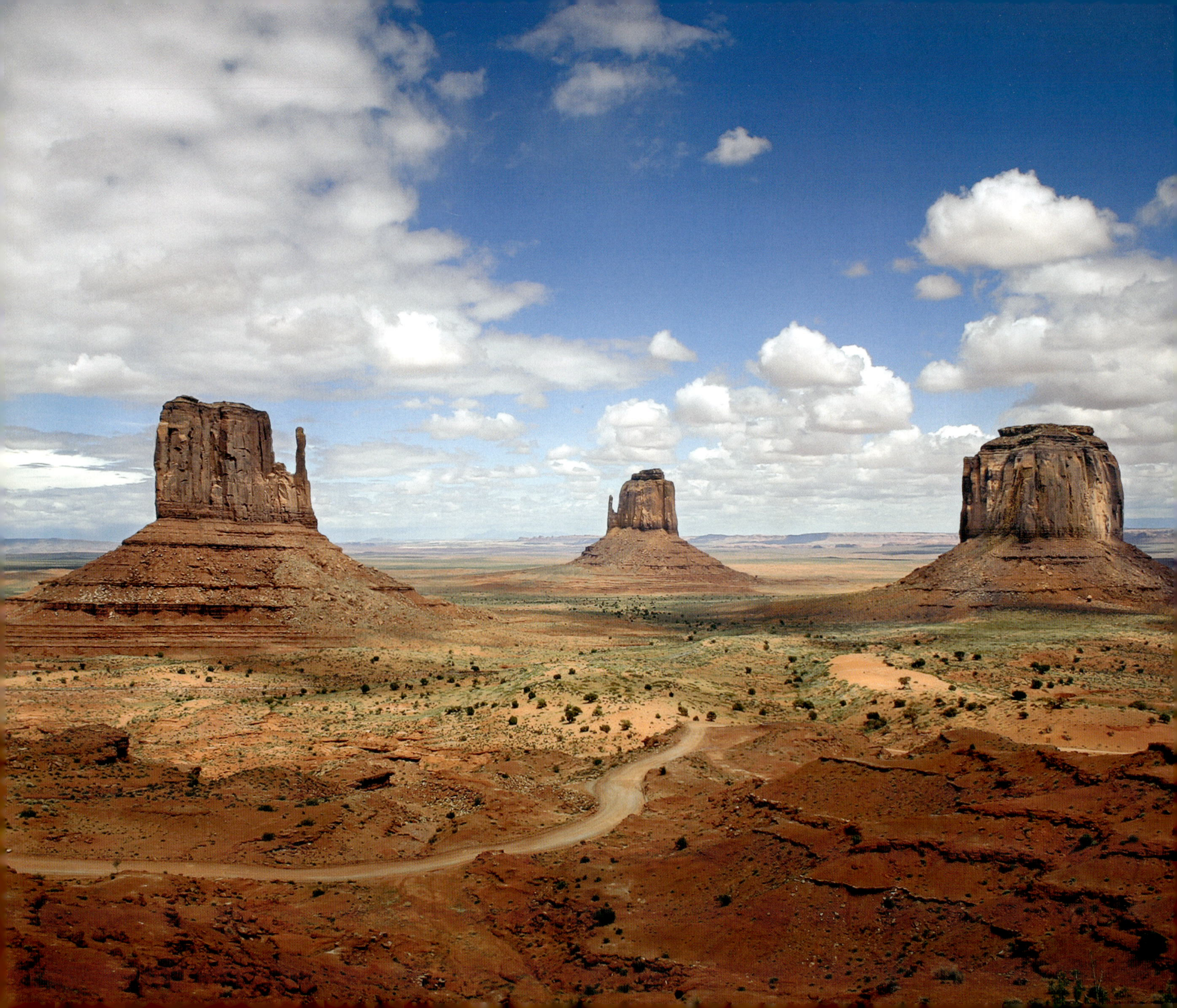

carried by His momentum

God's joy has a special momentum. As we are received into His arms, we cast off the plodding nature of the old self and, as new creations in Christ, rise into currents that propel us smoothly forward. It takes practice to be carried by the Lord. At times, our trust falters and we fall back into our former ways. We must release habits of thought that hinder hope and confidence, and give up all reliance on ourselves. But as we do, we find that His joy can be stunning.

REFLECT

Those who wait for the LORD *will gain new strength;*
they will mount up with wings like eagles, they will run
and not get tired, they will walk and not become weary.

ISAIAH 40:31

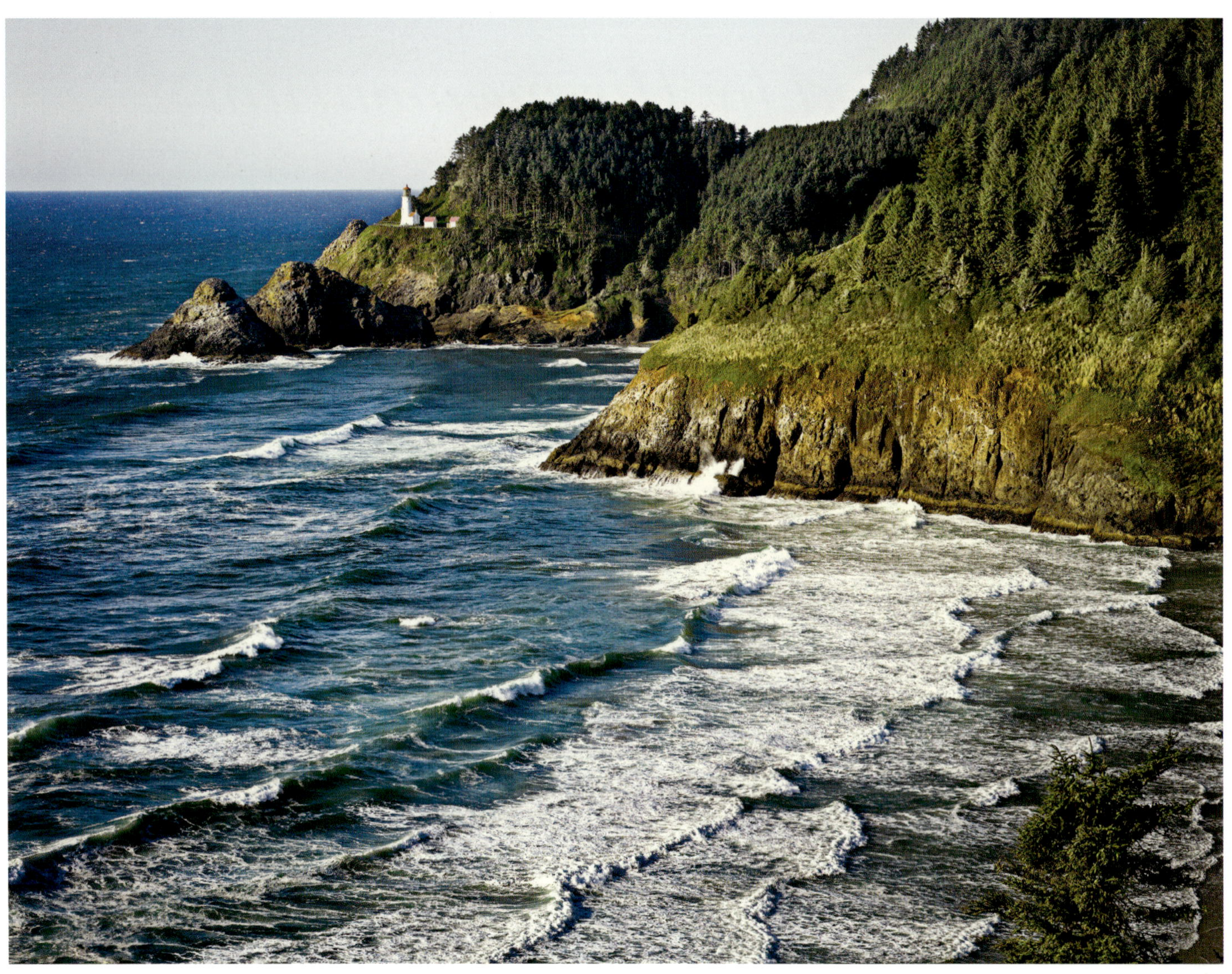

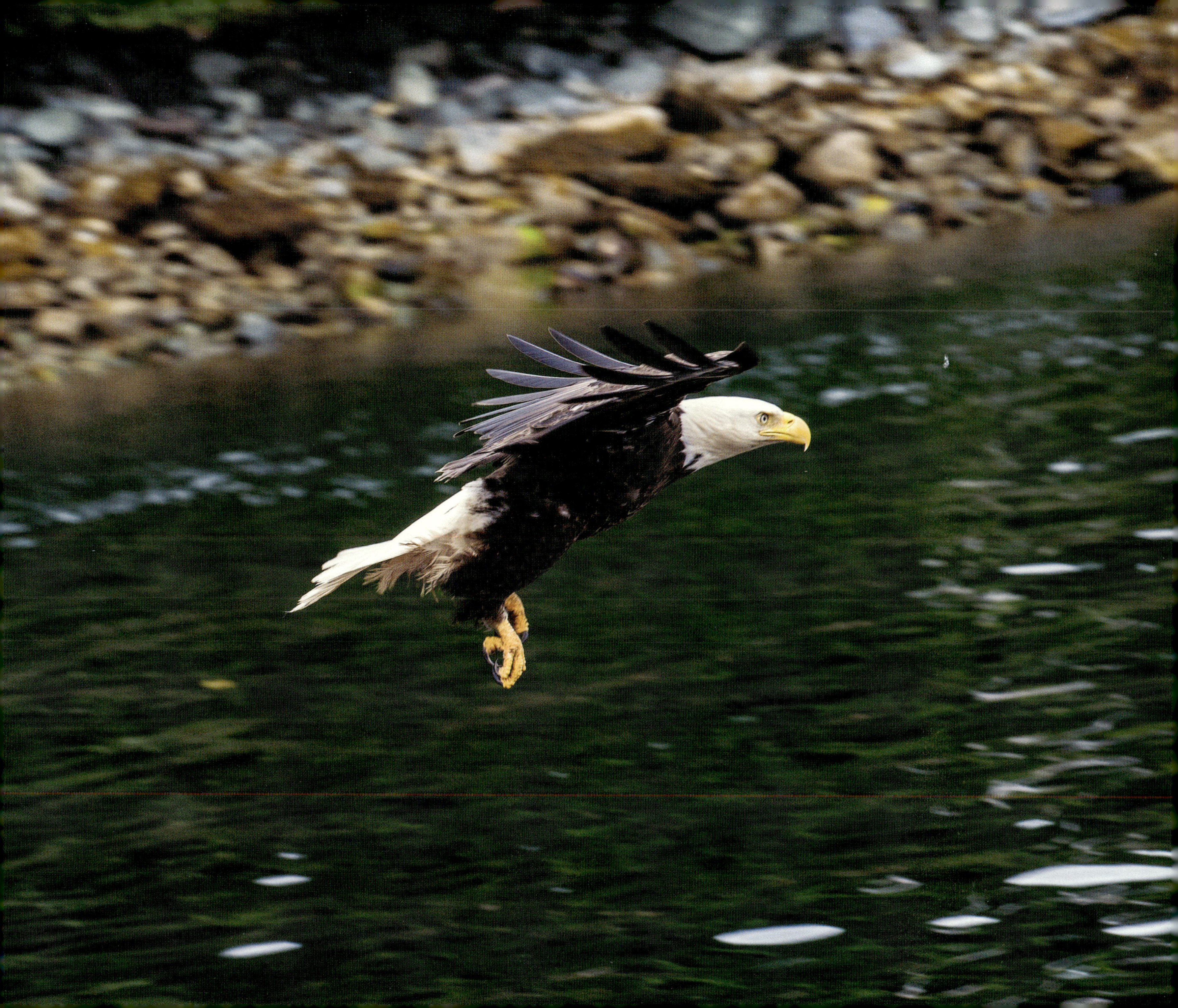

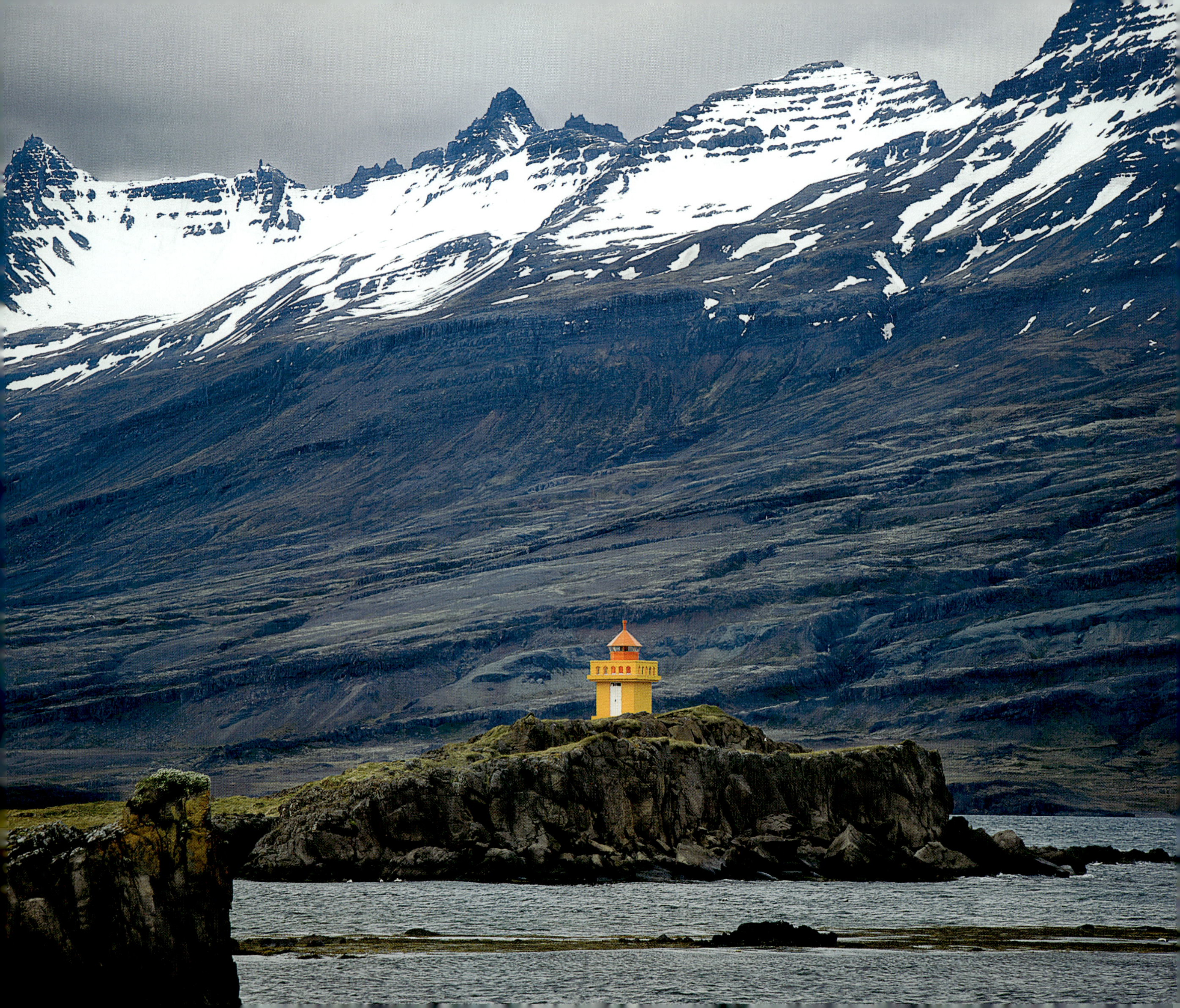

His joy makes us strong!

The joy that comes from belief in Jesus is true strength. At first glance, joy may seem like weakness—a moment of unwise vulnerability, a chink in the armor. But the joy of our Lord is like a parade of columns marching proudly around a stately building. Though it may have the appearance of gaps, it is filled with divine strength to uplift and support, and helps us endure, conquer, and press forward. It transforms our hearts into sturdy vaults of power.

REFLECT

Go and celebrate ... This is a sacred day
before our Lord. Don't be dejected and sad,
for the joy of the LORD is your strength!

NEHEMIAH 8:10 (NLT)

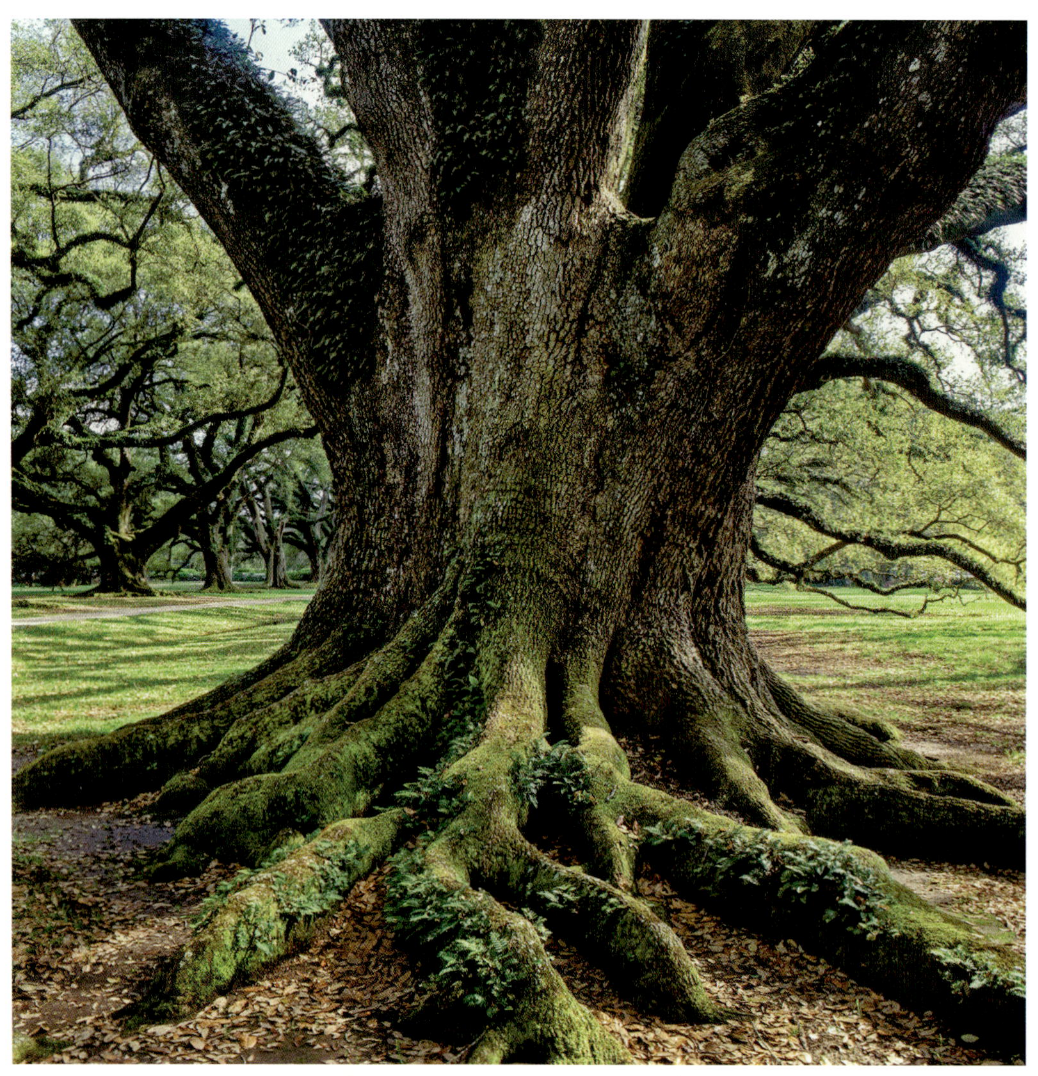

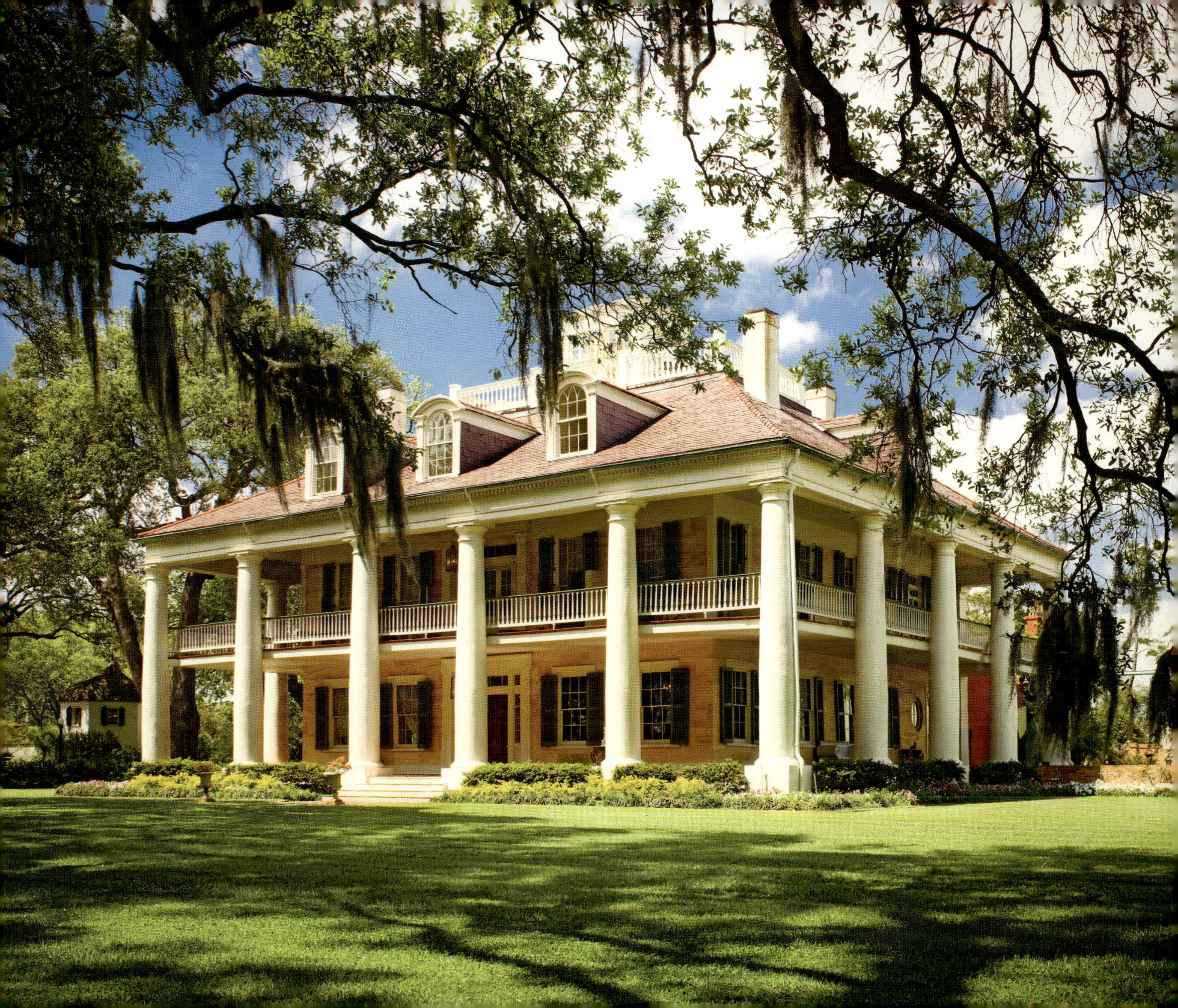

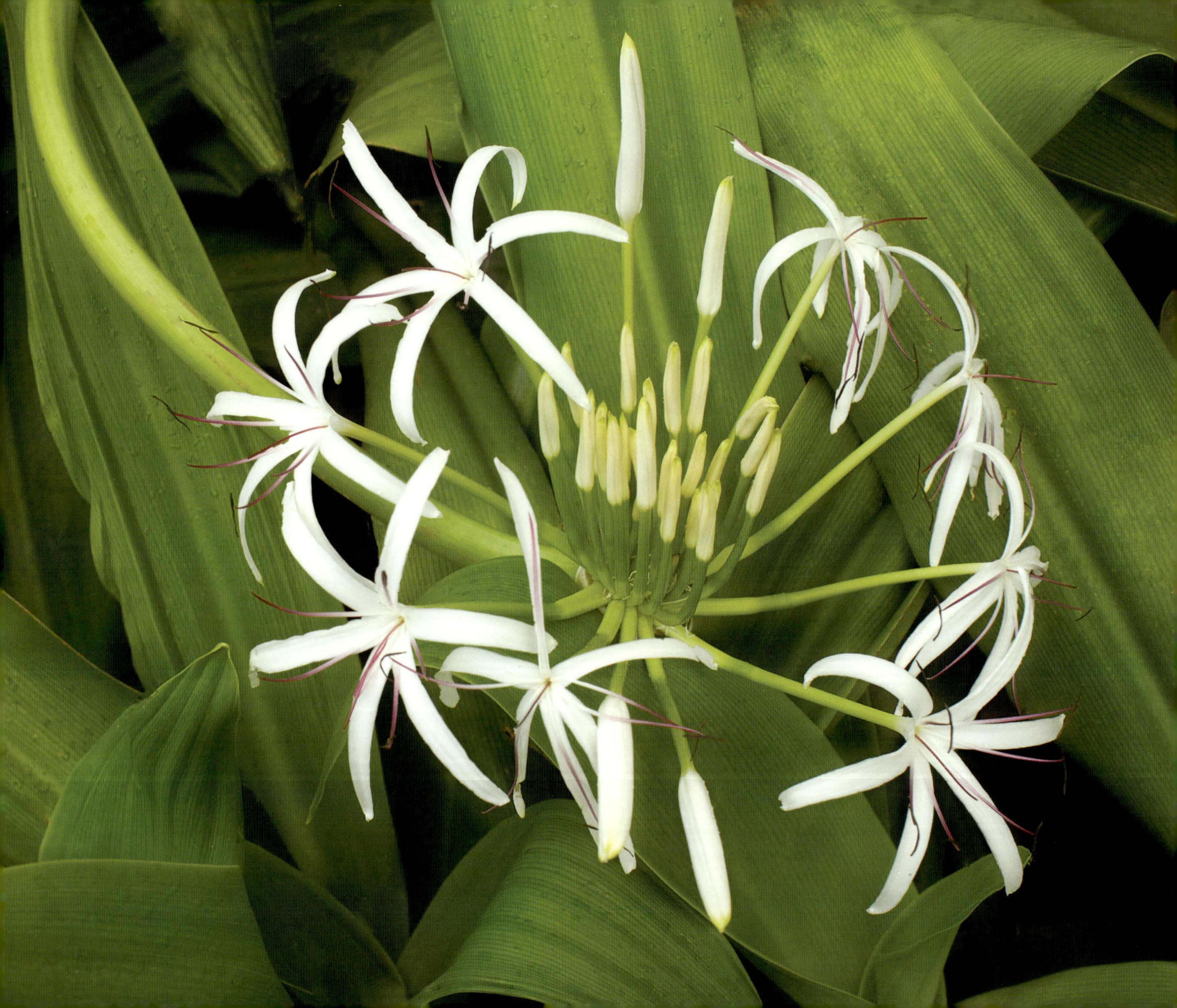

REFLECT

Now may the God of hope
fill you with all joy
and peace in believing,
so that you will abound in hope
by the power of the Holy Spirit.

ROMANS 15:13

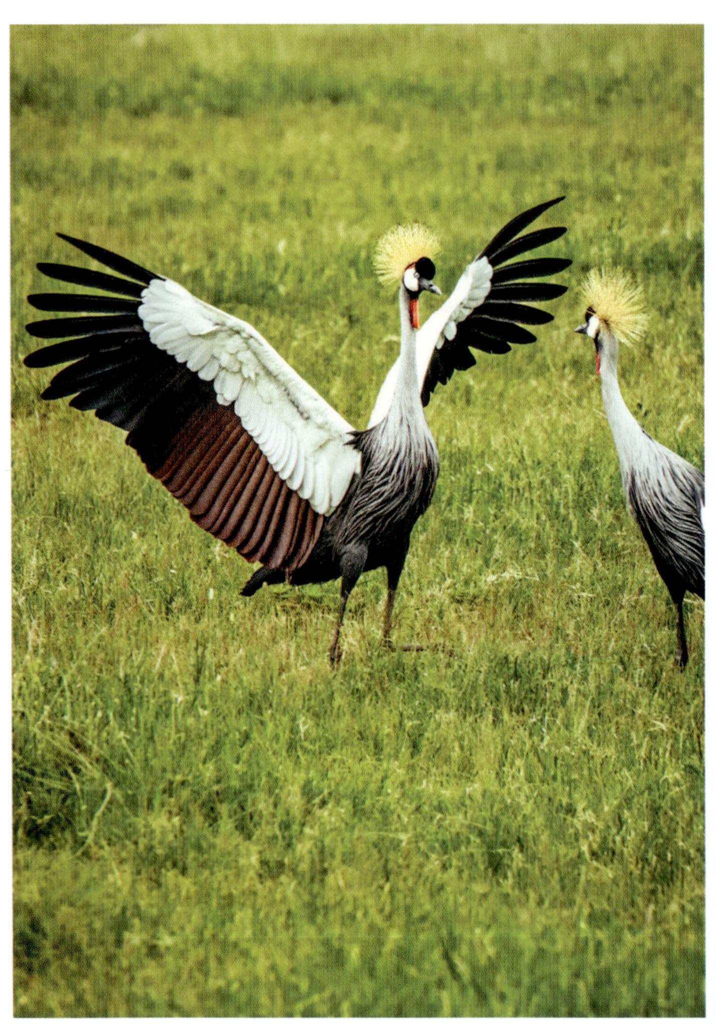

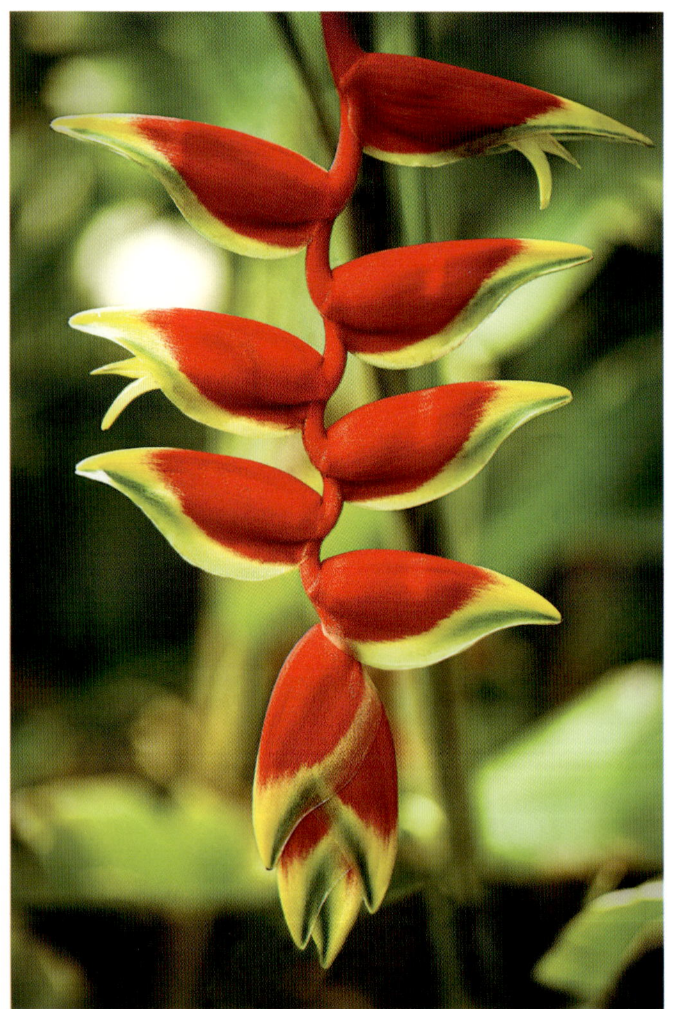

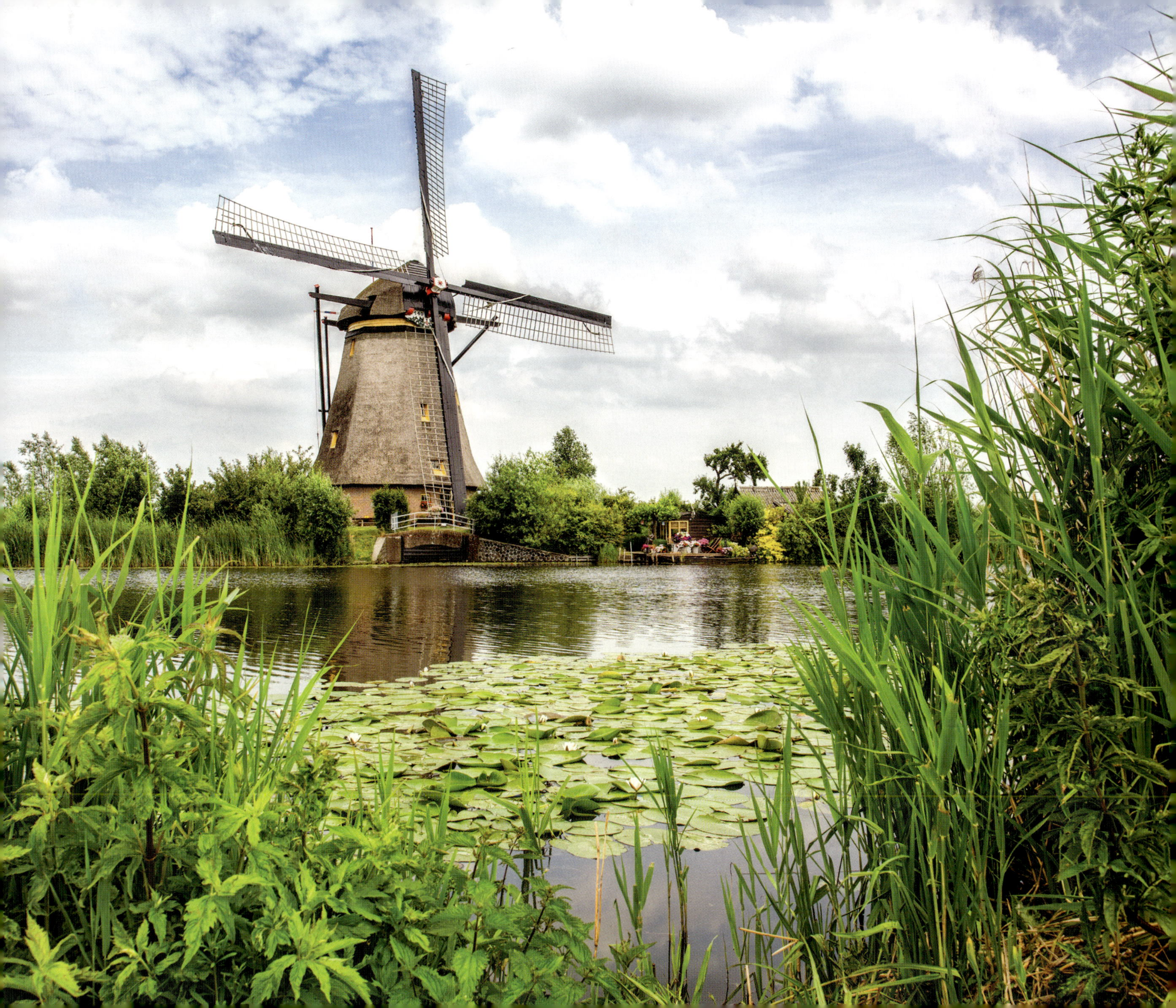

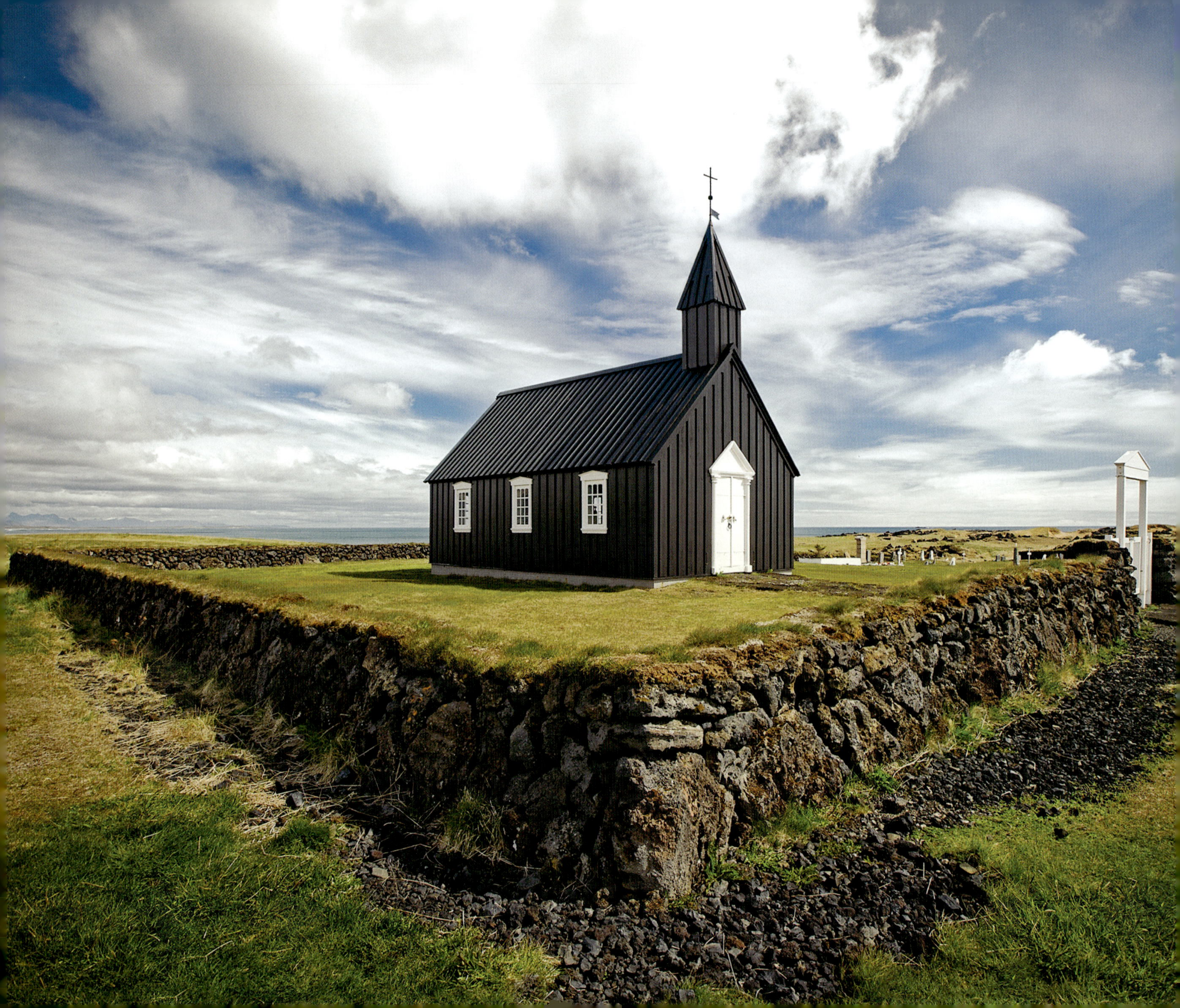

CHAPTER SIX

THE BLESSING OF CHRIST'S BODY

To the delight of every child of faith, there is kinship in the family of God. We sense ties of love with our brothers and sisters by the blood of Jesus, and together our spirits rejoice. But beyond familial bonds, we also share an astonishing oneness. By a mysterious and divine fusion, all believers in Christ are united together as His body here on earth. This means we are linked by the spiritual tissue that makes up a dwelling for our King: love, prayer, tenderness, fellowship. Such a communion is a most precious thing. It is also very powerful.

God gives each of us spiritual gifts to build up and encourage one another. And He entrusts us with treasures in many different forms, so we can serve others and glorify Him. All good things are a gift from Him and show others His great love. And God's greatest gift, of course, is Jesus. Filled with the peace, joy, and strength of the Savior, His earthly body, the church, gives witness to His matchless excellence and calls the world to seek true life in Him.

The family of God brings order and completeness back into the world. Made whole in Christ, we provide a contrast to the brokenness that still surrounds us—we become a beacon of hope in the dark. A ravaged place can become bright with life again through the presence of Christ in the touch of His people. As His light radiates through us, we bless others and bear fruit for His purposes, to His unending glory and the praise of God forever.

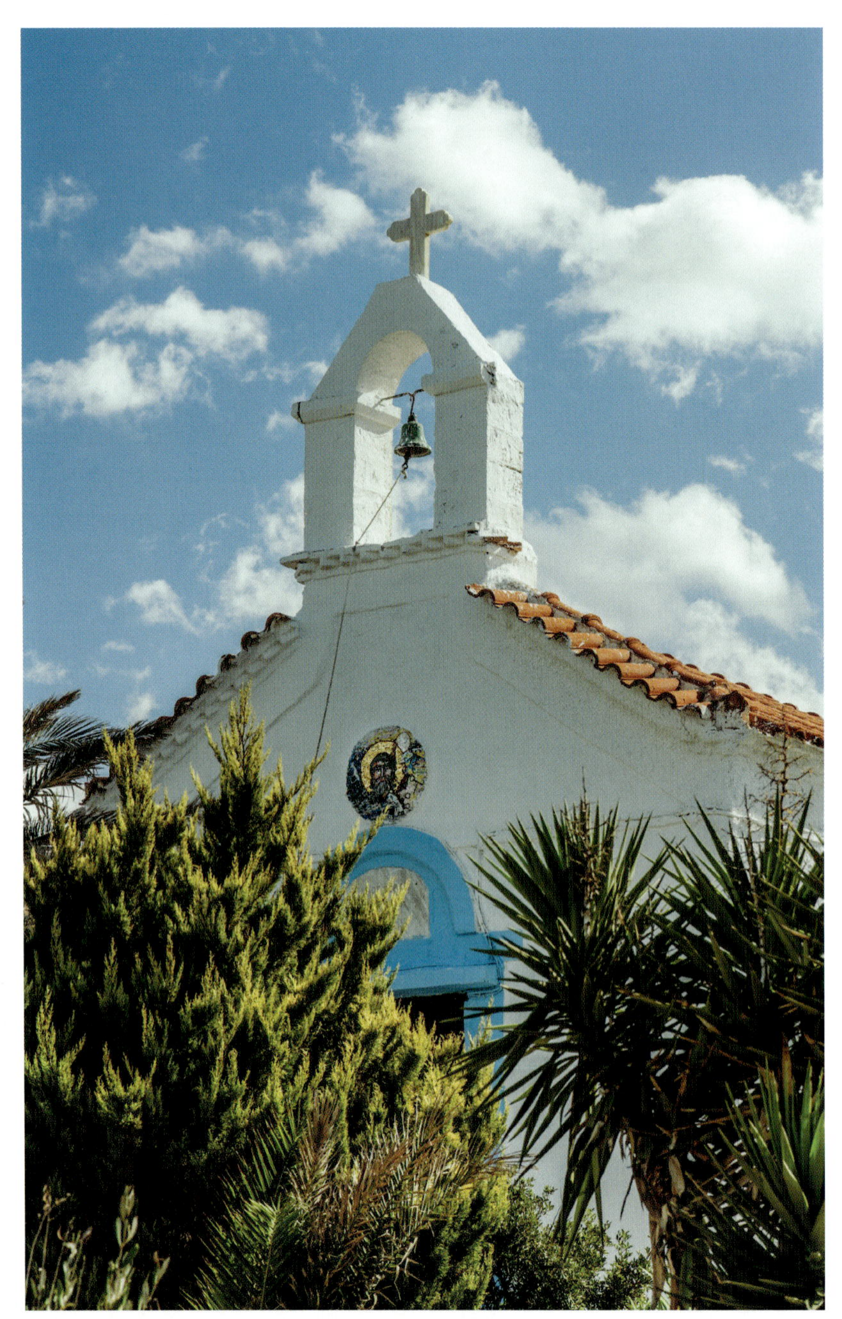

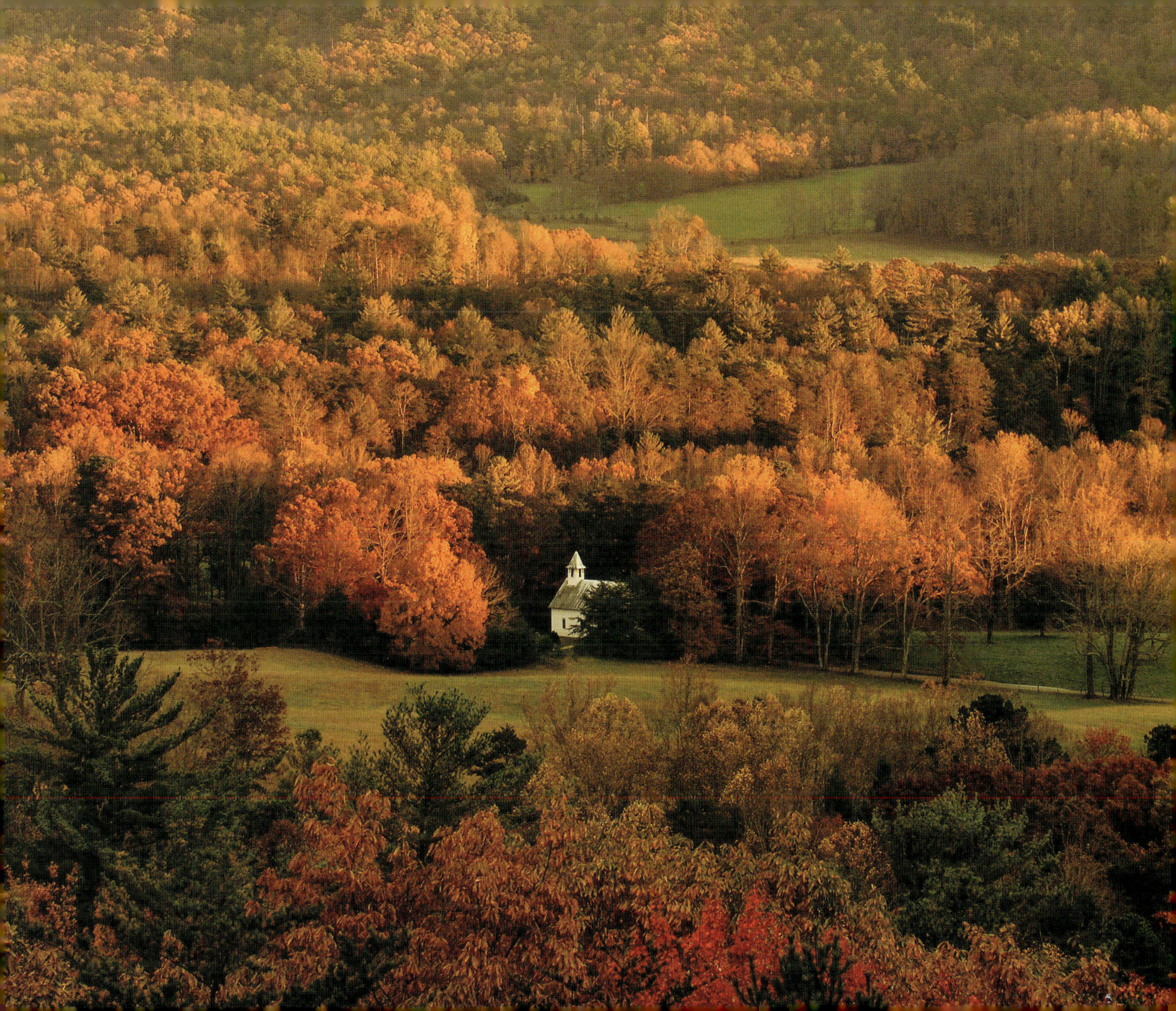

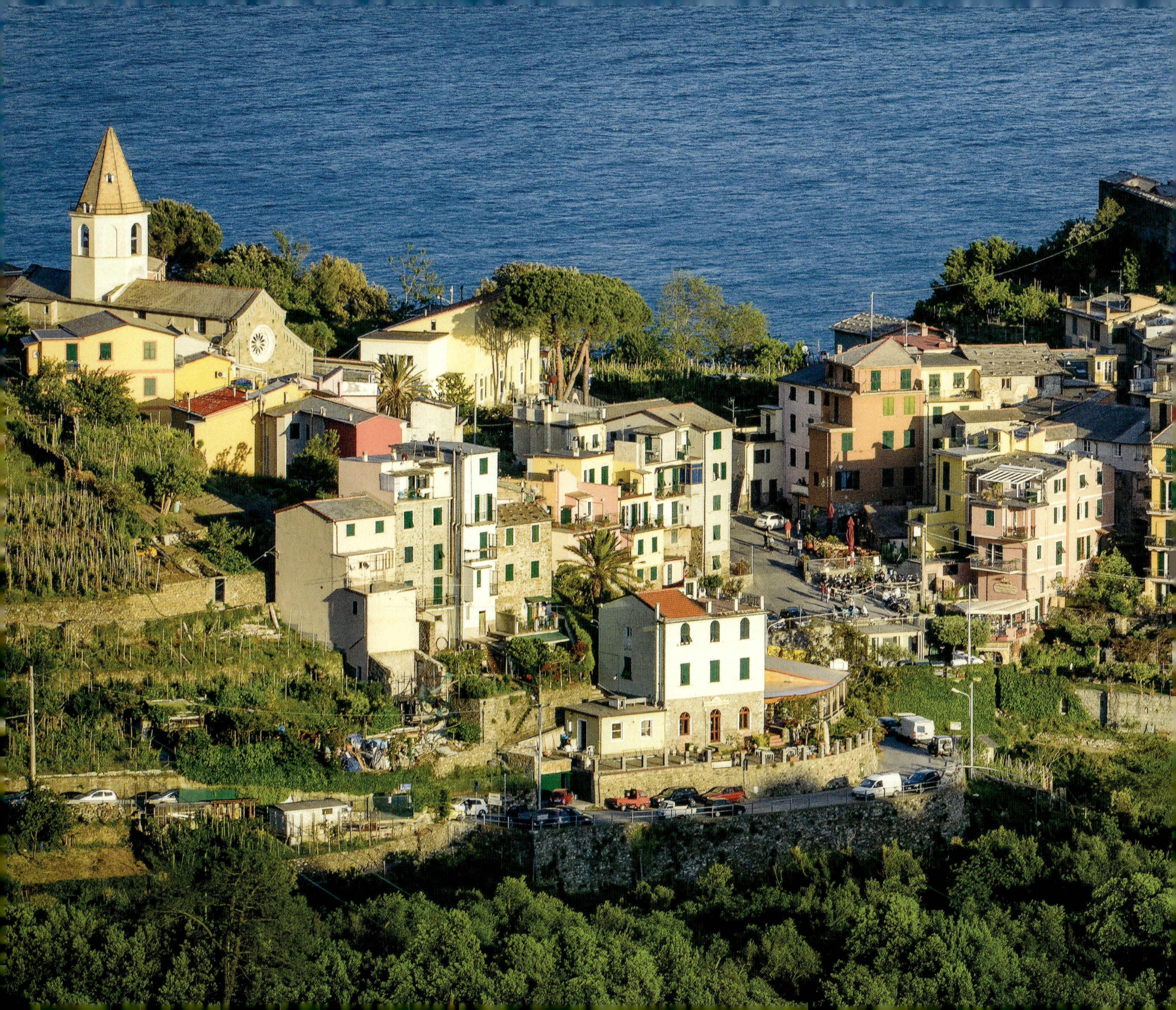

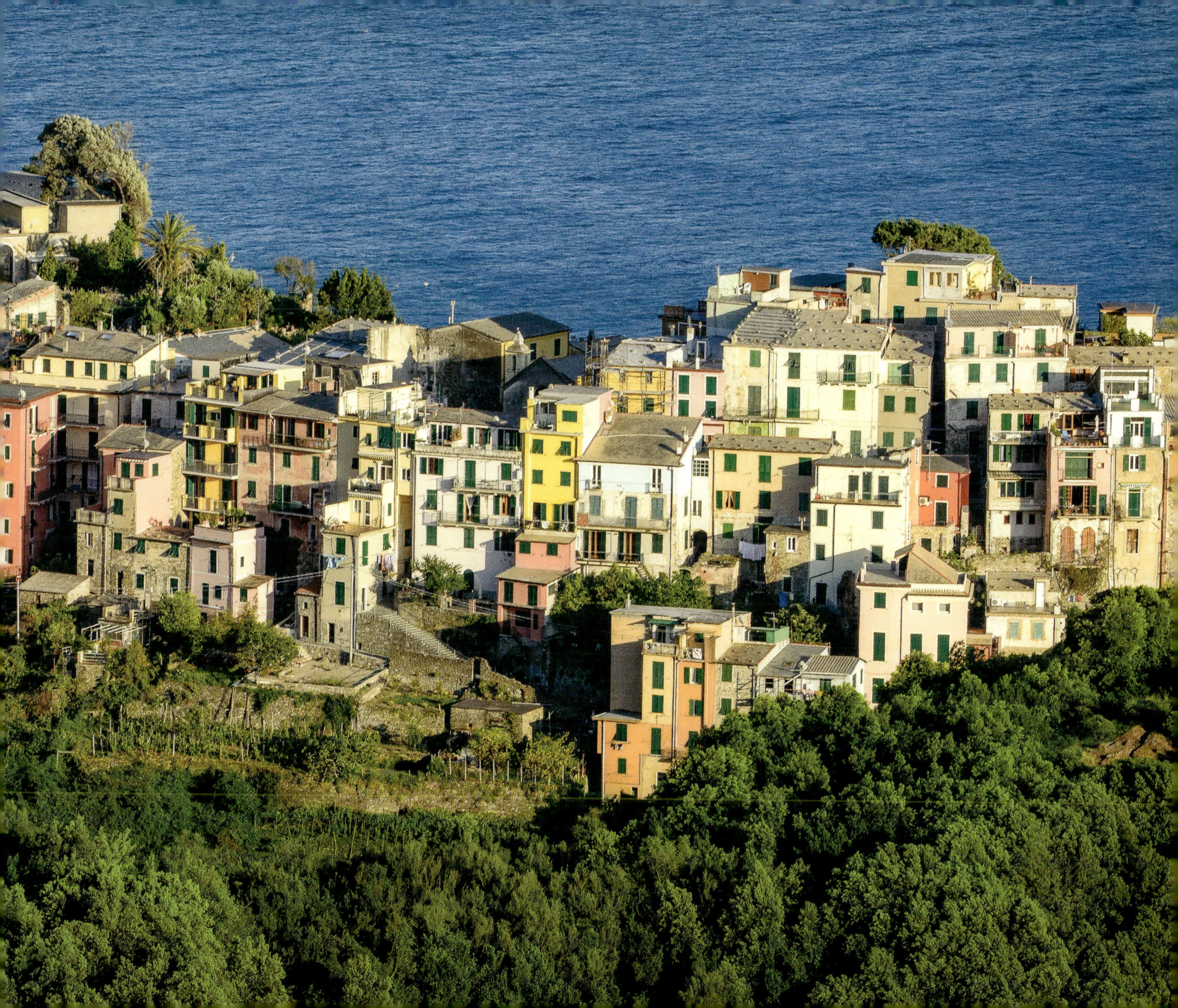

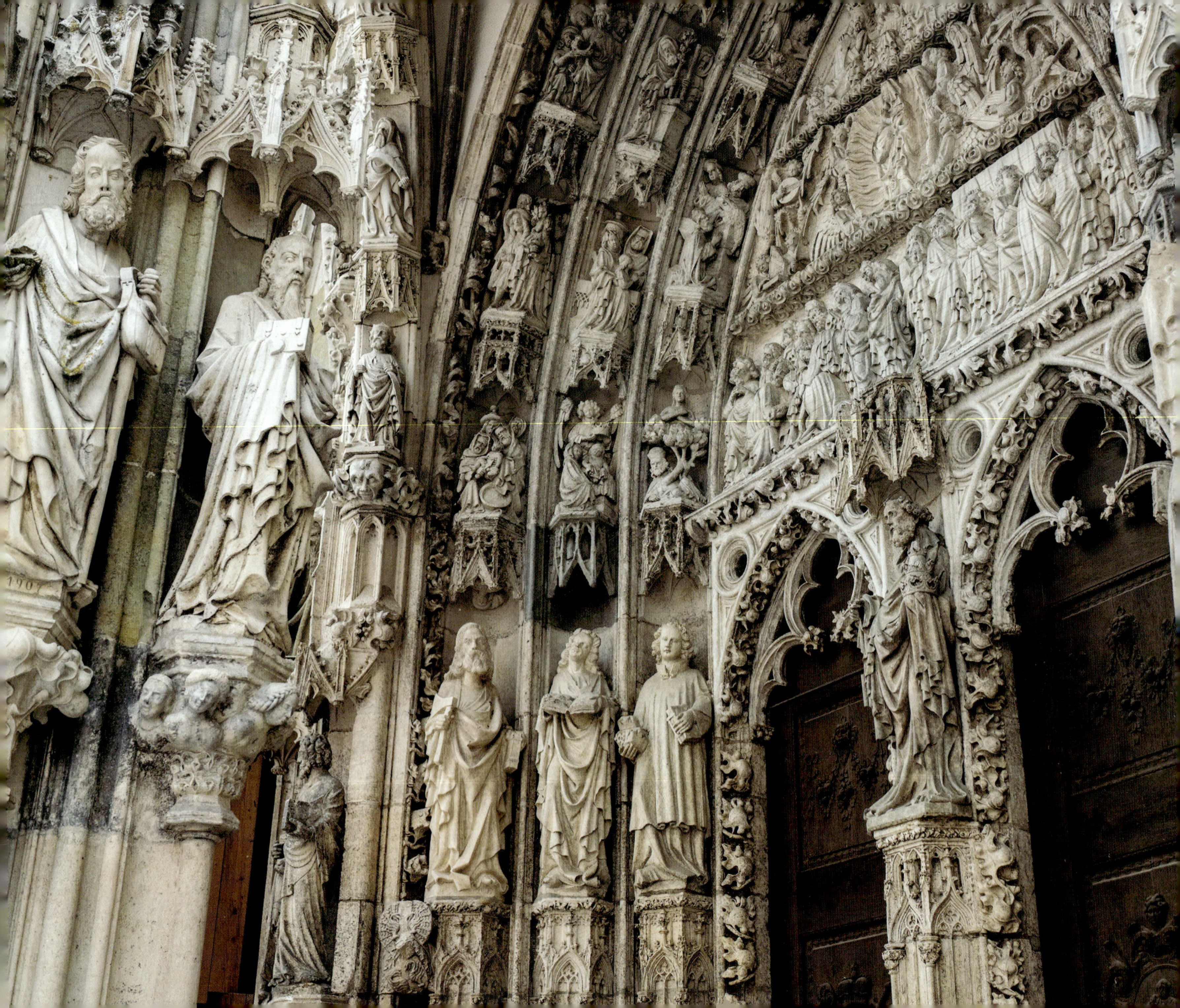

we bring You our best, Lord

Born again into Christ, we become the building blocks that make up His living church, His body on earth. Just as we are being built up as part of that body, each of us is also building upon Him as the foundation of our new life. All we say, do, and accomplish rests on this bedrock, and is meant to be a contribution to Christ, worthy of presentation to our heavenly Father.

REFLECT

You also, as living stones, are being built up
as a spiritual house for a holy priesthood,
to offer up spiritual sacrifices acceptable to God
through Jesus Christ.

1 PETER 2:5

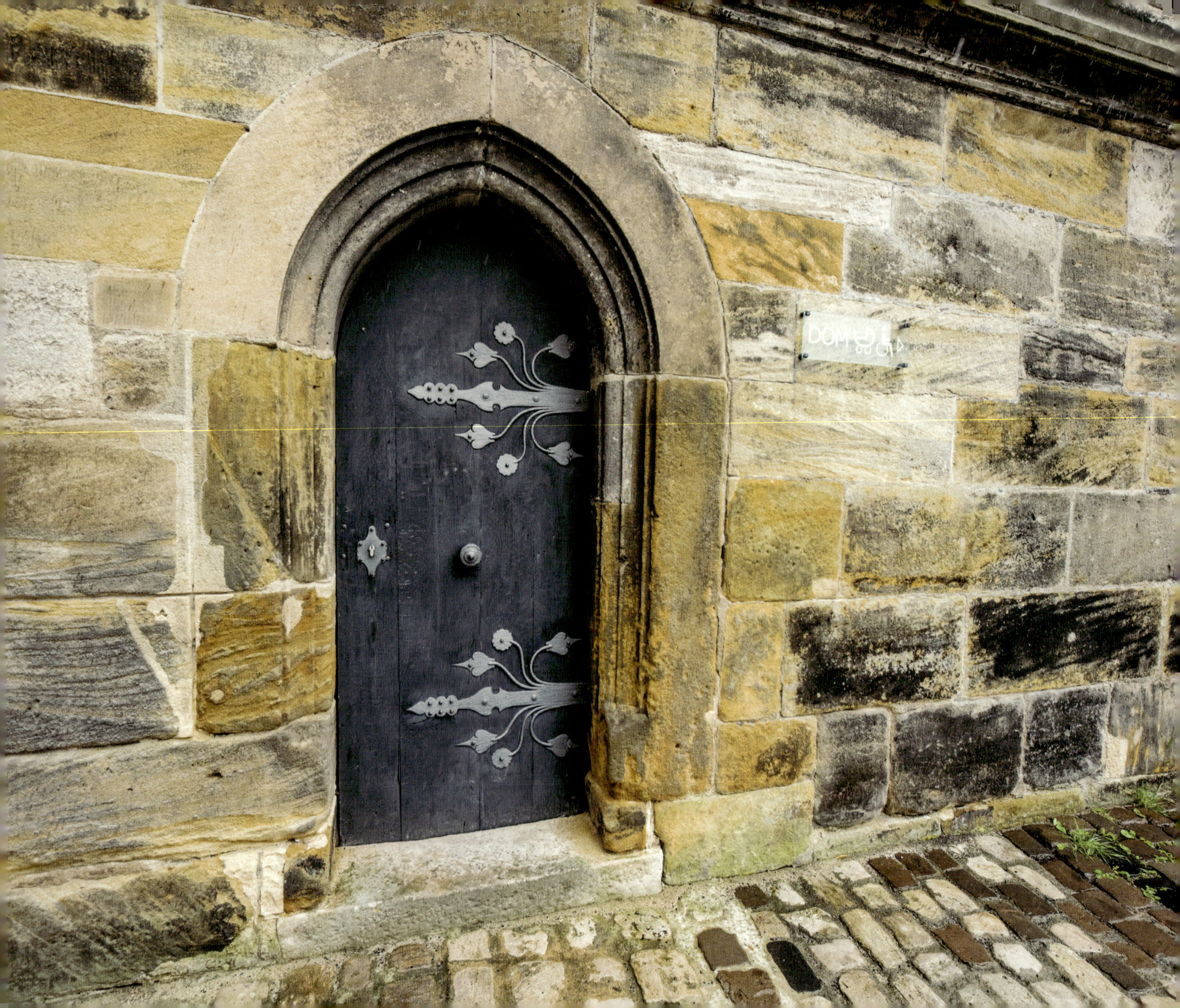
DOM

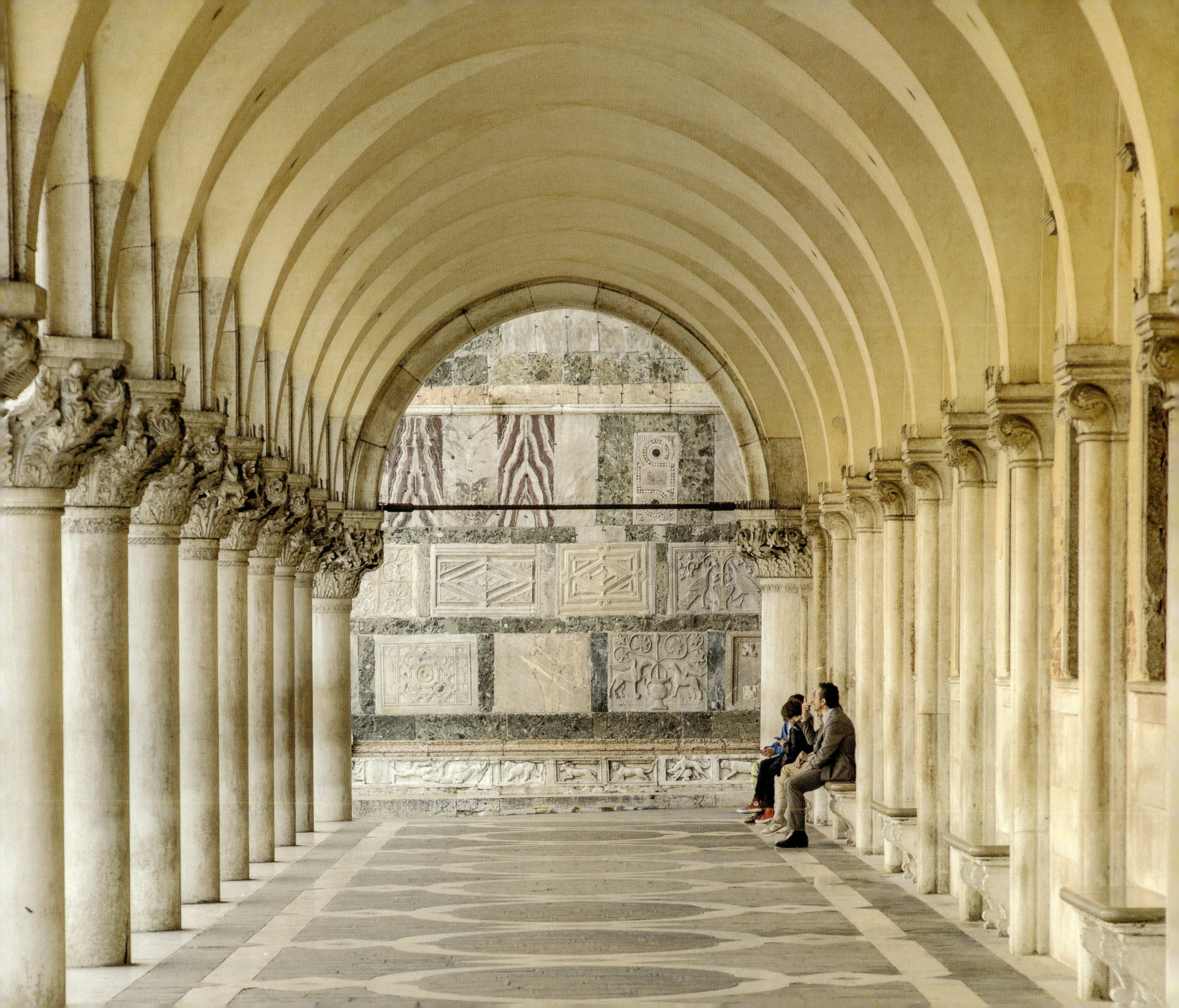

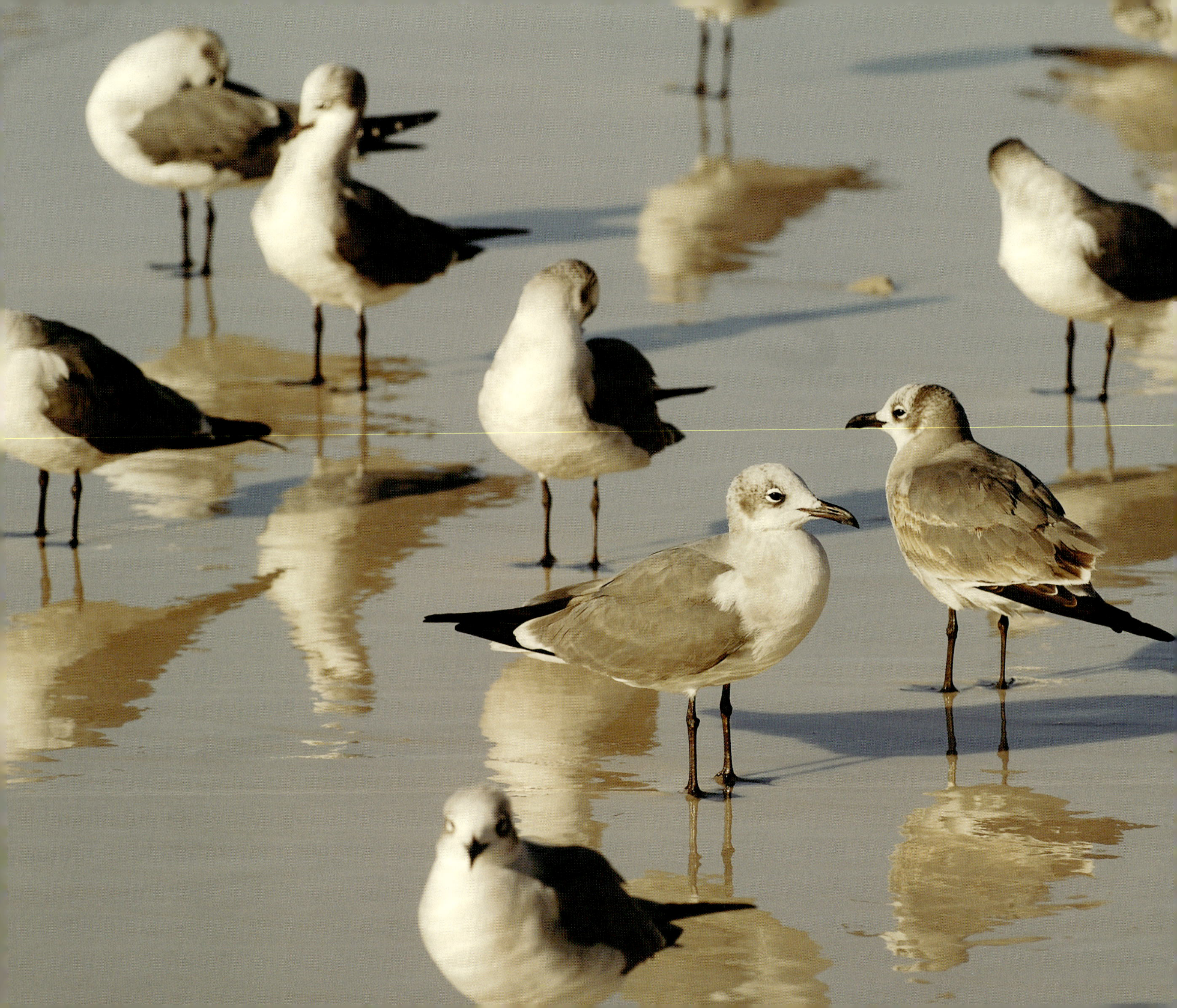

Jesus Christ is the head of the church, and we are the body. All believers everywhere have been baptized by the Holy Spirit into Christ's body. God has put the whole body together to function as one beautiful unit, diversified in our gifts and talents and abilities. Every single member of the body is important. God has placed each of them just as He desired. With all the members operating jointly and lovingly together, the whole body functions properly, glorifying Him and fulfilling His work on earth. What a beautiful sight we must make before God! The body of Christ is His most precious possession on earth.

— DR. CHARLES STANLEY —

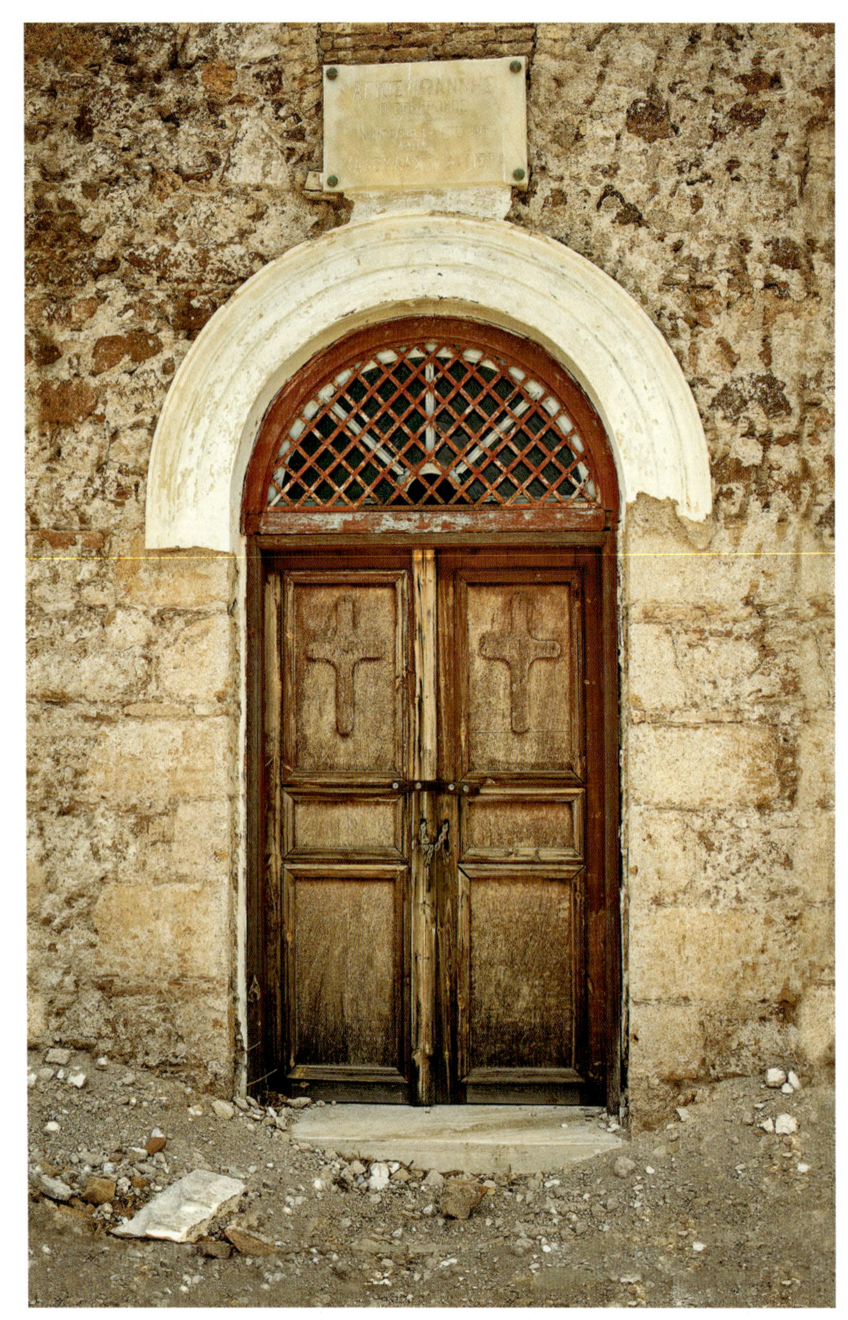

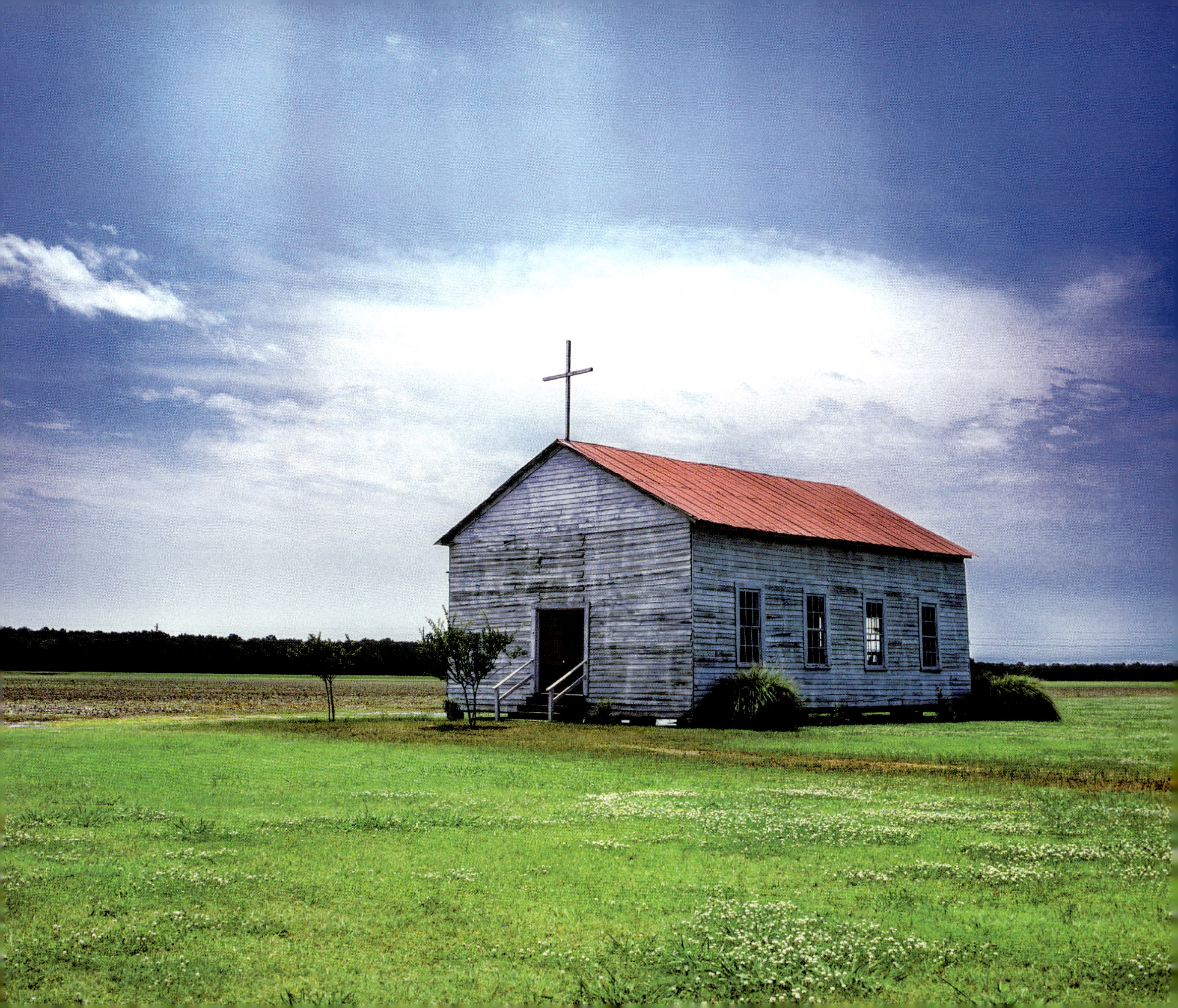

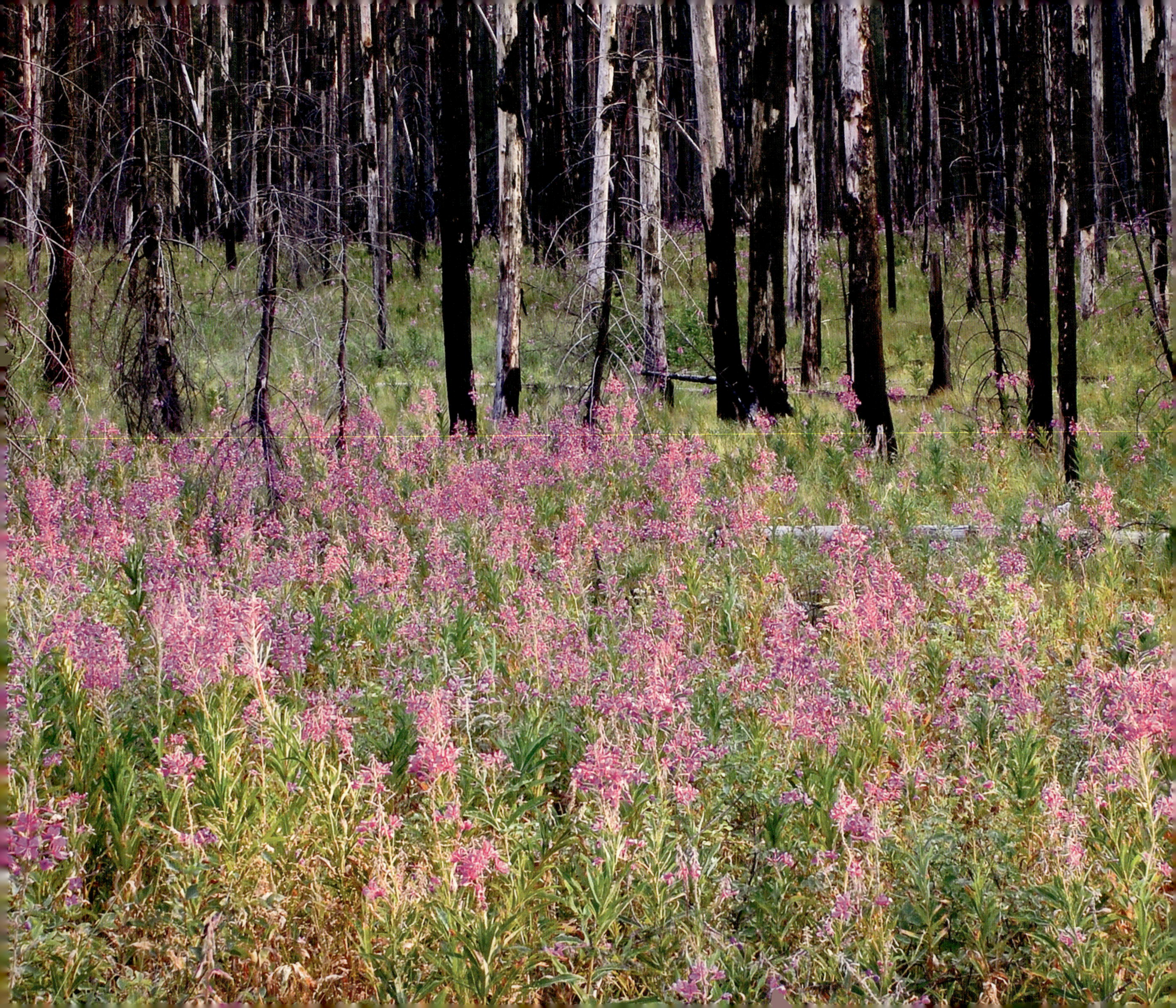

caring for His treasures

Like a gardener with a basket of seedlings and a plot of soil, we stand in the world holding the treasures of God's kingdom in our hands. The presence of Christ within us is the priceless rose of our basket, to be cherished above all else. We also tend His many gifts to us—time and talents, property, knowledge, or family. Through love, study, diligence, communication, and ingenuity, we can use them all to exalt our God and point to His Son, Jesus.

REFLECT

Blessed are those you choose and bring near
to live in your courts! We are filled with the good things
of your house, of your holy temple.

PSALM 65:4 (NIV)

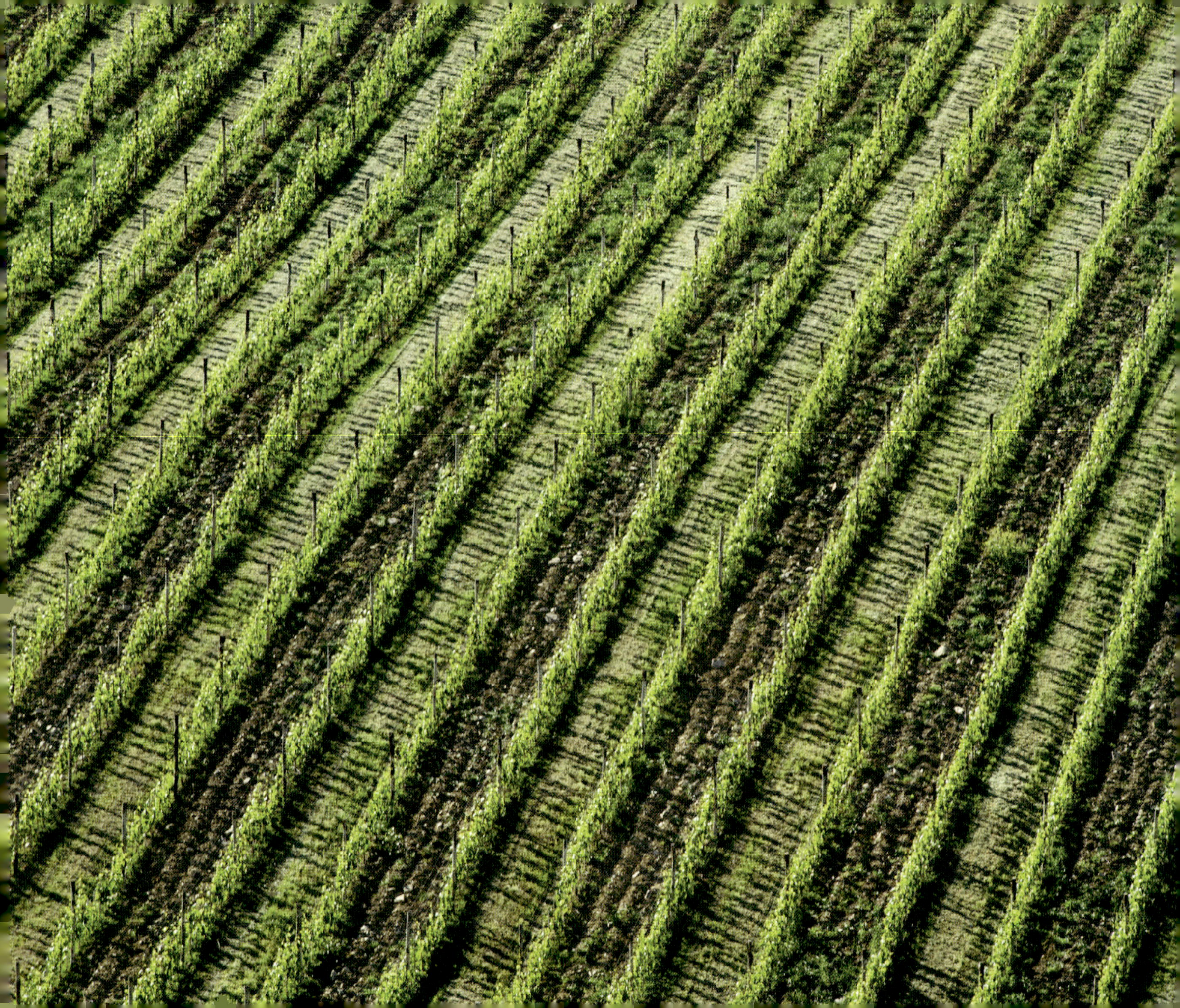

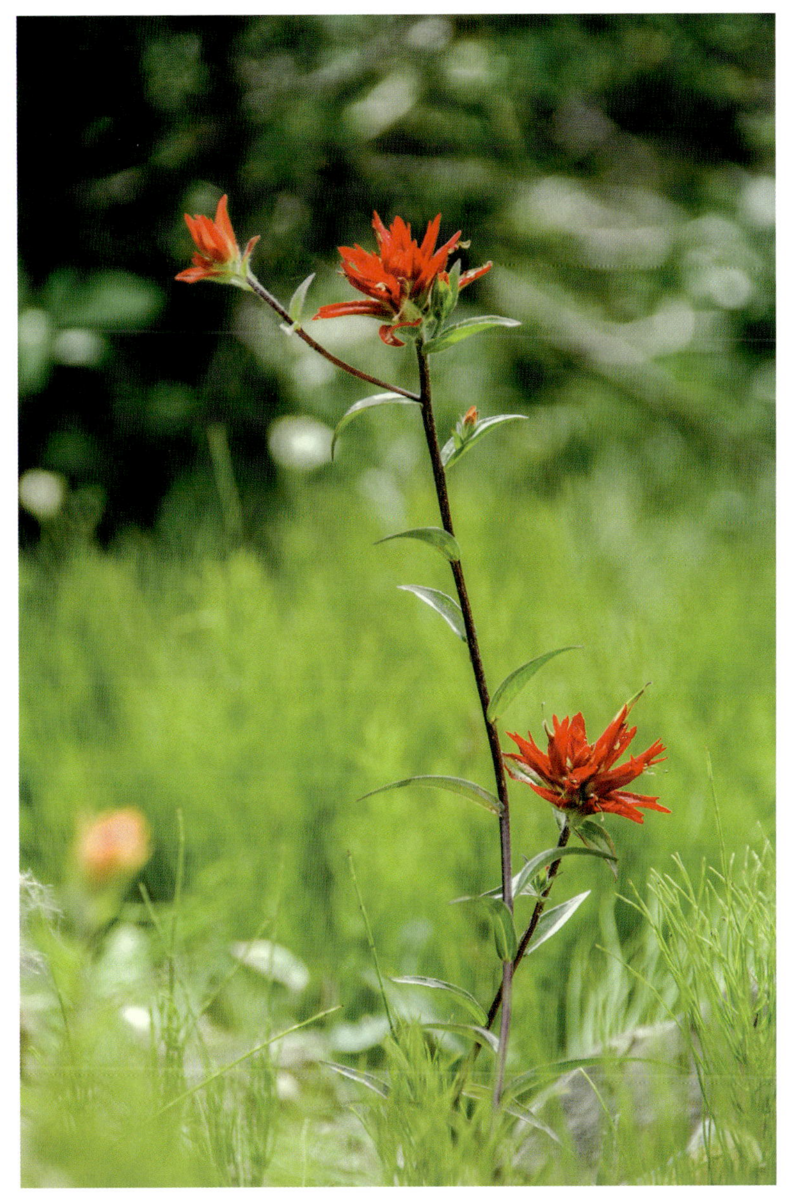

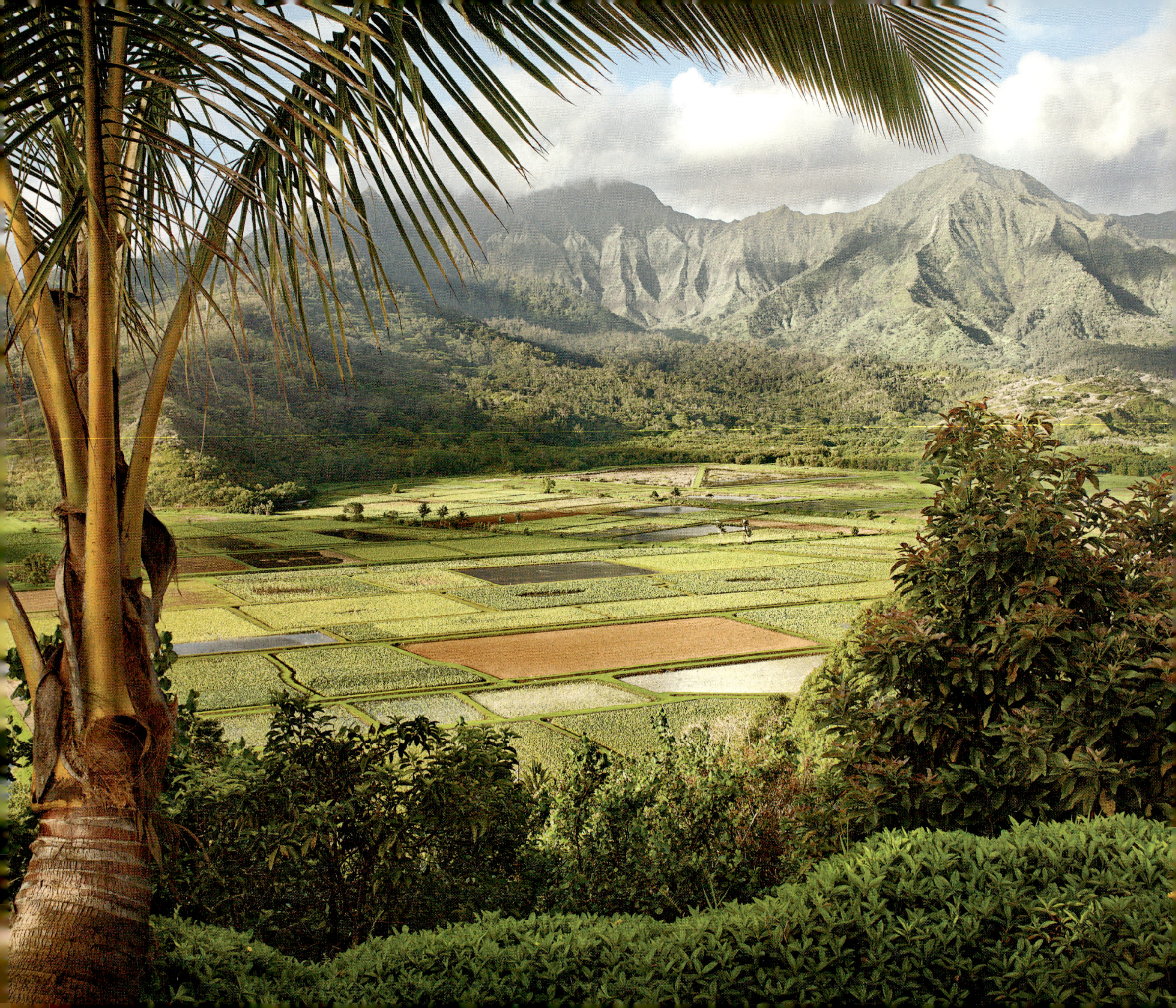

seeds of mercy and love

We cultivate the earth with the plow of truth and plant seeds of mercy and love. Every blessing given to another is sown for God's glory. A helping hand, an act of forgiveness, a gift of kindness, a word of encouragement, a cup of cold water—nothing is lost, but germinates beneath the ground of time for a harvest of honor to the Lord, who inspires it all.

REFLECT

Let us not lose heart in doing good, for in due time
we will reap if we do not grow weary. So then,
while we have opportunity, let us do good
to all people, and especially to those who are
of the household of the faith.

GALATIANS 6:9-10

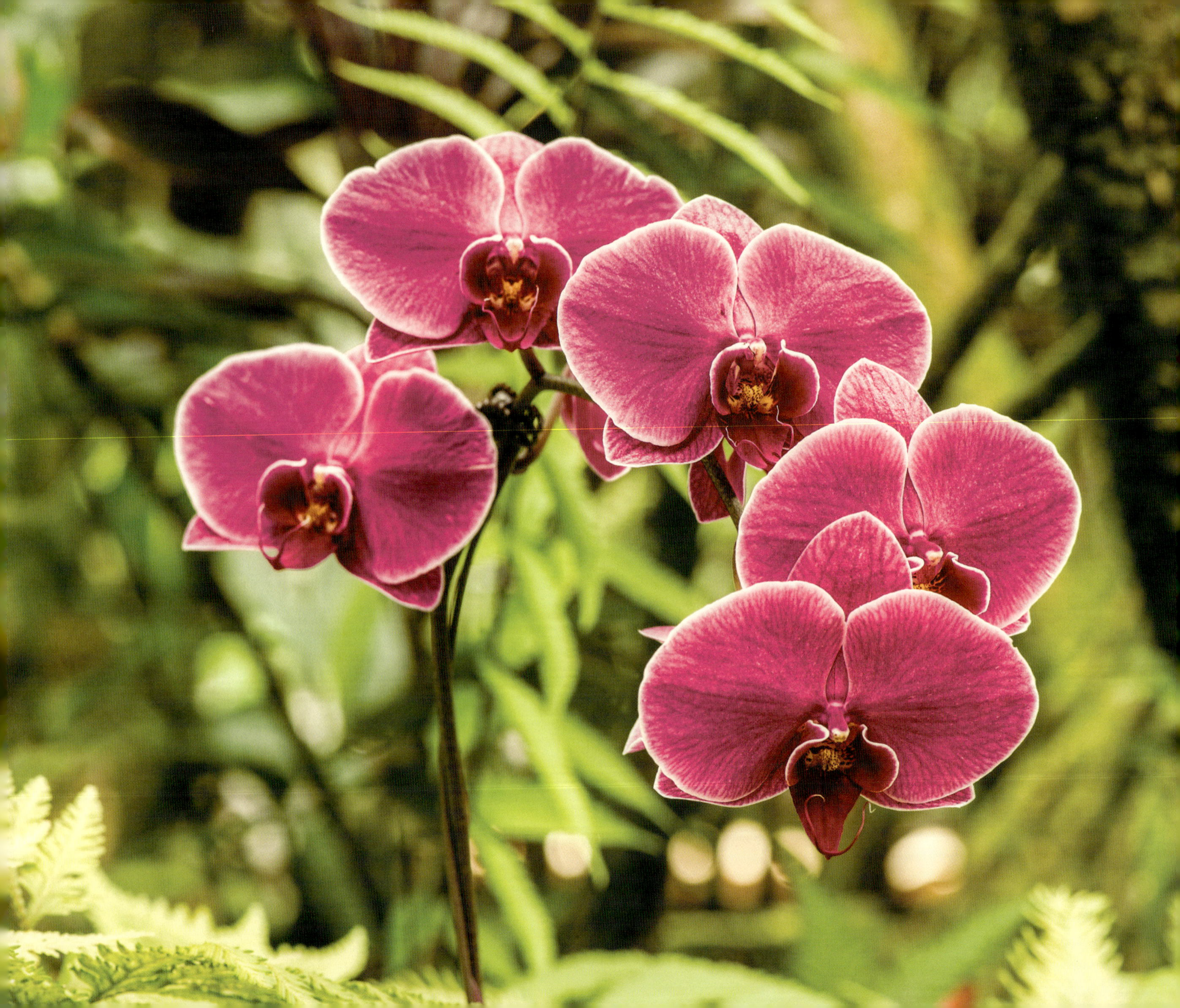

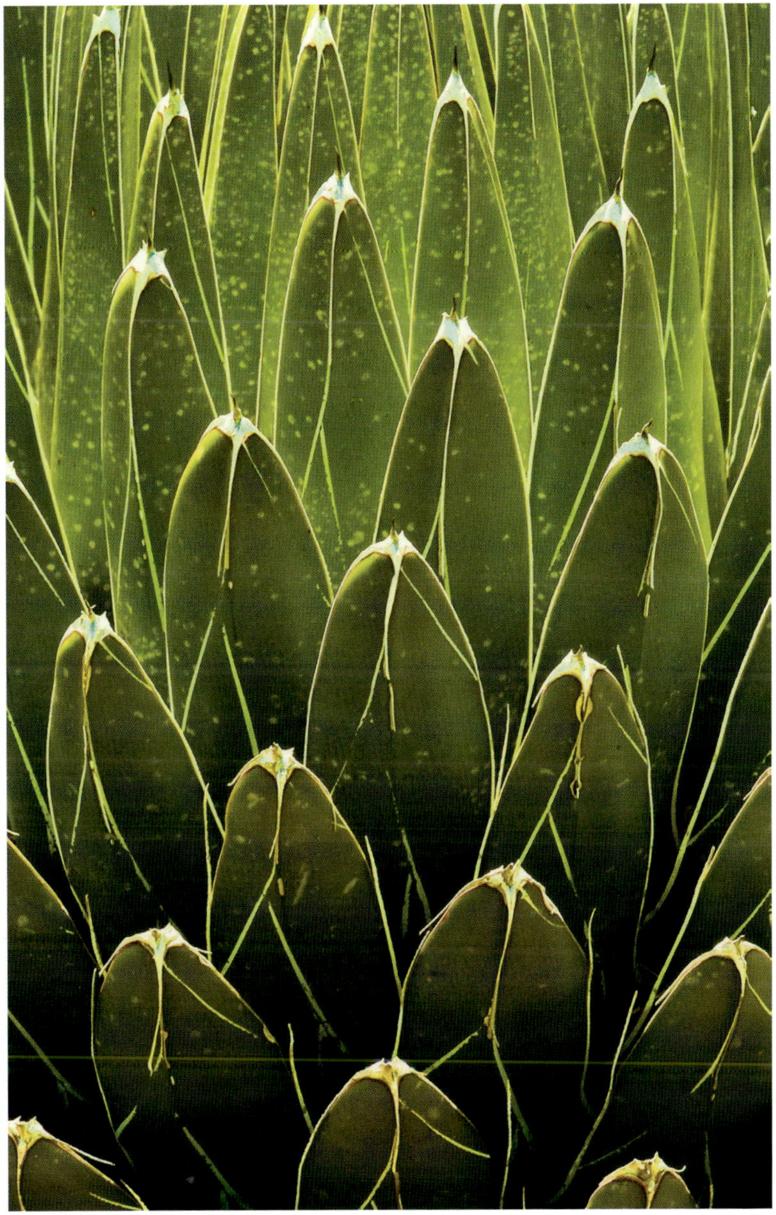

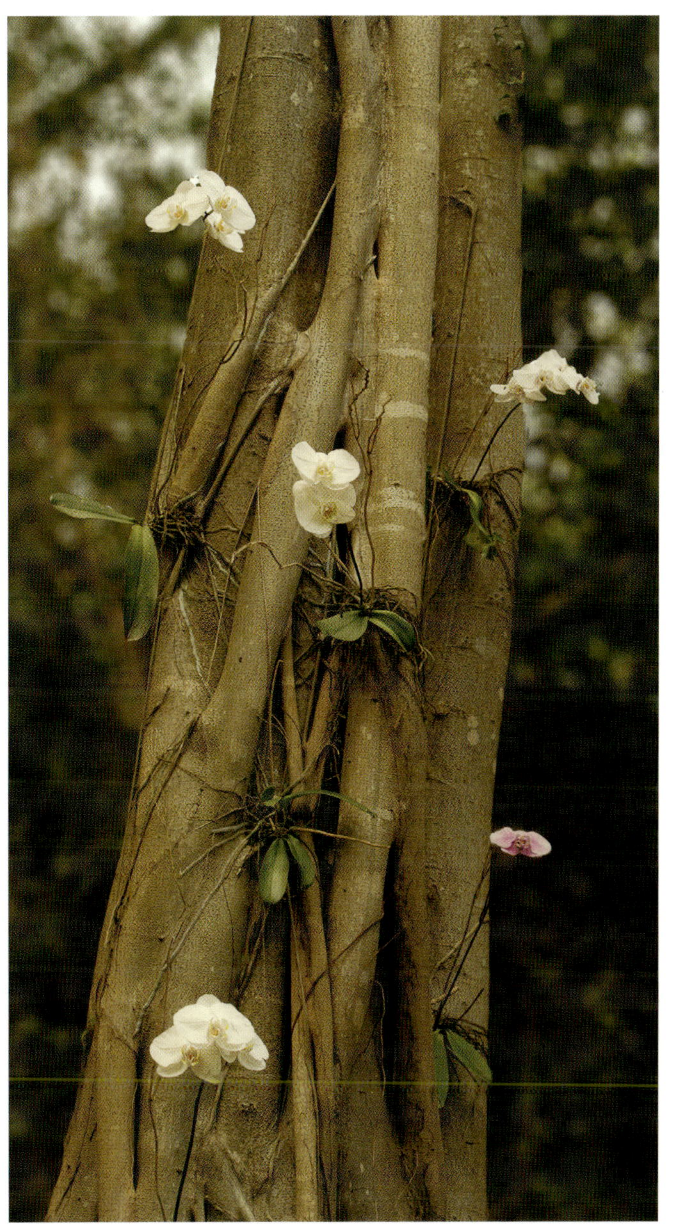

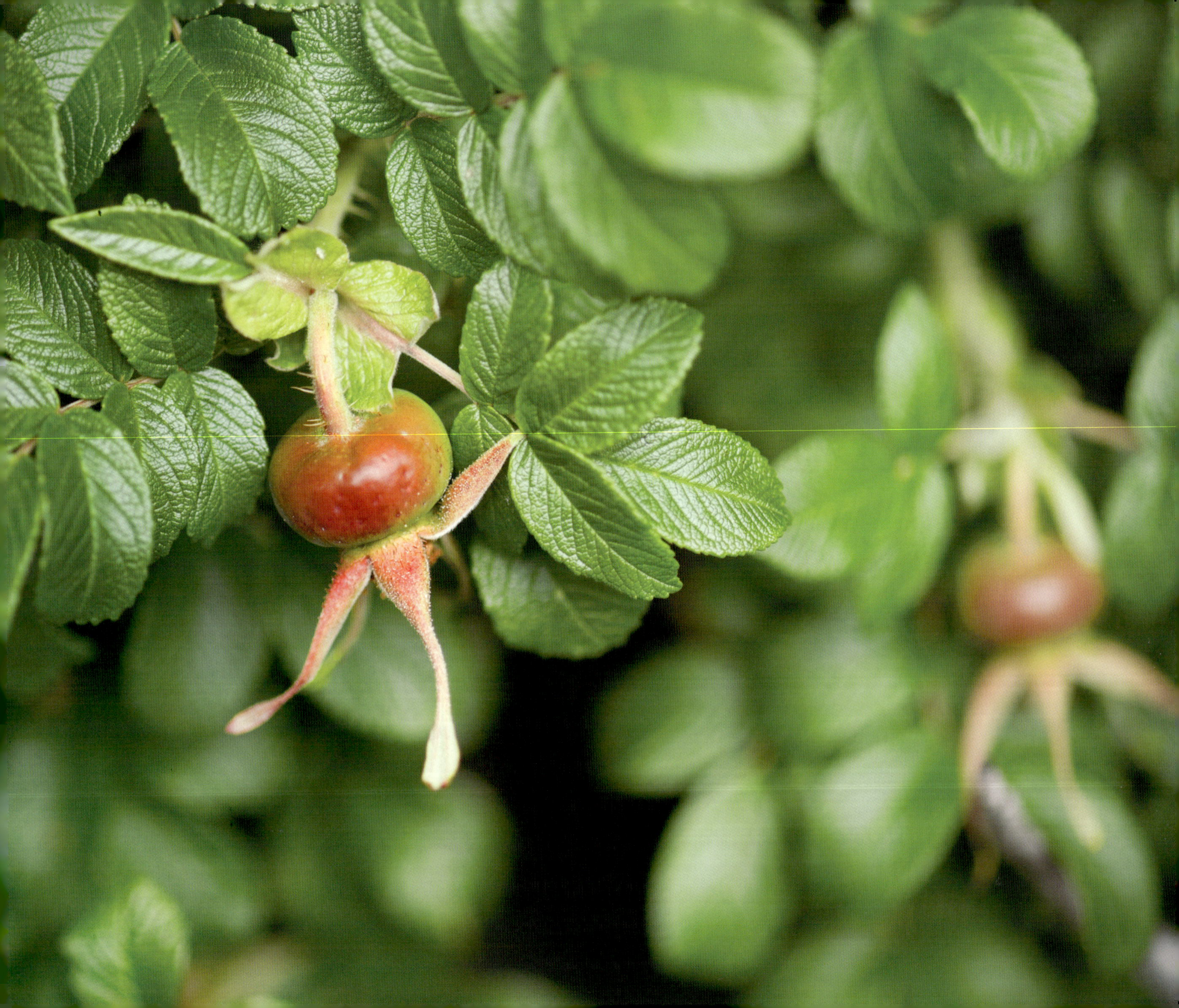

bearing fruit

The sap of life is found in Jesus Christ. Bonded together with Him through faith, we have access to an incredible miracle—true life, once so elusive, begins to run through our veins with undeniable power. We see buds on our branches, then blossoms, and finally, the sweet fruits of His presence in us: love, joy, peace, service. Any plot of dry land becomes, with such cultivation, a radiant garden in full flower. We need only to remain in Jesus, follow Him, trust Him, and yield to Him. His riches, birthed through us, can sustain multitudes.

REFLECT

"I am the vine, you are the branches; he who abides in Me and I in him, he bears much fruit."

JOHN 15:5

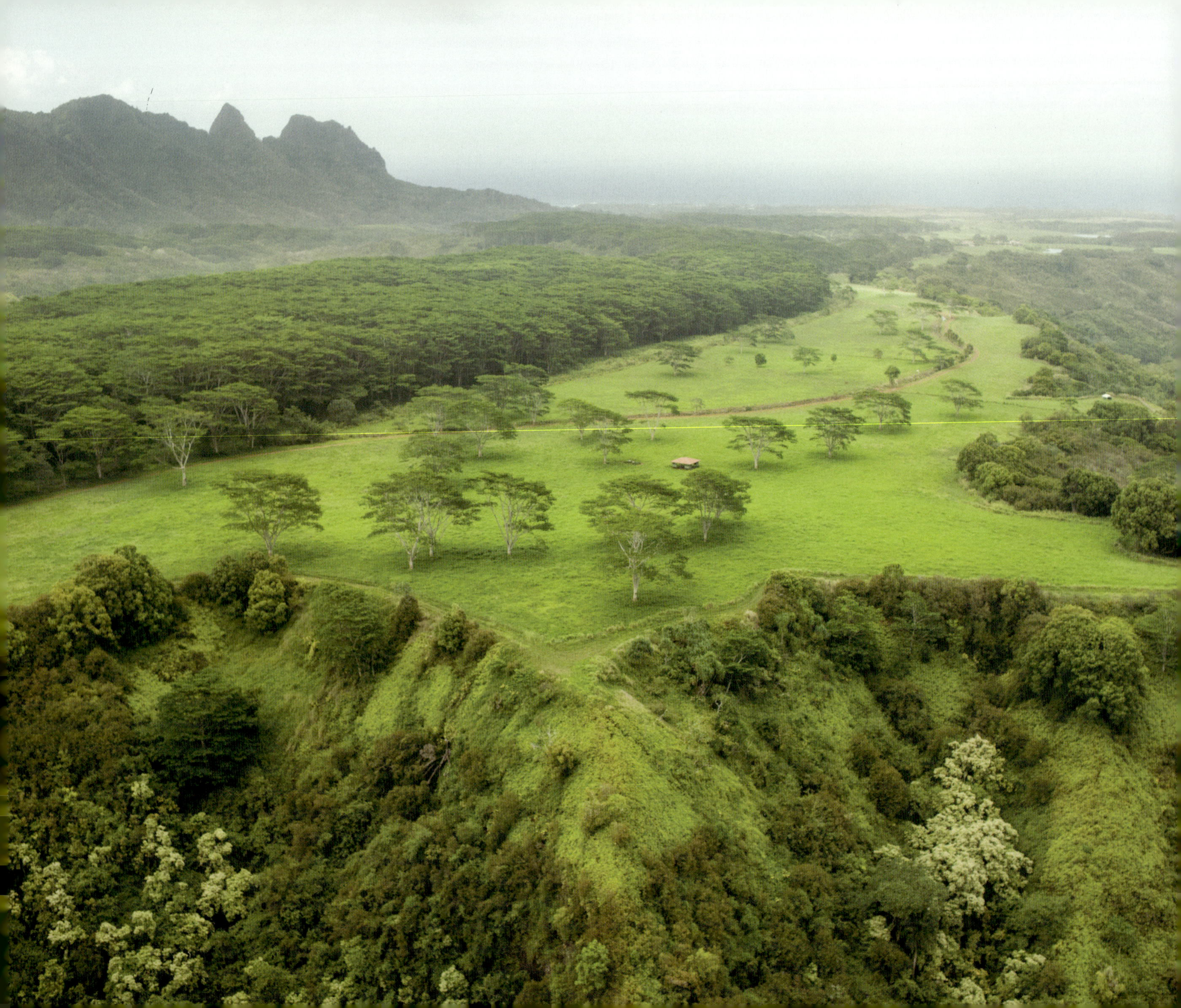

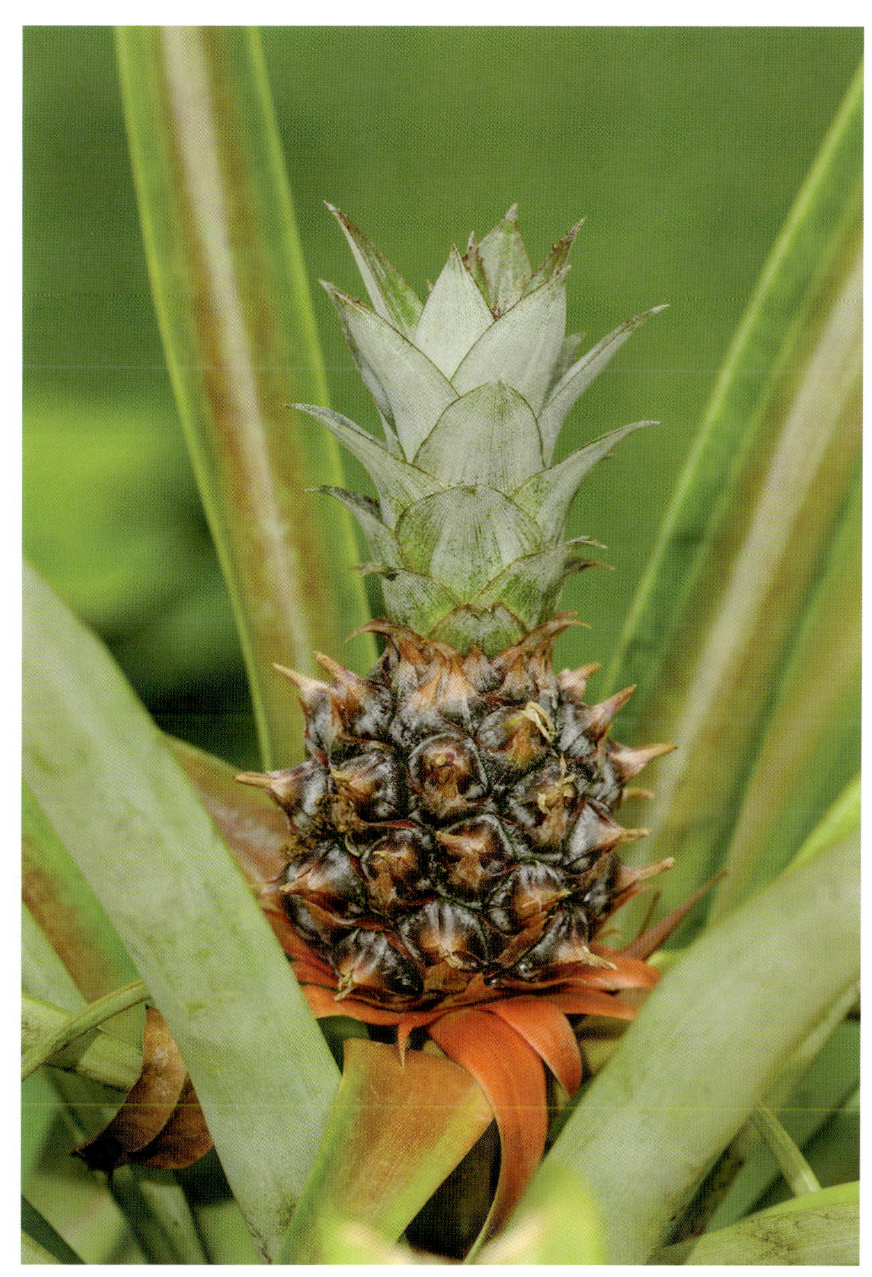

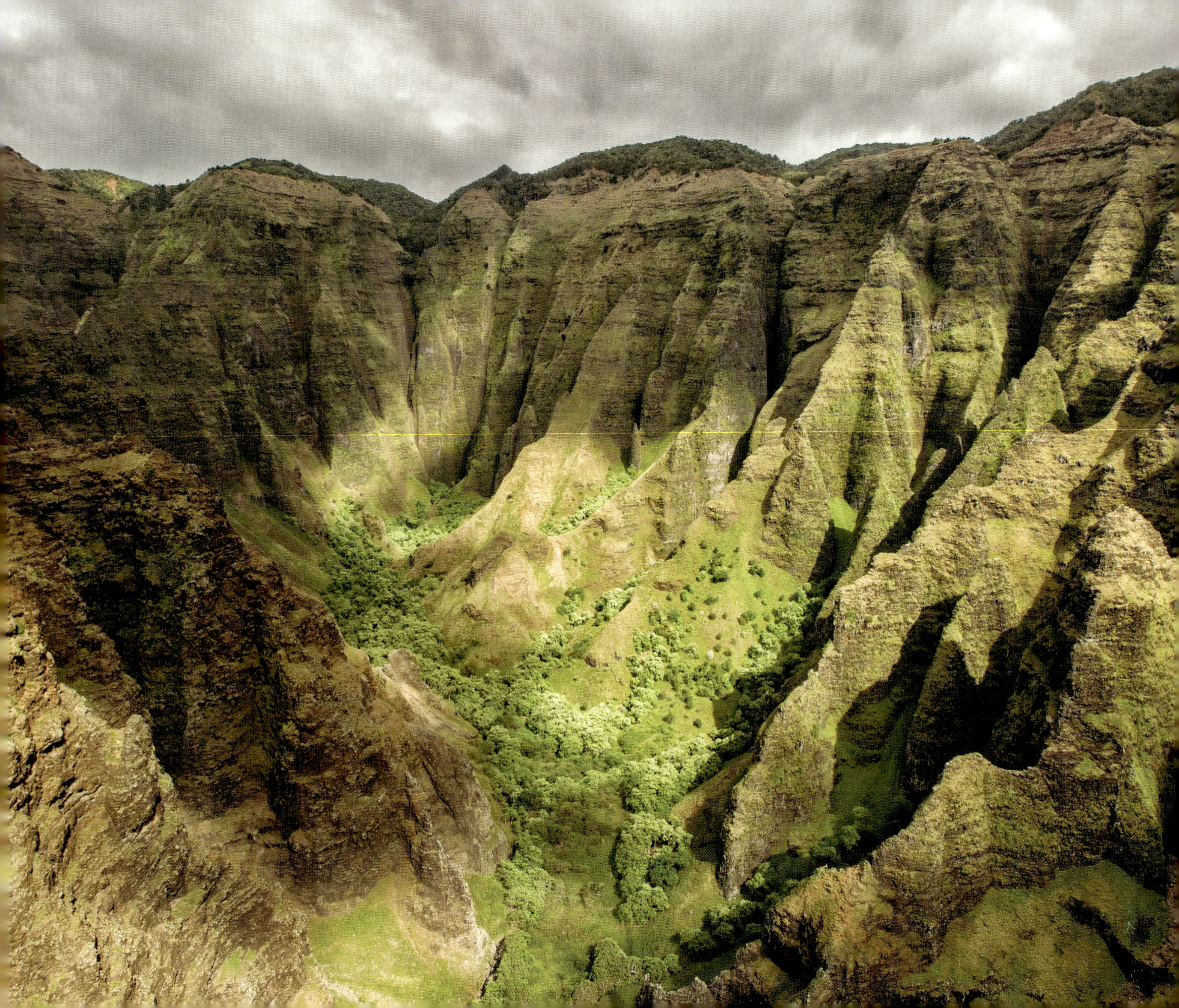

REFLECT

God is able to make all grace
abound to you,
so that always having
all sufficiency in everything,
you may have an abundance
for every good deed.

2 CORINTHIANS 9:8

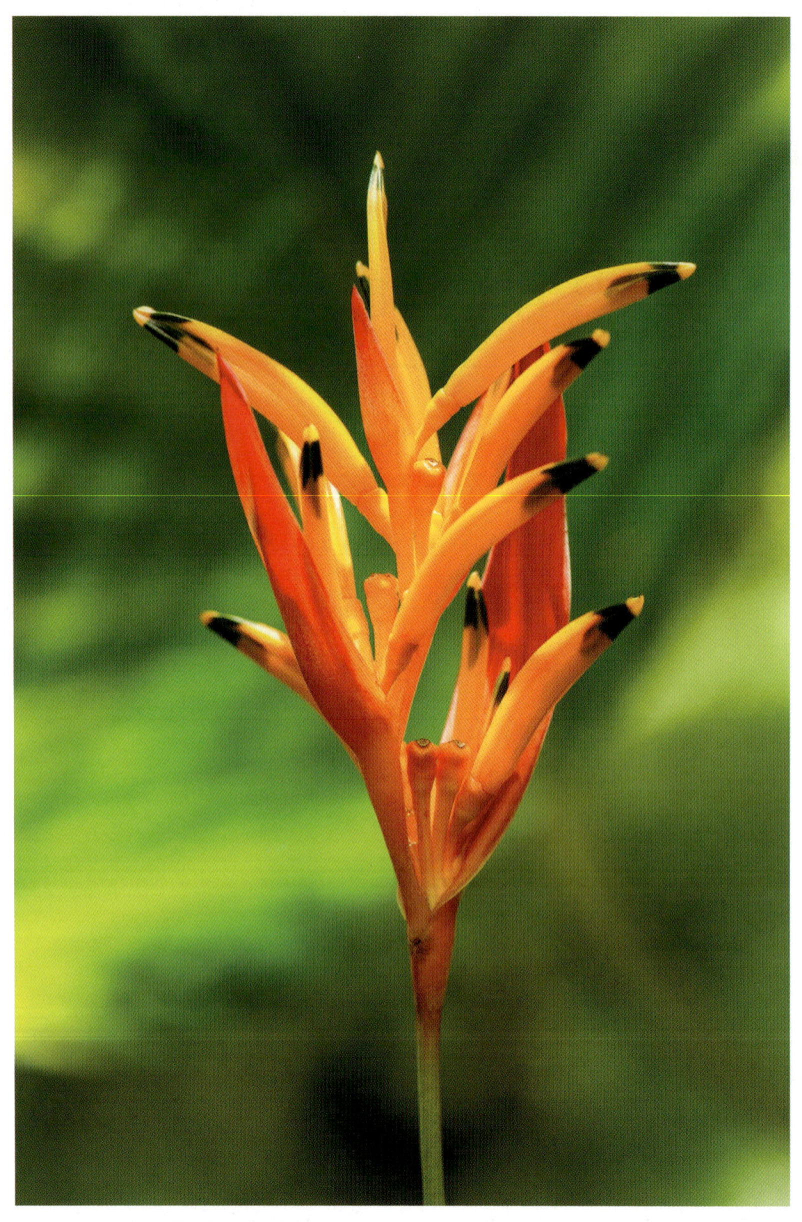

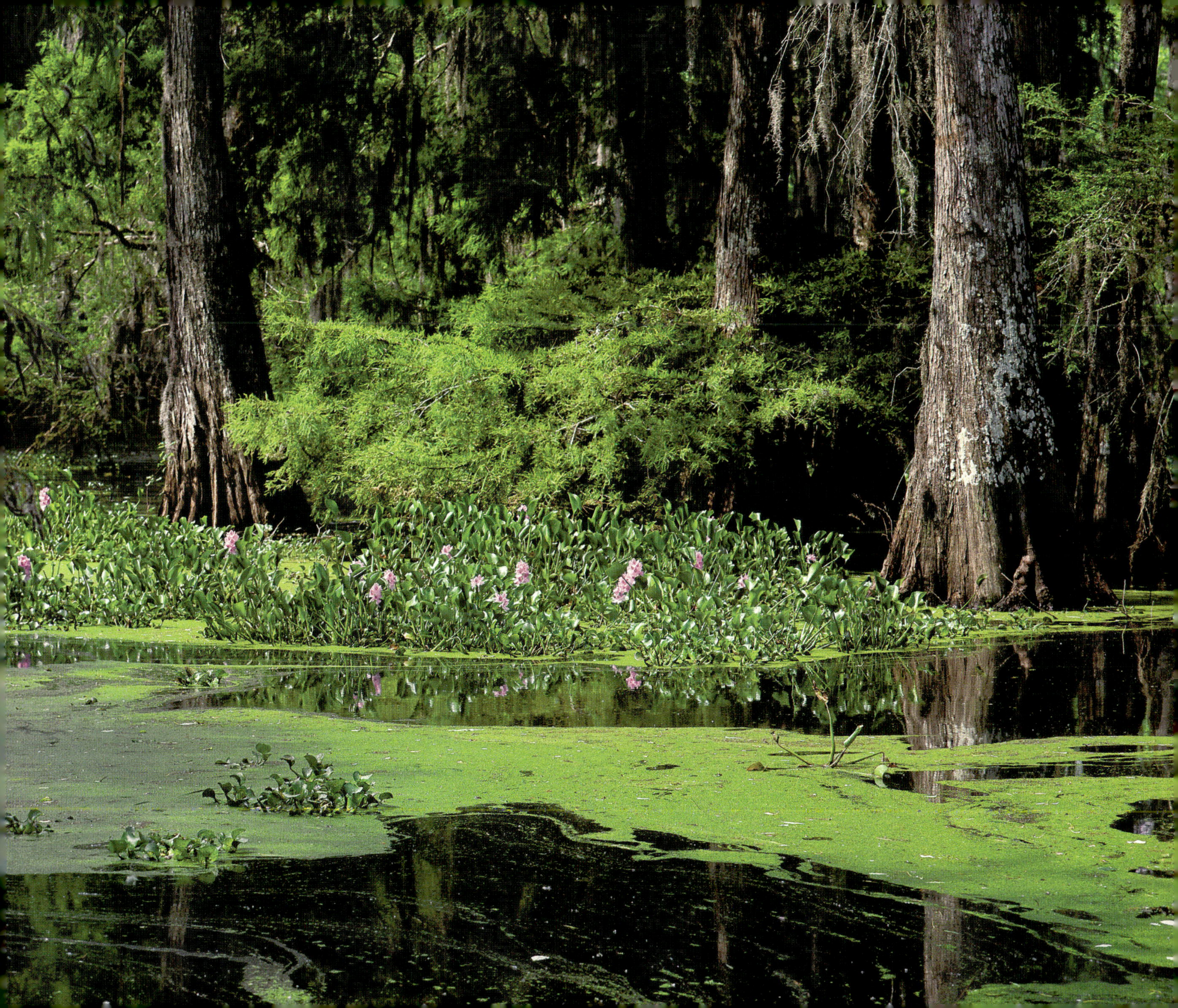

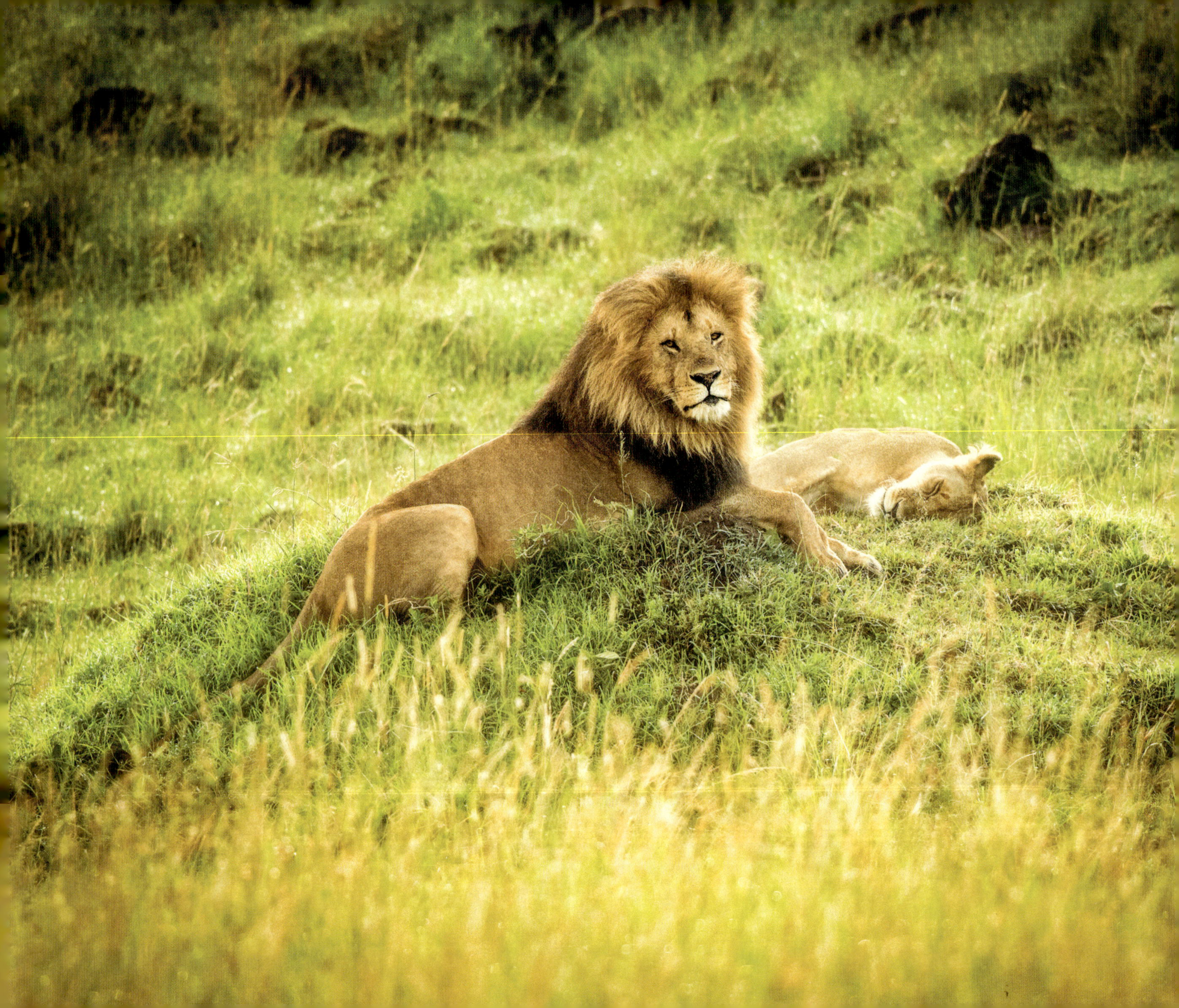

CHAPTER SEVEN

A LITANY OF PRAISE

Scripture says that all God's creation is waiting eagerly to see the children of God revealed. While we still have our feet on this earth, we'll continue to grow in Christ. But we can look forward with joy to the day God unveils the work He has promised to complete in us.

This final chapter is a "visual feast" in celebration of the incredible story of our salvation through the blood of Jesus, the story of God's infinite love for us. The better we understand this miracle, the more astonished we are at His grace, and the fuller we become with ever-increasing gratitude. No matter what the circumstances of life bring, no hardship and no worldly blessing compares to the presence of Jesus—to our fellowship with Him, His Father, and the Holy Spirit.

God's created world, seen through the eyes of this new life, becomes a catalogue of divine splendor and anticipation. Mountain peaks strive to exalt Him. Crashing waterfalls thunder His praise. Flower petals sing of His kindness. Birds soar, wildlife roars, and the varied works of human hands tell of the glory, honor, and magnificence of our God. To contemplate our world in this state is to be fulfilled, to be comforted, and to overflow with an exuberance born of His mercy and grace. Praise Him!

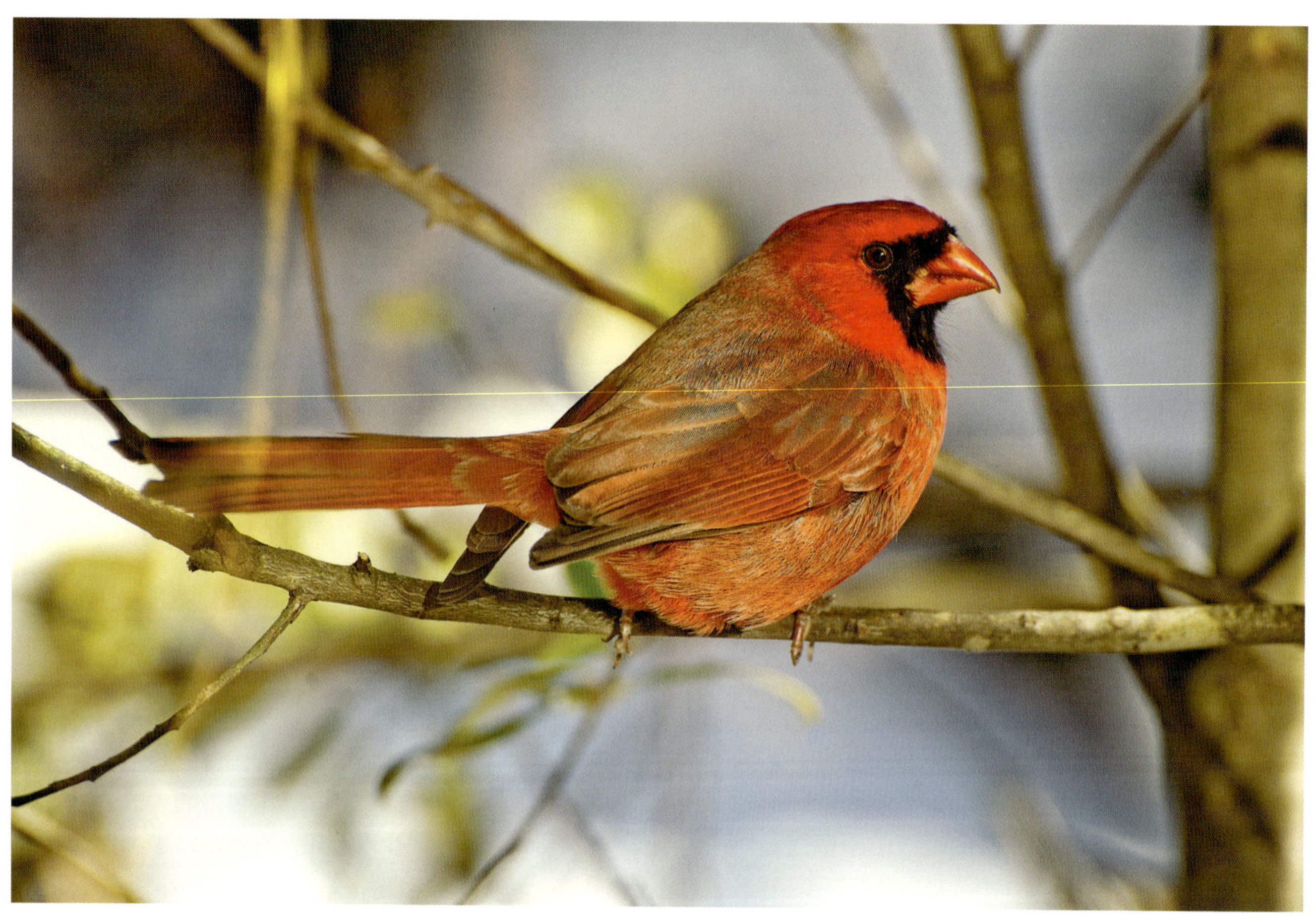

Sing a new song to the L*ORD*! *Let the whole earth sing to the* L*ORD*!

PSALM 96:1 (NLT)

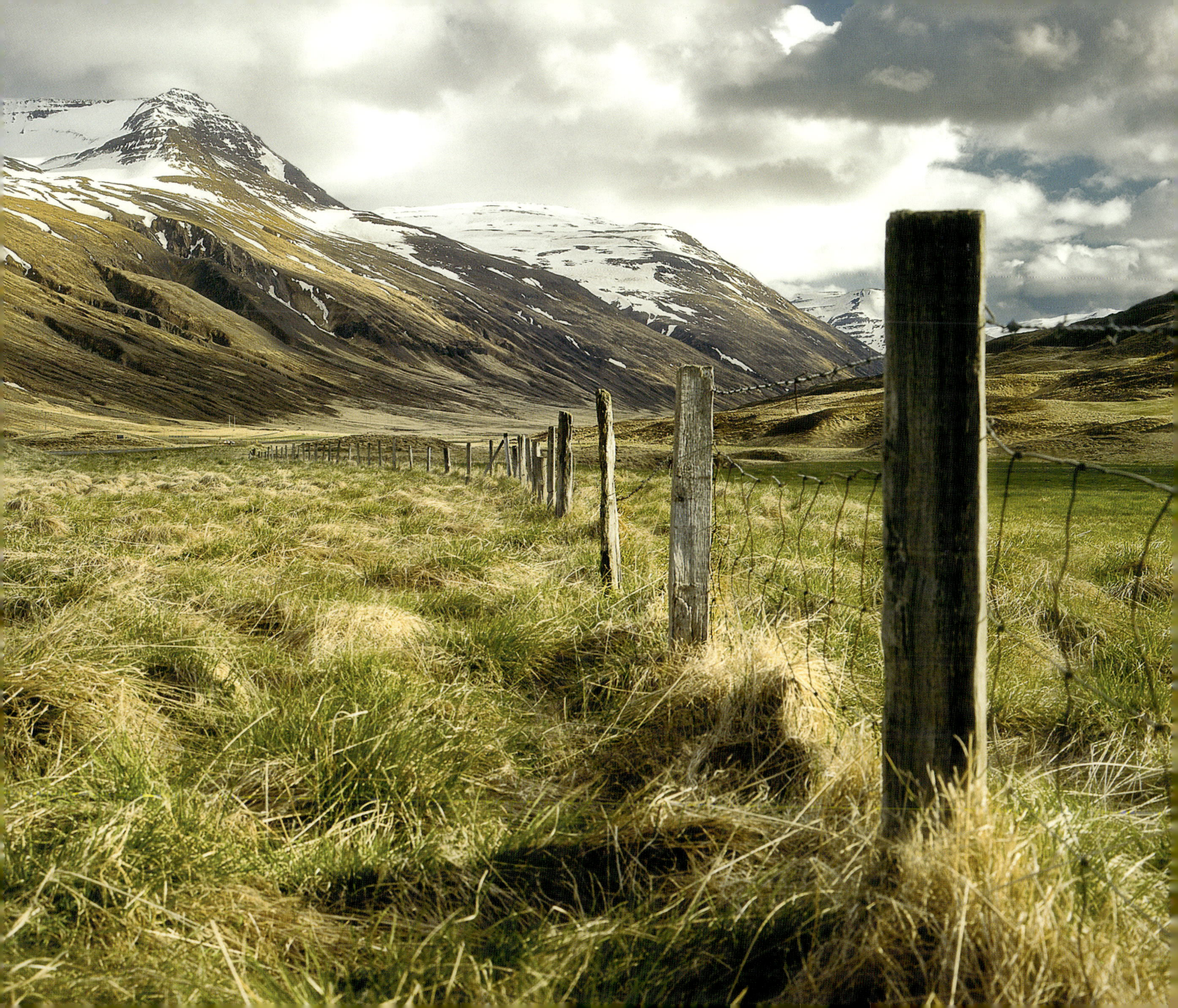

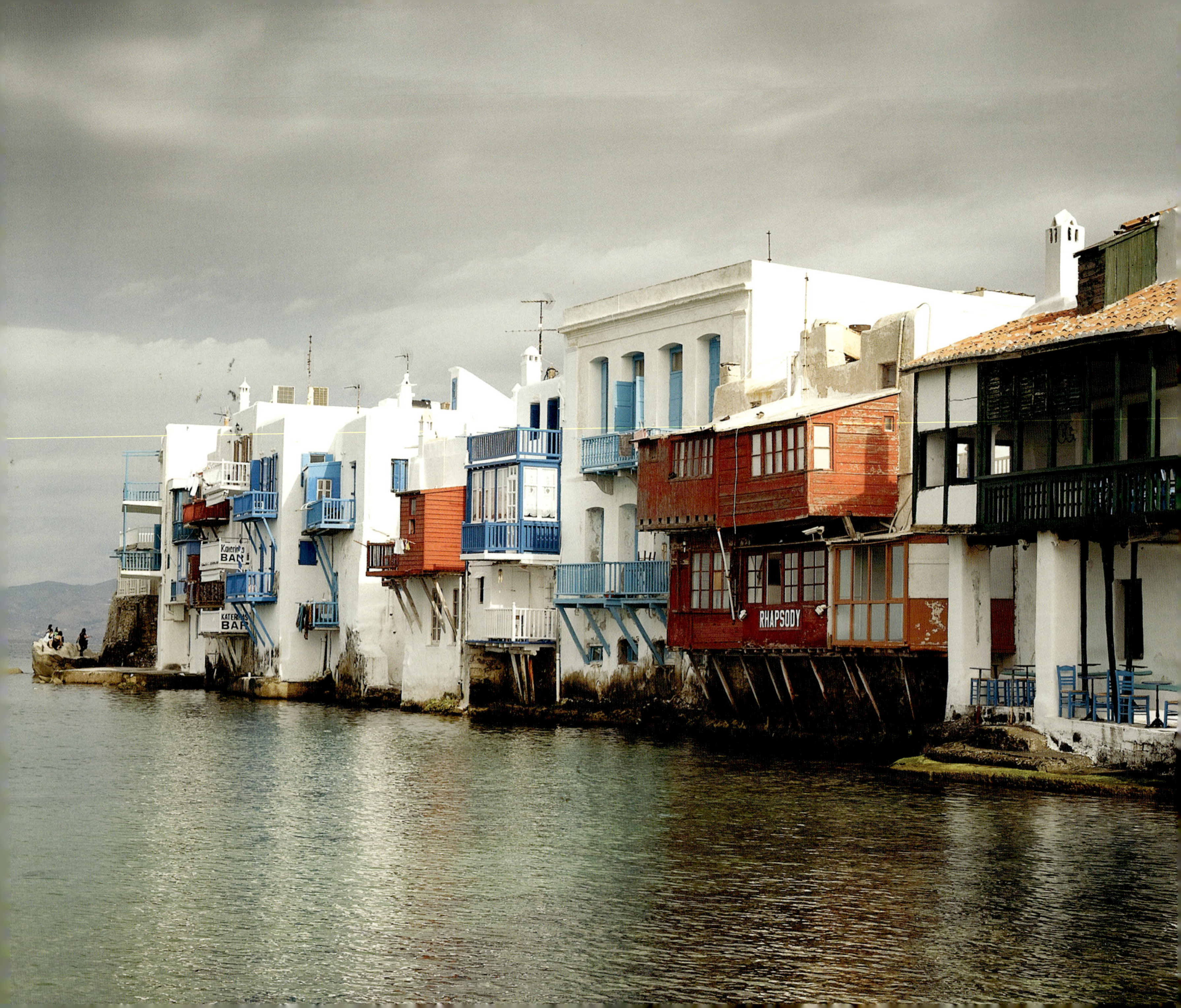
BAR
BAR
RHAPSODY

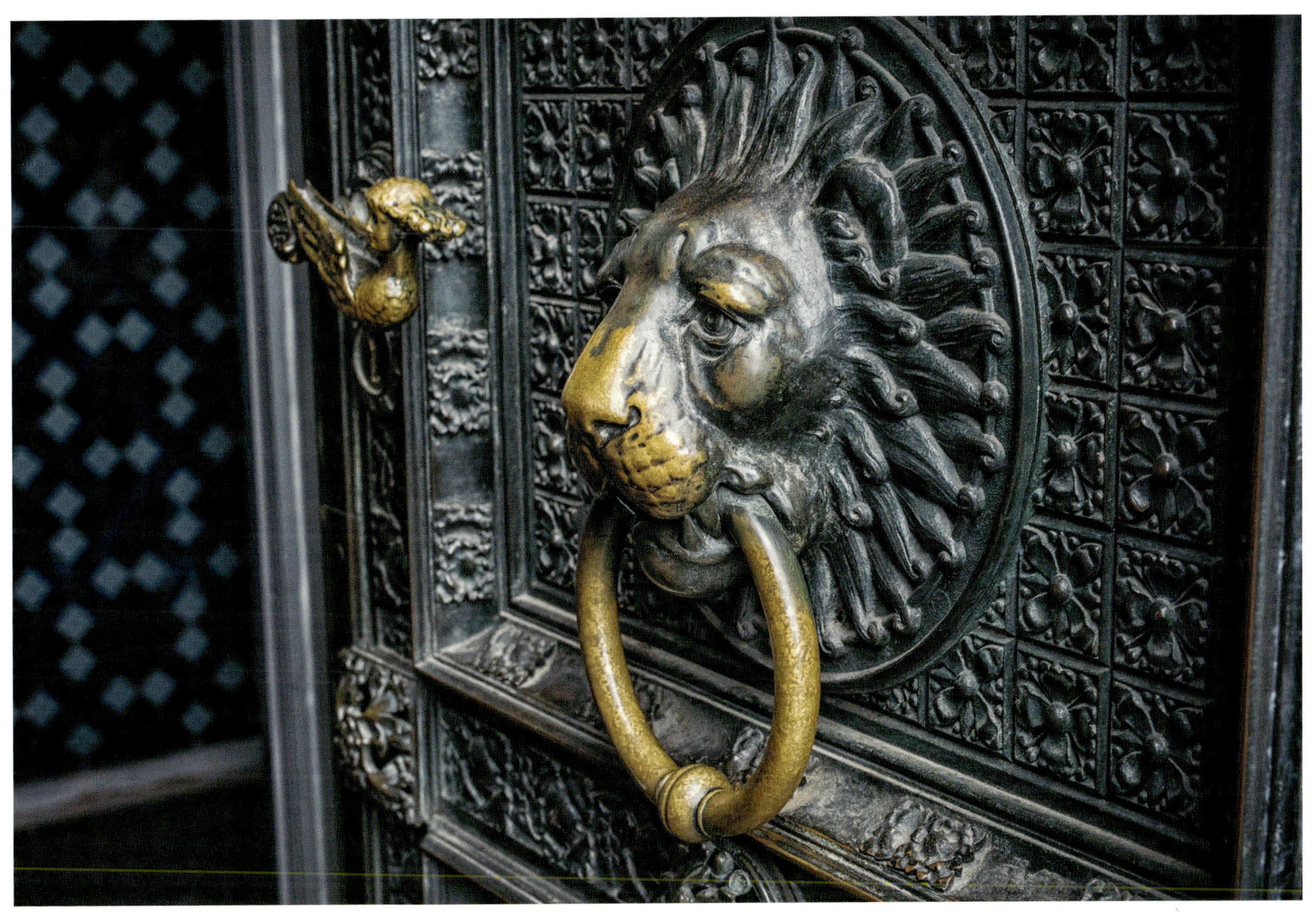

Sing, all you who sail the seas, all you who live in distant coastlands ... shout praises from the mountaintops! ... Let the whole world glorify the LORD; let it sing his praise. The LORD will march forth like a mighty hero.

ISAIAH 42:10-13 (NLT)

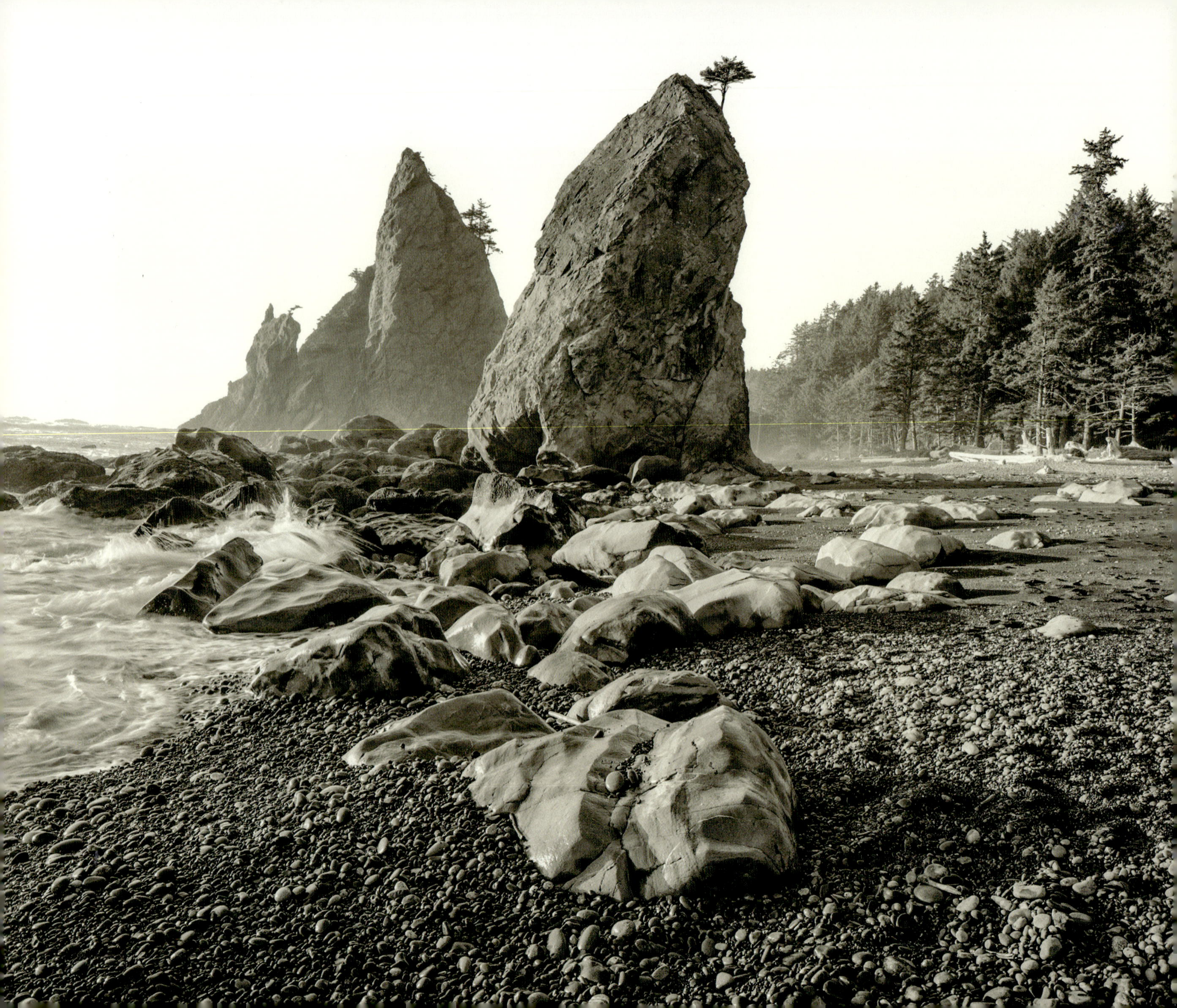

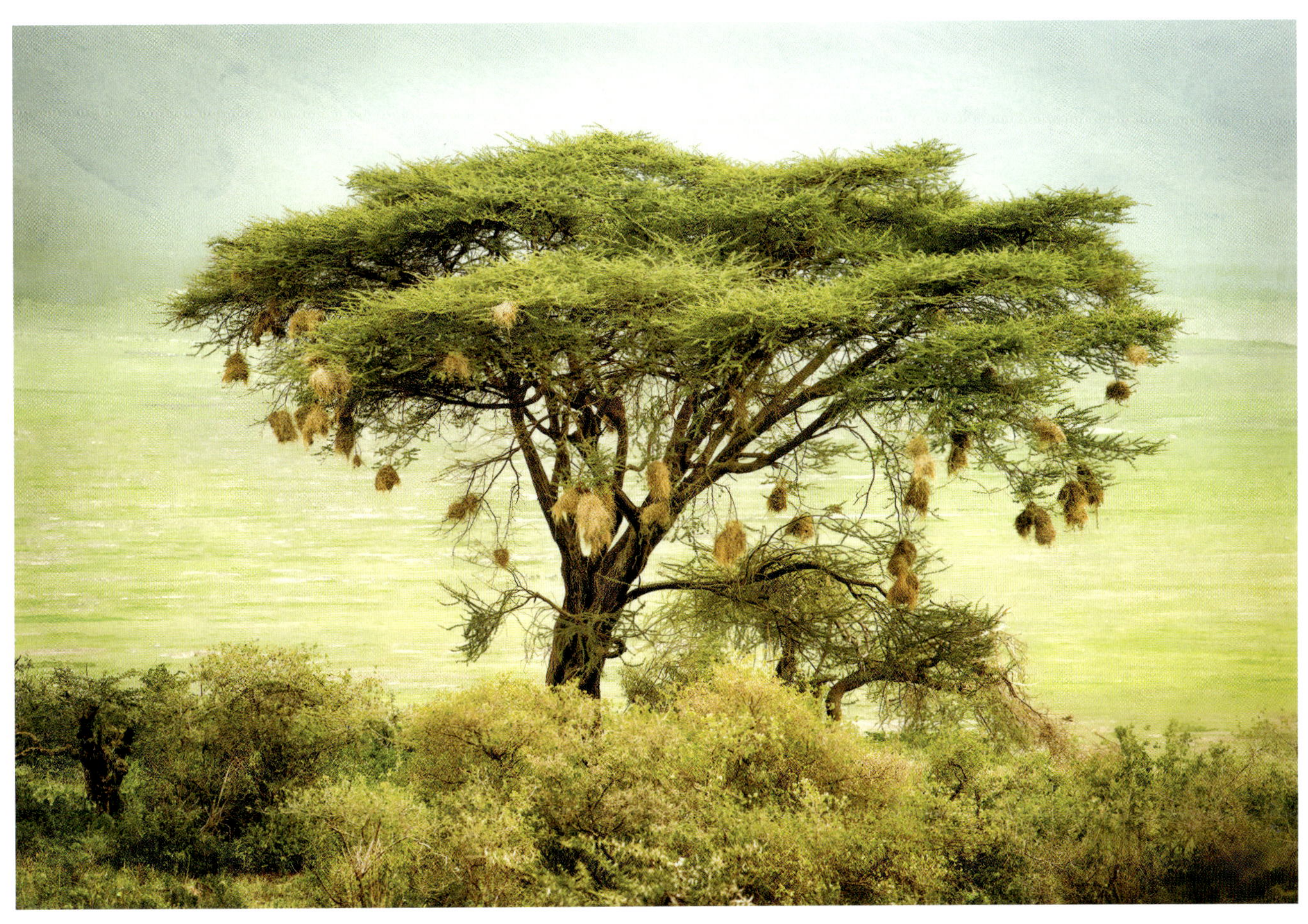

O Lord, You are my God; I will exalt You, I will give thanks to Your name; for You have worked wonders, plans formed long ago, with perfect faithfulness.

ISAIAH 25:1

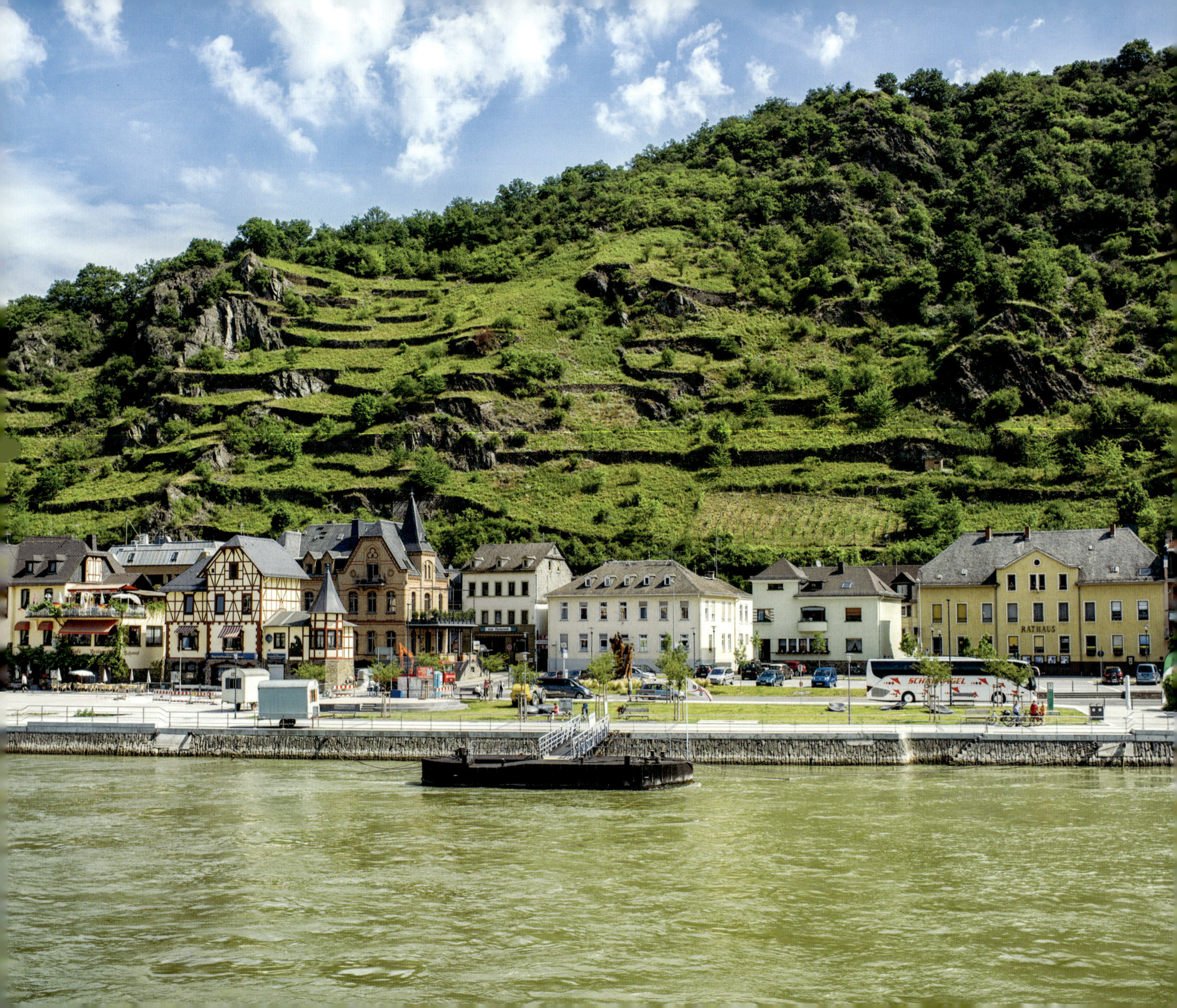
RATHAUS

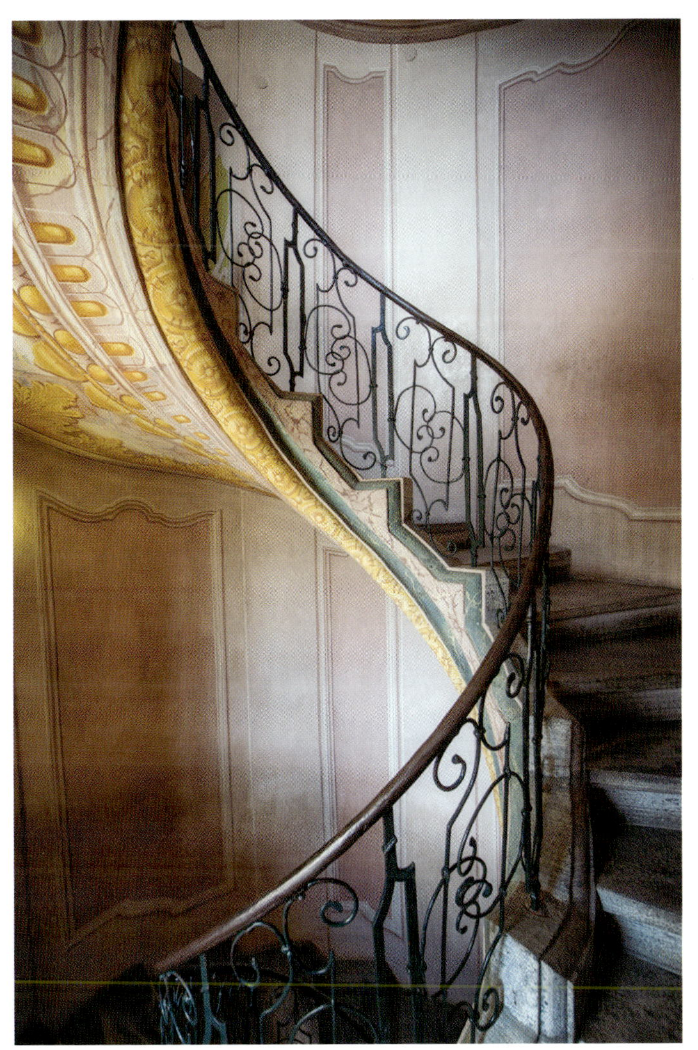

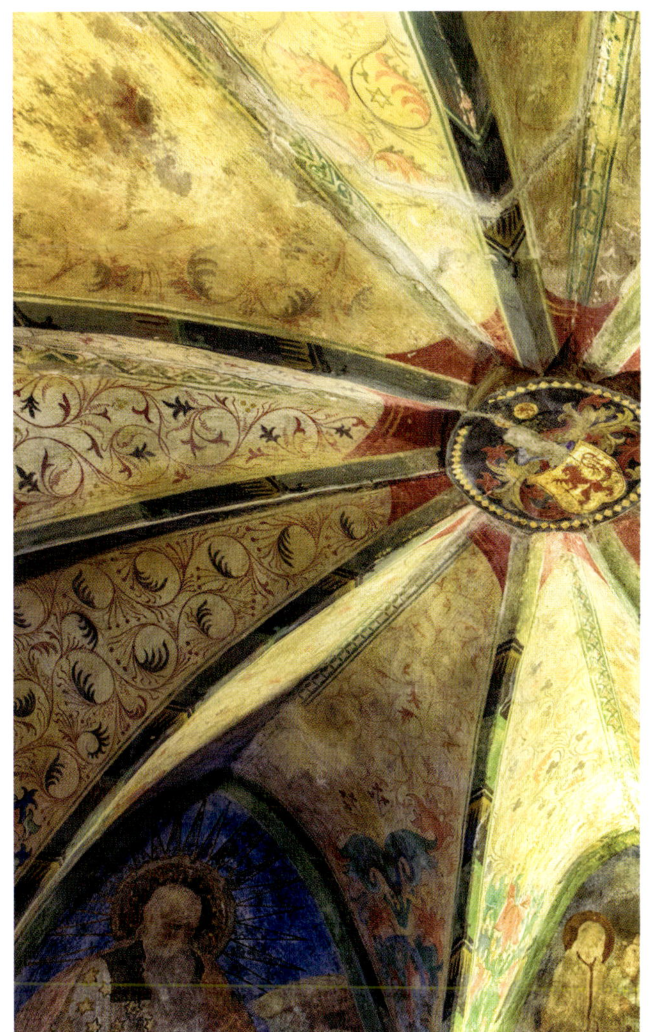

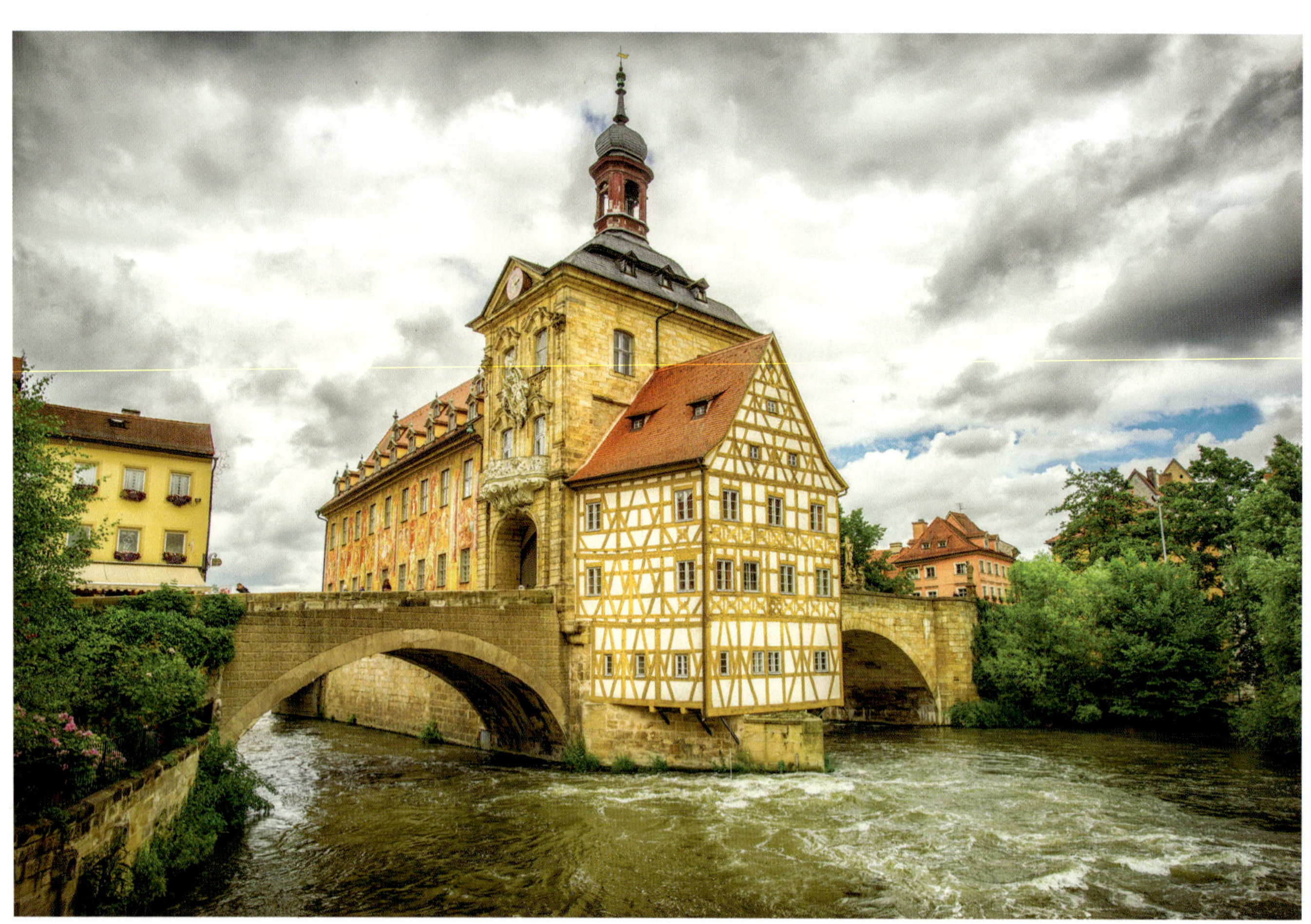

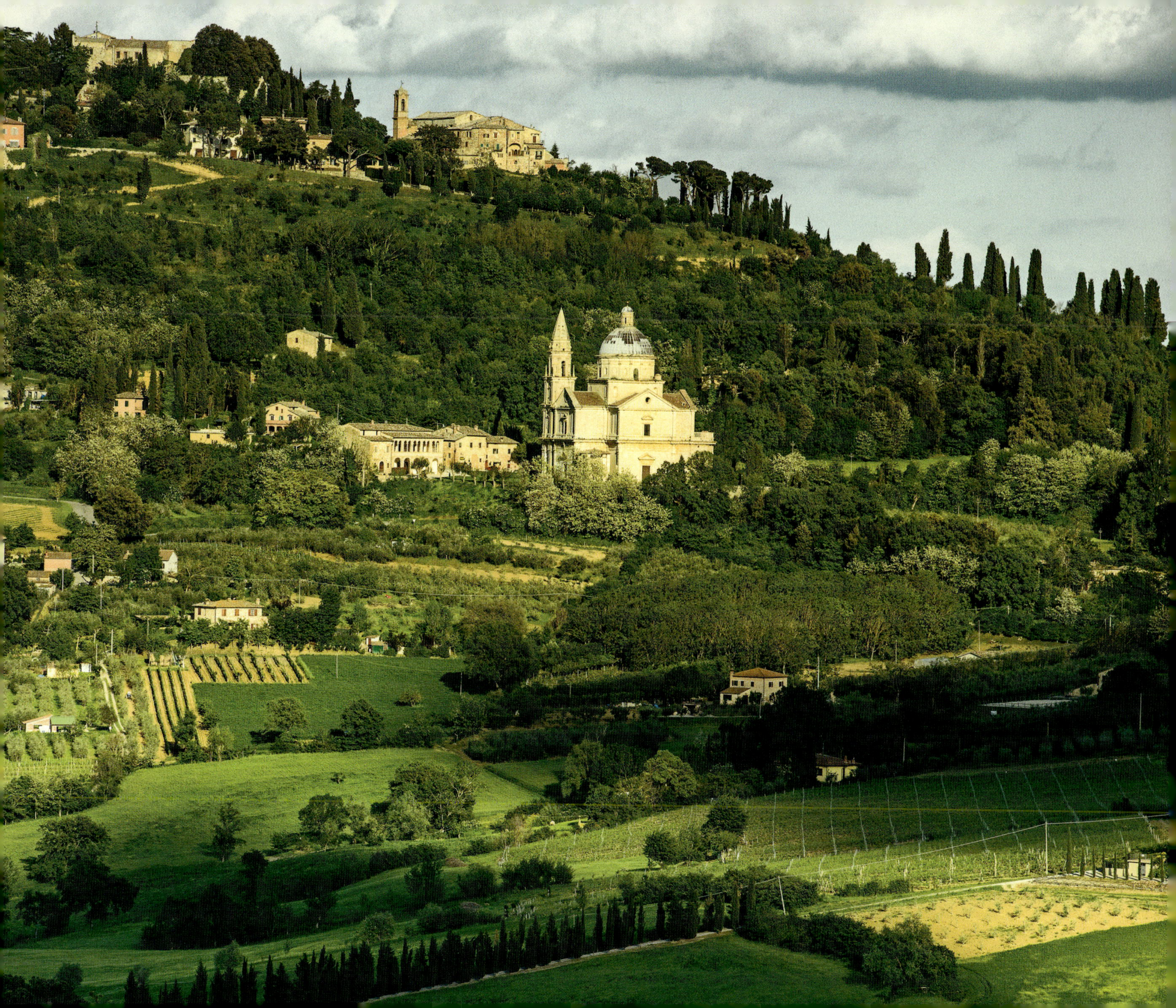

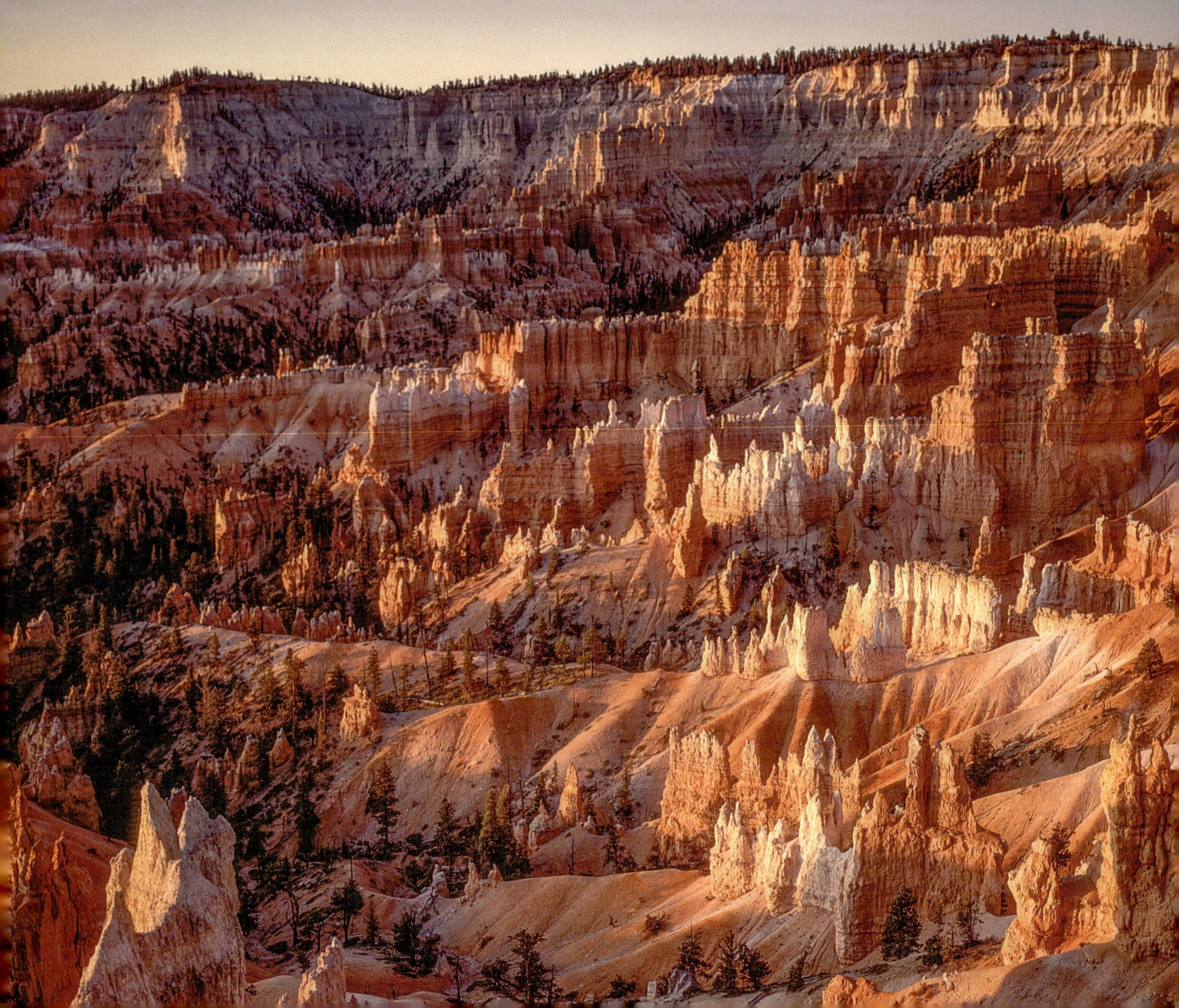

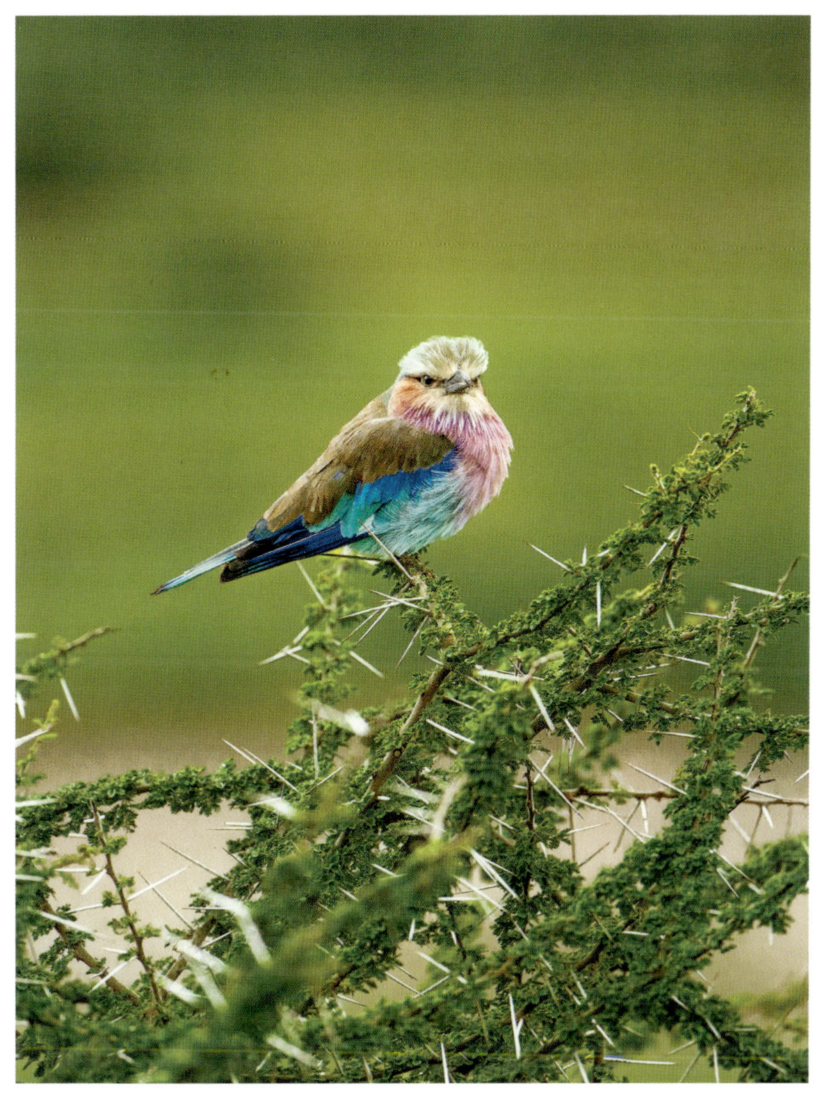

O LORD, our Lord, how majestic is Your name in all the earth, who have displayed Your splendor above the heavens!

PSALM 8:1

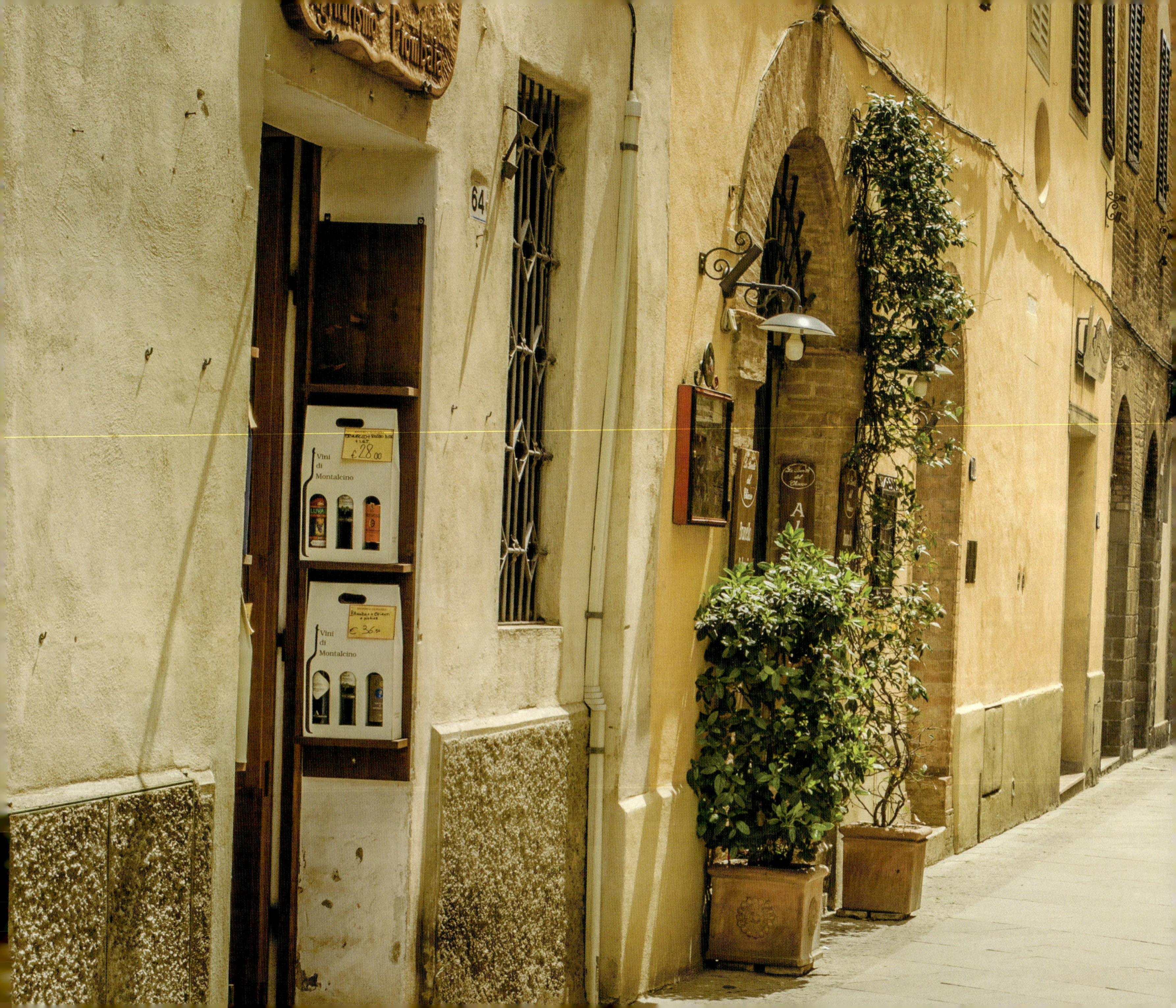
64
Vini di Montalcino
€28,00
Vini di Montalcino
€36,50

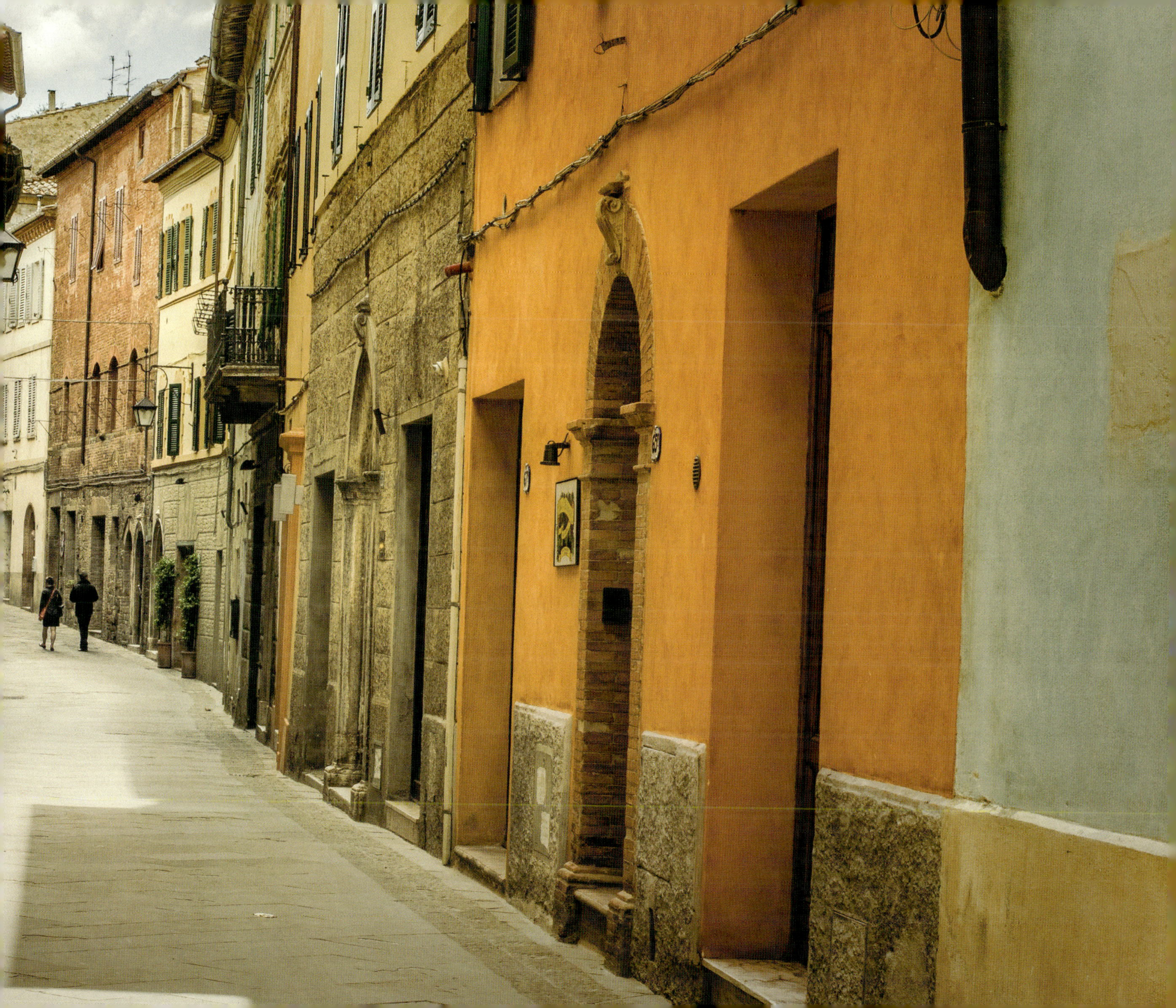

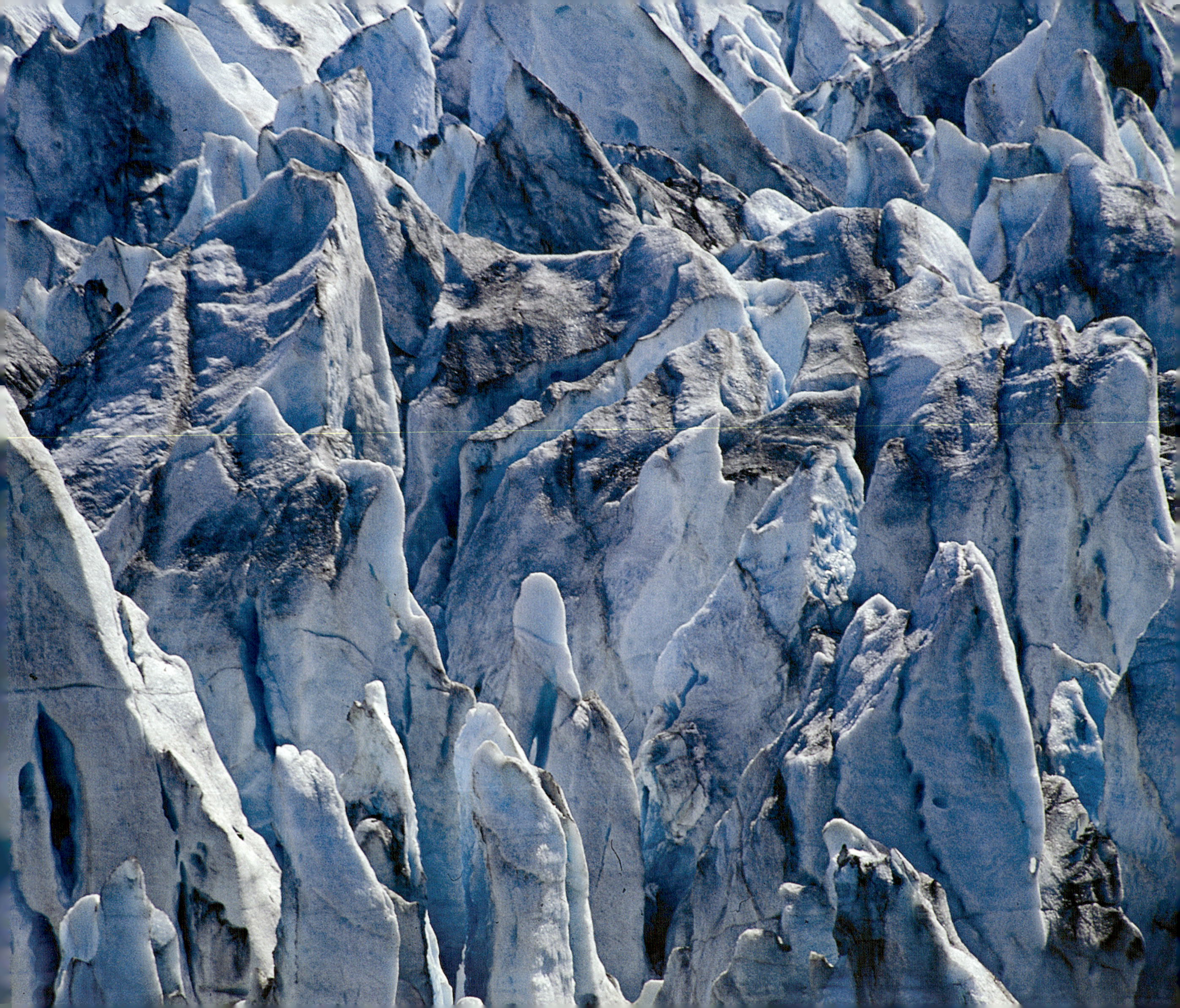

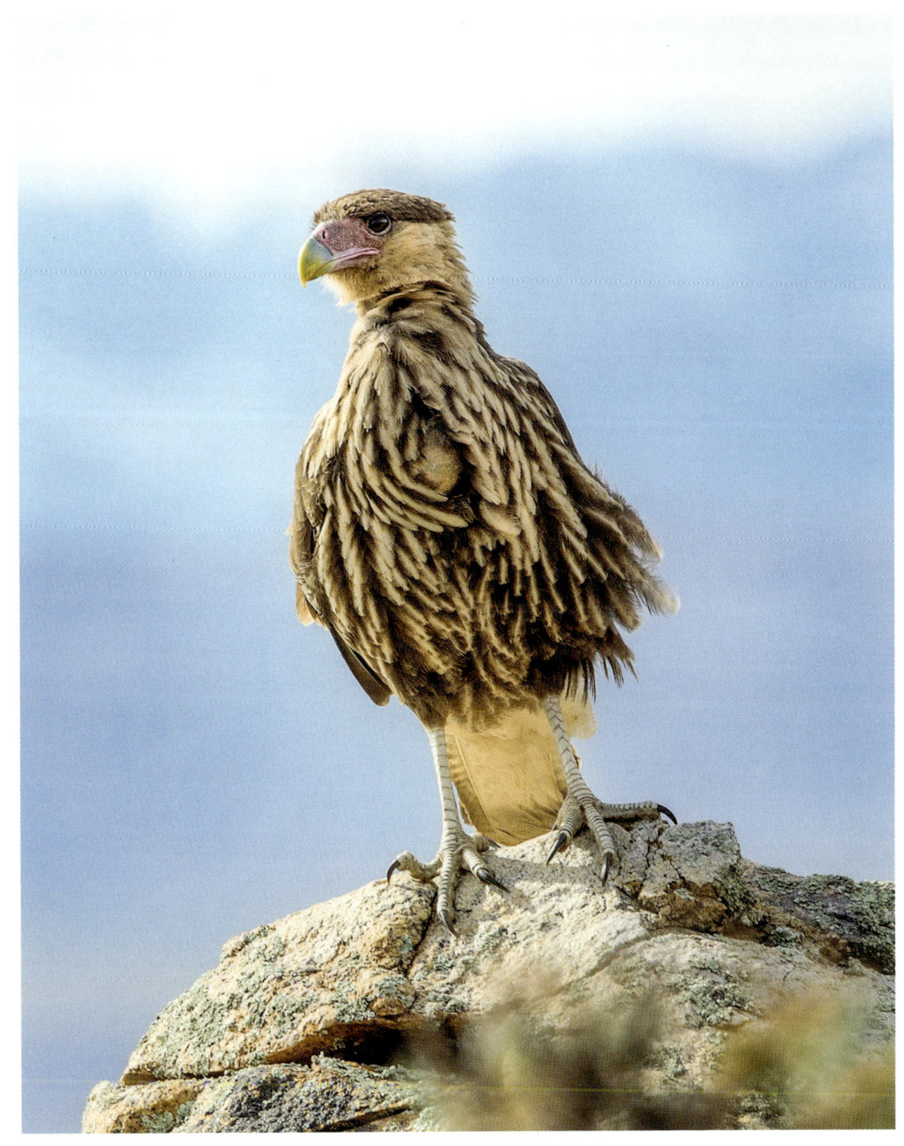

Praise the Lord! I will give thanks to the Lord with all my heart, in the company of the upright and in the assembly.

PSALM 111:1

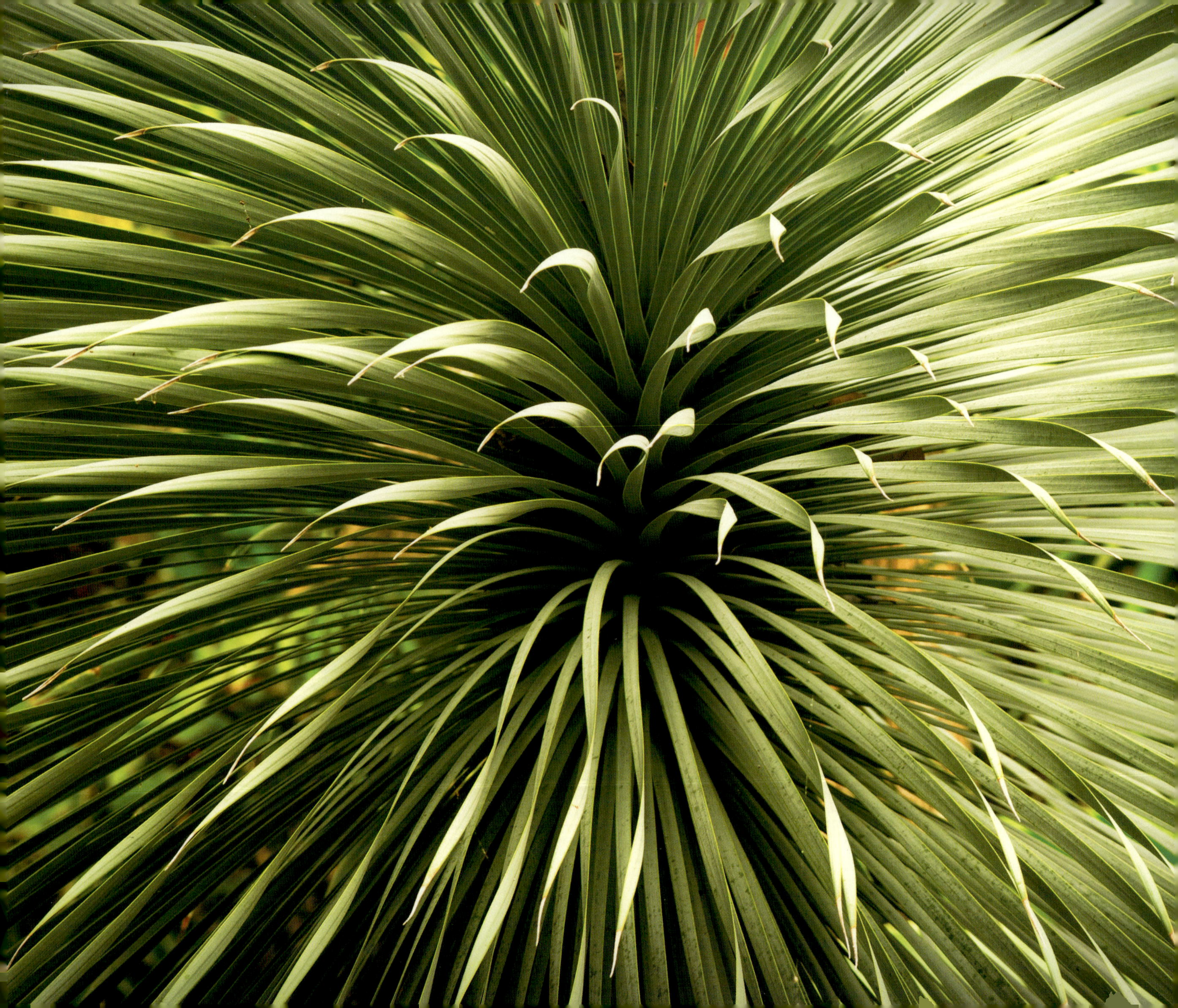

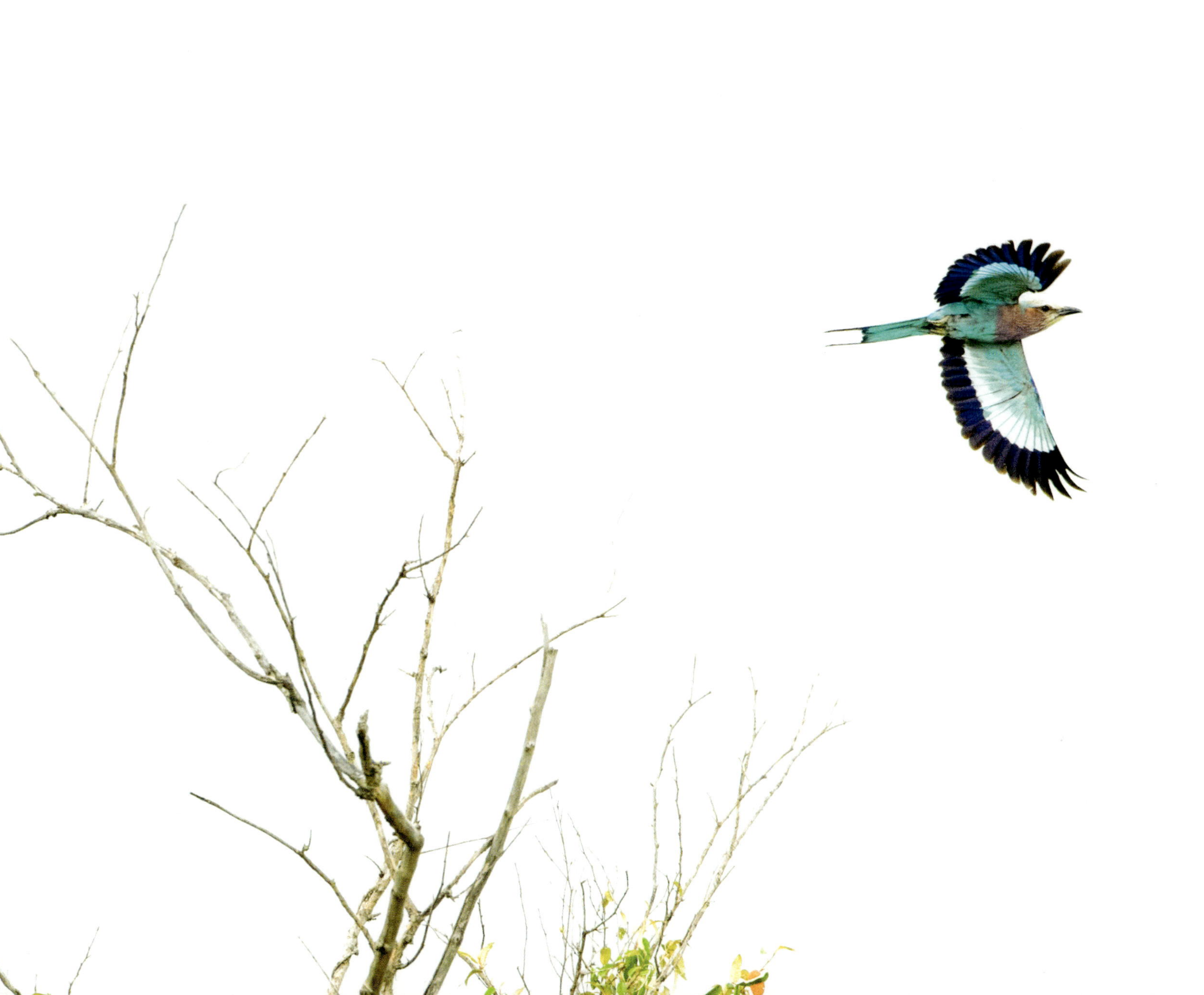

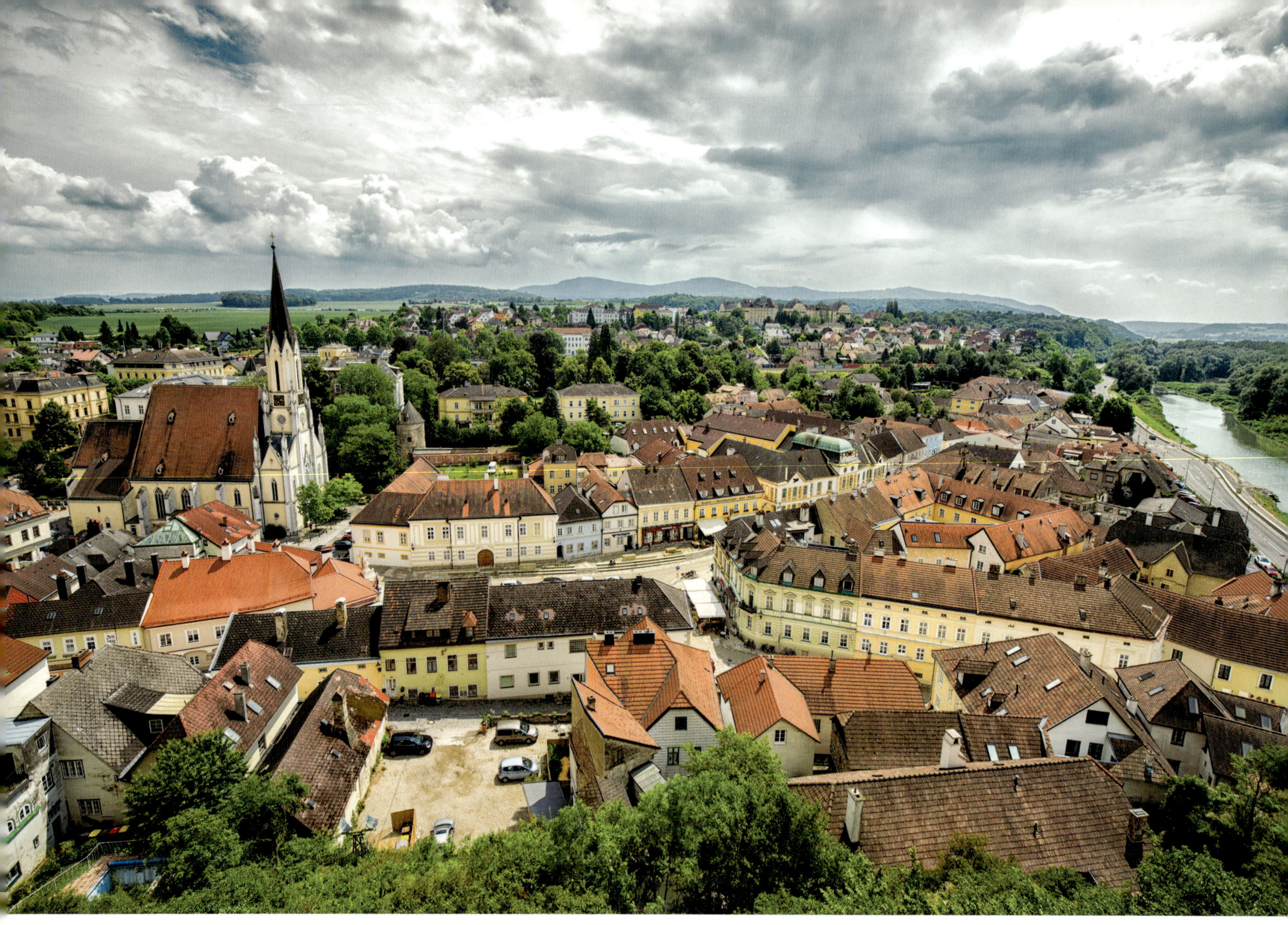

Praise be to the God and Father of our Lord Jesus Christ, who has blessed us in the heavenly realms with every spiritual blessing in Christ. For he chose us in him before the creation of the world to be holy and blameless in his sight.

EPHESIANS 1:3-4 (NIV)

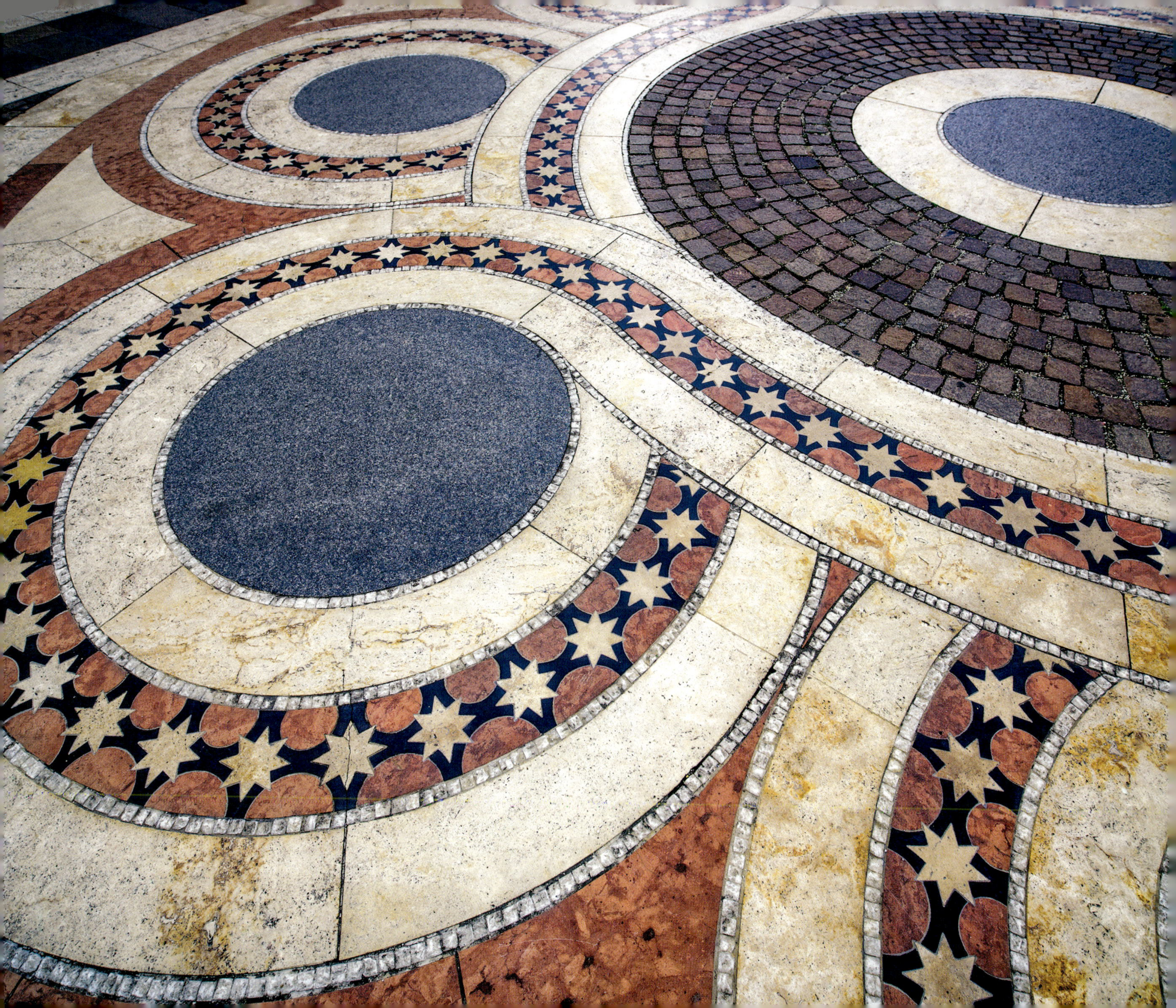

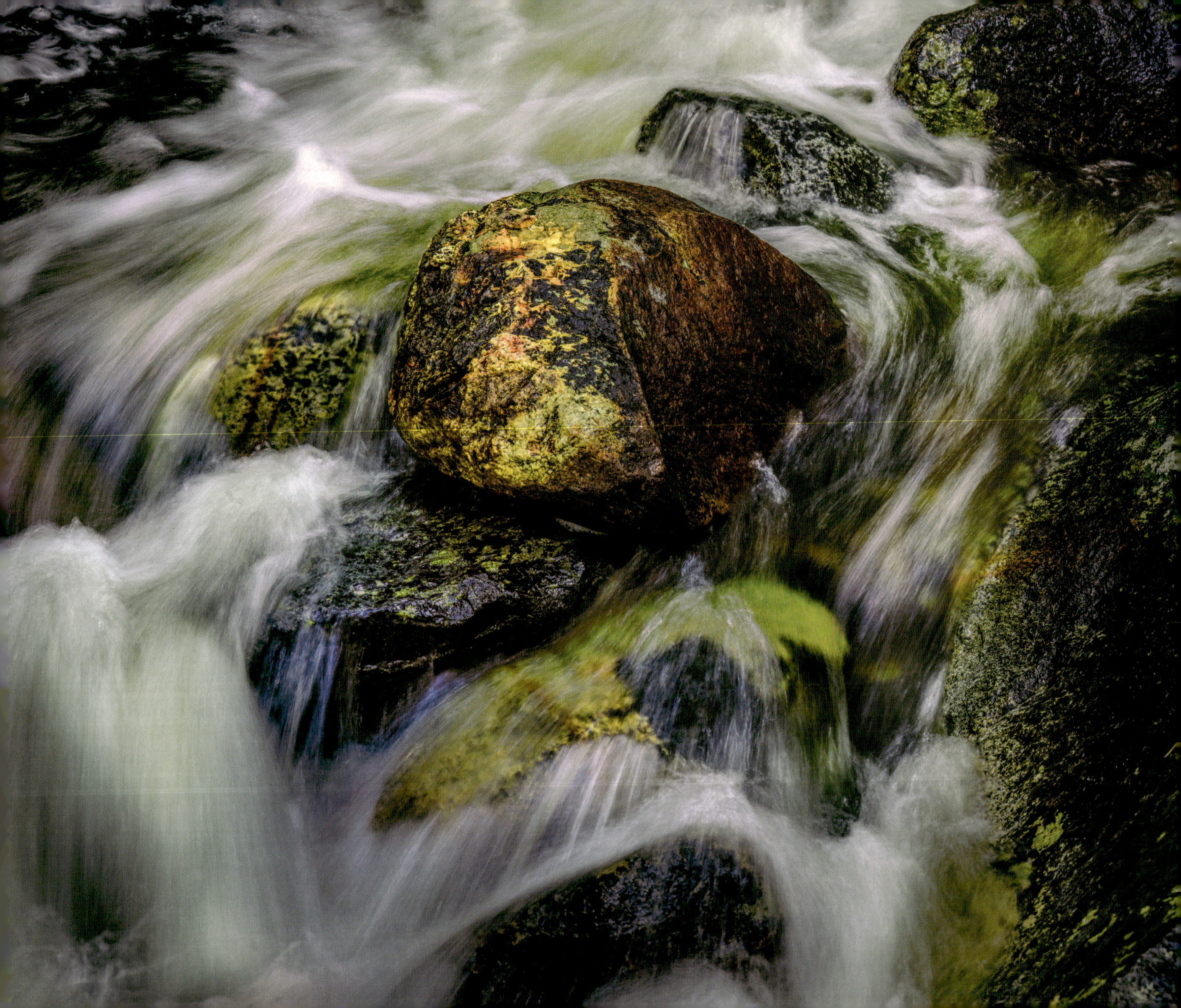

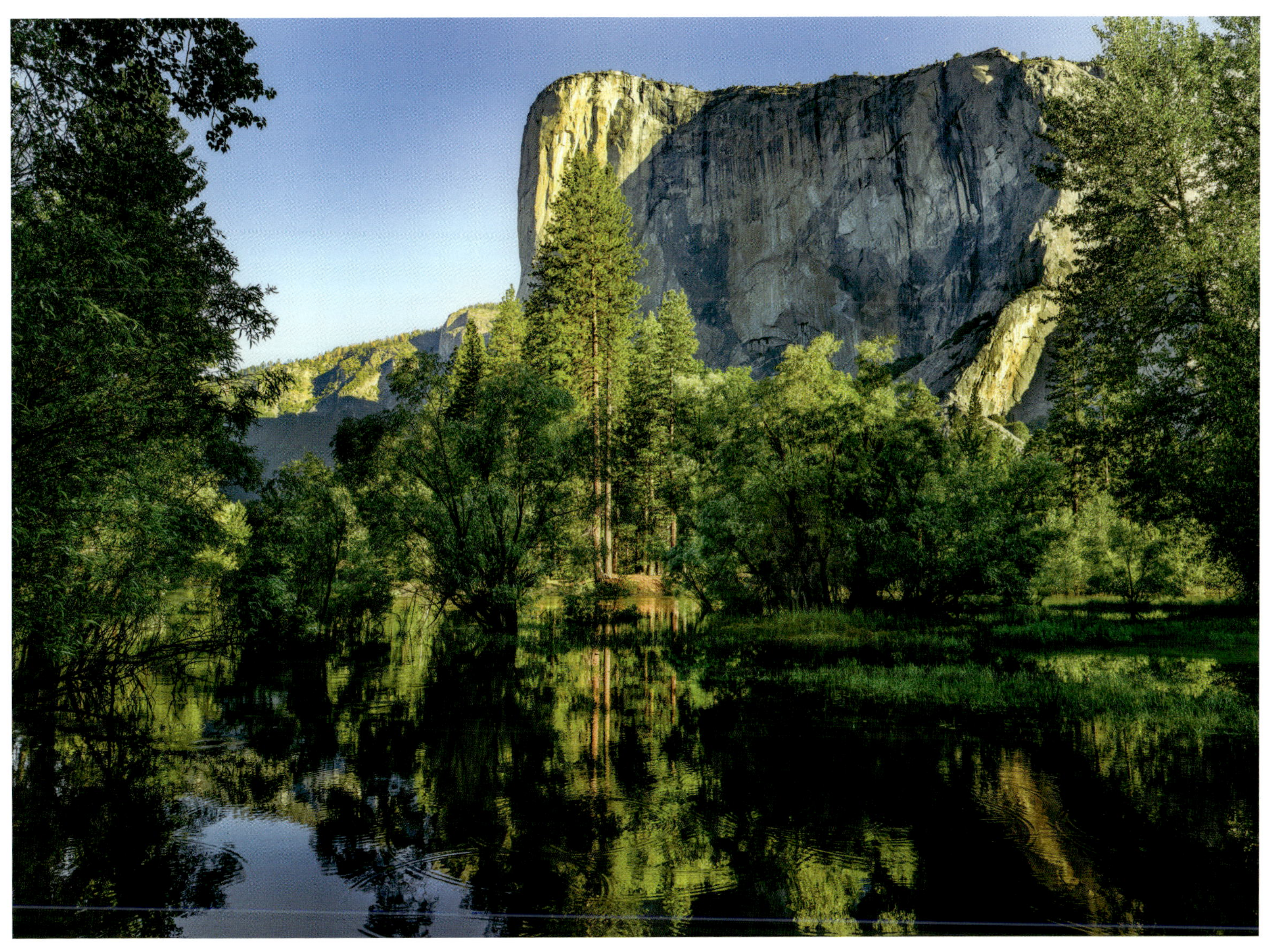

Shout for joy, O heavens, for the Lord has done it! Shout joyfully, you lower parts of the earth; break forth into a shout of joy, you mountains, O forest, and every tree in it; for the Lord has redeemed Jacob.

ISAIAH 44:23

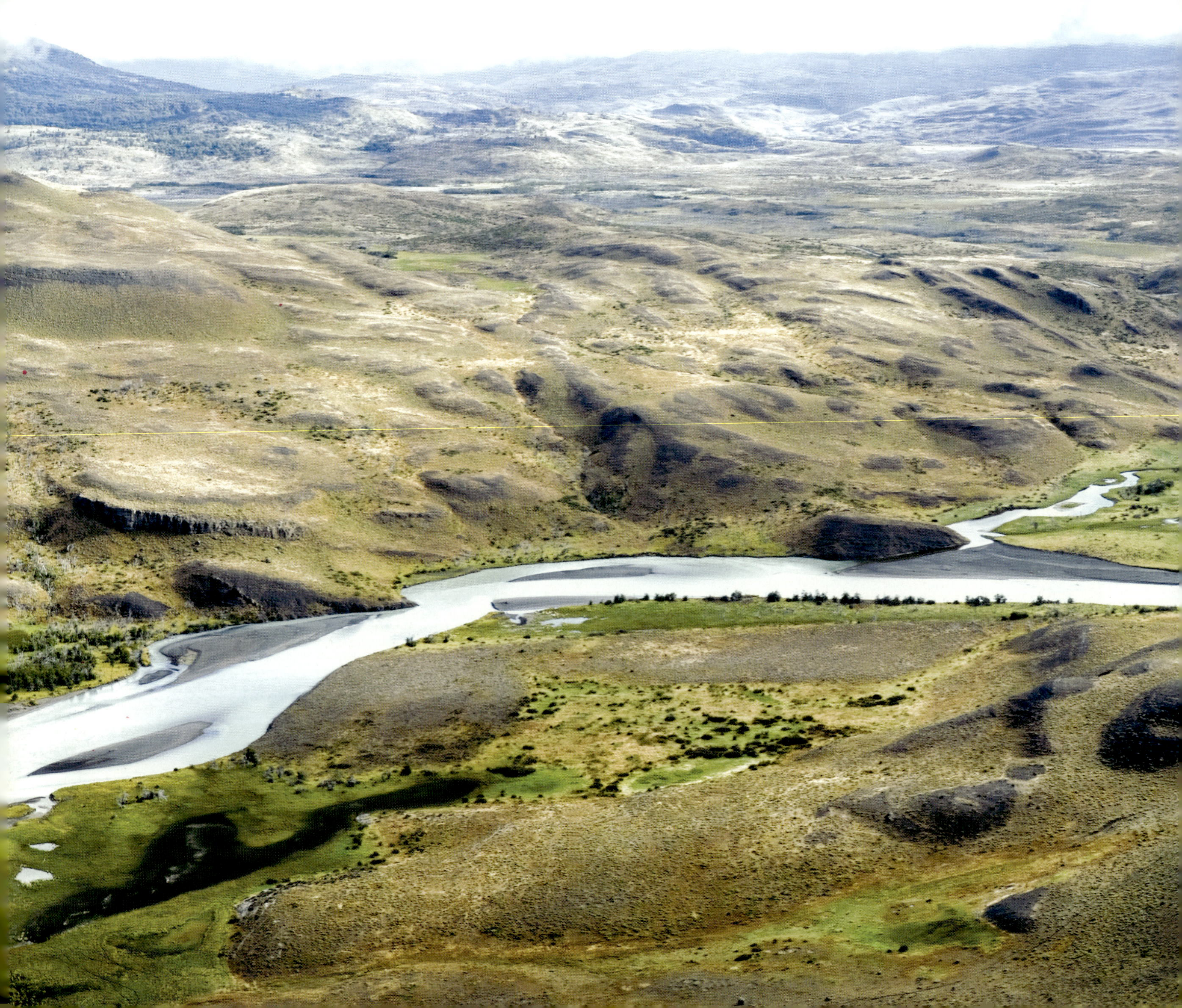

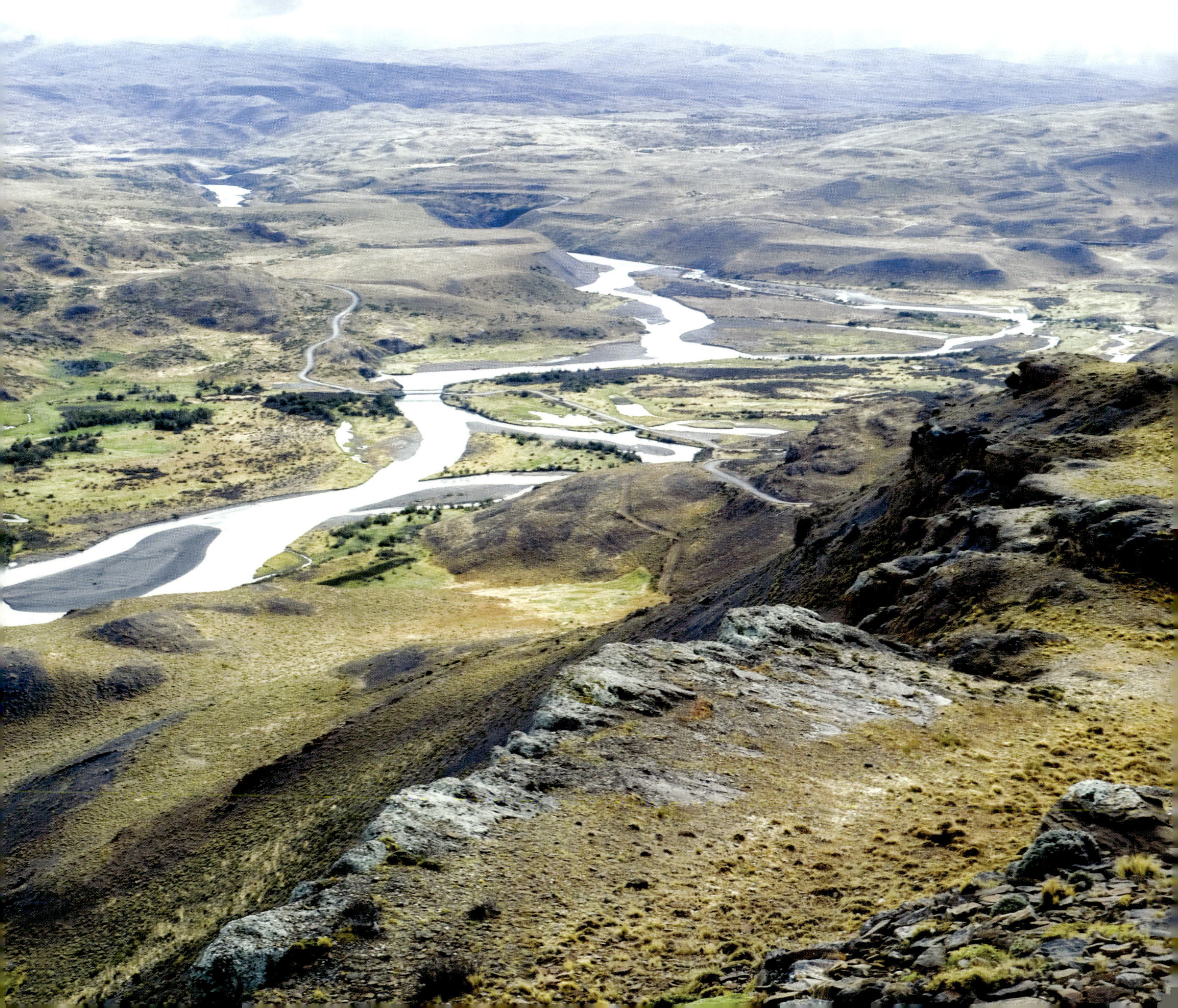

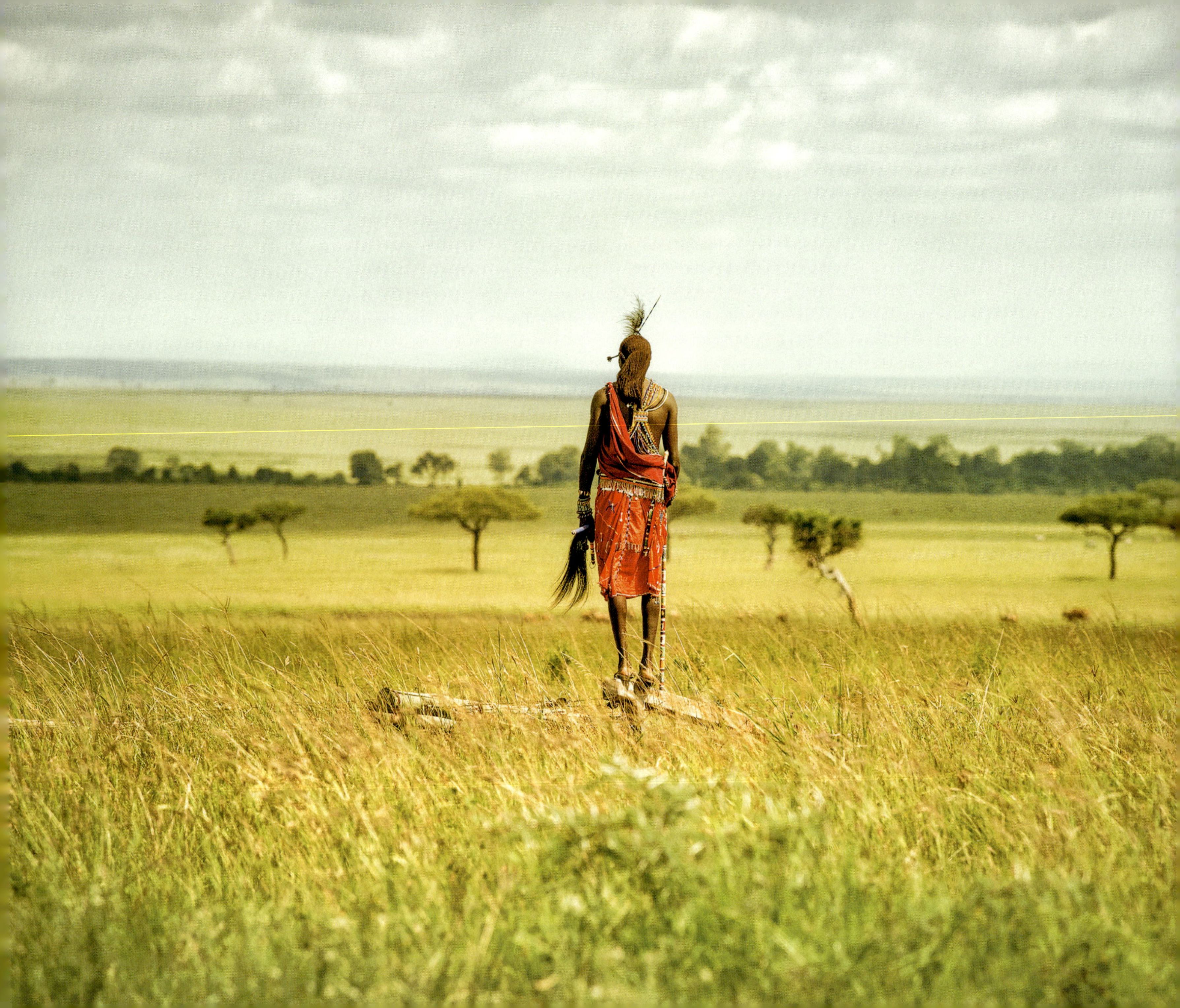

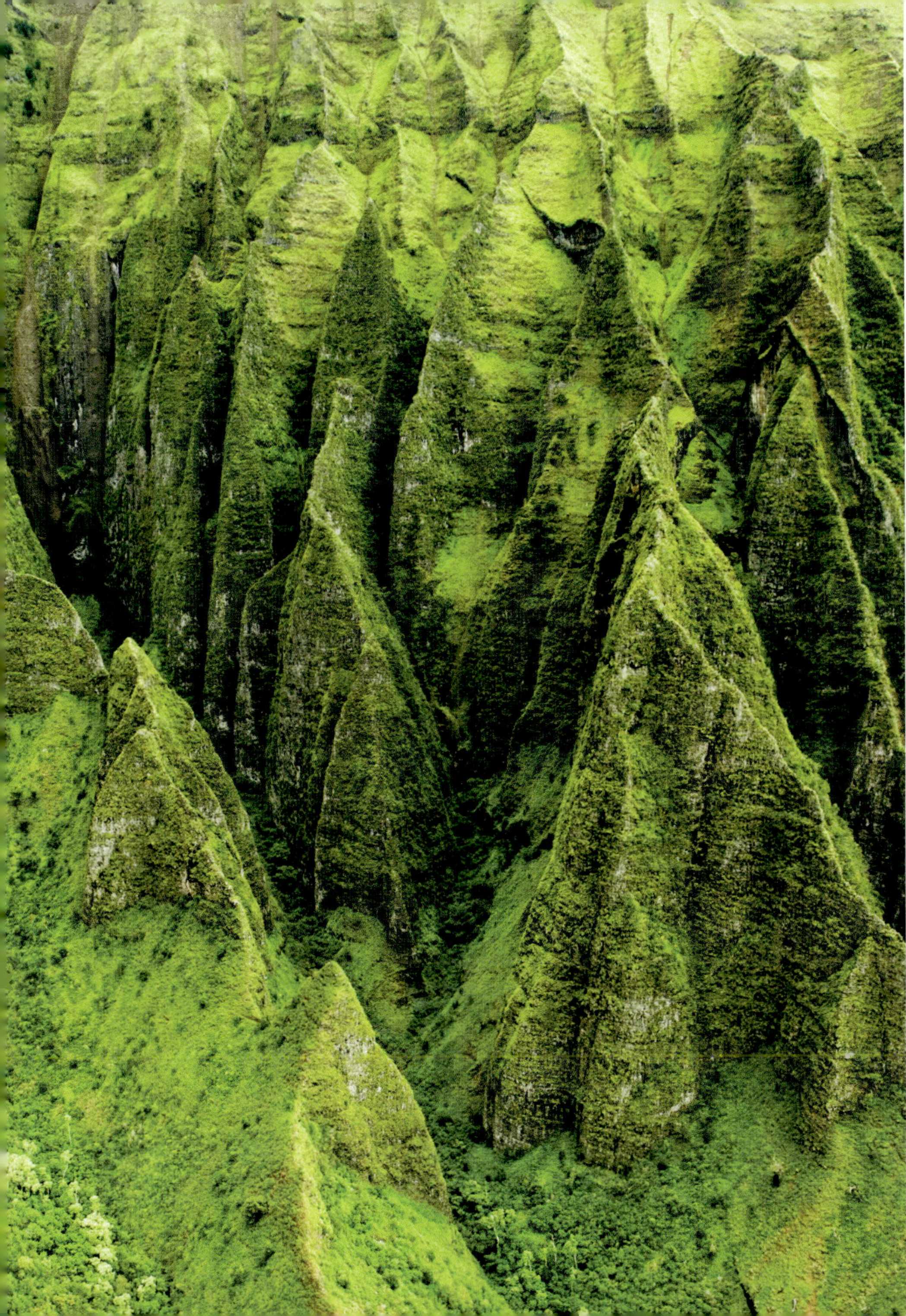

Awake, my soul!
Awake, harp and lyre!
I will awaken the dawn.
I will praise you, Lord, among the nations;
I will sing of you among the peoples.
For great is your love, reaching to the heavens;
Your faithfulness reaches to the skies.
Be exalted, O God, above the heavens;
Let your glory be over all the earth.

PSALM 57:8-11 (NIV)

A Word of Thanks

Thank you for taking this journey into God's heart, through His amazing, beautiful world and His wonderful Word. I hope you have been encouraged by His care for you, strengthened in your love for Jesus, and refreshed in your faith. Remember, your heavenly Father knows right where you are at all times—both physically and spiritually. He has many messages of encouragement all around you—signs of hope just waiting for you to look, listen, and enjoy.

As you continue on your walk of fellowship with the Lord, it's my prayer that you will seek Him continually and love Him with all your heart. And don't forget to "sing praises to Him; speak of all His wonders [and] glory in His holy name" (Ps. 105:2-3)! The more you do, the closer you will feel to the God who loves you with an everlasting love—and there's no better feeling than that.

Charles F. Stanley

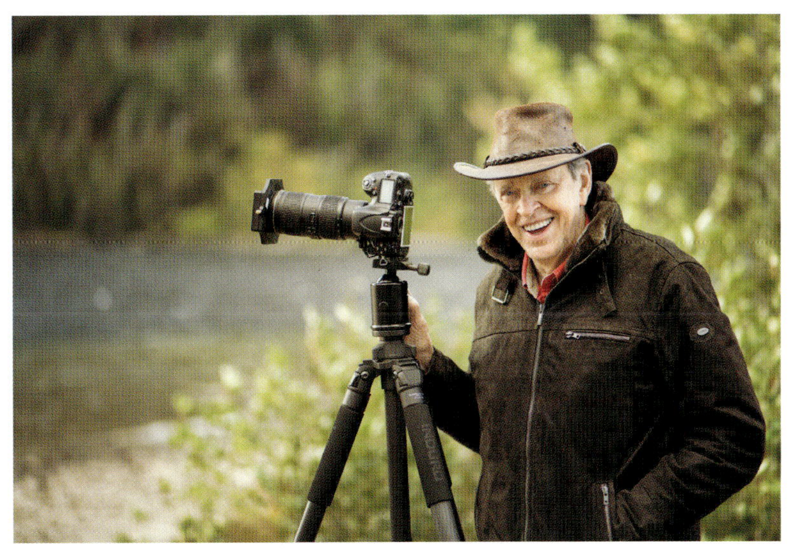

DR. CHARLES F. STANLEY is the senior pastor of First Baptist Church Atlanta and founder of In Touch Ministries, both located in Atlanta, Georgia. His first adventures behind the lens began with a borrowed camera on a mission trip to Haiti in 1962. Since then, Dr. Stanley has traveled around the globe capturing the beauty of creation and encouraging others to enjoy the wonders of God's world. Photography has become both a favorite pastime and a part of his ministry, as he seeks to share with audiences an awareness of the Lord's great power and love reflected in the world around us. Dr. Stanley believes, in accordance with Acts 20:24, that "my life is worth nothing to me unless I use it for finishing the work assigned me by the Lord Jesus—the work of telling others the good news about the wonderful grace of God."

Index of Photos

74. Summit Lake – Mount Evans, Colorado
75. The Coliseum – Rome, Italy
76. Mirror Lake – Yosemite National Park, California
77. Padlock – Maui, Hawaii
78. Pot in the garden – Louisiana
80. Pitcher in a window – Baton Rouge, Louisiana
81. Olive jar – Louisiana
82. Central coast of California
84. Hibiscus flower
85. Pigeon Point Lighthouse – Pescadero, California
86. Antelope Canyon – Page, Arizona
88. Door to Marienkapelle (Mary's Chapel) – Wertheim, Germany
89. Keyhole view from Malta doors – Rome, Italy
90. Orchid – Hawaii
92. Schwabacher Landing – Grand Tetons National Park, Wyoming
93. Pink Rose of Sharon
94. Statue of an angel in Gross Sankt Martin Church – Cologne, Germany
96. Statue of St. Peter in Cologne Cathedral – Cologne, Germany
97. Matthias Church – Budapest, Hungary
98. Northwest shore – Kauai, Hawaii
100. Winding creek – Wisconsin
101. Horseshoe Bend – Page, Arizona
102. Water lily – Smoky Mountains, Tennessee
104. Green rolling hills – New Zealand
105. Red skiff – Nova Scotia, Canada
106. Talking rocks – Glacier National Park, Montana
107. Denali (Mt. McKinley) sunrise – Denali National Park, Alaska
108. Akaroa Lighthouse – South Island, New Zealand
110/111. Gondolas – Venice, Italy
112. Torch ginger – Maui, Hawaii
114. Canadian Rockies – Jasper, Canada
115. Waterfall in Akaka Falls State Park – Big Island, Hawaii
116. Statue of Christ
118. African masked weaver – Africa
119. Zabriskie Point – Death Valley National Park, California
120. Loulu palm – Hawaii
122. Red ginger plant – Hawaii
123. Misty woods – North Carolina
124. Deer – Smoky Mountains, Tennessee
126. Yellow finch
127. Wild iris
128. Great egret – Louisiana
130. Kauai, Hawaii
131. Pink coneflowers
132. Mount Fitz Roy – Argentina
134. Pink strawflowers
135. Breaching whale – Juneau, Alaska
136/137. Fields of gold – Klausenpass, Switzerland
138. Valley at Going-to-the-Sun – Glacier National Park, Montana
140. Nā Pali Coast – Kauai, Hawaii
141. Lesser Flamingos – Africa
142. Creek in Greenbrier – Smoky Mountains, Tennessee
144. Hippopotamus – Africa
145. Lenticular cloud – El Calafate, Argentina
146. Blue heron – Atlanta, Georgia
148. Big creek – Ashford, Washington
149. Perito Moreno Glacier – Los Glaciares National Park, Argentina
150. Monument Valley, Utah
152. Heceta Head Lighthouse – Yachats, Oregon
153. Eagle – Alaska
154. Hafnarnes Lighthouse – Faskrudsfjordur Bay, Iceland
156. Oak tree trunk – Louisiana

157. Houmas House Plantation – Darrow, Louisiana
158. Spider flower – Big Island, Hawaii
160. Grey crowned Cranes
160. Lobster claw plant – Maui, Hawaii
161. Windmill – The Netherlands
162. Budir Church – Snæfellsnes Peninsula, Iceland
164. Church – Greece
165. Cades Cove Methodist Church – Smoky Mountains, Tennessee
166/167. Village of Corniglia – Cinque Terre, Italy
168. Exterior doorway – St. Peter's Cathedral, Regensburg, Germany
170. Exterior door – Bamberg Cathedral, Bamberg, Germany
171. San Marcos archway – Venice, Italy
172. Beach birds – Iceland
174. Church doors – Greece
175. Country church – Iceland
176. Fireweed – Yukon, Canada
178. Rows of fruitfulness – Italy
179. Indian paintbrush – Canadian Rockies, Canada
180. Kauai Valley – Kauai, Hawaii
182. Fuchsia orchid – Hawaii
183. Sparkling cactus – Tombstone, Arizona
183. Orchids on tree – Big Island, Hawaii
184. Rose hip
186. Moloaa Forest Reserve – Kauai, Hawaii
187. Pineapple plant – Hawaii
188. Kalalau Valley – Kauai, Hawaii
190. Parakeet flower – Hawaii
191. Louisiana swamp
192. Lions – Maasai Mara, Kenya
194. Cardinal – North Georgia
195. Northern Iceland
196. Greece
197. Lion's head door knocker, Cologne Cathedral – Cologne, Germany
198. Olympic Beach, Washington
199. Acacia tree
200. View along the Rhine River – Germany
201. Staircase at Melk Abbey – Melk, Austria
201. Prayer room ceiling at Marksburg Castle – Koblenz, Germany
202. Old Town Hall – Bamberg, Germany
203. Montepulciano – Tuscany, Italy
204. Bryce Canyon National Park – Utah
205. Lilac-breasted roller – Tanzania, Africa
206/207. Walk with me – Montalcino, Tuscany, Italy
208. Sawyer Glacier – Juneau, Alaska
209. Southern crested caracara chick
210. Spidery yucca plant – Big Island, Hawaii
211. Lilac-breasted roller in flight – Tanzania, Africa
212. Melk, Austria
213. Plaza mosaic at St. Stephen's Cathedral – Budapest, Hungary
214. Tenaya Creek – Yosemite National Park, California
215. El Capitan – Yosemite National Park, California
216/217. Snake River Overlook – Jackson Hole, Wyoming
218. Maasai warrior – Maasai Mara, Kenya
219. Mountains and valleys – Kauai, Hawaii
221. Dr. Charles Stanley